Praise for
Borderland

"A beautifully written evocation of Ukraine's brutal past and its shaky efforts to construct a better future. Reid succeeds in vividly conjuring up dozens of littleknown heroes and villains of Ukrainian history. Reid summons up the rogues and poets of Ukraine's past with a deft touch, but her real theme is the tragedy which has been Ukraine's lot for much of its history. *Borderland* is a tapestry woven of the stories of all its inhabitants, recording their triumphs and their conflicts with the fairness of a compassionate outsider." —*Financial Times*

"Reid has stepped forth with an ambitious, fluent, and remarkably comprehensive synthesis that should be required reading for anyone interested in the region." —*Boston Globe*

"Beautifully written and lovingly researched. This book brims with colourful historical personalities. The mixture of travelogue, history, political analysis and anecdote makes Anna Reid's account a highly digestible popular introduction to the tragic plight of a country whose very name means 'Borderland.' 'The West...had difficulty taking Ukraine seriously at all,' she writes. Her first (and I hope not her last) book is a noble and praiseworthy attempt to correct this gross historical injustice." —*Daily Telegraph*

"Gripping history. Reid writes with authority having lived for three years in Kiev as a reporter. She is remarkably clearheaded about the many competing versions of Ukraine's history and its mostly invented heroes. A wise and generous government in Kiev would give her a medal." —*Times* (UK)

BORDERLAND

BORDERLAND

A JOURNEY THROUGH THE HISTORY OF UKRAINE

REVISED AND UPDATED EDITION

ANNA REID

BASIC BOOKS

New York

Basic Books
Hachette Book Group
1290 Avenue of the Americas, New York, NY 10104
www.basicbooks.com

Printed in the United States of America

First published in Great Britain in 1997 by Weidenfeld & Nicolson
Originally published in hardcover in the United States by
Basic Books in June 1999
Third paperback edition originally published in Great Britain
in 2022 by Weidenfeld & Nicolson
Third U.S. trade paperback edition: February 2023

Published by Basic Books, an imprint of Perseus Books, LLC, a subsidiary of Hachette Book Group, Inc. The Basic Books name and logo is a trademark of the Hachette Book Group.

The Hachette Speakers Bureau provides a wide range of authors for speaking events. To find out more, go to www.hachettespeakersbureau.com or call (866) 376-6591.

Basic books may be purchased in bulk for business, educational, or promotional use. For information, please contact your local bookseller or Hachette Book Group Special Markets Department at special.markets@hbgusa.com.

The publisher is not responsible for websites (or their content) that are not owned by the publisher.

Typeset by Input Data Services Ltd, Somerset

Library of Congress Control Number: 2015938031

ISBNs: 9781541603486 (paperback), 9781541603493 (ebook)

LSC-C

Printing 1, 2022

For Charles

◆ CONTENTS ◆

◆ NOTE ON PLACE-NAMES ◆

Place-names are a touchy issue. When writing Part One of this book in the mid-1990s, I used Ukrainian-language place names in most instances, but English-language – which mostly meant Russian-language – ones for places well known to English-language readers. Hence Kiev rather Kyiv, Odessa rather than Odesa, the Dnieper River instead of the Dnipro. In Part Two, written a quarter of a century later, I have switched to today's usage, which is to transliterate from the Ukrainian in every case. To add to the complication, Communist place-names are gradually being replaced. Some cities have reverted to their pre-revolutionary names; others have been named for Ukrainian national figures. These changes are flagged in the text. For surviving inconsistencies (Crimea has not become Krim, for example), I beg the reader's forgiveness.

◆ CHRONOLOGY ◆

Mid 800's Scandinavians establish a trade-route along the Dnieper.

988 Prince Volodymyr baptised in Chersonesus.

1037 Santa Sofia Cathedral completed.

1240 Mongol army under Batu Khan captures Kiev.

1362 Lithuanian army under Grand Duke Algirdas captures Kiev.

1363 Lithuanian victory over the Mongols at the Battle of Blue Waters.

1386 Grand Duke Iogaila of Lithuania marries Queen Jadwiga of Poland, and is crowned Polish King.

Early 1400s First Cossack outposts established.

1553 Zaporozhian Sich founded.

1569 Union of Lublin creates the Polish–Lithuanian Commonwealth.

1596 Union of Brest creates the Uniate church.

1648 Khmelnystky Rebellion begins.

1654 Treaty of Pereyaslav. Khmelnytsky accepts Russian protection.

1657–'86 'The Ruin'. War between Russia, Poland, Turks and Cossacks for control of Ukraine.

1686 'Eternal Peace' between Russia and Poland hands Kiev and Cossack lands east of the Dnieper over to Russian rule.

1687 Mazeppa appointed Hetman of Russian-ruled Ukraine.

1708 Swedish army under Charles XII enters Ukraine. Mazeppa declares support for Charles.

1709 Battle of Poltava. Swedes and Cossacks defeated by Peter the Great.

1773 First partition of Poland. Galicia comes under Austrian rule.

1774 Treaty of Kuchuk Kainarji ends the Russo-Ottoman war.

1775 Catherine the Great destroys the Zaporozhian Sich.

1781 Catherine dissolves the Hetmanate.

1783 Catherine annexes Crimea.

1795 Third and final partition of Poland.

1830–'31 Polish rising.

1840 Shevchenko's *Kobzar* published.

1847 Shevchenko arrested and exiled.

1848 'Springtime of Nations'. Polish risings in Cracow and Lviv. Ukrainians' 'Supreme Ruthenian Council' declares loyalty to the Hapsburgs.

1861 Elected assemblies created in Vienna and Lviv, with limited Ukrainian representation.

1863–'64 Polish rising.

1876 Edict of Ems bans all Ukrainian-language publishing and teaching in the Russian empire.

1881 Alexander II assassinated by anarchists. Pogroms in Kiev, Odessa and Yelizavetgrad (Kirovohrad).

1890 First Ukrainian political party formed in Lviv.

1905 Nicholas II makes democratic concessions in face of strikes and mass demonstrations. Pogroms in Kiev, Odessa, Kherson and Nikolayev (Mykolayiv).

1908 Ukrainian student assassinates the Polish governor of Galicia.

March 1917 Nicholas II abdicates. Central Rada formed in Kiev.

November 1917 (October, old-style Julian calendar) Bolshevik coup in Petrograd (St. Petersburg).

January 1918 Red Army captures Kiev. Rada proclaims Ukrainian independence and flees.

March 1918 Treaty of Brest-Litovsk. German army occupies Kiev.

November 1918 West Ukrainian National Republic declared in Lviv. Ukrainian government flees to Stanyslaviv (Ivano-Frankivsk) in face of simultaneous Polish rising.

December 1918–August 1921 War between Red, White, Polish and Ukrainian armies, and 'Cossack' peasant bands, for control of Ukraine.

1923 Allies formally recognise Polish sovereignty in Galicia. *Korenizatsiya* launched in Soviet Ukraine.

1929 'Dekulakisation' and collectivisation begin.

1929–'33 Up to twelve million 'kulaks' deported.

1930 Ukrainian purges begin. Polish 'pacification' campaign in Galicia.

1932–'33 Up to five million peasants die of starvation in Soviet Ukraine.

1937–'39 Second wave of purges sweeps the Soviet Union. Up to one million Soviets executed, and up to twelve million sent to camps.

1939 Ribbentrop–Molotov Pact. Soviet Union occupies Galicia.

June 1941 Germany invades the Soviet Union. Massacre and deportation of Ukrainian Jews begins.

1942 Ukrainian Insurgent Army (UPA) formed.

1943–'44 Soviet army retakes Ukraine.

May 1944 Crimean Tatars deported.

1947 Last UPA units in Poland rounded up. Poland's Ukrainians deported to newly-acquired ex-German lands, and to the Soviet Union.

1954 Khrushchev hands Crimea to the Ukrainian SSR.

1965–'66 Arrest and showtrial of Ukrainian 'sixtiers'.

1972 Shcherbytsky appointed First Secretary of the Ukrainian Communist Party. Mass arrests of Ukrainian intelligentsia.

1976 Ukrainian Helsinki Group formed.

1986 Chernobyl explodes.

1988 First anti-communist demonstrations in Lviv and Kiev.

1989 Shcherbytsky sacked. Rukh holds its founding congress. Uniate parishes legalised.

March 1990 Semi-democratic elections to the Ukrainian Supreme Soviet.

September–October 1990 Mass demonstrations and student hunger strike in Kiev.

October 1990 Ukrainian Autocephalous Orthodox Church legalised.

August 1991 Attempted coup in Moscow. Ukrainian Supreme Soviet declares independence.

December 1991 Kravchuk elected president of Ukraine.

1993 Hyperinflation.

January 1994 Tripartite Agreement with Russia and America commits Ukraine to surrendering its nuclear weapons.

July 1994 Kuchma elected president.

1996 The hryvnya replaces the coupon.

1999 Former prime minister Lazarenko flees to the US. Kuchma wins a second presidential term, and appoints Yushchenko prime minister.

2000 Putin elected president of Russia. The Gongadze and Kuchmagate scandals break.

2001 Yushchenko resigns as prime minister.

2002 Tapes released in which Kuchma apparently agrees the sale of anti-aircraft systems to Iraq.

2003 Kuchma snubbed at a NATO summit.

2004 Yushchenko poisoned with dioxin in the run-up to presidential elections. The elections are rigged in Yanukovich's favour; the Orange Revolution forces a re-run; Yushchenko is elected president.

2008 Ukraine offered NATO membership in principle. Russia invades Georgia.

2010 Yanukovich elected president.

November 2013 Yanukovich abandons a trade deal with the EU. Mass demonstrations begin on Kiev's Maidan.

February 2014 Over a hundred protestors are shot dead by the security forces. Yanukovich flees to Russia; Russia invades Crimea.

April–May 2014 Pro-Russian militias take power in the eastern Donbass. Poroshenko elected president. Fighting begins between the militias and the Ukrainian army.

August 2014 Russia starts sending troops and heavy weaponry to the Donbass.

September 2014 Ceasefire and peace deal agreed in Minsk, but never implemented.

October 2014 Parliamentary elections produce a pro-European government.

February 2015 Putin and Poroshenko reach a second peace deal in Minsk, in talks brokered by Germany's Angela Merkel.

May 2015 Poroshenko signs 'De-Communisation' laws mandating the removal of Soviet-era monuments and place-names.

2017 Poroshenko signs an Education Law mandating Ukrainian-language teaching in most schools.

April 2019 Zelensky elected president.

May 2019 In his last days as president before Zelensky's inauguration,

Poroshenko signs a Language Law mandating the wider use of Ukrainian in local government, media, commerce and the arts.

July 2019   President Trump threatens Zelensky with a cut in military aid unless he helps him to discredit his Democrat rival, Joe Biden.

October 2021   Russian troops start to gather at the Ukrainian border.

24 February 2022   Russia invades Ukraine.

End February–early March 2022   Russian forces capture Kherson, surround and bombard Kharkiv, Mariupol and Chernihiv, and capture Kyiv commuter towns.

End March 2022   Russian forces withdraw from around Kyiv, Chernihiv and Kharkiv.

May 2022   President Biden signs a 'Ukraine Democracy Defense Lend-Lease Act', and Mariupol falls.

June 2022   European Union member countries agree dramatically to cut imports of Russian oil. Ukraine and Moldova are granted EU candidate status.

End June–early July 2022   Russian forces capture the Donbass towns of Severodonetsk and Lysychansk. Western long-range weapons systems start to arrive at the front.

◆ PREFACE TO 2023 EDITION ◆

This book is in two parts. The first was written in the mid-1990s, when Ukraine was a newborn state, in a state of economic collapse and still groping for a national identity. Because it gives a snapshot of the country at a formative time I have left the text unchanged, complete with then-current Russophone place-names – Kiev rather than Kyiv – and my then predictions as to Ukraine's future. Part Two was written and updated in stages, in the wake of three increasingly violent attempts by Russia to wrestle Ukraine back under its control. In 2004 President Putin tried and failed to rig a presidential election. In 2014 he seized Crimea and part of the Donbass, and in February 2022 he launched a full-scale war, which upended the post-Soviet world order and at the time of writing (summer 2022) is still hideously ongoing. But far from breaking Ukrainians' spirit, all Russia's attacks have done is make their sense of themselves and commitment to independence stronger. By 2014, Ukraine was already a completely different country from the one I lived in in the 1990s. And to travel there today is to see a sight unlike any since the Second World War: a large European democracy in arms, fighting tooth and nail against an invader that displays all the markers of fascism.

Shocked and horrified, the West's response has been to lend Ukraine money and send it increasing quantities of increasingly powerful weapons. Trade with Russia has not completely ceased. Nor, America's President Biden has made it clear, will NATO send troops or otherwise enter the conflict directly. Overall, though, governments have acted with unexpected firmness and speed. Public support for Ukraine may begin to wane as compassion fatigue sets in and fuel bills rise.

But for now it is sky-high and concretely expressed in a massive effort to help millions of Ukrainian refugees. May we keep it up, may they be able to return to a free, peaceful and prosperous country, and *vsye budye Ukraina!* – 'everything will be Ukraine!'

Anna Reid
London, July 2022

◆ PART ONE ◆

◆ CHAPTER ONE ◆

The New Jerusalem: Kiev

> But the brightest light of all was the
> white cross held by the gigantic statue
> of St Vladimir atop Vladimir hill.
> – *Mikhail Bulgakov, 1925*

UKRAINA is literally translated as 'on the edge' or 'borderland', and that is exactly what it is. Flat, fertile and fatally tempting to invaders, Ukraine was split between Russia and Poland from the mid seventeenth century to the end of the eighteenth, between Russia and Austria through the nineteenth, and between Russia, Poland, Czechoslovakia and Romania between the two world wars. Until the Soviet Union collapsed in 1991, it had never been an independent state.

Being a borderland meant two things. First, Ukrainians inherited a legacy of violence. 'Rebellion; Civil War; Pogroms; Famine; Purges; Holocaust' a friend remarked, flipping through the box of file-cards I assembled while researching this book. 'Where's the section on Peace and Prosperity?' Second, they were left with a tenuous, equivocal sense of national identity.

Though they rebelled at every opportunity, the few occasions on which they did achieve a measure of self-rule – during the Cossack risings of the seventeenth century, the Civil War of 1918–20, and towards the end of Nazi occupation – were nasty, brutish, and above all short. Moreover, until very recently Ukraine's neighbours did not see it as a separate country, or Ukrainians as a separate people, at all. To Russians it was part of Russia; to Poles, part of Poland. And many Ukrainians, Russified or Polonised by centuries of foreign domination, thought the same way. With inspiring moments in their schizophrenic history few and far between, and neighbours who refuse to acknowledge the existence of such a thing as 'Ukrainian' history in the first place, it is no wonder that Ukrainians are still puzzling out just who they are, and just what sort of place they want their country to be.

The story – Ukraine as borderland, Ukraine as battlefield, Ukraine as newborn state struggling to build itself a national identity – begins in Kiev. When I flew in, on a winter's night in 1993, the airport baggage hall was ankle-deep in lumpy brown slush. Our suitcases appeared on the back of a Kamaz truck, which dumped them in one large heap, leaving passengers to dig and scramble for their possessions. The road into the city – Ukraine's only four-lane highway, I found out later – was wrapped in Blitz-like blackness: no street lights, no crash barriers, no white lines. My companions smelt of wet clothes and old food, and carried large, oddly shaped bundles wrapped in string, with pieces of wood for handles. Deposited in a silent square in the middle of an invisible city, I went in search of a telephone box. What I found was a scratched bit of aluminium coping with an ancient Bakelite receiver attached – no instructions, no phone directory, no light. I didn't have any Ukrainian money either, but miraculously, it turned out not to matter. Inflation had done away with coinage, and Ukraine no longer used the Soviet roubles the phones had been designed for anyway, so now all calls were free. Suddenly things felt a little friendlier, more penetrable – my Ukrainian journey had begun.

Visitors to Kiev usually hate the place, but those who live there nearly always grow to love it. The staircase to my one-room flat might have stunk of urine and rotten cabbage, but outside raggedy black crows swung about in the poplars, shaking gobbets of frozen snow on to the rattling trams below. I liked the cobbled streets with their elaborately stuccoed turn-of-the-century houses, so dilapidated that the city authorities strung netting under the balconies to prevent chunks of plaster falling onto pedestrians' heads. I liked the hillside parks with their brick paths and rusty wrought-iron pavilions, where teenagers smooched in summer and children in rabbit-fur bonnets tobogganed in winter. I liked the old men playing chess on the benches round the pink-lit fountains on Independence Square, or shouldering home their tackle-boxes after a day's ice-fishing on the Dnieper. I liked the way dog-owners promenaded on Sunday mornings, gravely exchanging compliments on their exquisitely trimmed 'Jacks' and 'Johnnys'. I liked the echoey, pigeon-filled covered market, full of peasant women who called you 'little swallow' or 'little sunshine', and dabbed honey and sour cream onto one's fist to taste. I liked the couples dancing to an accordion – not for money, just for fun – in the dripping underpasses on Friday evenings. I liked buying posies of snowdrops, wrapped in ivy leaves and tied with green string, from the flower-sellers who appeared outside the metro stops early each spring. And in autumn I liked the bossy *babushki* who, passing on the street, told you to button up your coat and put on a hat, for the first snowfall had come. I even – sign of the true convert – grew to like *salo*, the raw pig-fat, eaten with black bread, salt and garlic, that is the national delicacy and star of a raft of jokes turning on the Ukrainian male's alleged preference for *salo* over sex.

All the same, Kiev was a melancholy city. Its defining features were failures, absences. Some were obvious: only one supermarket (dollars only), few private cars (six at an intersection counted as a traffic jam), a joke of a postal service (to send a letter, one went to the railway station, and handed it to a friendly face going in the right direction). Others one only felt the force of after a time. With benefits and pensions virtually non-existent, the crudest health care (drugs had to be paid for; doctors wanted bribes), and no insurance (a few private firms had sprung up, but nobody trusted them with their money), Kievans were living lives of a precariousness unknown in the West, destitution never more than an illness or a family quarrel away. It showed in their wiry bodies and pinched, alert, Depression-era faces; the faces of people who get by on cheap vodka and stale cigarettes, and know they have to look after themselves, for nobody else will do it for them.

The absences were physical too. Though better preserved than many ex-Soviet cities, ghosts haunted every corner. Here, an empty synagogue; there, the derelict shell of the once-grand Leipzig Hotel, left to rot by a corrupt city government. The pavement bookstalls sold a heartbreaking little brochure entitled *Lost Architectural Monuments of Kiev*, listing all the churches and monasteries demolished under Stalin – St Michael's of the Golden Domes, St Basil's, SS Boris and Gleb's, St Olga's, and on and on. With so many gaps, with so much missing, searching out the past required a sort of perverse enthusiasm, an archaeologist's eye for small clues and empty spaces.

The easiest of Kiev's pasts to re-create in the imagination is the raucous commercial city of the pre-revolutionary sugar boom. The novelist Aleksandr Kuprin, writing in the 1910s, described a town full of stevedores and pilgrims, Jewish hawkers, German madams, down-at-heel Russian officers, students, card-players, cigar smoke and cheap champagne. Most of Kiev's surviving historic centre – ponderous opera house, cobbled boulevards and the extraordinary Chimera House, barnacled with frogs, deer and rhinoceroses, that advertised the city's first cement factory – dates from then, and on summer evenings the streets still smell, as in Kuprin's day, of 'dust, lilac and warm stone'; riverboats whistle on the Dnieper and men drink *kvass* out of jam jars at little booths under the chestnut trees. A museum on Andriyivsky Uzviz, the helter-skelter lane that plunges down from Catherine II's rococo St Andrew's Church to Contract Square, once the site of a great annual fair, houses an atmospheric ragbag of period ephemera: sepia photographs of uniformed cadets lounging against a studio balustrade, a pair of white suede gloves, a painted umbrella, ivory elephants, a stereoscope, a curlicued shop-till, a velvet opera cloak trimmed with ostrich feathers.

But the past that gives Kiev unique glamour, that made it 'the City' to the novelist Mikhail Bulgakov and the 'Joy of the World' to the medieval chroniclers, is not the brash boom town of the turn of the last century, but the Kiev of a thousand years ago. From the tenth century to the thirteenth it was the capital of the eastern Slavs' first great civilisation, Kievan Rus. And here Ukraine's fight for an identity commences. Generations of scholars have bandied insults about how Rus began, how it was governed, even about how it got its name. But the biggest argument of all is over who Rus belongs to. Did Kievan Rus civilisation pass eastward, to Muscovy and the Russians, or did it stay put, in Ukraine? 'If Moscow is Russia's heart,' runs a Russian proverb, 'and St Petersburg its head, Kiev is its mother.' Ukrainians, of course, say Kiev has nothing whatsoever to do with Russia – if she mothered anybody, it was the Ukrainians themselves.

Kievan Rus's founders were neither Russians nor Ukrainians, but the same Scandinavians – variously known as Vikings, Varangians, Normans or Norsemen – who conquered Iceland and parts of England, Ireland and France in the ninth and tenth centuries. Their arrival in Slav lands, according to the earliest Rus history, the *Chronicle of Bygone Years*, was by invitation of the quarrelsome tribes scattered along the forest-bound rivers south of the Gulf of Finland:

5

There was no law among them, but tribe rose against tribe. Discord thus ensued among them, and they began to war one against another. They said to themselves, 'Let us seek a prince who may rule over us, and judge us according to the Law.' They accordingly went overseas to the Varangian Russes ... The Chuds, the Slavs, the Krivichians and the Ves then said to the people of Rus: 'Our land is great and rich, but there is no order in it. Come to rule and reign over us.'[1]

The *Chronicle* may be overstating the Scandinavians' importance. Some historians think there were never enough of them to have had much influence; others believe that one of the local tribes, the Polianians, built the foundations of Rus before their arrival. Either way, they came not as rulers but as merchants, along a trade route connecting the Baltic and Black seas via the river Dnieper. Sometime in the eighth century, they built their first outpost on Lake Ladoga, near present-day St Petersburg, and in 830, according to the *Chronicle*, they sailed their dragon-headed longboats downriver to the little wooden settlement atop sandstone bluffs that became the trading centre of Kiev. Byzantium's Emperor Constantine VII Porphyrogenitus, writing a memorandum on imperial administration in the tenth century, described boatfuls of slaves, fur, wax and honey floating down the Dnieper tributaries when the ice broke each spring. In Kiev they refitted with sails and oars, and in June they set off in armed convoy for the Black Sea and Constantinople. Hoards of the silver coins the Scandinavians got in return still turn up all the way from Ukraine back to Sweden. It was a dangerous journey, especially so 250 miles south, where a series of rapids meant the boats had to be unloaded and dragged overland, leaving them vulnerable to attack by fierce nomadic Pechenegs. Thus what started out as a commercial venture turned – like the Hudson's Bay and East India companies in centuries to come – into a political one. Trading posts turned into forts, forts into tribute-collecting points, and tribute-collecting points, by the end of the tenth century, into the largest kingdom in Europe, stretching from the Baltic to the Carpathians. In the process the Scandinavians' ruling dynasty, the Riuriks, adopted native customs and language, intermarrying with the local clans and Slavicising their names. Helgi became Oleh; Ingwarr, Ihor; Waldemar, Volodymyr.

The best surviving key to Rus greatness is Kiev's Saint Sofia Cathedral, built in 1037 by one of the greatest Riurik princes, Prince Yaroslav the Wise. From the outside it looks much like any other baroque Ukrainian church, its original shallow Greek domes and brick walls long covered in gilt and plaster. But inside it breathes the splendid austerity of Byzantium. Etiolated saints, draped in ochre and pink, march in shadowy fresco round the walls; above them a massive Virgin hangs in vivid glass mosaic, alone on a deep gold ground. Her robe, as described by the travel-writer Robert Byron in the 1930s, is of a 'tint whose radiant singularity no one that has seen it can ever forget . . . a porcelain blue, the blue of harebells or of a Siamese cat's eyes'.[2] On her feet she wears the crimson slippers of the Byzantine empresses, and she is framed by an inscription taken from Constantinople's Hagia Sofia: 'God is in the midst of her, therefore shall she not be moved; God helps her from morning to morning.' On the twin staircases leading to an upper gallery, imported Greek craftsmen painted holiday scenes from home – almost the only pictures we have of secular Byzantine life. Fourhorse chariots (or the bits of them that survived nineteenth century overpainting) race up the walls, cheered on from windows and balconies, while outside the hippodrome gates a clown dances and musicians play pipes, cymbals, flute and a bellows-organ.

Built to celebrate Yaroslav's father Volodymyr's conversion to Christianity, Saint Sofia's was intended as, and remains, a place of huge political and spiritual significance. Under the tsars, pilgrims came in millions. (A mournful early graffito reads, 'I drank away my clothes when I was here'.)[3] The Bolsheviks desanctified but never quite dared demolish it; during perestroika Ukrainian nationalists demonstrated outside it; in 1993 members of a New Age sect sprayed it with fire extinguishers while threatening mass suicide; and in 1996 Orthodox believers tried – illegally since it is now a museum – to bury their patriarch within its walls, making do with the pavement outside after scuffles with police. Although of course neither 'Ukraine' nor 'Russia' existed in his day, Volodymyr – Vladimir in Russian – became the patron saint of both Ukrainians and Russians, celebrated in countless folk-tales and in the large statue, erected by the Ukrainian diaspora, that puzzles residents of London's Holland Park.

For all Saint Sofia's passion-stirring power, the conversion that it was built to celebrate was a thoroughly pragmatic one. By the time Volodymyr came to the throne in 980, Christianity was already making itself felt in Rus; his grandmother Olha had privately taken baptism some years earlier. To start with, however, Volodymyr was an enthusiastic supporter of the pagan party. The *Chronicle of Bygone Years* says he 'set up idols on the hills outside the castle . . . one of Perun, made of wood with a head of silver and a moustache of gold, and others of Khors, Dazhbog, Stribog, Simargl and Mokosh. The people called them gods, and sacrificed their sons and daughters to them . . .'[4] Worse, the pious chroniclers go on, he was 'overcome with lust for women . . . he had three hundred concubines at Vyshorod, three hundred at Belhorod, and two hundred at Berestrovo. He was insatiable in vice. He even seduced married women and violated young girls, for he was a libertine like Solomon.'[5]

Despite these unpromising beginnings, Volodymyr must at some point have decided that to keep pace with its neighbours his empire needed an up-to-date religion. All that remained was to choose which one. The first people he consulted, according to the *Chronicle*, were the Muslim Bulgars: 'Volodymyr listened to them, for he was fond of women and indulgence, regarding which he had heard with pleasure. But circumcision and abstinence from pork and wine were disagreeable to him: "Drinking," said he, "is the joy of the Russes, and we cannot exist without that pleasure."'[6] Following this disappointment, he despatched fact-finding missions to research the remaining options. The Jews and Catholic Germans failed to impress. 'We saw them performing many ceremonies in their temples,' the emissaries reported back, 'but we beheld no glory there.'[7] But Hagia Sofia bowled the Kievans over: 'the Greeks led us to the edifices where they worship their God, and we knew not whether we were in heaven or on earth. For on earth there is no such splendour or beauty, and we are at a loss how to describe it. We only know that God dwells there among men, and their service is fairer than the ceremonies of other nations . . .'[8]

So Orthodoxy it was. In 988 Volodymyr ordered that the old thunder-god Perun be dragged down to the river and beaten with sticks, and herded the Kievans into a tributary of the Dnieper for mass baptism. 'Some stood up to their necks,' wrote the chroniclers, 'others to their breasts, and the younger nearer the bank, some of them holding children in their arms . . . there was joy in heaven and upon earth to behold so many souls saved.'[9] It was one of the single most important events in the history of Europe. By choosing Christianity rather than Islam, Volodymyr cast Rus's ambitions for ever in Europe rather than Asia, and by taking Christianity from Byzantium rather than Rome he bound the future Russians, Ukrainians and Belarussians together in Orthodoxy, fatally dividing them from their Catholic neighbours the Poles.

The drawbacks of the new religion lay in the future; its benefits made themselves felt straight away. By the time of its conversion, Rus already had well-established contacts with Byzantium. In 911 the first historically verifiable Riurik, Oleh, had raided Constantinople, nailing his shield, legend says, to the city gates, and outfitting his homebound fleet with sails of silk. Half a century later Princess Olha fascinated Emperor Constantine when they met to negotiate trading treaties, and her son Svyatoslav allied with Byzantium in a war against the Bulgars. With the Riuriks' accession to religious respectability the foreign-policy field widened, and they set about forging dynastic alliances with half the royal houses of Christendom. Having

captured Chersonesus, a Greek town on the Black Sea, Volodymyr forced Byzantium's Emperor Basil II to let him marry his
sister Anna, a move which enormously enhanced Rus's prestige.
His son Yaroslav earned the nickname 'Father-in-law of Europe'
by marrying his sons to Polish and Byzantine princesses, and his
three daughters to the kings of Hungary, Norway and France.

Unlikely though they seem, these were not unequal matches,
for Kievan Rus impressed Europeans with its sophistication as
well as its size and power. Bishop Gautier Saveraux, sent by
Henri I of France to ask for Yaroslav's daughter Anna's hand in
marriage, reported home that 'This land is more unified,
happier, stronger and more civilised than France herself.'[10]
Dispossessed princes such as Olaf of Norway and Aethelred and
Edward (later the Confessor) of England, were happy to while
away exiles at the Kievan court, and Anna amazed the Franks by
being able to read and write: a document from her brief regency
after Henri's death shows her signature – 'Anna Regina' – in
Cyrillic alongside illiterate French crosses. Hundreds of Byzantine clerics and scholars came to Kiev to staff Yaroslav's new
churches and translate the scriptures, and Kievan nobles adopted Byzantine dress – illuminated manuscripts show them in red
and purple silks cuffed and belted with gold brocade. Good
manners, as laid down by one of Yaroslav's successors, required
them to get up early, praise God, 'eat and drink without
unseemly noise' and refrain from beating their wives. Customary law, codified on Yaroslav's orders, was remarkably humane,
stipulating fines rather than corporal punishment.

But Kievan Rus's glory days were short-lived. Lying on his
deathbed in 1054 Yaroslav had pleaded with his offspring to
'love one another' for 'If ye dwell in envy and dissension,
quarrelling with one another, then ye will perish yourselves and
bring to ruin the land of your ancestors . . .'[11] They took no
notice, and the empire disintegrated into a clutch of warring
princedoms: Kiev, Chernihiv and Turov in the south; Galicia
and Volhynia in the west; Novgorod, Polotsk and Smolensk in
the north; Vladimir-Suzdal, Ryazan and Tver on the Volga. Kiev

itself degenerated from imperial capital into just another petty fiefdom, ruled by twenty-four different princes in a hundred years. A twelfth-century ballad, 'The Song of the Host of Igor', deplored the mess:

> brother says to brother:
> 'this is mine
> and that is mine too'
> and the princes have begun to say
> of what is small: 'this is big'
> while against their own selves
> they forge discord
> while from all sides with victories
> pagans enter the Russian land.[12]

Nemesis came in the thirteenth century, at the hands of the Mongols. Originating on the north-western borders of China, these superbly organised warrior nomads had already conquered southern Siberia, Central Asia and Iran. In 1237 an army under Batu Khan, a grandson of Genghis, swept across the Urals into Rus, as swift and terrifying, in the words of an Arab chronicler who saw them strike elsewhere, as 'a darkness chased by a cloud'. Swearing to 'tie Kiev to his horse's tail', Batu captured the city in 1240, after a long siege and savage street fighting. All but a handful of its 400 churches were burned, and its earth ramparts, pierced by the three Great Gates, were razed to the ground.

When the Mongol army withdrew two years later Kiev went into a long, near-terminal decline. Trade along the Dnieper had already dried up following the Crusades, which opened the eastern Mediterranean to Christian shipping. In 1299 Kiev lost its religious status too, when the Metropolitan, Rus's senior churchman, transferred his see to Vladimir, and thence, a few decades later, to Moscow. Constantly raided by Crimean Tatars, the city shrank to three barely connected settlements – the 'High City' around Saint Sofia's and the old Golden Gate, the

Cave Monastery on the hills opposite, and Podil, the old trading district on the river flats.

For the next half-millennium Kiev languished, a stagnant, forgotten backwater. A Venetian visiting in the 1470s described it as 'plain and poor'.[13] Catherine the Great, passing through on her way to Crimea in 1787, could hardly believe that this was Kiev the City of Glory, Kiev the New Jerusalem. 'From the time I arrived,' she complained, 'I have looked around for a city, but so far I have found only two fortresses and some outlying settlements.'[14] On into the 1800s, visitors bemoaned its wood-paved streets, crowds of crippled beggars, frequent floods and fires, lack of good stone buildings and dreadful drinking water – so bad, apparently, that even horses wouldn't touch it. The city only began to revive mid-century, with the arrival of the railways and the sugar boom.

Despite its short lifespan Kievan Rus – ancient, vast, civilised, impeccably European – makes history to be proud of. But whose history is it? According to the Russians, on the Mongols' retreat the population of Kievan Rus migrated north-east, taking their culture and institutions with them. While the old capital crumbled, Kievan splendour was reborn in Moscow, the fast-expanding principality that became Muscovy and thence Great Russia. Thus the heirs of Rus are not the Ukrainians, with their funny language and quaint provincial ways, but the far more successful Russians themselves.

Ukrainians, led by the turn-of-the century historian Mykhaylo Hrushevsky, say this is all nonsense. Muscovy bore no more relation to Kievan Rus than Gaul to Rome, and treating one as the continuation of the other is like tacking the history of France on to that of the Roman Empire. As for the actual population of Rus, it stayed exactly where it was – or if a few people did move north, they quickly came home again. 'The Kievan State, its laws and culture, were the creation of one nationality, the Ukrainian-Rus,' Hrushevsky wrote firmly, 'while the Volodimir-Moscow State was the creation of another nationality, the Great Russian.'[15] Russia, in other words, is not Ukraine's 'elder brother', but the other way round. Rather than calling Ukrainians 'Little Russians', perhaps Russians should be calling themselves 'Little Ukrainians'.

The official Soviet line on the dispute emphasised harmony, homogeneity, Brotherhood. Kievan Rus was inhabited by a single monolithic 'ancient Rus' nationality, from which Russians, Ukrainians and Belarussians all descended; for them to argue over Volodymyr and Yaroslav made no more sense than for the Germans and French to squabble over Charlemagne. The languages of all three nations descend from the ancient Slavs', and all three inherited Orthodoxy.

The Soviets had a point. But even as far back as Yaroslav, there were differences between northern Rus (the future Russia), and southern (future Ukraine and Belarus). The most obvious derived from climate and geography. Northerners lived in pine-forests, in log cabins; southerners amid oak and ash, in cottages of wattle and daub. Northerners, with their poor soil and nev-erending winters, ate black bread made from rye; southerners, with their rich black earth and longer growing season, ate white bread, made from less hardy wheat. Only the northerners took steam baths. 'They warm themselves to extreme heat,' the chroniclers had St Andrew, on a mythical journey from Kiev to Novgorod, report, 'then . . . take young reeds and lash their bodies . . . so violently that they barely escape alive. Then they drench themselves with cold water and are revived. They think nothing of doing this every day, and actually voluntarily inflict such torture upon themselves.'[16]

Distinctions between north and south were apparent in contemporary nomenclature too. Byzantium's Emperor Constantine VII Porphyrogenitus refers, in his *De Administrando Imperio* to 'near Rus', around Kiev, and 'distant Rus', on the peripheries. Though the term 'Ukrainian' did not come into general use until the end of the nineteenth century, the word *Ukraina*, denoting the lands around Kiev, first appears in a chronicle of 1187. Muscovites started calling themselves the

Russky, and their state by the Greek word for Rus, *Rossiya*, in the fourteenth century, while the future Ukrainians and Belarussians carried on referring to themselves as Russes or *Rusyny*, rendered in English as 'Ruthenians'.

What widened the split between the two halves of Rus dramatically was the arrival of the Mongols. Kiev and southern Rus suffered devastation, but were abandoned again in little over a century. The northern principalities, in contrast, became permanent tributaries of the Golden Horde.

The Mongols ruled by proxy, granting charters to local leaders in exchange for tribute. The most successful northern princes became those who could squeeze most men and money out of their territories for delivery to the khan at his capital on the Volga. Failure to pay was punished in the cruellest manner, and the death penalty, rare in Kievan Rus, became widespread. Tellingly, the Russian words for 'chain' and 'whip', as well as 'money', all have Mongol roots. 'The Russians learned from the Mongols,' writes the historian Richard Pipes, 'a conception of politics which limited the functions of the state to the collection of tribute (or taxes), maintenance of order, and preservation of security, but was entirely devoid of any sense of responsibility for public well-being.'[17] Towards the end of the fifteenth century, invaded from the east in its own turn, the Golden Horde fell apart, and the northern princes stopped paying tribute and ruled independently again. But by then the habit of violent, Asiatic-style despotism was there to stay. Scratch a Russian, as the saying goes, and you find a Tatar.

Whereas northern Rus fell to the Horde, southern Rus went to the Lithuanians. Warlike and turbulent, worshippers of trees, snakes, hares and streams, they were the only Baltic people to have successfully resisted the efforts of the mighty Teutonic Knights to convert and rule them. When Rus collapsed after the Mongol withdrawal, they filled the vacuum, quadrupling the size of their Duchy in less than a hundred years. In 1362 a Lithuanian army under Grand Duke Algirdas took Kiev, and the following year it inflicted a crushing defeat on the Mongols at the battle of Blue Waters in the bend of the Dnieper. The Lithuanian Grand Duchy now occupied roughly half the territory of old Rus, extending all the way from the Baltic to the Black Sea.

Despite their fierce reputation, the Lithuanians proved relatively gentle rulers. Without the numbers or resources to colonise or occupy, they adapted to existing arrangements, co-opting the old Rus nobility into government under the motto 'We do not change the old, nor do we bring in the new'. Many Lithuanians adopted Orthodoxy, and Ruthenian – the precursor to Ukrainian and Belarussian – became the Duchy's *lingua franca*. 'Magdeburg Rights', common throughout medieval Europe and granted to Kiev and the other old Rus cities in 1494, let burghers elect their own mayors and magistrates, and exempted them from various taxes. All this, according to Ukrainian historians, is why the traditions of Kievan Rus lived on in what was to become Ukraine, while they perished in Mongol-ruled Muscovy.

In reality, it is doubtful whether much of Kievan Rus survived anywhere. What the Lithuanians did do, with endless consequences for East European history, was forge Ukraine's centuries-long link with Poland. Soon after conquering southern Rus, the Lithuanians decided that to hold on to their new empire they needed an ally – in practice either the Teutons or the Poles. The Poles seemed the lesser of two evils, and in 1385 Grand Duke Iogaila opened negotiations for the hand in marriage of Poland's eleven-year-old girl-queen Jadwiga. The Polish barons, preferring a non-interfering Lithuanian to a powerful Hapsburg, agreed, and the following year the hastily baptised Iogaila was solemnly crowned King of Poland.

For Jadwiga, the marriage was a disaster. Handed over to a hairy heathen instead of her promised Austrian fiancé, she pined away, devoting herself to good works and dying childless at the age of twenty-four. Politically, however, it was a resounding success, climaxing with the Union of Lublin in 1569, which turned two separate states with a shared monarchy into 'The Most Serene Commonwealth of the Two Nations'. From the late fourteenth century until Russia took its first big bite out of the Commonwealth in the mid seventeenth, therefore, nearly the whole territory of present-day Ukraine, including Kiev, was ruled from the Polish royal capital of Cracow.

Here begins Ukraine's great debate – still raw, still undecided: are Ukrainians Central Europeans, like the Poles, or a species of Russian? Poles used to call western Ukraine 'Eastern Little Poland'; the Russian name for Ukraine was 'Little Russia'. The Ukrainian spoken in western Ukraine has lots of Polish words; the Ukrainian of central Ukraine is full of Russian ones. West Ukrainian men, like Poles, are addressed as 'Pan So-and-So'; central and eastern Ukrainians, like Russians, are 'Gospodin'. Most Ukrainians are Orthodox, but in the west a separate 'Uniate' church, founded at the end of the sixteenth century, combines Orthodox liturgy with obedience to the Pope. Western Ukraine has ruined Renaissance palaces, walled towns, oniondomed churches. Villages dot its rolling valleys, in Joseph Conrad's words, 'like clusters of boats hidden in the hollows of a running sea'. It is, in short, a far-flung slice of Mitteleuropa. Eastern Ukraine is flat, dreary and covered in beet-fields and slag-heaps – the western edge of the thousand-mile-wide Russian steppe.

Kiev is where the two legacies meet. The Dnieper, Ukraine's only major natural feature and the boundary which used to divide the country between Russia and Poland, also splits the city into two. The golden domes of its great Orthodox monasteries and the neo-Gothic spire of its Catholic cathedral jostle on the skyline, and Ukrainian and Russian mingle in a crude slang known as *surzhik* in the trolley-buses and on the streets.

The result, surprisingly, is lassitude rather than tension, shadowy cross-hatching rather than stark black and white. Ask a Kievan his background, and his reply will probably be something along the lines of 'My father is a Ukrainian raised in Siberia, my mother a Russian from Odessa, and our surname sounds Polish.' Unlike the burningly self-aware inhabitants of Vilnius or Tblisi, Kievans aren't yet quite sure who they are, and don't much care. Six years after independence, hammer-and-sickle emblems still top the parliament and foreign ministry buildings, and at the end of the central highstreet, the Khreshchatyk, Lenin stretches out an ox-blood marble hand to a billboard advertising a newly privatised bank. Engels Street has been renamed, but Karla Marksa has stayed in place. All these survivals are less a product of nostalgia than of a pragmatic inclination to let sleeping dogs lie.

One of the clues to Kiev's lack of ethnic or ideological fire is its resolute provincialism. For 700 years it has been a borderland city, a sleepy periphery to a buzzing centre elsewhere. Thrust to stardom on independence, it has not let fame change its style. Newspapers carry little but domestic news, several days late. The state-owned television channels subsist on folk-dancing footage intercut with shaky helicopter shots of Santa Sofia. (Viewing, as one Ukrainian-Canadian diplomat puts it, is 'an act of patriotism'.) Occasions on which Kiev is required to play the national capital tend to end in farce. When Bill Clinton visited in the spring of 1995 the government asked him to sleep in the presidential jet because none of the hotels were grand enough, and a reception for Prince Charles at the Mariyinsky Palace the following year was thrown into confusion when all the lights went out – a problem cunningly solved by shining police-car headlights in through the windows. Most Kievans have not travelled much, and the lucky exceptions are touchingly proud of the fact: a deputy foreign minister I interviewed had a map on his office wall with coloured pins marking all the places in the world he had been to. Foreigners in general, though no longer rarities, are still objects of polite interest and surmise.

Despite a population of 3 million, Kiev is a small place. Everyone who is anyone – Russians and Ukrainians, communists and nationalists, *biznesmeny* and politicians – knows everyone else. They studied at the same institutes, have relatives who work at the same ministries, eat beetroot-and-prune salad out of miniature pastry-cases at the same few sepulchral restaurants, and go to the same gloriously awful productions of *Tosca* and *Traviata* at the State Opera House in the evenings. The curtain rises, and the chorus is revealed lined up in height order, men in one corner, women in the other. The men wear preposterous beards, peeling around the ears. The women wave dead carnations from side to side, out of time with the music. Clouds of condensed breath spiral up from the orchestra pit to the nymphs on the ceiling, and in the interval there is a scramble for tepid orangeade and synthetic cream-cakes in the bar upstairs.

Indubitable proof of the slim talents required to win fame in Kiev came soon after my arrival, when my 'fixer' Sasha – combined impresario, computer-games importer and estate agent – persuaded me to record a song he had composed with English lyrics. The recording took place in a freezing flat in a suburban housing block. In a squeaky schoolgirl voice, I warbled over and over the words 'Dreaming girl/In the sky/Have a ball/ Live your lie'. A few weeks later we were filmed for television. Tucked away in a basement of the sports stadium, the studio had been decked out with bottles of vodka, a tinsel Christmas tree and posters of AEG white goods. I came on after a group called the 'Twenty Verhovinas' – a brand of cigarette. The compère asked me to introduce myself. 'Well, actually' – nervous giggle – 'I'm a journalist.' Sasha kicked me under the table: 'Anna is an artist, a singer from misty Albion!' The result – vodka-flushed face, hopeless lip-synch, novelty camera-work – went out nationwide on New Year's Eve. I was a Ukrainian pop-star.

Seven hundred years of provincialism has had its advantages. Third city of the empire, Kiev never felt the grip of government in quite the same way as Moscow and St Petersburg. An early traveller to say so was Paul of Aleppo, an Orthodox cleric who accompanied his father Macarius, Patriarch of Antioch, on a fund-raising mission to the tsar in the 1650s. Landing at the mouth of the Dnieper, this smooth Mediterranean pair were initially not much taken with Ukraine. The mosquitoes bit, the food was dreadful, and the services went on for ever. 'We never left church,' Paul confided to his diary, 'but tottering on our legs after so much standing.'[18]

Moscow, though, was far worse. 'Anyone wishing to shorten his life by five or ten years,' Paul wrote, 'should go to Muscovy.' In the monasteries 'mirth and laughter and jokes' were forbidden, and spies watched through cracks in the doors to see 'whether the inmates practise devotional humility, fasting and prayer; or whether they get drunk and amuse themselves'. Drinkers, he was told, were sent to Siberia; smokers were liable for execution – news which put him 'in great fear' on his own account.[19] After all this, as he wrote on his journey home, Ukraine seemed like paradise:

> For during those two years spent in Muscovy a padlock had been set on our hearts, and we were in the extremity of narrowness and compressure of our minds; for in that country no person can feel anything of freedom or cheerfulness . . . The country of the Kosaks [Ukrainian Cossacks], on the contrary, was like our own country to us, and its inhabitants were to us boon companions and fellows like ourselves.[20]

The battered pair were even happier to reach Moldova, where they 'entered the bath, after twenty-seven months, during the whole of which time we had neither entered a bath nor washed ourselves with water'.[21]

As under the tsars, so under communism. Touring churches in the early 1930s, Robert Byron found that Moscow suffered from 'a stifling air – how stifling I only realised on reaching Kiev, which preserves in some indefinable way its old university tradition of the humanities and allows one to breathe normally again'.[22] An elderly professor showed him round Santa Sofia, the Academy of Sciences and the antiquarian bookshops, introducing him to friends on the way. It was all just like an afternoon in

Oxford and 'quite abnormal after the ferocious isolation of Moscow'.[23]

John Steinbeck, on an epic pub-crawl round the Soviet Union with the photographer Robert Capa soon after the war, was similarly struck:

> Everyone had told us it would be different once we got outside of Moscow, that the sternness and tenseness would not exist. And this was true . . . the people in Kiev did not seem to have the dead weariness of the Moscow people. They did not slouch when they walked, their shoulders were back, and they laughed in the streets.[24]

Even the girls were prettier: 'mostly blond, with fine, womanly figures'.

Unfashionable, easy-going, simultaneously of east and of west, in many ways Kiev represents the country whose capital it has become rather well. But to equate Kiev with Ukraine is to make an error. The 'real' Ukraine, the Ukraine that has outlived armies and ideologies, lies in the countryside. Half an hour's drive out of the city one enters a pre-modern world of dirt roads and horse-drawn carts, of outdoor wells and felt boots, of vast silences and velvet-black nights. The people here live off their own pigs and cows, fruit-trees and hives; they drink themselves to death on home-brewed vodka, roll cigarettes out of old newspapers, and curse 'American spaceships' for dropping Colorado beetles on the potato-plants. In winter they wrap their two-room cottages in dried maize stalks for extra insulation, and in spring they drown in Bruegelesque seas of knee-high mud. So closed, so absolutely basic is this world that Kievans treat trips out of town like treks through a wilderness, equipping themselves with portable water-heaters and several days' worth of picnic.

The man who best drew the contrast between Kiev and Ukraine was the novelist Mikhail Bulgakov. Son of a theology professor, he was brought up in a small house on Andriyivsky

Uzviz, the steep cobbled lane that winds down from the High City to Podil. His Kiev, immortalised in *The White Guard*, is the middle-class city of the years just before the revolution – the Kiev of the La Marquise confectioner's and the Fleurs de Nice flower shop, of chiming clocks and Dutch-tiled stoves, of sugar tongs and the green-shaded lamp in his father's study. Writing from the inflation-wracked Moscow of the early 1920s, Bulgakov turned these vanished comforts into something rich and strange:

> Beautiful in the frost and mist-covered hills above the Dnieper, the life of the City hummed and steamed like a many-layered honeycomb. All day long smoke spiralled in ribbons up to the sky from innumerable chimney-pots. A haze floated over the streets, the packed snow creaked underfoot, houses towered to five, six and even seven storeys. By day their windows were black, while at night they shone in rows against the deep, dark blue sky . . . [25]

But for Bulgakov – a conservative middle-class Russian – Kiev and Ukraine were two different things. Kiev stood for trams, electric light, the civilised and familiar; Ukraine for low dark horizons, a strange language, fear of the unknown. 'Although life in the City went on with apparent normality,' he wrote of Kiev during the Civil War, 'not a single person in it knew what was going on around and about the City, in the real Ukraine, a country of tens of millions of people, bigger than France . . . They neither knew nor cared about the real Ukraine and they hated it with all their heart and soul.'[26]

The battle *The White Guard* describes – between Reds, Whites and Ukrainian partisans – is not only a battle for a city, but a battle for an identity, for an imprimatur from something far older and grander than the participants themselves – in other words, for Kievan Rus. St Volodymyr – the polygamous prince who ordered Perun to be drowned and beaten – hovers above the action in the form of the cast-iron statue, holding an illuminated cross, which still stands above the Dnieper in one of Kiev's parks. At the close of the book, as the Bolsheviks prepare to take the city from the partisans, Bulgakov turns the saint back into a warrior:

> Above the bank of the Dnieper the midnight cross of St Vladimir thrust itself above the sinful, bloodstained, snowbound earth toward the grim, black sky. From far away it looked as if the cross-piece had vanished, had merged with the upright, turning the cross into a sharp and menacing sword.[27]

For Bulgakov, Volodymyr was defending a lost empire, perhaps a lost way of life. For Ukrainians, he stands for a lost history; the first equivocal staging post in a battle which stretches over a millennium.

◆ CHAPTER TWO ◆

Poles and Cossacks:
Kamyanets Podilsky

You boast, because we once
Brought Poland to calamity.
And so it was; Poland fell,
But you were crushed by her fall as well.
– Taras Shevchenko, 1845

May you croak in the faith of the Poles!
– Traditional Ukrainian curse

KAMYANETS PODILSKY HAD one functioning café, a dark, damp
cell built into the medieval city walls. It sold ersatz 'Jacky'
coffee and cardboard biscuits, and its only other customer was a
wispy young man in a tweed jacket and fogeyish leather
brogues. Hearing foreign voices, he came over and produced a
business card, a flimsy photocopied rectangle with a home-
drawn logo above the words 'Valery Chesnevsky, Architect'.
Underneath, in careful Latin lettering, he pencilled in the word
'Unemployed'. The reason he was unemployed, he said, was that
he was a Pole – the only one left in Kamyanets.

Kamyanets used to guard Poland's south-eastern border
against the Turks. Encircled by the rocky gorge of the Smotrych
river and accessible only by soaring single-span bridges, it was
one of Christendom's mythic outposts, remote yet uniquely

impregnable. A Turkish sultan, passing by at the head of his army, is said to have asked who fortified the city. 'God himself,' came the answer. 'In that case,' replied the sultan, 'let God himself storm it.' In 1672 the Turks did capture the city, albeit briefly, and the spell was broken. A minaret went up in the courtyard of the SS Piotra i Pawla Cathedral, and the words 'There is no God but God, and Mohammed is the Apostle of God' were inscribed in Arabic – as reported by a startled Victorian missionary – over the door. The nearby Polish fortress of Khotyn, its curved curtain walls the work of Genoese military engineers, housed the local pasha's harem: the young Prince Adam Czartoryski, touring with his tutor in the 1780s, when the region had fallen to the Turks for a second time, thought its women 'very untidily dressed'.[1] Today there is nothing to show that Khotyn was built by Italians on behalf of Poles, the guidebook on sale at the ticket-booth baldly informing visitors that it symbolises 'the struggle of the Ukrainian people against foreign invaders'.

Being an architect in Kamyanets, said Valery, was a depressing business. Run by Ukrainian nationalists, the local government would not give work to a Pole. Outdoors, hunched against a bitter wind, it didn't look as if there was much work to be had anyway. From a distance the city – all pepper-pot fortress and baroque bell-towers – had looked picturesque, poster-cute. Close up, it was falling to bits. Stained, cracked, swathed in black plastic and wooden scaffolding, its historic buildings stood about like relics of some lost civilisation, as irrelevant to their surroundings as Inca temples to a Peruvian peasant. There were no shoppers, no strollers, no tourists; in the weed-grown central square, the only sign of life was an old woman grazing a scabby pony. Passing a buttressed wall, Valery made me kneel down and peer between a pair of wooden doors, half off their hinges. All I could see was a mess of rubble and puddles, bird-droppings and fallen beams. This, he told me, had been a Benedictine monastery. A clothing factory had set up shop in the medieval cloisters the previous summer, and some bales of cotton had caught fire. 'The fire station isn't far away, but they mainly tried to save the factory. Nobody cared about the church, so it burned out.'

Not all Kamyanets's churches were as forsaken. Walls might sag and ceilings might drip, but bit by bit some at least were coming back to life. Catholic monks from Cracow had put a new copper roof on the cathedral and installed two or three pews – all they needed, since most of the city's Poles were deported by Stalin after the war. A card pinned up by the door outlined a four-point plan for new communicants: '1. GET BAPTISED. 2. GET MARRIED IN CHURCH. 3. HAVE YOUR CHILDREN BAPTISED. 4. SEE OUR PRIEST.' The other churches were being taken over by the Orthodox and the Uniates. In Trinity Church technicolored icons, draped with embroidered napkins, filled the niches where Polish madonnas once stood; the nave of St George's, a planetarium under communism, had been cut in two by a new plywood iconostatis. Valery's star exhibit was in the cathedral vestry, a leftover from its days as a Museum of Atheism. On a window-sill stood a knee-high mechanical model of a monk shouldering a wicker basket. Valery turned a handle and the lid of the basket opened, revealing a naked girl. 'This is how they taught us that monks were not monks, and monasteries were whorehouses.'

Ukraine's relationship with Poland is difficult and contradictory. For 500 years they shared a common history, first under the Polish kings, then under the Russian tsars. But like rival siblings they define themselves more by their differences than their similarities – Poland glamorous and self-dramatising; Ukraine inarticulate and put-upon. Ukraine resents Poland for hogging the limelight; Poland resents Ukraine for stealing its lines. Ukrainians, like the Irish, rebelled against their Polish landlords at every opportunity; Poles, like the English, responded with a curious mixture of affection, scorn and fear. The Ukrainians, one interwar Polish memoirist wrote of the tenants on her lost Volhynian estates, were 'singers of songs as beautiful as any in the whole world; a slothful bovine people whose torpor concealed an element which might break out into a hurricane at any moment . . .'[2]

That the relationship would end in acrimony was not a foregone conclusion, for the Poland that Ukraine joined with Iogaila's marriage to Jadwiga was a country ahead of its time. Power was divided between the king and the Sejm, a representative assembly elected by the nobility or *szlachta*. Uniquely, the *szlachta* comprised around 10 per cent of the population, giving a level of representation that would not be bettered elsewhere until the nineteenth-century British Reform Acts, and forcing princely magnates to share power on an equal basis, in theory at least, with poor smallholders whose pride was the only thing differentiating them from the surrounding peasantry. Only the Sejm could make legislation, and the king could not raise taxes or troops without its consent. From the late sixteenth century onward the *szlachta* also appointed the king himself, at a rowdy gathering in a field outside Warsaw. Poland thus became that constitutional oddity, an elective monarchy, and a Republic of Nobles.

Compared to *szlachta* status, religion and race were unimportant. The nobility included Ruthenians (the Polish name for what were to become Ukrainians and Belarussians), Lithuanians, Jews, Germans, Moldovans, Armenians, Italians, Magyars, Bohemians and even Muslim Tatars. 'One is born noble, not Catholic' was the motto. Catholics, Protestants and Orthodox all served in the upper house of the Sejm, and the legal system used six different languages – Ruthenian (precursor to Ukrainian and Belarussian), Polish, Hebrew, Armenian, German and Latin. The Reformation saw an influx of recherché nonconformist refugees, who were allowed to build churches and proselytise. Lviv, in present-day western Ukraine, became the only city in the world besides Rome to host three Christian archbishoprics – Catholic, Orthodox and Armenian. Zygmunt August, last of Iogaila's descendants, called himself 'King of the people, not of their consciences', and his father Zygmunt the

Elder put down a bumptious cleric with the words 'Permit me, Sir, to be King of both the sheep and the goats'.[3]

But the virtues of the Polish system were also its weaknesses. Unfettered by a strong monarchy, the wealthiest magnates – Ruthenians and Lithuanians as well as Poles – operated like independent rulers. In the wide, underpopulated eastern border-lands they accumulated vast estates as big as many a Western kingdom. Guillaume Le Vasseur, Sieur de Beauplan, a French military engineer who worked for the Polish crown in Ukraine through the 1630s and '40s, wrote that these 'kinglets' had 'the right to place crowns on their coats of arms, in the manner of minor sovereigns, to cast as much cannon as they please, and to build fortresses as strong as their means may permit. Neither the king nor the Commonwealth may prevent them. Indeed, they lack only the right to coin money to be sovereign.'[4] Quarrels between 'kinglets' were frequent, and settled in full-scale battles involving thousands of armed retainers. Judicial rulings from Cracow were routinely flouted: one magnate paraded at court in a suit fashioned from all the writs he had received and ignored. Poles still use the expression 'Write to me in Berdychiv' – a small town west of Kiev – to mean 'Catch me if you can'.

With the rise of the great landowners, Polish society, once so tolerant and inclusive, began to atrophy and fossilise. In the early sixteenth century, just as the rest of Europe was abandon-ing serfdom, Poland introduced it, the better to exploit an export boom in grain. Rather than extract money rents from peasant farmers, landowners preferred to take the land in hand and turn it over to wheat, using the peasantry as free labour. 'Ukraine was treated,' in the words of the historian Adam Zamoyski, 'by its own élite as well as by the Poles, as a sort of colony.'[5] Laws were passed making it difficult for peasants to leave the land, and they lost their rights of appeal, leaving them at the mercy of local manorial courts. De Beauplan described the results:

The local peasants are in a very miserable state, being obliged to work, with their horses, three days a week in the service of their lord, and having to pay him, in proportion to the land they hold, many bushels of grain, and plenty of capons, hens, goslings and chickens, at Easter, Pentecost and Christmas. What is more, they must cart wood for their lord, and fulfil a thousand other manorial obligations, to which they ought not to be subject . . . the lords have absolute power not only over their possessions, but also their lives, so great is the liberty of Polish nobles (who live as if they were in paradise, and the peasants in purgatory). Thus if it happens that these wretched peasants fall into the bondage of evil lords, they are in a more deplorable state than convicts sentenced to the galleys . . .[6]

The weirdest manifestation of the new exclusivity was the cult of 'Sarmatism', based on the lunatic notion that the Polish nobility were descended from a mythic eastern warrior-tribe called the Sarmatians, justifying an imaginary racial divide with the rest of the population. In line with their newly-invented Sarmatian credentials, the *szlachta* developed a bizarre taste for the bejewelled and exotic. Turkish carpets and enamelled coffee pots started appearing in wood-girt Polish manor houses; Polish knights shaved their heads, wore Arab-style chain-mail armour, and dyed their horses' hides cochineal pink or patriotic red-and-white on special occasions. Poles ended up looking so oriental, in fact, that at the battle of Vienna in 1683 Jan Sobieski had to order his troops to wear straw cockades so as to distinguish them from the enemy Turks.

With serfdom and Sarmatism came the end of religious toleration. Towards the end of the sixteenth century, with the Counter-Reformation and Poland's wars against the Swedes and Turks, Polishness became increasingly identified with Catholicism. Nonconformists were banished, entry to the *szlachta* was barred to non-Catholics, and a new chain of Jesuit colleges set about converting the sons of the Orthodox nobility. The high point of the Catholic push came when Piotr Skarga, an influential Jesuit divine, persuaded a group of Orthodox bishops, hopeful of being admitted to the upper house of the Sejm, to acknowledge papal supremacy while retaining their own Slavonic liturgy and their priests' right to marry. In 1596 an Act of Union was signed at Brest creating the 'Greek-Catholic' or Uniate Church, which dominates western Ukraine to this day. The rest of the Orthodox were furious, denouncing the Union and calling for an anti-Catholic alliance with the Protestants. Alarmed by the uproar, two of the four new Uniate bishops turned tail and reverted to Orthodoxy. 'Your dear Union,' the chancellor of Lithuania wrote to one of the remainder, 'has brought so much bitterness that we wish it had never been thought of, for we have only trouble and tears from it.'[7]

Though Catholic proselytising soured relations between the Commonwealth and Ruthenians in general, it did stunningly well within an important group – the Ruthenian nobility. A mournful work of 1612, entitled 'Trenos or Lament of the Holy Eastern Church', asked what had happened to the old families of ancient Rus:

> Where are the priceless jewels of [Orthodoxy's] crown, such famous families of Ruthenian princes as Slutsky, Zaslavsky, Zbarazky, Vyshnevetsky, Sangushsky, Chartorysky, Pronsky, Ruzhynsky, Solomyretsky, Holovchynsky, Koropynsky, Masalsky, Horsky, Sokolynsky, Lukomsky, Ruznya, and others without number? Where are those who surrounded them . . . the well-born, glorious, brave, strong, and ancient houses of the Ruthenian nation who were renowned throughout the world for their high repute, power and bravery?[8]

It was a rhetorical question. Vyshnevetsky had turned into Wisniowiecki, Sangushsky into Sanguszko, Chartorysky into Czartoryski – the Ruthenian nobility, in other words, had adopted the faith, language and manners of the ruling Poles. By the mid seventeenth century, according to de Beauplan, Ukraine's nobles seemed 'ashamed of any religion but the Roman, to which more of them are converting every day, even though the great men of wealth and all those who bear the title of prince issue from the Greek religion.'[9]

Though as individual families the Ruthenian nobility flourished, providing many of the greatest names in Polish history, as a distinct group it disappeared. For the rest of the Ruthenians – later to re-identify themselves as Ukrainians and Belarussians – this was a long-term disaster. Shorn of their native élite – the class that founded and filled schools and universities, patronised the arts, built churches and palaces, invested in trade and manufacturing – they turned into a leaderless people, a 'non-historic nation'. Ruthenian became the language of serfs and servants, barn and byre. Right up to the First World War the words 'Ruthenian' and 'peasant' were virtually synonymous, used interchangeably in Polish letters and memoirs. Ukrainians and Belarussians did not get their own national leaders again until the mid nineteenth century, when a great wave of ethnic consciousness, borne along by the Romantic fascination with all things folkloric and obscure, swept the whole of Eastern Europe. The new enthusiasts were not the descendants of the old Rus princes, but writers, teachers and antiquarians, offspring of a fledgling educated middle class.

Polish rule robbed Ukraine of its nobility. But it also saw the emergence of a new power in the region – the Cossacks. Outlaws and frontiersmen, fighters and pioneers, the Cossacks are to the Ukrainian national consciousness what cowboys are to the American. Unlike the remote and sanctified Rus princes, the Cossacks make heroes Ukrainians can relate to. They ranged the steppe in covered wagons, drawing them up in squares in case of Tatar attack. They raided Turkish ports in sixty-foot-long double-ruddered galleys, built of willow-wood and buoyed up with bundles of hollow reeds. They wore splendid moustaches, red boots and baggy trousers 'as wide as the Black Sea'. They danced, sang and drank *horilka* in heroic quantities. 'No sooner are they out of one state of inebriation,' wrote de Beauplan, 'than they set about drinking again as before.'[10]

Though the historical Cossacks ceased to exist in the eighteenth century, they lived on powerfully in the Ukrainian imagination. The anarchic peasant armies of the Russian Civil War called themselves 'Cossacks', as do a few fringe nationalists today, turning out in astrakhan hats and home-made uniforms at anti-communist rallies. *Khokhol* – the name of the long pony-tail, worn with a shaven head, which was the Cossack hallmark – is still derogatory Russian slang for a Ukrainian.

Cossackdom had its beginnings in the early fifteenth century, when the Grand Dukes of Lithuania built a line of forts on the edge of the empty 'wild field' between the Duchy and Tatar-ruled Crimea. Initially garrisoned with Tatar mercenaries called 'kazaks' or 'free adventurers', they soon attracted runaways of every class and nationality – escaped serfs, indebted nobles, defrocked priests. By the end of the century these makeshift frontier communities had turned into a semi-independent society with its own elected leaders – called 'hetmans' and 'otamans' – army, laws and vocabulary. Epitome of Cossackdom was the Zaporozhian Sich, a stockaded wooden barracks-town on a remote island south of the Dnieper rapids. Symbol of freedom for generations of Ukrainians, it was where the wildest outlaws gathered, the most daring raids were plotted, and the most *horilka* drunk. No women were allowed to enter the Sich, and important decisions were taken by the Rada, a rough-and-ready open-air assembly where, in theory at least, everybody had an equal voice. 'This Republic could be compared to the Spartan,' wrote a seventeenth-century Venetian envoy, Alberto Vimina, 'if the Kozaks respected sobriety as highly as did the Spartans.'[11]

Despite Ukrainian wishful thinking, Cossackdom never formed anything approaching a state in the modern sense of the word. It had no borders, no written laws, no division between army and administration, and no permanent capital (the Sich moved several times in its career). Nor, since not all Ukrainians were Cossacks and not all Cossacks Ukrainians, did Cossackdom form an embryo Ukrainian nation. As Zamoyski says, the Cossacks were not a people, but a way of life.

What they also certainly were was a military power. Most of the time they worked on the land as ordinary farmers and craftsmen. 'Among these people,' wrote de Beauplan, 'are found individuals expert in all the trades necessary for human life: house and ship carpenters, cartwrights, blacksmiths, armourers, tanners, harnessmakers, shoemakers, coopers, tailors, and so forth.'[12] But when inclination and the hetman dictated, they took up horse-tail banners and spiked maces, and launched fearsome raids deep into Poland. In 1498 they reached Jaroslaw, west of Lviv; four years later they got all the way to the Vistula.

Poland's response, never more than partially succesful, was to try to redirect Cossack aggression eastwards, towards the Muscovites and Turks. In 1578 King Stefan Batory granted the wealthier, town-dwelling Cossacks stipends in exchange for military service against Muscovy and the wild outlaws of the Sich. The move split Cossackdom into three – the 3,000 'registered' Cossacks loyal to the Poles, the 5,000 or 6,000 independent Cossacks of the Sich, and the remaining 40,000 or so who pitched in on either side as whim and circumstance dictated.

As far as attacking Turkey was concerned, Batory's arrangement worked brilliantly. Between 1600 and 1620 the Cossacks mounted sea-raids against Akkerman, Trabizond, Kaffa, Perekop, Varna, Kilia and Ismail, and burned Constantinople twice. The price of captured slaves fell so low, according to Paul of Aleppo, that 'Every gentleman of fortune owns seventy or eighty Tatar males, and every rich matron fifty or sixty women or girls'.[13] Europe rang with the Cossacks' praises: from scrubby renegades they had turned into latter-day Crusaders, new paladins in a holy war against the godless Mohammedan. 'The horrible Turk opened his mouth,' wrote a Polish polemicist approvingly, 'but the brave Rus thrust his arm within. When Turkey rushed upon Poland with a mighty army, it was stopped by the Ruthenian force.'[14] But what the Polish stipends signally failed to do was to stop the Cossacks attacking Poland herself. A series of uprisings – in 1591, 1595, 1625, 1635 and 1637 – was met with equally vicious pacification campaigns, culminating in 1648 with the biggest and bloodiest Cossack rebellion of them all, under Hetman Bohdan Khmelnytsky.

Of all the endlessly mythologised figures of Ukrainian history, Khmelnytsky is both the most influential and the most mysterious. For Ukrainians he is the leader of the first Ukrainian war of independence; for Poles he is the misguided peasant rebel who split the Commonwealth, pushing Poland into her long pre-Partition decline. For Jews he is the prototype *pogromshchik*, author of the infamous Khmelnytsky massacres; for Russians he is the founder of the Great Slav Brotherhood, the Moses who led Ukraine out of Polish bondage into the welcoming arms of Muscovy. In Kiev, the tsars erected a statue of him astride a rearing charger, pointing his mace towards the north-east and Moscow. According to its original design, the hetman was to have been represented trampling the cowering figures of a Polish nobleman, a Catholic priest and a Jew. Wiser councils prevailed, and today a solitary Khmelnytsky slices the uncomplaining air on a traffic island outside Santa Sofia Cathedral.

It is hard to make out what kind of man Khmelnytsky was in real life. Polish tradition paints a lurid picture of a half-mad drunkard surrounded by necromancers, terrified by his own runaway success. But contemporary accounts from outsiders describe a quite different figure: plain, judicious and oddly at variance with the chaotic rebellion to which he gave his name. The Venetian envoy Vimina, in Ukraine in 1650, reported Khmelnytsky to be 'of more than middle height, with wide bones and of a powerful build. His utterances and his system of governing indicated that he possesses judicial thinking and a penetrating mind. In his manner he is gentle and unaffected, thereby winning the love of the Kozaks.' Though the hetman conversed happily in Latin, his surroundings were austerely military: 'There is no luxury of any kind in his room; the walls are bare. The furniture consists of rough wooden benches covered with leather cushions ... A damask rug lies before the hetman's small bed, at the head of which hang a bow and a sabre.'[15] A couple of years later, Paul of Aleppo was surprised to find this 'old man, possessing every quality of a leader' having dinner in 'a small and mean shelter . . . with the table spread before him and no other dish laid on it but a mess of boiled fennel'.[16]

For the first fifty years of his life, Khmelnytsky pursued a perfectly conventional *szlachta* career. Born around 1595 of noble Orthodox parents, he was educated by Jesuits at Jaroslaw, before joining the Polish army. Serving in Moldova, he fell prisoner to the Turks and spent two years in captivity. In 1622 he came home to the family estate in central Ukraine, where he spent the next twenty-five years farming and bringing up his family, avoiding involvement in the uprisings of the 1620s and '30s and climbing steadily up the ranks of loyal registered Cossacks. What induced this respectable middle-aged figure to start a rebellion that would last eight years, lay waste Ukraine, kill hundreds of thousands of people and almost destroy the Commonwealth of which he had hitherto been a loyal and successful member?

The answer, apparently, was a personal grudge. In 1646, while Khmelnytsky, now a widower, was away on business, a Polish neighbour with whom he had quarrelled raided his estate, beating to death his young son and kidnapping the woman he had been planning to marry. Having failed to win redress from the local courts or the Senate in Warsaw, in January 1648 the infuriated Khmelnytsky fled to the Sich, where he succeeded in persuading the Zaporozhians to rise once more under his leadership. At the same time he concluded an alliance with the Tatar khan, giving him a force of 4,000 cavalry, vital against the Poles' fearsome Husaria, who galloped into battle with twenty-foot lances and feather-covered wooden wings hissing above their heads. Forewarned, the Poles marched south, and in April the two sides came face to face at a village north-west of the Sich called Yellow Waters, where a 3,000-strong Polish advance guard was surrounded and cut to pieces.

That spring and summer Khmelnytsky seemed invincible. Marching north-west towards Warsaw, his raggle-taggle army scored victory after victory, leaving the Commonwealth in tatters. Registered Cossack troops came over to the rebels in droves, and all over the country peasants took the opportunity to loot and massacre. 'Wherever they found the *szlachta*, royal officials or Jews,' says the nearly contemporary *Eye-Witness Chronicle*, 'they killed them all, sparing neither women nor children. They pillaged the estates of the Jews and nobles, burned churches and killed their priests, leaving nothing whole. It was a rare individual in those days who had not soaked his hands in blood . . .'[17] Jarema Wisniowiecki, leader of an earlier pacification campaign and the most powerful magnate in Ukraine, raised his own army and instituted savage reprisals, ordering captives to be tortured 'so that they feel they are dying'. Imitating the Tatars, both sides took to using prisoners for target practice, or impaled them alive upon wooden stakes.

For three years Khmelnytsky held all of present-day western and central Ukraine, from Lviv in the west to Poltava in the east. His luck ran out in 1651, when the Cossacks were deserted by their Tatar allies and suffered a crushing defeat at Berestechko, north-east of Lviv. Beaten and betrayed, Khmelnytsky needed an ally. Fatefully – some would say fatally – for the whole of Eastern Europe, he found it in Russia.

By now Muscovy was already a vast empire. Ivan IV ('The Formidable' to Russians, 'The Terrible' to everyone else) had conquered the Muslim khanates of Kazan and Astrakhan, taking the border south to the shores of the Caspian. Trappers and traders had crossed the whole length of Siberia, followed by officials staking out taiga and pine-forest for Moscow. But compared to their neighbours the Russians were still backward and thinly spread. With about 8 million inhabitants, Russia's population was about the same size as Poland's and only half as large as that of France. To turn into a true European power Russia needed to push towards the rich, populous West. Though nobody saw it that way at the time, its alliance with Khmelnyt-sky was the first step in a process which came to an end only with the collapse of the Soviet Union – and perhaps not even then.

The transfer of Ukraine's loyalties from Cracow to Moscow took place in January 1654 at Pereyaslav, a small town on the eastern bank of the Dnieper, not far south of Kiev. From the beginning, the partnership was an unhappy one. The two delegations, headed by Khmelnytsky and the Russian envoy Vasiliy Buturlin, met in a church. Khmelnytsky had expected that in exchange for an oath of loyalty on the Cossacks' side, Buturlin would, on behalf of Tsar Alexey, swear 'that he would not betray the Cossacks to the Poles, that he would not violate their liberties, and that he would confirm the rights to their landed estates of the Ukrainian *szlachta*'. Buturlin refused. Polish kings might make oaths to their subjects, he said, but they also often broke them, whereas 'the tsar's word is unchangeable'. Furious, Khmelnytsky stalked out of the church, only to stalk back in again a few hours later, and sign a unilateral oath of obedience. The tsar's title changed from 'the autocrat of all Russia' to 'the autocrat of all Great and Little Russia', and the Cossack hetman took a new seal substituting the tsar's name for that of the Polish king.

Symbolism aside, Pereyaslav's significance became apparent only with hindsight. Over the next thirty years Russian, Polish, Cossack and Tatar armies swept repeatedly through Ukraine in a series of formless wars dubbed 'The Deluge' by Poles and 'The Ruin' by Ukrainians. The situation did not stabilise until 1686, when Poland and Russia – this time without even consulting the Cossacks – signed a so-called 'eternal peace', handing Kiev and all lands east of the Dnieper over to Muscovy. For the next three and a quarter centuries Kiev would be ruled from Moscow.

Khmelnytsky left lots of unanswered questions behind him. Historians disagree about why he started his rebellion, the extent to which he controlled its course, and why he ended it the way he did. Easier than saying what his rebellion was is saying what it was not. One aim he certainly did not have was to free Ruthenian peasants from serfdom. Their interests were consistently ignored during the various treaty negotiations, and one of the prices Khmelnytsky paid for his alliance with the Tatars was allowing them to march whole villages away to the Crimean slave-markets for auction. Nor is it clear that the rebellion – initially at least – was even anti-Polish. Marching westward at the outset of the 1648 campaign, Khmelnytsky wrote letters to the Polish king in the style of a loyal subject protesting his grievances, signing himself 'Hetman of His Gracious Majesty's Zaporozhian Host'. For much of the time, the rebellion looked more like a war between different Ruthenian interest groups than an ethnic conflict. Wisniowiecki and Adam Kysil, the chief general and chief negotiator on the Commonwealth side, were both Polonised Ruthenian magnates. Kysil was Orthodox; Wisniowiecki was a great-nephew of the founder of the Zaporozhian Sich and had converted to Catholicism only sixteen years previously.

The Ukrainian version of events, of course, is that Khmelnytsky led an early, failed, war of independence. Probably he never aimed that high. But that the Cossacks did want political and religious autonomy is clear, as proved by the demands they laid down in their various treaty negotiations with the Poles. The abortive treaty of Hadziacz, for example, would have allowed the Cossacks to choose, subject to crown approval, their own treasurer, marshal and hetman. It would have given them their own courts, mint and army, and it would have banished Polish soldiers, Jews and Jesuits from Cossack lands. From whose hands the Cossacks took autonomy, though, seems to have been immaterial. At one point, Khmelnytsky was even in talks with the Ottoman Porte about establishing the same sort of loose protectorate enjoyed by Moldova and Crimea. Pereyaslav itself may only have been intended as a temporary alliance, one more move in the Cossacks' long juggling act between powerful, threatening neighbours.

Like the historians, today's Ukrainians are not quite sure what to make of Khmelnytsky. On the one hand he beat the Poles; on the other he delivered up Ukraine to the even tenderer mercies of the Russians. But they are reluctant to jettison him altogether. Ukrainians have not hit the history books often, and under Khmelnytsky, for a while at least, they were genuinely a power to be reckoned with. For a country short on heroes, he is simply too prominent to pass up. Instead, he and his Cossacks have once again been recast to suit the mood of the times – Khmelnytsky as the leader of Ukraine's first failed stab at independence; the Sich with its Rada as a prototype democracy.

On Khortytsya island in Zaporizhya, now a smoggy industrial city and once the site of the Sich, the local museum has installed a new Cossack exhibition, financed by the Ukrainian diaspora. My friend Roma Ihnatowycz – a Ukrainian-Canadian journalist – and I arrived on a bleak Sunday in February, when the museum was half-closed and the surrounding park thigh-high in grimy snow. The curator was surprised to see anyone in such weather, and pleased that a foreigner was writing about Ukraine. She showed us hetmans' batons and model Viking ships, Scythian arrowheads and a panorama of the Rada in full raucous swing. Did we know, she asked, that Marx had called the Sich the 'first democratic Christian republic'? Did we know that the Cossacks had helped France defend Dunkirk during the Thirty Years' War? Did we know that Orly airport, in Paris, was named after Pylyp Orlyk, author of the first Ukrainian constitution? Some might pretend, she said, that the Cossacks were nothing but bandits, but all cultured, scientific people knew they were early social democrats. The Cossack experience might even help the Ukrainian government work out its new constitution. Ukrainians didn't need to copy America or Germany, for 'we have our own history, our own system'.

The drive home to Kiev took us through the old Cossack heartlands – the gently folded plains which skirt the northern edge of the Ukrainian steppe. Covered in snow, the countryside looked one-dimensional, like an overexposed black-and-white photograph. Crows, fluffed into balls against the cold, crouched motionless in the bare trees either side of the empty road. Concrete signposts, topped with hammer-and-sickle or block-jawed proletarian, marked the entrances to 'Labour-loving' village or 'Peace' collective farm. As the monochrome landscape lurched past, I suggested to Roma that as national figureheads the Cossacks weren't up to much. Weren't they violent? Weren't they drunk? Above all, weren't they failures? Didn't even Gogol make fun of his Cossack hero Taras Bulba? Roma got cross. 'Cossacks,' she said, 'are all we've got. Other people's heroes might be a bit more polished, but for Ukrainians the rawness of it all, the down-to-earthness of it all is just what we like.' Persuading her to forgive me took the rest of the trip.

The end of Polish rule over Ukraine turned, a century and a half later, into the end of Poland. Weakened by war, peasant uprisings, foreign machinations and the fecklessness of its own nobility, by the mid eighteenth century Poland was, in the words of Frederick of Prussia, 'like an artichoke, ready to be eaten leaf by leaf'. Shorn of two-thirds of its territory in the Partitions of 1773 and 1793, the Commonwealth finally collapsed for good in 1795. The eastern half of the old Commonwealth lands fell to Russia, the remainder to Prussia and Austria. Like Kievan Rus, Poland had fallen off the map. Like the Ukrainians, the Poles were now a nation without a state.

Shared misfortune did not turn them into friends. During the Polish rising of 1863, Ukrainian peasants rounded up insurgents and turned them over to the Russian authorities. At the end of the First World War Polish and Ukrainian partisans fought over Galicia, left vacant by the collapsed Austro-Hungarian empire. Between the wars Ukrainian nationalists in Polish-ruled western Ukraine mounted an assassination campaign against Polish government officials, and the two partisan armies fought again at the end of the Second World War, as the Germans retreated west before the Red Army. The bickering continued right up to

1945, when a wholesale population exchange brought about a crude but effective divorce.

The reason for conflict was simple. Ukrainians regarded Ukraine as Ukrainian. Nineteenth- and early twentieth-century Poles regarded it – along with the rest of the old eastern borderlands – as immutably Polish. The borderlands, in fact, were even *more* Polish than Poland proper, because the provincial nobility, unlike the sophisticates of Warsaw, had stuck to old-fashioned *szlachta* ways. The fact that the actual population of those borderlands was mostly of a different nationality was immaterial. Hence Adam Mickiewicz, Poland's national poet and a man who never visited Warsaw in his life, was able to open his patriotic epic *Pan Tadeusz* with the words 'Oh Lithuania'.

The other great example of the borderland mentality is Joseph Conrad. Born Jozef Teodor Konrad Korzeniowski, he grew up in Terehovye, a small village eighty miles south-west of Kiev. His family were crazily, pathologically, patriotic. Jozef's father Apollo celebrated his birth in 1857 with a poem entitled 'To My Son, born in the 85th Year of Muscovite Oppression'. With baptism came another poem: 'Tell yourself that you are without land, without love, without Fatherland, without humanity – as long as Poland, our Mother, is enslaved.' Conrad's own earliest surviving work is a note to his grandmother, thanking her for sending cakes to Apollo, by then in gaol for anti-Russian agitation in a Warsaw coffee-shop. The six-year-old solemnly signs himself 'grandson, Pole, Catholic, nobleman'. Later, his most vivid childhood memories were of his mother wearing black in mourning for Poland's demise, and of a great-uncle's tales of eating roast dog on the retreat from Moscow with Napoleon. When Conrad set off, aged sixteen, to join the French merchant navy, a family friend saw him on to the train with the words 'Remember, wherever you sail you are sailing towards Poland!'. Surfeited with Polishness, Conrad only ever went back home once, ending his days in the undemanding county of Kent.

His Canterbury tombstone muddles up his English and Polish names, rechristening him 'Joseph Teador Conrad Korzeniowski'.

The Korzeniowskis' house is still there in Terehovye, used now as the village school. Though not very big, one can see that it once belonged to gentry. The doors are thick and panelled, the walls have cornicing round them, and plaster rosettes show where chandeliers once hung. The drawing room has been turned into the school gymnasium – lines painted on to the parquet, basketball hoops screwed to the walls, and a portrait of Lenin propped up behind a pile of hockey-sticks in a boarded-up bay window. Outside a line of lime trees marks the edge of what was once a terraced garden.

The village is a tiny place, silent save for a chained dog, and smelling of melting snow and horse manure. But it has not forgotten its famous writer. A very deaf old man with gold teeth and a fur hat let me into the collective farm headquarters, where alongside the obligatory pictures of astronauts and folk dancers sepia photographs hung of Conrad on a pony, Conrad at his desk, Conrad in naval uniform. Down at the bottom of the hill, by a frozen lake, he drew a dipper from a square, brick-lined well. 'Conrad drank this water. It's a very good well – it never freezes.' But since Conrad was a Pole who lived abroad most of his life and wrote in English, why should the villagers care? 'They don't,' he said; 'they think – what did Konrad give us? Nothing!'

Despite their antagonism, matched circumstances pushed Poland and Ukraine into matching survival strategies. For Poles in the nineteenth century and for Ukrainians right up until 1991, the idea of nationhood took on a religious, almost metaphysical significance. Just as diaspora Ukrainians still tend to regard themselves as part of Ukraine despite having been born and brought up in Canada or Australia, exiled nineteenth-century Poles felt they were no less part of Poland for having spent their lives in Paris or Moscow. Their countries existed in a sort of mental hyperspace, independent of such banalities as governments and borders. 'Poland is not yet lost' was the title of a Napoleonic Polish marching song; 'Ukraine is not dead yet' is the less-than-inspiring opening line of the present-day Ukrainian national anthem.

With this state of mind went a peculiar approach to the writing of history. In the imagination of both countries, as the historian Norman Davies puts it, 'the "Word" has precedence over the "Fact" . . . more attention is paid to what people would have liked to happen than to what actually occurred.'[18] National leaders and national uprisings – no matter that they failed – are given more space and weight than the foreign governments who actually dictated events. Poles revere their 'Constitution of May 3rd', Ukrainians, their so-called 'Bender Constitution'. Never mind that neither even came close to being put into practice, for intentions are more important than results.

This heroic imaginative effort did not make the political re-emergence of either country any easier. Both have had enormous difficulty persuading the rest of the world to take them seriously. The British historian E.H. Carr, a delegate at the Paris peace talks of 1919, called reborn Poland 'a farce'. For Keynes it was 'an economic impossibility whose only industry is Jew-baiting'; for Lloyd George, 'a historic failure' – he would no more hand over Upper Silesia to Poland, he swore, than he would give a clock to a monkey. George Bush, had he been around at the time, would undoubtedly have joined this chorus in favour of the status quo, his only contribution to Ukrainian independence being the infamous 'Chicken Kiev' speech of August 1991, in which he urged Ukrainians to stay loyal to the Soviet Union. But at least Bush knew Ukraine existed. Six years after independence, many otherwise well-informed Westerners have either completely failed to register that they have a country called Ukraine as a neighbour, or have vaguely heard of it but have no idea where it is, throwing out guesses – Somewhere on the Baltic? Next door to Kazakhstan? – with the gay abandon of a child playing Pin the Tail on the Donkey.

For both Poland and Ukraine, the best way to get the West's attention has been to stress their impact on Russia. Nineteenth-century liberals argued that unless Russia freed Poland, it would never be able to undertake its own constitutional reform. The effort of holding down its most intransigent colony trapped Russia in the role of tyrannical autocracy, hurting ordinary Russians as much as the Poles themselves – hence the slogan of the 1831 Polish rebellion: 'For our freedom and yours.' The argument Poland used in pleading for military aid last century, Ukraine employs in making the case for IMF funds and diplomatic support today. The (Polish-born) American Sovietologist Zbigniew Brzezinski writes that 'without Ukraine, Russia ceases to be an empire, but with Ukraine suborned and then subordinated, Russia automatically becomes an empire.' The bottom line is that 'Russia can either be an empire or a democracy, but it cannot be both.'[19] If Ukraine does not stay independent, in other words, Russia will not remain a democracy, so Ukrainian independence is as much for Russia's good as Ukraine's.

Russians, of course, have some difficulty taking this concept on board. Just as the Polish risings turned even diehard anti-establishmentarians like Pushkin into raging Slavophiles, today's independent Ukraine brings out the empire-builder in the best of Russian liberals. 'When you look at nineteenth-century Russian treatments of the Polish problem,' says Roman Szporluk, head of Ukrainian studies at Harvard, 'you really think you're reading all those Moscow think-tankers today on Ukraine.'[20]

Today, Polish–Ukrainian relations are rather muted – surprisingly so given their long and scratchy common history. Polish and Ukrainian presidents exchange visits, and Polish economists turn up at Kiev conferences on free-market reform. Numberless Ukrainians do private trade across the border, heaving suitcases full of smoked sausage and tacky clothing on to trains going west, and returning with car parts and kitchenware. In Lviv, near the Polish border and a Polish city before the war, Ukrainian yuppies like to assert their Western credentials with a Warsaw-style kiss to the hand. But aside from Ukrainian resentment at the missionary activities of the Polish Catholic Church, the relationship, on the Ukrainian side at least, is a curiously bloodless one. Despite centuries under Polish rule, Ukrainians have none of the fierce love–hate for Poland that they have for Russia – probably simply because Poland no longer affects them much. The number of ethnic Poles left in Ukraine is tiny, and Poland has no leverage over Ukrainian affairs. Whereas Khmelnytsky tried to play off Muscovy against the Poles, today's Ukraine balances Russia against America.

Ukraine may have ceased to care about Poland, but Poles have not stopped caring about Ukraine. Ukraine might be an economic joke, a place to make cracks about, but it is also a vital buffer-state. With Ukraine independent, the Russian border stays 600 miles to the east and Poland can convincingly call itself part of Central, not Eastern, Europe. Were Ukraine – or more likely Belarus – to lose its independence, Russia would be back glowering over the frontier wire, and Europe's centre of gravity would shift away westwards. Solidarity sent representatives to the founding conference of Rukh, the opposition coalition that took Ukraine to independence, and Poland was the first country to give Ukraine diplomatic recognition, the day after the independence referendum of 1 December 1991.

In 1883 the young Polish novelist Henryk Sienkiewicz published his best-selling epic *By Fire And Sword*. A Hollywoodian drama set during the Khmelnytsky rebellion, the book is not historically accurate. Never having visited Ukraine, Sienkiewicz based his descriptions of the Dnieper on his travels up the Mississippi, decorating its banks with mangrove swamps and 'vast reptiles'. Nevertheless, it perfectly sums up the mixture of nostalgia, condescension and self-interest with which Poles view their erstwhile borderlands. The novel has two parallel story-lines: Khmelnytsky's war with Wisniowiecki for Ukraine, and the battle between a savage Cossack otaman and a relentlessly virtuous Polish knight for the hand in marriage of a Ruthenian princess. The Pole ends up getting the girl, but the Polish army does not end up getting Ukraine.

Instead the country descends into chaos: the book's notorious final sentence reads, 'And hatred swelled in people's hearts and poisoned the blood of brothers.' The moral of the story, not lost on the palpitating contemporary readership, was that history should not be allowed to repeat itself. To get rid of Russia, Poles and Ukrainians had to stop fighting, and stick together.

◆ CHAPTER THREE ◆

The Russian Sea:
Donetsk and Odessa

Shall the Slav rivers merge into the Russian sea?
Or shall the sea itself run dry?
  – Aleksandr Pushkin, 1831

'WE CALL THESE things "Stalin's hands",' said Alexey, pointing at a pair of hinged metal hooks at the bottom of a rusty conveyor-belt. Impervious to the freezing wind, he led me round snow-whipped slag-heaps and half-buried bits of rotting machinery, explaining just what each object was for. 'These,' he said, pointing to a stack of pine logs, 'hold up the walls of the tunnels. The problem is that nowadays they're very expensive and we don't have enough of them.' Earlier, an official at the local branch of the coal ministry had told me that 212 men had died in mining accidents in the Donetsk region the previous year, 32 of them in a single gas explosion. He hadn't been at all embarrassed about the number: at four lives per million tonnes of coal produced it was well within normal ratios.

Alexey was in his early thirties, and had lived in Donetsk all his life. All his family were miners: during the war even his grandmother had worked down the shafts, losing the fingers of her left hand under the wheels of a runaway trolley-car. Though he had gone into a white-collar union job after college, he still thought of himself as a miner, a *shakhtyor* – in Russian the word still has a faint heroic ring – too. But beyond that Alexey wasn't too sure what he was. Like most people in Donetsk he spoke only Russian, no Ukrainian. His family had come here from Russia, as far as he knew, in the late 1800s, when industrialisation was just getting under way. Did I know that Donetsk used to be called Yuzovka, after a Welshman, John Hughes, who opened the first foundry on the site? Did I know that Donetsk was twinned with Cardiff? Alexey had been there once on an exchange programme, and kept a little wooden shield painted with the Cardiff city arms in a glass-fronted cabinet in his office. 'When we told them how we worked here they just couldn't believe it. We looked at everything they had – the special baths, the clothes, the equipment – and we practically burst into tears.'

Inside the corrugated-iron shed at the top of the mine-shaft we watched the day-shift clocking off. Bent and ragged, with bloodshot eyes and gold teeth shining out of filthy faces, the men looked almost too miner-like to be true – blacked-up actors, perhaps, in some clichéd documentary on the horrors of the Industrial Revolution. Most were in their forties or older. The younger ones, Alexey said, had found better jobs elsewhere, driving taxis or trading over the Russian border. He called a group over to meet the foreign journalist. They didn't want to answer questions, jerking their heads when I asked them what they thought of their new Ukrainian government. As we shook hands, I noticed that many, like Alexey's grandmother, had fingers missing.

In truth, Alexey said, the 'Red Guard' men didn't much care who they were governed by. 'Some of them demand that we go back to Russia, but this is just kitchen-talk. We know that Russia doesn't need us – it already wants to close its own mines.

Moscow, Kiev, it's all the same.' What they did want was better
pay – any pay at all, in fact, since they hadn't received a kopek
for six weeks – and freedom to run their mine the way they
wanted. 'It takes six months to make any decision, because
everything has to go through Kiev. The energy ministry takes
our coal at three dollars a tonne, but we the producers aren't
allowed to sign our own contracts, though we could sell the
same coal at $20 or even $60 a tonne.' Dolefully Alexey shook
his head, the flaps of his fur hat waggling like spaniel's ears.
Outside the snow swirled, the slag-heaps loomed, the tumble-
down sheds and bits of broken machinery disappeared into the
gathering dusk. It was time to go. As we said our goodbyes he
pulled a bundle out of his pocket: two enamelled badges in the
shape of his union's initials, and a triangular banner in shiny red
nylon. 'For you – so you can remember Donetsk.'

Ukraine's Russians are fairly recent arrivals. They came in
waves that mirrored the empire's belated industrial revolution:
at the end of the nineteenth century, with the first industrial
boom; in the 1920s and 1930s, with the Five-Year Plans; and
again after the war. By 1989, according to the last Soviet census,
they made up 11 million of Ukraine's 52 million population. In
the Donbass coal basin, equidistant from Kiev and Moscow,
they form a majority.

To stay independent, Ukraine has to keep its Russian-speaking east sweet. Densely populated and heavily industrialised, it
already has a big say in the country. In the first post-independence presidential elections it was the weight of eastern votes
that handed victory to Leonid Kravchuk, an ex-Party boss, over
Vyacheslav Chornovil, a former dissident and leader of the
independence movement. And in 1994 it was eastern votes that
threw out Kravchuk, by then the darling of the nationalists, in
favour of Leonid Kuchma, ex-director of a missile factory in the
Russian-speaking city of Dnipropetrovsk. The previous year,
ironically, Kuchma had been forced to resign as prime minister
when thousands of Donbass miners arrived in Kiev demanding

pay rises. Ukrainian politicians' worst nightmare is Donbass separatism, the fear that one day eastern Ukraine will want autonomy, or even bid to rejoin Russia.

Ukraine's Russians, though, are neither the oldest nor the most problematic legacy of Ukraine's 300 years inside the Russian empire. Far more invidious was the effect of Russian rule on the Ukrainians themselves, beginning with the decline and fall of the Cossack hetmanate. Khmelnytsky's Pereyaslav Treaty had not, in the Cossacks' eyes at least, made Ukraine east of the Dnieper part of Russia, but simply given it Russian protection. Though subject to increasing Russian interference, the Cossacks still chose their own hetmans (subject to the tsar's approval), ran their own army, and collected their own taxes. Loyalty to Russia was conditional, a matter of mutual rights and promises. The arrangement fell to pieces at the beginning of the eighteenth century, with the disastrous hetmanate of that most un-Cossack of Cossacks – Ivan Mazeppa.

Suave and subtle, famous for his love affairs and his deft hand at political intrigue, Mazeppa was an even unlikelier rebel than Khmelnytsky. Born into a noble Orthodox family in Polish-ruled 'right-bank' Ukraine, he was schooled at a Jesuit college in Warsaw before entering the court of King Jan Kazimierz as a gentleman-in-waiting. Keen to create a cadre of Ruthenian nobles loyal to the crown, Kazimierz sent him to study in Holland before putting him to work on diplomatic errands to the left-bank hetmanate. In 1663 the promising young favourite suddenly left Cracow and joined the Polish-ruled Cossacks on the western bank of the Dnieper. Legend – as embroidered by everyone from Byron to Tchaikovsky – has it that he had been discovered in bed with the wife of a neighbour, who stripped him naked and sent him galloping off into the steppe on the back of a wild horse. Whatever the truth, Mazeppa spent the next few years travelling back and forth to the Crimean khanate as the Polish Cossacks' envoy. In 1674, journeying home from one of these missions, he was captured by the Zaporozhians and turned over to the rival left-bank hetmanate as a spy.

At this point, one might have thought Mazeppa's career was over. Not a bit of it. Deploying his already legendary charm, Mazeppa sweet-talked his way out of captivity and into a job as assistant to Ivan Samoylovych, the left-bank hetman. Thirteen years later, having ingratiated himself with Moscow and manufactured a conspiracy framing Samoylovych for treason, he was hetman himself. A nonpareil at sizing up the endless intrigues of the Russian court, he managed to stay in favour when Peter the Great overthrew his sister Sophia in 1689, and quickly became one of the young tsar's closest confidants. Mazeppa sent Peter wines from Crimea; Peter replied with gifts of fish from the Baltic, as well as the new Order of St Andrew and vast Ukrainian estates. 'The tsar would sooner disbelieve an angel,' rivals muttered, 'than Mazeppa.'[1] The French diplomat Jean Baluse, on a visit to the Cossack capital of Baturin in 1704, described him at the height of his power:

> Conversation with this Prince is extremely pleasant. He has unusual experience in politics, and, contrary to the Muscovites, follows developments in other countries . . . On several occasions I tried very assiduously to direct our conversation toward the present political situation, but I must confess I could find out nothing definite from this Prince. He belongs to that category of people who either prefer to keep completely silent or to talk and say nothing. But I hardly think that he likes the Muscovite Tsar, because he did not say a word against my complaints about Muscovite life. But in the case of the Polish crown, Monsieur Mazepa did not hesitate to declare that it is heading, as did ancient Rome, toward decline. He spoke about the Swedish King with respect, but deems him too young . . .[2]

As Baluse guessed, Mazeppa's loyalty was wavering. Apostasy came four years later, precipitated by Peter's long Northern War with the austere young Charles XII of Sweden. In September 1708 the conflict reached a crisis-point. Charles had already swept over Poland, putting a Swedish puppet on the Polish

throne, and now his armies threatened Moscow and St Petersburg. But at the village of Lesnaya, in present-day eastern
Belarus, the Swedes suffered their first serious setback, when
Russian troops cut off and burned the wagon-train carrying the
army's supplies of powder, food and winter clothing. Unable to
push on east, and with winter drawing near, Charles turned
southwards to what he had been told was a 'country flowing
with milk and honey' – to Ukraine.

Here Mazeppa's genius for picking winners failed him for the
first time in his life. Faced with a choice between hostile
occupation by Charles's brutal army, or supporting the Swedes
and risking Russian fury later on, Mazeppa stalled, excusing
himself from joining Peter by pretending to be mortally ill, then
declared for Charles, taking 2,000 of his Cossacks with him.
Peter was amazed and furious. 'It was with great wonderment,'
he wrote, 'that I learned of the deed of the new Judas, Mazeppa,
who after twenty-one years of loyalty to me and with one foot
already in the grave, has turned traitor and betrayer of his own
people.'[3] Peter immediately ordered that Baturin's 7,000 inhabitants be put to the sword, and the following month, at a solemn
ceremony in Moscow's Uspensky Cathedral, Mazeppa's name
was pronounced anathema, a ritual that was to be repeated
annually in all Russian churches for the next 200 years.

Exactly what Mazeppa hoped to get out of his U-turn is a
mystery. He may have dreamed of putting himself on the throne
of a genuinely independent hetmanate with Swedish backing.
He may simply have been infuriated by Russia's failure to
honour the Pereyaslav Treaty by helping defend Ukraine against
threatened invasion by the Poles. (Peter's reply to earlier pleas
had been 'I cannot even spare ten men; defend yourself as best
you can.')[4] He was certainly jealous of Peter's favourite, Aleksandr Menshikov. But whatever his motives, he had picked the
wrong man. The following summer, just outside Poltava, a small
town east of Kiev, Charles's and Peter's armies finally came face
to face. Wounded in the foot, Charles could only watch the
battle from a litter, leaving command split between bickering

generals. Demoralised and badly led, the Swedes suffered one of the most decisive defeats of European history. Sweden's dreams of the Kremlin were over; Russia, with its first major victory against a modern army, was on its way to becoming one of Europe's great powers. After the battle Charles and Mazeppa fled west across the steppe to Bender in Ottoman-ruled Moldova, leaving most of their army stranded on the wrong side of the Dnieper. Mazeppa died three months later, his head propped on saddle-bags full of looted diamonds. Charles was killed by a stray bullet in 1718, while besieging a town in Norway. Descendants of the soldiers they abandoned can be found outside the Swedish embassy in Kiev, forlornly applying for citizenship of a country their ancestors left three centuries ago.

In Poltava I stayed with a family of Baptists, introduced by my temporary interpreter Taras, a spotty youth who spent his spare time reading *Pilgrim's Progress* ('What, please, is a Slough of Despond? Who is Mr Valiant-for-Truth?') and distributing American-produced leaflets showing believers climbing ladders to heaven, and unbelievers burning in hell-fire. (Religious tolerance, in Taras's book, was 'a typical decadent Western idea'.) Grandparents, two sets of parents and eight children all shared a newly built, immaculately tidy house on the outskirts of town. Lined up in height order like the Family von Trapp, the children gave their names – Irina, Kristina, Slavik, Yulya . . . – and sang an evangelical hymn: 'My Father is waiting for me in heaven/ Where He has made a crown for mee-eee.' Afterwards they went back to watching *Stop Or My Mom'll Shoot!* on video. Though all the characters were dubbed by the same bored voice, they didn't seem to mind, laughing uproariously at every joke. The machine, little creamy-cheeked Irina explained, was a present from South Carolinan missionary dentists, who had given them all fillings while spreading the Word. So too was the shiny new poster on the wall, with coloured time-lines showing mankind's progress from Adam to Last Judgement, via the Deluge and the Tower of Babel. But what had really impressed her was the dentists' remarkable bulk. 'There was one' – a conspiratorial whisper – 'called Phil. When he sat down his legs went like *that!*' And she spread her hands in the manner of a fisherman describing a monster missed catch.

Poltava, it turned out, hadn't yet decided whether to treat its famous battle as a glorious Russian victory or as a tragic Ukrainian defeat. In the meantime, successive ideologies were being allowed to accumulate, like strata in a sort of historio-graphical ocean bed. In the middle of town, in a square full of cigarette kiosks and shuffling trolley-bus queues, stood a tsarist monument, all cannons, eagle and laurel wreaths, celebrating the battle's first centenary. Next came the inevitable Lenin, one hand outstretched, the other deep in his pocket ('Looking for money for the budget,' said my driver). Opposite Lenin a big hand-painted billboard had gone up: 'The Flower Poltava in the Wreath of Independent Ukraine!' The newest monument of all was a giant stone cross, inscribed 'To the Cossack Dead' in folksy Ukrainian lettering. The central post office, a white pillared building that had housed the local Nobles' Club, chipped in with a mercifully apolitical message of its own: 'CITIZENS! USE THE SIX-DIGIT POSTAL INDEX!'

In the little museum on the battlefield site – a snowbound muddle of factory buildings and straggling woodland – the traditional Russian version of events held undisputed sway. Socialist-realist oils showed Peter at his more sympathetic pursuits: rolling up his sleeves in a cannon foundry; dividers in hand in the Volga shipyards; spotlit through storm clouds aboard a rearing charger. The grand finale was a diorama of the battle itself – real wagon wheels and cannon balls in front of a painted scene of galloping horses, flying banners and puffs of smoke, all 'created by artists of the Grekov studio of the Ministry of Defence of the USSR'. But why hadn't the museum got anything about Mazeppa? The attendant, a pretty blonde in anorak and padded boots, rifled through her desk, produced keys, and led me along a corridor to a distant room. Here, she said, was their new exhibition. It had pictures of Mazeppa in beaten copper, bits and pieces of weaponry and Ukrainian folk costume, and a wobbly fibreglass Cossack gravestone. It was behind locked doors, she said, because 'we don't have a man to look after it. If anyone asks, we just let them in.' Hadn't the museum come under any pressure to ditch its old, pro-Russian displays? A sigh. 'At first, yes, but now it has faded away. Nobody's interested in history any more.'

Following the disastrous Mazeppa adventure, the hetmanate went into rapid decline. The Cossack capital was moved from Baturin to Hlukhiv, closer to the Russian border, and Russians were given command of the Cossack regiments. Government was overseen by a 'collegium' of Russian officials, and hetmans who stood on their rights were imprisoned or replaced. Royal favourites were granted vast Ukrainian estates, and began building themselves the neoclassical mansions, designed by Scots and Italians, whose dilapidated hulks still brood over the villages east of Kiev today.

The last of the hetmans was Kyrylo Rozumovsky, younger brother of Oleksiy, an affable but illiterate Ruthenian who caught Empress Elizabeth's eye while singing in the imperial choir, and subsequently became her lover, maybe even her husband. He was removed by Catherine II in 1764, following his petition for a return to full autonomy and for the hetmancy to be made hereditary in the Rozumovsky family. Now that the hetmans were gone from 'Little Russia', Catherine declared, 'every effort should be made to eradicate them and their age from memory.'[5] In 1781 she did away with the hetmanate altogether, splitting its territory into three provinces organised on the same lines as the rest of the Russian empire. The Sich had been razed by Russian troops six years earlier, and its lands given over to Russian grandees and German and Serbian colonists. The surviving Zaporozhians were deported to the Kuban, north-west of the Caucasus, leaving Ukrainians to sing ballads in their memory – and scour the Dnieper reed-beds for their hidden treasure – for ever after.

One of the reasons Catherine felt able to do away with the Cossacks was that she no longer needed their help against the Turks. In 1774 she had signed a peace treaty with the Sultan handing the Crimean khanate, formerly an Ottoman protectorate, over to Russia. With the khanate came control of the 'wild field', the fertile, uninhabited no-man's-land between Crimea and the Sich lands to the north. The treaty meant that the centuries-old to-and-fro between Tatar and Cossack raiders was over. Ruthenian peasants would no longer be marched south for sale in the slave-markets of Kaffa and Constantinople; Tatars would no longer wake to find their ports torched by Cossack galleys. The 'wild field' had suddenly become a safe place.

According to the Russian scheme of things, the peace restored a rightful inheritance. By annexing the Black Sea steppe, Russia was 'gathering the Russian lands', rebuilding the ancient kingdom of Rus. Catherine had a commemorative medal struck, engraved with the words 'I have recovered what was torn away', and gave her new territories the name *Novorossiya* – New Russia.

Today, New Russia exists only in the imagination. The endless plains and vast skies are still there of course, but the grey-green grass, the bison, marmots and antelope, the buzzards and wild horses, have long since disappeared under the plough. People who did see and describe the virgin steppe all came up with the same image – the ocean. 'I sail a sea where waters never ran/My wagon like a boat,' wrote Mickiewicz.[6] Riders disappeared into the rippling grass like a fish into waves; canvas-covered ox-carts rolled over it like ships under sail. Nothing pierced the gently undulating horizon save the occasional line of willows by a river, or the distant gravemound of some Scythian warrior-princess, buried complete with horse and manservant, battle-axe and turquoise-studded jewellery. So featureless was the landscape that the wagoners, like sailors, steered by the stars.

For some the steppe was a desert, but for most, like Nikolay Gogol (a Ukrainian who wrote in Russian), it was an inspiration:

The surface of the earth appeared here like a golden-green ocean, flecked with the colours of a million different flowers. Through the tall, slender stalks peeped pale-blue and lilac cornflowers; the yellow broom thrust its spiky tips upwards; the white clover adorned the surface with its umbrella-like caps; an ear of wheat, blown God knows from where, stood ripening, deep in the grass. Partridges with craning necks darted hither and thither among the slender roots. The air was filled with the song of a thousand different birds. Hawks hung motionless in the air, their wings spread wide and their keen eyes fixed on the grass. The cries of a passing flock of geese carried to their ears from a distant lake. With measured strokes of its wings a gull rose from the grass and bathed luxuriantly in the deep-blue waves of the air . . .[7]

But once made safe for farmers, the steppe could not stay empty for long. For centuries tall stories had been told about its fertility. Leave a plough in a field overnight, it was said, and next morning you couldn't find it again for new grass. So numerous were the bison that hunters didn't even bother to eat their meat, just taking the hides. So packed were the rivers with fish that a spear would stand upright, unsupported, in the water. Growing up on the Sea of Azov in the 1870s, Anton Chekhov saw the wilderness eaten away by windmills and telegraph poles, villages and ploughed fields. His lyrical short story *The Steppe*, based on boyhood journeys with the old ox-drawn wagon-trains, was written as a memorial to a landscape that was vanishing for ever:

You drive on for one hour, for another . . . You meet upon the way a silent old barrow or a stone figure put up God knows when and by whom; a night bird floats noiselessly over the earth, and little by little those legends of the steppes, the tales of men you have met, the stories of some old nurse from the steppe, and all the things you have managed to see and treasure in your soul, come back to your mind . . . And in the triumph of beauty, in the exuberance of happiness you are conscious of tension and yearning, as though the steppe knew she was solitary, knew that her wealth and inspiration were wasted for the world, unsung, unwanted; and through the joyful clamour one hears her mournful, hopeless call for singers, singers![8]

Catherine gave the job of opening up 'New Russia' to her one-eyed lover Grigory Potemkin. His job was to attract new settlers into the countryside, and to found naval and commercial ports on the lower Dnieper and along the coast. In both enterprises he was spectacularly successful. Cheap government loans and remissions from serfdom and taxation brought in the farmers, and trading exemptions helped the towns. In 1787, to show off his achievements and celebrate the twenty-fifth year of Catherine's reign, Potemkin organised a royal progress down the Dnieper to Crimea. Catherine and her entourage left St Petersburg in early January, travelling in gilded coaches mounted on sleds. Reaching Kiev at the end of month, they waited three months for the ice to break on the Dnieper, before setting off downriver in a fleet of eighty boats led by eleven brocade-upholstered Roman-style galleys. At the new town of Yekaterinoslav, the present-day Dnipropetrovsk, Catherine was met by her ally Josef II of Austria, and the two laid foundation stones for a vast new cathedral. Though the city was still nothing more than a collection of wooden houses, Potemkin had grand plans for a university, law courts and a conservatoire. Josef was cynical: 'I performed a great deed today,' he wrote to a friend. 'The Empress laid the first stone of a new church, and I laid – the last.'[9] But further downriver at Kherson, where things were more advanced, the party could not but be impressed:

> Imagine on the one hand a quantity, increasing hourly, of stone buildings; a fortress, which encompasses a citadel and the best buildings; the Admiralty, with ships being built and already built; a spacious suburb, inhabited by merchants and burghers of different races; and, on the other hand, barracks housing about 10,000 soldiers. Add to this, almost opposite the suburb, an attractive-looking island with quarantine buildings, with Greek

merchant vessels, and with canals constructed to give these vessels access. Imagine all this and you will understand my bewilderment, for not so long ago there was nothing here but a building where beehives were kept for winter.[10]

The tour climaxed at Sevastopol, where Catherine reviewed her new sixteen-ship Black Sea Fleet, threw roubles to a troop of 'Amazons' done up in turbans and ostrich feathers, and enjoyed a spectacular fireworks display, which terrified the natives. As the coloured sparks faded into the hot Crimean night, the letter E – for Yekaterina – appeared on a hillside, etched in 55,000 torches. Potemkin had done well, and Catherine was delighted. An excellent portrait of the empress, taken in Kiev as she set off on her New Russian tour, still hangs in the city's Tereshchenko Gallery, former town-house of an artistically inclined sugar magnate. Direct, blue-eyed, Germanic, she resembles nothing so much as a shrewd and forceful headmistress.

New Russia may have been the work of the Russian monarchy, but 'New Russia' was still a misnomer. Potemkin's new cities, with their newfangled boulevards and fancy classical names, were certainly not very Ukrainian places. But they were not very Russian either. From the first, New Russia depended on foreigners.

The place that epitomised this was Odessa. Its history begins with the capture by a Spanish-Irish mercenary in Russian pay of a small Turkish fortress called Khadzhibey. A Dutch engineer, Franz de Voland, recommended to Catherine that the fort, with its good natural harbour, be turned into New Russia's capital. Catherine approved, and gave him the money to build break-waters. Her city, she decided, should be female – hence Odessa, after the ruins of the ancient Greeks' Odessos along the coast to the east.

The man who turned Odessa from idea into reality was Armand-Emmanuel, Duc de Richelieu. A great-nephew of the cardinal, he had sat out the French Revolution in Russian service, fighting under Suvorov in Turkey. In 1803 Tsar Aleksandr I made him governor of Odessa, and, two years later, of all three provinces of New Russia. A foreign exile who had done well under the expanding Russian empire, the 36-year-old de Richelieu populated his new kingdom with more of the same. Offering cheap land, religious toleration and exemption from military service, he attracted persecuted minorities from all over Europe and the empire. From the south came Bulgars, Serbs, Moldovans, Greeks and Armenians; from the north Jews; from the west Swiss and hard-working Mennonite Germans; from the east dissenting Molokans, Dukhobors and Old Believers. By 1817, when there was no more virgin land to be given away, Richelieu was able to report that 'Never, Sire, in any part of the world, have there been nations so different in manners, language, customs and dress living within so restricted a space.'[11] Remarkable as much for his incorruptibility as for his energy, when de Richelieu returned home to France to serve as prime minister under the restored monarchy he is supposed to have taken nothing with him but a suitcase containing his uniform and two shirts. A statue at the top of the Odessa Steps shows him in a Roman toga; in its plinth is lodged a piece of roundshot, fired by the British frigate *Tiger* during the Crimean War.

The next governor-general was another Frenchman, Count Alexandre Langeron. Unlike de Richelieu, he found the New Russian salad indigestible. 'The territory entrusted to me,' he wrote gloomily, 'is as large as all of France and is populated by ten different nationalities ... There are to be found also ten different religions and all ten are practised freely. One can judge the work which burdens me and the absolute impossibility of my doing it all.'[12] His successor, after a brief interregnum, was Mikhail Vorontsov, a Russian but also a passionate Anglophile. He had spent his childhood in London, where his father was Russian ambassador, and gone to university at Cambridge. His father had married an Englishwoman, and his sister an Earl of Pembroke. (Her portrait still hangs, surrounded by beefy in-laws, on the grand staircase at Wilton House in Wiltshire.) Arriving in

Odessa in 1823, Vorontsov brought his English tastes with him. On the cliffs near the Crimean fishing village of Alupka, English architects built him an extraordinary palace, half Moghul mosque and half Scottish castle, which he filled with Holbeins and statues of the Duke of Wellington. Suitably, it was in this monstrous piece of Victoriana that Churchill and his suite were housed during the Yalta conference of 1945.

Meanwhile Odessa was booming. When Vorontsov took office the population stood at 30,000. By the time he left it had more than doubled, and continued to grow at breakneck speed right up to 1914. Grain from the hinterlands rolled into the city by ox-cart, later by train, for export to the great corn-marts at Genoa, Leghorn and Marseilles. Laid out on a grid-shaped street plan and surrounded by sea and prairie, it reminded Mark Twain, researching a comic travel book in the 1860s, of the boom towns of the American West:

> It looked just like an American city; fine broad streets and straight as well; low houses (two or three stories), wide, neat, and free from any quaintness ... a stirring business-look about the streets and the stores; fast walkers; a familiar *new* look about the houses and everything; yea and a driving and smothering cloud of dust that was so like a message from our own dear native land that we could hardly refrain from shedding a few grateful tears and execrations in the old time-honored American way. Look up the street or down the street, this way or that way, we saw only America![13]

Foreigners founded Odessa; foreigners made it grow. The export trade was dominated by Greeks and Italians, prompting hand-wringing articles in the Russian press about the lack of native entrepreneurial drive. A German firm installed the gaslights, Belgians the trams, British the waterworks. The paving-stone for the roads came from Trieste; after the eruption of Mount Etna in 1900, some were re-covered in black Sicilian lava. The opera house, completed in 1887 after its predecessor burned down, was the work of Austrians, and the acacias shading the boulevards were descendants of trees imported by de Richelieu from Vienna. Even the famous Odessa Steps, nearly twice as wide at the bottom of the flight as at the top, were installed by a shady English engineer named Upton, who had fled Britain while on bail on a charge of forgery. In Odessa, wrote a visitor in the 1840s,

> the Russian jostles against a Turk, a German against a Greek, an Englishman against an Armenian, a Frenchman against an Arab, an Italian against a Persian or a Bucharestian ... Everything surges and mixes together: the dress coat, the swallowtail coat of the West European mixes together with the kaftan and robes of the oriental. Here there is glimpsed ... the modern hat of a Frenchman, the high towering cap of a Persian and the turban of an Anatolian and the fez of a Morean and a Dutch sailor in a wide-brimmed low hat.[14]

Commercial, apolitical, foreign, Odessa was a city for runaways, for outsiders. For the poor it was a place to change one's life, to make a fortune. Serfs fled there in their thousands, knowing that the demand for labour meant they were unlikely to be returned to their owners if discovered. They were nicknamed *neznayush-chiye* – 'I don't knowers' – for their refusal to say where they came from. Later most of the immigrants were Jews fleeing the impoverished *shtetlech* of the Pale. For the rich, it was an escape from the stifling atmosphere of St Petersburg – not quite abroad, but almost as good. Exiled from the capital, Pushkin and the Polish poet Mickiewicz both spent pleasant, frivolous summers strolling the boulevards and seducing star-struck poetry groupies – Pushkin going so far as to have an affair with Vorontsov's wife. Retiring world-weary Onegin to Odessa after his fatal duel with Lensky, he describes nights of oysters and opera; mornings smoking and sipping Turkish coffee while a doorman swept the pavement in front of the casino. 'But why succumb to grim emotion?' asks Onegin. 'Especially since the local wine/Is duty free and rather fine./And then there's

Southern sun and ocean./What more my friends, could you demand?'[15]

Odessa is still a lovely city. Unspoilt by war or planners, it is a place for idling away one's time in outdoor cafés – it has more of them than anywhere else in Ukraine – and quizzing the passing crowds. In most ex-Soviet cities people shuffle; they keep their eyes to the ground and don't swing their arms or legs. Not so in Odessa. Odessans have style, self-confidence. In winter they eat stuffed pike in little basement restaurants, in summer they snorkel for mussels on the breakwaters, and brew their own wine from the vines trailing across their sagging balconies. Their city is somewhere everyone in the Soviet Union used to dream about, and they know it. After the helpless degradation of places like Donetsk, watching Odessans go about their business is a relief and a pleasure.

Quicker than anywhere else, Odessa is stripping away its monochrome Soviet varnish to reveal the old multi-ethnic identity underneath. Ulitsa Karla Marksa has turned back into Yekaterinskaya, Lenina into Richelyevskaya, Karla Libknechta into Grecheskaya – 'Greek Street'. Babelya, named after the great Odessan novelist Isaac Babel, has become Yevreyskaya – 'Jewish Street'. Just as foreigners built the city, foreigners are bringing it to life again. A Swiss firm has done up the grand old Londonskaya Hotel, now a favourite haunt of conspiratorial businessmen. Cypriots have opened a casino in the old stock exchange building, staffing it with bemused Liverpudlian croupiers, and Italians have renovated the port, from which boats full of petty traders and prostitutes ply again the old routes to Haifa, Alexandria, Istanbul.

The most remarkable bit of foreign-led reconstruction is of the city orchestra. Odessa has a proud musical history. 'All the people of our circle – brokers, shopkeepers, bank and steamship office employees – taught their children music,' wrote Babel of his turn-of-the-century childhood in the poor Jewish quarter, the Moldavanka.[16] Though Babel himself made noises 'like iron filings' before running off to play hookey on the beach, it was a tradition that produced great violinists, among them Jascha Heifetz and David Oistrakh. So I went to hear a concert – a concert, as it happened, celebrating the fiftieth anniversary of VE Day.

It took place in the old stock exchange building, downstairs from the Cypriot casino. A riot of barley-sugar columns, Egyptian friezes and Gothic heraldry, the hall was filled with the kind of people who look as though they march on May Day and want to rebuild the Soviet Union. Old boys in boxy blue uniforms, dangling tiers of medals, sat next to their tiny, fierce wives. Schoolgirls in long white socks and frilly pompoms bobbed up and down expectantly. The orchestra came on and struck up tunes for each of the Allies – Bizet for the French, Elgar for the British, de Souza for the Americans, a grand, grim bit of Shostakovich, all snowy plains and rumbling tank columns, for the Russians. The conductor, a handsome young man, was obviously something of a local hero. In between numbers, the girls and grannies lined up in front of the stage and handed him bunches of lilac wrapped in silver paper. But there was something odd here. The figure at the centre of this festival of Soviet valour wasn't a Russian, he wasn't even a Ukrainian. He was, in fact, an American: *nash Hobart* – 'our Hobart' to Odessans.

Visiting Odessa as a guest conductor a few years previously, Hobart had fallen in love with the place and decided to stay. When he arrived the woodwind had run out of reeds, the strings hadn't had their bows re-haired for years and the trombones were using washing-up bottles as mutes. The repertoire was antiquated. 'In Soviet days,' a clarinettist told me, 'we had a kind of percentage plan – so much modern music, so much Ukrainian music, and so on. If Schnittke wasn't a favoured composer we didn't play him. You didn't actually get a letter or a phone call – it was just kind of in the air.' Now that Our Hobart was in charge, the players were still only being paid ten dollars a month, but life had begun to perk up. There was new music to learn and they had performed abroad in Germany, Spain and Britain, even in America. To save money on these trips they took all their food with them and busked in shopping malls between concerts. I asked Hobart if he ever worried that his orchestra might simply melt away mid-tour, resurfacing as a bunch of illegal waiters and cleaning ladies. He didn't. 'We had one musician who went to Poland where he earned ten times as much on a building site. But he came back. He missed the orchestra, he missed Odessa, and he missed me.'

For Ukrainians, Russia's conquest and settlement of New Russia was something of a sideshow. The Black Sea steppe had never been part of Ukraine anyway. If it had belonged to anyone, it was to Tatars and Greeks. What affected them much more was the beginning of 'Russification', the insidious centuries-long process whereby not only the Ukrainians' political institutions, but their culture and identity, were fitted to the Russian mould.

Russification did not only happen in Ukraine. All the nations of the empire suffered it, under tsarism as well as Communism. But Russification was more determined and more successful in Ukraine than elsewhere. First, Ukraine joined the empire early: Ukrainian lands east of the Dnieper went to Russia in 1686, Estonia and Latvia were conquered twenty years later, the Caucasus and Finland not until the nineteenth century. Ukraine thus became to Russians what Ireland and Scotland were to the English – not an imperial possession, like Canada or India, but part of the irreducible centre, home. Hence Lenin's (probably apocryphal) remark that 'to lose Ukraine would be to lose our head', and the dream of romantic nationalists such as Solzhenitsyn that Russia, Ukraine and Belarus will one day be reunited.

Second, Russians regarded – and still regard – Ukrainians as really just a subspecies of Russian in the first place. Any differences that did demonstrably exist between them were the artificial work of perfidious, Popish Poles – replaced in today's Russian imagination by the meddling West in general. Rather than attacking Ukrainians and Ukrainian-ness as inferior, therefore, Russians deny their existence. Ukrainians are a 'non-historical nation', the Ukrainian language a joke dialect, Ukraine itself an 'Atlantis – a legend dreamed up by Kiev intellectuals' in the words of a parliamentary deputy from Donetsk. The very closeness of Ukrainian and Russian culture, the very subtlety of the differences between them, is an irritation. Why Lithuanians and Kazakhs refuse to consider themselves Russians is perfectly obvious. But that Ukrainians should choose to do the same is simply infuriating. A Ukrainian friend who used to live in Moscow described to me the appalled reaction of her impeccably anti-communist Russian friends to Ukrainian independence:

> When we were part of the empire it was very well taken to be Ukrainian. They patted you on the back, they were very friendly, and they loved your Ukrainianism. We were all brothers in grief. But when Ukraine became independent – horrors! The best democrats immediately became so imperialistic. I had neighbours on my landing – very nice people, very liberal. But when it all happened and I was trying to decide whether to move back to Kiev, they said 'You're mad! Ukraine? What kind of Ukraine? What are you talking about?'

The ethnic Russian I got to know best in Kiev was Yuriy – George as he preferred to be called – Pestryakov, a retired physicist. Speaking courtly English gleaned from Dickens and Maugham, and liable to recite Kipling's *If* off by heart at a moment's notice, he was the model of the old-style *intelligent*. Many of his friends had emigrated to Israel or America, leaving him rather lonely in a tiny flat dominated by massive mahogany furniture and an out-of-tune grand piano stacked with old newspapers. But for all his devotion to Kipling and the World Service, for all his long years spent debating *samizdat* in smoky kitchens, Yuri was appalled both by the West – 'The Americans, they're robots, they never read, all they do is *barbecue*!' – and by Ukrainian nationalism – 'It's not renaissance, it's Nazification!'

Though his father's family came to Kiev in the 1850s, and his own grandfather, an Orthodox priest, was shot by the Bolsheviks during the Red Terror, he considered himself a Russian through and through. Still, after 150 years in Ukraine? 'Look. Before 1989, there was never any antagonism between Ukrainians and Russians, never in anything. The only exceptions were some people from the Union of Writers who were unhappy about their inability to distinguish themselves in any other way.' Ukrainianism, in other words, was a fraud, the self-justifying invention of second-raters.

Like Polonisation before it, the Russification of Ukraine started at the top. One of the reasons Catherine the Great was able to dissolve the hetmanate so easily was that she simultaneously extended Russian noble privileges to the Cossack ruling class. In 1785, along with the rest of Russia's nobility, they were exempted from taxes, from government duties, and from military service. In another sop to Cossack self-interest Ukrainian peasants, like Russian ones earlier, were forbidden to leave their landlords, reducing them to the status of serfs.

Since Peter's time, Ukrainians had done well in Russian service. As the Russian empire expanded, their opportunities widened. Though a few continued to mourn the hetmanate, secretly circulating fantastical histories of Khmelnytsky and Mazeppa, most were happy to treat it as a piece of out-of-date antiquaria, taking jobs in the imperial administration and preaching loyalty to the empire. Typical of the loyalist attitude was Viktor Kochubey, chairman of the Imperial Council in the 1830s. 'Although I was born a *khokhol*,' he told the governor-general of Ukraine, 'I am more Russian than anybody else ... My calling and the position I hold put me above all sorts of petty considerations. I look at the affairs of your province from the point of view of the common interest of our country. Microscopic views are not my concern.'[17] Gogol lampooned 'those mean Little Russians ... droves of whom can be found in council chambers and government offices, who squeeze every kopek they can out of their fellow-countrymen, flood St Petersburg with denunciations, finally amass a fortune and solemnly add to their surnames ending in O the letter V.'[18]

Throughout the nineteenth century Russification of Ukrainians proceeded hand in hand with the emasculation of Ukraine's Poles, who still made up most of the landowning class west of the Dnieper. In 1833 Kiev was given a new Russian university named after St Vladimir and designed, according to the Russian education minister, to 'disseminate Russian education and Russian nationality in the Polonised lands of western Russia'.[19] Thousands of Poles involved in the risings of 1831 and 1863 lost their estates, and were sent, often in chains and on foot, to Siberia. Those left behind were subject to intense surveillance: the novelist Balzac, revelling in the luxury of his Polish mistress's house near Zhytomyr ('The servants literally throw themselves on their stomachs when they enter one's presence, beat the ground three times with their foreheads, and kiss one's feet')[20], found his post ransacked by customs. Poorer nobles lost their patents of nobility, reducing them to the status of peasants, and Polish schools were closed, a move which hurt Ukrainians especially, since they could rarely afford to educate their children at home instead. As a result literacy rates actually fell. Better educated than Russia under the hetmanate, by the end of the century Ukraine was producing more illiterate army conscripts than any other part of the empire.

A campaign against the Uniates, begun by Catherine, recommenced under Nicholas I. Whole parishes were converted at the point of the bayonet, and in 1839 the Orthodox and Uniate faiths were officially 're-unified'. This was followed by confiscation of the property of Uniate monasteries and the arrest, deportation or imprisonment of hundreds of monks and priests. New laws forbade marriages between the religions, and conversion from Orthodoxy to other faiths.

As with Ukraine's Western-influenced religion, so with its Western-derived legal system. In 1831 municipal privileges based on the ancient Magdeburg Law were rescinded, and in

1840 Ukraine's separate legal code, the 'Lithuanian Statute', was replaced by ordinary Russian law (though a few obscure legal quirks, last remnants of Duchy rule, survived right up to the revolution). A ballad of the period, 'The Lament of the Kievans on the Loss of the Magdeburg Law', decried the fact that 'the bearded ones' had taken over Kiev, and condemned the old city government for having lost its rights through corruption and gambling, concluding that now 'the Muscovite will rule'.[21]

In 1876 Russification climaxed with the Edict of Ems. Taking the waters in that German spa, Aleksandr II signed a decree banning all import and publication of Ukrainian books and newspapers, all stage-shows, concerts and public lectures in Ukrainian, and all teaching in Ukrainian, even for infants. Ukrainian-language books were to be removed from school libraries, and Ukrainophile teachers transferred to Great Russia. During cholera outbreaks, even public health notices were to be posted in Russian alone.

Russification almost succeeded. By the 1840s, writes the Ukrainian-Canadian historian Orest Subtelny, 'the political significance of Ukraine and the Ukrainians' had become almost terminally 'vague and emasculated'. Neither the Decembrist rebellion of 1825 nor the Polish rising of 1831 included Ukrainian claims in their programmes, although they took place partly on Ukrainian soil and included Ukrainians among their leadership. In 1825 peasants in the villages around Kiev even helped round up rebel soldiers and hand them over to the authorities.

Cooperating with Russian government, though, was not the same thing as being Russian. The cities might be largely Russian-speaking, and the nobility Russified to the point of indistinguishability from the genuine article. But the process, like Polonisation before it, never went more than skin deep. In the villages, peasants took orders from their landlords in Russian, but still spoke Ukrainian among themselves. And though they did not yet call themselves 'Ukrainians' – the term, unlike the ancient word *Ukraina*, was not widely used until the end of the century – they knew very well that they were something different from the loathed Muscovites, the *moskali*. 'The worst label that a Little Russian pins on a Pole,' wrote Johann Georg Kohl, a German anthropologist who travelled through Ukraine in the 1830s, 'is a "senseless Pole"; while a Muscovite in the imagination of the Little Russian is always "cursed". The Little Russians have such widely used proverbs as: "He is a good man but a Muscovite!"; "Be friendly with the Muscovite, but keep a stone under your coat!"'[22] Kohl's remarkably prescient conclusion is worth quoting in full:

> Before their subjection, all Little Russians were freemen, and serfdom, they maintain, had never been known among them. It was the Russians, they say, that reduced one-half of the people to slavery. During the first century after the union, Little Russia continued to have her own hetmans, and retained much of her own constitution and privileges, but all these have been swept away by the retrograde reforms of the last and present century . . . Should the colossal empire of Russia one day fall to pieces, there is little doubt but that the Little Russians will form a separate state. They have their own language, their own historical recollections, seldom mingle or intermarry with the Muscovite rulers, and are in number already more than ten million. Their national sinews may be said to lie among the rural nobility living in the villages, from among whom every great political movement has hitherto emanated.[23]

Kohl got it half right. The Russian empire did fall to pieces, and Ukrainians did get their own separate state, but not under the leadership of the old, suborned Cossack nobility. The authors of modern Ukraine were a brand-new class that rose from the ranks of the peasantry – the Ukrainian intelligentsia.

CHAPTER FOUR

The Books of Genesis: Lviv

Only look well, only read
That glory through once more,
From the first word to the last,
Read, do not ignore
Even the least apostrophe,
Not one comma even,
Search out the meaning of it all,
Then ask yourself the question:
Who are we? Whose sons? Of what sires?
– *Taras Shevchenko, 1845*

All that I can find to say is that a nation
exists when a significant number of people in
a community consider themselves to form
a nation, or behave as if they formed one.
– *Hugh Seton-Watson, 1977*

IHOR PODOLCHAK IS an artist, and like all good artists, he has a mission. He is trying to persuade the Lviv city authorities to erect a statue to Count Leopold von Sacher-Masoch, the erotic novelist who gave his name to masochism. Sacher-Masoch was born in Lviv in 1836, son of the local police chief. 'We have three problems,' admits Ihor. 'His father was an Austrian official, he wrote in German, and he left Lviv when he was aged fourteen. But I say he was one of the greatest Ukrainian writers because his creative work was very closely connected with Ukrainian culture. It doesn't matter what language he wrote in –

there are more important things.' Lviv remains unconvinced. 'The official reaction,' says Ihor, 'is – "so now we have people who want to make out that Ukrainians are masochists!"' But Ihor has achieved the impossible before. A few years ago he arranged for one of his lithographs to be taken aboard the space station Mir – demonstrating, as he puts it, that 'art can exist outside the cultural context'. A video of the event shows a grinning astronaut floating in zero gravity, picture in hand. To celebrate the millennium, Ihor wants the billionaire financier George Soros to fund the construction of an ice pyramid on top of Mount Everest, symbolising 'humanity's striving for eternity in time and space'. Even if the ice pyramid doesn't happen, the project won't have been a failure, because it's the idea that matters, not the actuality. As if Ukraine didn't have problems enough already, Ihor is determined to give it conceptual art.

That Lviv should adopt an Austrian novelist as a local celebrity is actually not such a bizarre idea. Fifty miles east of today's Polish–Ukrainian border, Lviv was ruled by Austria from the first partition of Poland in 1773 until the collapse of the Austro-Hungarian empire in 1918. Christening the city Lemberg, the Austrians made it the capital of the 'Kingdom of Galicia', a patched-together province stretching east from Cracow to the river Zbrucz. With the rebirth of Poland the city went back to its ancient Polish name of Lwow, and in 1945 it fell, for the first time in its history, to the Russians, who deported the Polish population and renamed it Lvov. It only became Lviv in 1991, with Ukrainian independence.

Visually, it is Polish Lwow and Austrian Lemberg that have survived best. The Poles built a forest of churches – Dominican, Carmelite, Jesuit, Benedictine, Bernadine – and the inevitable monument to their beloved poet Mickiewicz. The Austrians gave it parks, cobbled boulevards, Jugendstil villas, a flamboyant opera house, municipal buildings painted the Hapsburgs' reassuring mustard yellow, and the matronly bronze caryatids that grace the lobby of the George Hotel. Though the Austrians themselves have long gone, Lviv is still a Mitteleuropean city, full of students carrying violin cases, the smell of warm poppyseed buns, the tap of footsteps on stone – a shabbier Salzburg, blessedly devoid of von Karajan posters and Mozart souvenirs. In the overgrown Lychakiv cemetery, the initials K & K – *Kaiserlich und Königlich*, motto of the old Austria – can still be made out on the tumbled gravestones, epitaph to bygone generations of colonial bureaucrats. For them, Galicia was a far-flung posting, chilly with 'the vast breath of the huge hostile tsarist empire', a place where, in the words of the novelist Joseph Roth, 'the civilised Austrian was menaced . . . by bears and wolves and even more dreadful monsters, such as lice and bedbugs' and soldiers in forgotten barrack-towns 'fell prey to gambling and to the sharp schnapps . . . sold under the label 180 Proof'.[1]

Of all Lviv's rulers, it is only the Austrians for whom Ukrainians retain any sneaking fondness. It is still just possible to find old men who can whistle the marching song 'Ich hat' einen Kamaraden', and *babushki* who, when asked the time, reply 'Old or new?', their clocks still being set to the hours kept under benign, bewhiskered Emperor Franz-Josef. The Hapsburgs might have been foreign autocrats, but at least they weren't as bad as the tsars. And it was under their indulgent rule, in Galicia, that the Ukrainian national movement was able to take root and flourish, providing Ukrainians with their first modern political parties, and, eventually, with their first short-lived Republic.

Ethnically and socially, nineteenth-century Galicia was an unbalanced, unhappy place. Poles owned the land; Jews the shops and inns. Ukrainians – 40 per cent of the province's population overall, the majority in the east – laboured out of sight in cottages and fields. Over this uneasy mixture lay a thin layer of Austrian officialdom (among them Oberpolitzmeister Sacher-Masoch). Lviv itself was not a Ukrainian, far less a

Russian city, but a Polish-Austrian-Jewish one. A Baedeker of 1900 makes the point:

Lemberg. – Hotels. HOTEL IMPERIAL; GRAND HOTEL; HOTEL METROPOLE; HOT. DE L'EUROPE; HOTEL DE FRANCE; HOT. GEORGE.
Cafés. THEATRE CAFE, FERDINANDS-PLATZ; VIENNA CAFE, HEILIGE-GEIST PLATZ.

Lemberg, Polish Lwow, French Léopol, the capital of Galicia, with 135,000 inhab. (one-fourth Jews), is the seat of a Roman Catholic, an Armenian, and a Greek Catholic archbishop. There are fourteen Roman Catholic churches, a Greek, and Armenian, and a Protestant church, two synagogues, and several Roman Catholic and Greek convents . . .

The handsome Polytechnic Institution, in the Georgs-Platz, completed in 1877, contains a large chemical-technical laboratory and is otherwise well-equipped. In the Slowacki-Str., opposite the Park, is the large new Hall of the Estates. In the Kleparowska-Strasse rises the fine Invaliedenhaus, with its four towers. At the Theatre (closed in summer), in the Skarbkowska-Str., Polish plays and Polish-Italian operas are performed (the solos generally in Italian, the chorus in Polish).

Ossolinski's National Institute, in the Ossolinksi-Strasse, contains collections relating chiefly to the literature and history of Poland, including portraits, antiquities, coins, and a library . . .

To the S. of the town is the extensive Kilinski Park, the favourite promenade of the citizens, with a statue of Jan Kilinski (1760–1819), the Polish patriot, by Markowski. Fine views of the town may be enjoyed from the Unionshügel, and from the top of the Franz-Josef-Berg.

But out of sight of the Franz-Josef-Berg, the views were not fine at all. Like Ireland, Galicia was a byword for rural poverty. In the 1880s it was calculated that of all the ex-Polish territories, Galicia had the highest birth and death rates and the lowest life expectancy. The average Galician ate less than half the food of the average Englishman, yet paid twice as much of his income in taxes. Every year 50,000 people in the province died of malnutrition, and only one in two children reached the age of five. The population grew regardless, and peasant plots shrank from an average of twelve acres to six. What spare cash the peasants did have went on drink: in 1900 eastern Galicia had one tavern per 220 inhabitants, compared to one hospital per 1,200, and one elementary school per 1,500. Though speculators struck oil in the region in the 1860s, the resulting wealth flowed away to London and Vienna. A joke of the period has a Polish socialist being stopped by a policeman as he crosses the Galician frontier. Asked what he means by socialism, he says it is 'the struggle of the Workers against Capital'. 'In that case,' replies the policeman, 'you may enter Galicia, for here we have neither the one nor the other.'[2]

The escape route for many was emigration. In the twenty-five years before the First World War more than 2 million Ukrainian and Polish peasants left Galicia, including an extraordinary 400,000 people, or almost 5 per cent of the province's population, in 1913 alone. Some went to the new factories of Polish Silesia, some to France and Germany. But most took ship to Canada and the United States, founding today's 2.4-million-strong North American Ukrainian diaspora. The New World was glad to have them. Some of the first Ukrainians into America were shipped over as strikebreakers by a Pennsylvania coal mine; the Canadian government used them to settle the prairie – not very different, they were assured, from the Ukrainian steppe. Fleeced by predatory commission agents, their first homes were often no more than brushwood wigwams; in time they progressed to mud-and-thatch huts and elaborate wooden churches just like the ones back home. As a Canadian home minister wrote: 'I think a stalwart peasant in a sheepskin coat, born on the soil, whose forefathers have been peasants for ten generations, with a stout wife and half-a-dozen children, is good quality.'[3]

The second great wave of emigration came at the end of the Second World War, when hundreds of thousands of Galicians fled west before the advancing Red Army, finding their way via

Displaced Persons' Camps in Allied-occupied Germany to Canada, America and Britain's industrial Midlands. The stories they have to tell are amazing: tales of midnight knocks, abandoned feather beds and dowry chests, carts strafed from the air, divided families, last trains. The journey was well worth it, for no better argument for nurture over nature exists than the tragicomic contrast between the escapees' 'hyphenated' descendants – multilingual, well travelled, university-educated – and their cousins who were left behind to grow up in the Soviet Union. One young Ukrainian-American Reuters journalist I knew always had her swish Kiev flat piled high with sacks of potatoes, lugged into town by kindly relatives on a remote collective farm. 'They really think,' she would groan, 'that otherwise I won't have anything to eat.'

Born of a mixture of political rivalry and Romantic preoccupation with peasant culture, the nineteenth-century Ukrainian national movement relied, like all national movements, on a large element of invention, not all of it even on the part of the Ukrainians themselves. Though it came to fruition in Galicia, it had its roots in eastern Ukraine, where Russia saw the Ukrainian peasantry as a potential counterweight to Polish influence. Most early Ukrainophile writing and research came out of Kharkiv University, founded in 1805 to train imperial bureaucrats, and one of the first histories of Ukraine, *History of the Russes or Little Russia*, was published by Moscow's Imperial Society for the Study of Rusian History and Antiquities. In the 1860s the movement passed into the hands of a group of young Kiev-born Poles, who took to the villages in embroidered peasant shirts to demonstrate their opposition to serfdom and discreetly lobby for support for Polish emancipation, and towards the end of the century it drew encouragement from Austria, which intermittently used the Ukrainians to counter Polish pretensions in Galicia.

For the educated inhabitant of Ukraine, national identity was a question of personal taste. In many families, some individuals turned into prominent 'Ukrainians', while others continued to think of themselves as Russians or Poles. Volodymyr Antonovych, professor of history at Kiev University and leader of the Ukrainian national movement in the 1860s and '70s, was born of a noble Polish family, as was Andriy Sheptytsky, Metropolitan of the Uniate Church in Galicia from 1900 to 1944. Asked his nationality, he would say that he was 'like St Paul – a Greek to the Greeks, a Jew to the Jews'. Andriy's brother Stanislaw, meanwhile, remained a conventional Roman Catholic Pole, spelling his surname Szeptycki and ending up as minister of defence in one of the interwar Polish governments. Though the Ukrainian peasant knew very well he was not a hated Pole or *moskal*, it was not until the end of the century that he started thinking of himself as a 'Ukrainian'. Asked his identity, he would probably have replied that he was a *muzhik* – a peasant – or 'Orthodox', or simply one of the *tuteshni* – the 'people from here'.

In the absence of a large body of people consciously identifying themselves as Ukrainians, the early evangelists for Ukrainianism had to stress what distinguishing features were to hand – history and language. At the beginning of the nineteenth century knowledge of either was rare. Tales of the Cossack uprisings had become the preserve of folk-tale and legend, transmitted by wandering bards. Ukrainian itself had turned into a peasant tongue, the language in which one addressed the servants, if one spoke it at all. In the cities, it was hardly heard. For a long time even Ukrainophiles expected it to die out completely, comforting themselves with the thought that Irish nationalism had survived the demise of Gaelic.

The first man to try producing literature in Ukrainian was a Russian-speaking bureaucrat, Ivan Kotlyarevsky. Significantly, he used the language for comic effect – his ballad *Eneida*, published in 1798, is a burlesque on Virgil's *Aeneid*, full of rollocking Cossacks and lusty village maidens. Though *Eneida* was a bestseller, even Kotlyarevsky did not think Ukrainian could be used for serious writing. But at the same time, work began on codifying the language. Ukrainian got its first grammar in 1818 (the compiler thought he was recording 'a disappearing dialect')[4] and its first short dictionary in 1823. Given birth by eccentric antiquarians, national consciousness remained incongruously bound up with the dusty world of libraries and learned journals, academic rivalries and obscure linguistic disputes. It is no coincidence that the president of the first Ukrainian Republic, of 1918, was a historian.

The lateness and fragility of the Ukrainian cultural revival was nothing unusual. Czech, Hungarian, Bulgarian, Romanian and Russian itself were all only just beginning to turn into literary languages. Czech got its first dictionary in 1835, and for a long time the language of the Bohemian cities was German. The first Hungarian grammar appeared in 1803, at which stage the Magyar nobility still spoke a mixture of French, German and dog-Latin. The Russian Academy published its pioneering six-volume Russian dictionary in the 1790s, followed by an official grammar in 1802. Pushkin, the first great writer in the vernacular, worked in the 1830s, and for much of the century the Russian nobility preferred French. Pushkin's Onegin is charmed by girls who can't speak their own language correctly – 'I find a faultless Russian style/Like crimson lips without a smile'[5] – and Tolstoy has Anna and Vronsky quarrelling in French as late as the 1870s. Hence, perhaps, Russia's vicious defensiveness over the development of rival Slavic tongues.

Ukraine's equivalent to Pushkin, and the man who contributed more than any other single individual to the creation of a Ukrainian sense of national identity, was Taras Shevchenko. Though rather scorned by young Ukrainians today, who have been force-fed his works at school, he single-handedly turned Ukrainian into a literary language, remains Ukraine's greatest national hero, and led a life that must surely be one of the most remarkable in all literature.

Shevchenko was born in 1814 in a village south-west of Kiev, to a poor serf family. His father worked as a carter in summer and a wheelwright in winter; his mother died when he was nine. From an early age he struck people as an unusual little boy, scratching pictures on walls and fences with lumps of coal or chalk, making clay whistles in the shape of nightingales, and getting lost in the fields looking for the 'pillars that hold up the sky'. His father, whose death left Shevchenko an orphan aged eleven, is supposed to have bequeathed his odd son nothing, on the grounds that he would obviously grow up a ne'er-do-well or a genius, and money would be no help either way.

Aged fourteen or fifteen, Shevchenko joined the household of the local landowner – Pavel Engelhardt, a great-nephew of Potemkin and a fashionable lieutenant in the Guards – as a servant-boy. His tasks were to wash the dishes, heave wood and empty slops. But at night, so tradition has it, he crept down the manor-house corridors making sketches of Engelhardt's paintings. One account even has him hanging his drawings, Orlando-like, from the trees in the park. Later the same year he was sent to Warsaw, where Engelhardt had been posted to the Russian garrison. Here Shevchenko met and fell in love with a young seamstress – not, like him, a serf. 'It was the first time,' he wrote later, 'that I began to wonder why we unlucky serfs were not free people like everyone else.' The romance was not destined to last: November 1830 saw the outbreak of the Polish rising and the Engelhardt ménage decamped to St Petersburg.

In the capital, Shevchenko's life changed. Apprenticed to a house-decorator, he painted friezes on palace walls by day, and spent the eerie 'white nights' sitting on a paint pot in the Summer Gardens, taking copies of its mythological sculptures. Early one morning he struck up conversation with another Ukrainian, a student at the Academy of Fine Arts, Ivan Soshenko. Soshenko showed him how to use watercolours, took him to galleries, and introduced him to friends – including Karl Bryullov, creator of a celebrated salon picture of the time, the melodramatic *Last Days of Pompeii*. Bryullov took an instant liking to the 'unserflike' young artist, and called on Engelhardt to try to talk him into granting Shevchenko freedom. The meeting was not a success. Bryullov ended by calling Engelhardt 'a feudal dog-trader' and 'a swine in slippers'; Engelhardt thought Bryullov a 'real American madman'. The only way to get Shevchenko's release would be to buy it. After much negotiation this was finally accomplished, the necessary 2,500 roubles being raised by Bryullov's donation of a portrait to a charity raffle. Aged twenty-four, Shevchenko ceased to be a serf.

A free man at last, he started enjoying himself. 'At that time,' wrote Soshenko disapprovingly, 'he changed entirely. Introduced by Bryullov to the best St Petersburg families, he frequently went out in the evenings, dressed smartly, even with some pretensions to elegance. In a word, he became possessed, for a while, with the social demon.'[6] In his memoirs, Shevchenko remembered gloating 'like a child' over a new coat:

> Looking at the skirts of this shining coat, I thought to myself: was it so long ago that, wearing a dirty smock, I did not even dare to think about such shining clothes? But now I spend a hundred roubles on a coat . . . Truly, the metamorphoses of Ovid![7]

At the same time he began to write. In 1838 he was showing verses to friends, and in 1840 he published his first collection, titled *Kobzar* after Ukraine's race of wandering bards. The book created a sensation. The Ukrainophile intelligentsia instantly recognised it as a landmark – 'so good', wrote one, 'that you can smack your lips and clap your hands';[8] Russians, of course, couldn't understand why anyone should want to write in Ukrainian at all.

Shevchenko's poems are an odd mixture of pastoralism, xenophobia and self-hatred. His themes are the beauty of Ukraine's landscape, her lost Cossack greatness and her shame in labouring under the Russian and Polish yokes. Though Russians, Poles (and, embarrassingly, Jews) all get short shrift, most of his bile is directed at the treachery and complacency of the Ukrainians themselves. Ukraine is a serf-girl seduced and abandoned by a heartless officer, a widow deserted by ungrateful children, a plundered grave, 'mould-grown', 'rotting', 'covered in

weeds'. Ukrainians are 'asleep', 'worse-than-Poles', even canni-
bals. Again and again, he lets fly at Russified compatriots:

> Here and there; they carry on
> In Russian, laugh, and curse
> Their parents who'd not had them taught
> To jabber, while still children,
> The German language, so that now
> They would not be ink-pickled . . .
> Leeches, leeches! For, maybe,
> Your father had to sell
> His last cow to the Jews, till he
> Could teach you Russian well![9]

Russian reviewers praised Shevchenko's talent, but regretted
that it should be put to work on a useless peasant tongue.
Ukrainian was 'artificial', 'dead', 'a joke and a whim'. It was
incomprehensible that writers should 'occupy themselves with
such stupidities'. The Ukrainian 'dialect' was fated to 'die in the
archives' and it was sad to see it 'used by people who might
adorn the all-consuming Slavic [i.e. Russian] literature'.[10] The
best-known critic of the day, Vissarion Belinsky, took him to
task – with some justification – for 'naïveté'. 'There is everything here which can be found in every Ukrainian poem,' he
wrote of Shevchenko's *Haydamaky*, a long and gory ballad on
the peasant rebellions of the eighteenth century. 'The Poles, the
Jews, the Cossacks; they swear a lot, drink, fight, set things on
fire, and butcher each other; in the intervals, of course, there is a
kobzar (for what Ukrainian poem can be without one?) who
sings his elevated songs without much sense, and a girl who
weeps in a raging storm.'[11]

Shevchenko had his reply ready:

> . . . If you want to sing
> For money and glory,
> Then you must sing about Matriosha
> And Parasha, and subjects

Like the sultans, parquet floors, spurs,
That's where glory lies. But
He sings – 'The blue sea is playing.'
While he himself is crying. Behind
Him stands a whole crowd,
All in peasant coats . . .[12]

Between 1843 and 1847 Shevchenko made two year-long trips to Ukraine, being lionised by the Ukrainophile intelligentsia and sketching Cossack monuments. Accounts from the period describe a short, thickset man with reddish hair, a plain face and strikingly bright and intelligent eyes. He made friends everywhere, and was evidently good company: Princess Varvara Repnina, who fell in love with him while he was painting her father's portrait, described him to a friend as 'one of those who are so congenial in the country . . . and whom one can leave alone without any fear that some trifle will offend him'. He was 'simple and unpretentious', 'relaxed and tactful in society, and never used clichés'.[13]

In the spring of 1846 Shevchenko fell in with Mykola Kostomarov, a young historian at Kiev's St Vladimir University. Kostomarov was leader of the Brotherhood of Saints Cyril and Methodius, one of the many semi-secret discussion groups which produced the radical political thinking of the time. Comprising only a dozen or so members, the Brotherhood's utopian aim was to abolish serfdom and monarchy and form a new pan-Slavic democratic federation, with Ukraine at its head. This programme was set out in 'The Books of Genesis of the Ukrainian People', a pseudo-biblical document which Shevchenko may have helped write. Early in 1847 the Brotherhood fell prey to an informer. Disembarking from a Dnieper riverboat on his way to act as best man at Kostomarov's wedding, Shevchenko was arrested and sent to St Petersburg for interrogation by Count Alexey Orlov, head of Nicholas I's secret police. Orlov decided he was not actually a member of the Brotherhood, but an 'important criminal' none the less. 'Shevchenko has acquired among his friends,' he reported, 'the reputation of a brilliant Ukrainian writer, and so his poems are doubly harmful and dangerous. His favourite poems could be disseminated in Ukraine, inducing thoughts about the alleged happy times of the hetman era, the exigency of a return to those times, and the possibility of Ukraine's existence as a separate state.'[14] The tsar's reply was unequivocal. All the Brotherhood members were to be sent into internal exile, and Shevchenko was to be consigned to penal service with the Orenburg Corps, on the Ural river near Russia's present-day border with Kazakhstan. A note appended to Orlov's report in Nicholas's own hand reads: 'Under the strictest surveillance, prohibited from writing or painting.'

Shevchenko's ten years of exile took up over a third of his adult life. But they were not as grim as they could have been. Merciless in theory, the tsarist penal system was notoriously slapdash in practice. Exiles with contacts, charm or money could live in relative ease, and Shevchenko had all three. The bored governors of distant barrack-towns were not about to let this charismatic celebrity – with his ability to sing, paint, tell funny stories and dance the *hopak* – pass unappreciated, and put him to use tutoring their children, taking portraits of their wives or directing amateur theatricals. Though there were periods when Shevchenko was forced to stay in barracks doing drill and guard duty, and suffered acute boredom and loneliness, most of the time he was able to paint, send and receive letters and books, wear civilian clothes and live in private quarters. He also continued to write poetry, hiding his notebooks with friends or tucking them inside his boots.

By far the harshest period of his exile were two and a half years with a military expedition sent to chart the Aral Sea. In May 1848 a caravan of 2,500 carts, 3,500 camels, 600 Bashkir cavalry, 200 Ural Cossacks and an entire disassembled schooner, the *Constantine*, set off south from Orenburg. Shevchenko's role, despite Nicholas's ban on painting, was as official artist. As the caravan crawled across the steppe – as flat 'as if it were covered with a white tablecloth' – he took sketches of a huge grass fire and of a holy poplar-tree, to which the Bashkirs made sacrifices. The expedition safely crossed the Karakumy desert – a waste of sand-hills and glaring salt-plains, strewn with skeletons of men and animals – arriving at the bleak coastal fortress of Raim in June. Here the *Constantine* was reassembled, and with surveyors and a geologist as well as Shevchenko aboard, embarked on a two-year odyssey of gales and rocks, scurvy and boils. At one point the ship spent a fortnight anchored at sea riding out a storm, and the entire crew was forced to drink salt-water. Having mapped hundreds of miles of coastline and discovered several new islands, the expedition finally returned home in the autumn of 1850. The following year Shevchenko accompanied a much less arduous geological expedition to the coal-rich Mangyshlak peninsula on the Caspian Sea, spending pleasant days riding into the mountains with a sketch-pad, or reading and writing with friends in the back of a covered cart.

In 1855 Nicholas I died, to general rejoicing. Two years later Aleksandr II gave permission for Shevchenko to return from exile, on condition that he submit to police surveillance and not 'misuse his talent'. Fêted by admirers all the way, Shevchenko sailed from Astrakhan up the Volga to Moscow, and on home to the 'sinful paradise' of St Petersburg. In astrakhan hat and grizzled Cossack moustache, he resumed life as a literary celebrity, campaigning for an end to serfdom and joining Turgenev and Dostoyevsky at public poetry readings. A final trip to Ukraine, in the spring of 1859, ended in arrest and despatch back to the capital. There, after a tipsy night's Christmas carolling, Shevchenko developed dropsy and died, aged forty-seven. Twelve days earlier he had written a final poem:

> Should we not then cease, my friend,
> My poor dear neighbour, make an end
> Of versifying useless rhymes?
> Prepare our waggons for the time

When we that longest road must wend?
Into the other world, my friend,
To God we'll hasten to our rest . . .
We have grown weary, utter-tired,
A little widsom we've acquired,
It should suffice! To sleep is best.[15]

Straight away, Shevchenko's supporters began elevating him to sainthood. After lying in state in the chapel of the Academy of Arts, his corpse was given temporary burial in a St Petersburg cemetery. Two months later it was disinterred, put inside a new metal coffin draped with red taffeta, and borne by students down Nevsky Prospekt to the railway station. At Orel and Moscow the coffin left the train for requiem masses, and on arrival in Kiev it was met by a large crowd and shipped, amid much speech-making, downriver to Kaniv, a picturesque village where Shevchenko had been planning to buy a house. Here, on a high bluff overlooking the river, the poet was finally laid to rest. The grave was covered with a Cossack-style mound and marked with an oak cross. In the 1880s the wooden cross was replaced with an iron one, in 1931 with an obelisk, and in 1939 with a hideous monumental bronze statue, which still stands today.

In death, Shevchenko has been subjected to serial hijack, dragooned in support of a string of causes which he never knew or dreamed of. For nineteenth-century Russians he was an icon of liberal opinion. In Ilya Repin's conversation-piece, *They Weren't Expecting Him*, which depicts a family open-mouthed at the reappearance of an exiled relative, a portrait of Shevchenko hangs in the background, silent marker of the family's progressive political sympathies. The Soviets recast him as a prototype revolutionary, erecting busts and statues all over Ukraine. (One, opposite Kiev University, replaced a statue of Nicholas I; the plinth, thriftily, remained the same.) Trees under which he might have mused turned into sacred 'Shevchenko oaks' – the Ukrainian equivalent of Russia's omnipresent 'Pushkin rocks'. Beetle-browed and glowering, this Bolshevik

Shevchenko is a massive, militant presence, equally at odds with the snub-nosed, twinkling fellow of the sketches made from life and with the dreamy, Byronic figure of the self-portraits.

His latest reincarnation is as hero of Ukrainian independence. The man who in life loved pig-roasts, rum and servant-girls (his last romance fell to pieces when he found the girl in question in the arms of the butler) has been turned into Ukraine's national martyr, doe-eyed embodiment of a suffering people. Nationalist parliamentary deputies sport the Shevchenko moustache, bushy and turned down at the ends, and his works are quoted *ad nauseam*, in the portentous singsong of Slavic poetry recital, on every conceivable occasion. The first of many times I heard Shevchenko quoted aloud was, unsuitably enough, in the company of a tipsy Russian businessman. Taking me to dinner at the Salyut Hotel, a feast of beige carpeting, foxed cheeseplants and Rosa Klebb-lookalike waitresses, he lifted a vodka glass, told me his wife did not understand him, and proceeded to recite Shevchenko's famous *Testament* in a resonant baritone: 'When I die, then make my grave/High on an ancient mound,/In my own beloved Ukraine ...'[16] Knowledge of Shevchenko, I was intended to understand, was proof positive of sound democratic principles. As a pass-making technique it was a non-starter – but it sounded terrific.

A well-known joke has two old men sitting on a bench drinking beer – *pyvo* in Ukrainian. 'You know what the filthy Russians call this?' asks one, '*Pi-i-i-vo!*' 'Horrible!' replies the other, spitting on the ground; 'I could shoot them for it!' Despite its similarity to Russian (the two are about as close as Dutch and German, or Spanish and Portuguese), the Ukrainian language plays a starring role in the Ukrainians' sense of national identity, making it a delicate political as well as cultural issue. If an Englishman cannot open his mouth without half his compatriots hating him for his accent, a Ukrainian cannot utter a word without half his fellow-citizens despising him for his choice of language.

For people who speak Ukrainian as a first language, those who have no Ukrainian at all, or who speak it badly, are not true co-nationals. Russian-speakers, on the other hand, suspect determined Ukrainian-speakers of zealotry or opportunism. In Bulgakov's *The White Guard*, set in Kiev during the Civil War, the reader immediately realises that the Turbins' Baltic-German brother-in-law is a bad hat when he is spotted poring over a Ukrainian grammar. Today's born-again Ukrainian – the political hanger-on who was never heard to utter a word of Ukrainian until 1991, or the pundit who speaks Ukrainian on the conference platform, and switches back to Russian in his office – is still a stock figure of fun. Prominent among them is President Kuchma himself, who was rumoured to be taking two Ukrainian lessons a day during the election campaign of 1994. 'You ask them to speak Ukrainian,' my friend Roma would complain of her interviewees, 'and they say fine. But then all of a sudden they start sticking in Russian words every now and then, and the next thing you know they've switched completely to Russian.' Even the sincerest Ukrainophiles are prey to this tendency. The director of the Kiev City Museum, a nice man beset with worry that his beloved collection was about to lose its premises to the new High Court, once gave me a peroration on the superiority of Ukrainian over Russian culture. 'When *we* were building Santa Sofia, over *there*' – waving an arm vaguely eastwards – 'there was nothing but *wolves*.' For my benefit, he said, he was talking in Russian. But did he speak Ukrainian at home? He blushed a little and shifted in his chair: 'Well, you know how it is, it isn't easy . . .'

Ukrainian is still in a state of flux. Its technical vocabulary is underdeveloped, necessitating extensive borrowings from German and English (anything but Russian.) There are also variations between the Russian-influenced Ukrainian of the central provinces and the Polish-influenced Ukrainian of Galicia, anathematised under the Soviets as not Ukrainian at all, but a bastard form of Polish. A Ukrainian friend brought up near Lviv remembers being told at school that 'the language we were talking was improper, very bad, incorrect, some kind of dialect . . . and that somewhere there is this correct Ukrainian language, but somehow different – not the language we were talking of course'. There is also a gap between the everyday Ukrainian of the street and the formal, flowery language of books, speech-making and television. People who actually speak the literary version in real life are rare enough to be celebrated for it. 'You must go and interview him,' I would be told of this or that person, 'he speaks *such* beautiful Ukrainian' – as though speaking the language 'properly' were an achievement in itself.

Despite pressure from nationalists, the post-independence governments have held to a sensible line on the language issue. Unlike the ethnic Russians of Latvia and Estonia, Ukraine's Russians do not have to pass language tests to get voting rights and citizenship, and Ukrainianisation of the education system is taking place on a gentle *ad hoc*, school-by-school basis. Students have to master basic Ukrainian to enter university, but once there, many of their books and lectures are still in Russian. In the Donbass and Crimea, contrary to what the Russian press would have one believe, nearly all schools remain Russian-speaking. In Lviv, on the other hand, a generation of schoolchildren is growing up, for the first time in fifty years, who speak no Russian at all. But through most of the country, urban Ukrainians look set to become what many of them are already – bilingual. Though the language problem is not going to fade away – Russian is too deeply entrenched for that – it has already ceased to be quite the political football it was in the immediate post-independence years.

Shevchenko's work, though a great boost to Ukrainophiles, did nothing to soften government hostility to Ukrainian cultural revival. His death in 1861 was followed by the century's second great Polish uprising, provoking a new wave of Russian paranoia. All religious and educational publications in Ukrainian were banned, and a new generation of activists was sent into exile. 'A Little Russian language never existed, does not exist and never shall exist,' the interior minister instructed the censors. 'Its dialects as spoken by the masses are the same as the Russian language, with the exception of some corruptions from Poland.'[17] Restrictions eased slightly in the early 1870s, only to tighten again with the Edict of Ems in 1876. Under the Edict's malign influence, the national movement evaporated. Dissent flowed instead into the empire-wide anarchist and revolutionary movements, climaxing with Aleksandr II's assassination (by a terrorist group led by a Ukrainian from Odessa) in 1881. From the mid-1870s, therefore, the pressure for national revival came not from Kiev but from Austrian-ruled Lviv. Small, poor and backward, Galicia became the unlikely Piedmont of Ukraine.

As in Kiev, the national movement in Lviv got much of its initial impetus from imperial efforts to play Ukrainians off against the more powerful Poles. Austria experimented with the technique in 1848, during the Europe-wide popular risings known as the 'Springtime of Nations'. When the barricades went up in Cracow and Lviv, the governor of Galicia, Count Franz Stadion, encouraged Ukrainian leaders to submit a loyal petition to the Emperor, asking for official recognition for their nationality and for Galicia to be split in two. He helped organise a 'Ruthenian Supreme Council' under a Uniate bishop, and gave funding for the first Ukrainian-language newspaper. An elected parliament with Ukrainian representation was, however, dissolved once order had been restored.

In 1861, following Austria's defeat at the hands of the French in Italy, parliament and constitution reappeared, this time permanently. As well as sending delegates to the Reichsrat in Vienna, each province had its own local Diet, with jurisdiction over schooling, health and trade. But the electoral system was designed to give solid majorities to the conservative landowning class – which in Galicia meant the Poles. Whereas only fifty-two votes were needed to elect a deputy to the landlords' curia, peasant delegates needed almost 9,000, and urban workers had no votes at all. The result was that although Ukrainians made up about half Galicia's population, they never held more than a third of the seats in the Lviv Diet. Moreover, the Galician government was notoriously addicted to vote-rigging: ballot-box stuffing, intimidation and non-registration of candidates and voters were all common. Though Galicia introduced direct and universal suffrage in 1907 – several years after Vienna, thanks to Polish opposition – Ukrainians remained heavily under-represented.

In 1867 Austria lost another war, this time with the Prussians. The result was the Austro-Hungarian Compromise, giving the Hungarians direct rule over about half the empire, and reducing the Austrian–Hungarian connection to a shared monarchy and army. In exchange for Polish support for the battered empire, from then on Vienna gave the Poles a free hand in Galicia. Poles replaced Germans and Austrians in the local bureaucracy, Polish became the language of education, and Poles took the Galician governorship. 'Whether and to what extent the Ruthenians may exist,' said an Austrian politician, 'is left to the discretion of the Galician Diet.'[18] Ukrainians' acquiescence in the arrangement, and continued loyalty to the Hapsburgs, was bitterly satirised by the Ukrainian socialist Ivan Franko in his short story, 'Budget of the Beasts'. In it the Lion, ruler of the animal kingdom, proposes a 'budget' of Sheep and Chickens (Ukrainians) for the Wolves, Bears and Eagles (Poles) to eat:

> Pages distributed the printed figures among all the animal deputies. The deputies glanced at the figures and icy shivers ran up their backs. But what could they do now? . . . 'Secretary,' ordered the Lion, 'read the budget aloud, maybe someone will want to take the floor in debate on this question!' Then one very old Ass rose and said: 'I move that the secretary be relieved of the necessity of reading it. We have all read the budget, and we realised at once that we couldn't manage without a budget. We all have faith in our emperor and are ready to do anything for his sake. Therefore, I move that this House adopts this budget at

once and without debate. Everybody in favour, please stand.' All rose. The budget was adopted. From that time on true heavenly peace reigned in the animal kingdom.[19]

Despite everything, Galician Ukrainians were far better off than their cousins over the Russian border. With freedom to publish and associate, real though limited participation in imperial politics, and the proverbially well-organised Czechs and Germans on hand as inspiration, they developed a remarkable penchant for activism. The largest and oldest of the Ukrainian organisations in Galicia was the *Prosvita* or 'Enlightenment' society. Established in 1868, it concentrated on teaching peasants to read. By 1914 it had 200,000 members and nearly 3,000 village libraries and reading-rooms. Around the reading-rooms sprang up choirs and theatre groups, gymnastics clubs and voluntary fire-fighting associations, taken from Czech models. The 1880s and '90s saw the appearance of hundreds of rural cooperatives and credit unions, allowing peasants to raise cheap loans and cut out middlemen. Ukrainian-language newspapers multiplied, and in 1890 the Galicians finally formed their first political party, a decade before Russia's Ukrainians were able to follow suit. Led by Franko, it put socialism before independence. The rival National Democratic Party made its appearance nine years later, quickly overtaking the Radicals on a platform of loyalty to the Hapsburgs and moderate liberal reform.

As well as a literary language and a burgeoning sense of national identity, Ukrainians now had a full roster of cultural and political institutions. But as the Ukrainians gathered strength, they came into increasingly sharp conflict with the Poles. For both, Galicia was the place where their political opportunities were greatest and their national movement strongest, and they clashed on all fronts. Ideally, the Ukrainians would have liked Galicia to be split into eastern and western halves, each with its own Diet. Failing this, they wanted more Ukrainian schools and their own university. In 1894 they won what turned out to be an important victory, when the Austrian government reluctantly allowed the foundation of a new chair of Ukrainian history at Polish-controlled Lviv University. ('Ruthenian history,' the Austrian education minister had complained, 'is not real scholarship.'[20]) Given the euphemistic title 'The Second Chair of Universal History with special reference to the History of Eastern Europe', the professorship went to 28-year-old Mykhaylo Hrushevsky, one of a string of bright young Kievans who were making their way to Lviv. His agenda – establishing a historical basis for the Ukrainian identity – was clear right from the start. The 'nation', he told the audience at his inaugural lecture, was 'the alpha and omega of historical discourse', 'the sole hero of history'.[21] His ten-volume *History of Ukraine-Rus*, published over the next several decades, did for Ukrainian history what Shevchenko had done for Ukrainian literature. Henceforth nobody, whatever else they might say about it, would be able to pretend it didn't exist.

Despite the Ukrainians' gains, relations with the Poles went from bad to worse. Students fought in the lecture-halls, and in 1908 the Polish governor of Galicia was assassinated in protest at continued vote-rigging. It is hard to imagine how the two sides could have been reconciled. Both saw Galicia as an integral part of a future nation-state. Poles called the province 'Eastern *Malopolska*' or 'Little Poland'; Ukrainians were already talking about it as a potentially independent 'Western Ukraine'. In July 1914, during a massive Ukrainian rally in Lviv, news came through of the assassination of Archduke Ferdinand in Sarajevo. Here, in a war which was to destroy both the empires – Romanov and Hapsburg – which ruled them, Poles and Ukrainians each had their chance to turn dream into reality.

What Lviv was to Ukraine in the late nineteenth century, it was again in the closing years of the Soviet Union. It produced most of Ukraine's dissidents and demonstrators, and the political party – Rukh – which led the movement for Ukrainian independence. Uncompromisingly Ukrainian (speak Russian on the street, and you will get some dirty looks), it still epitomises the enthusiastic sense of self of western Ukraine over the downbeat cynicism of Kiev, and the grim disillusion of places like Donetsk.

But now that it is no longer a political centre – on independence, politics moved to Kiev – the old city is having to learn new tricks. The first person I got to know well in Lviv was Oleh, a gangling youth full of political theory and burning ideals, deeply into the student movement. I took him to the Grand Hotel, a Western-owned outfit with real linen napkins, proper cutlery and fleets of nervous newly trained waiters. Oleh was nervous too – he'd never been anywhere like this before, and seven dollars was a terrifying amount of money to be spending on lunch. When we next met, gangling Oleh was transformed. He produced roses, chocolates: this time, he was taking me out to supper. We went to a newly opened café round the corner from his flat. Since we had seen each other last, he said, he had got into the printing trade. Here was a calendar his firm had produced – the butterflies had come out well, but he'd got the dates muddled, so they'd had to do a rerun. He was exporting Christmas cards to Austria and Hungary, and he'd worked out a nice little arrangement with the manager of a local bottling plant: 'Two hundred dollars for him; 100,000 labels for me.' Things were going so well that he was even having to pay protection money – 25 per cent of profits – to local racketeers. Wasn't that rather a lot? 'No, because they don't know how much profit we're making.' A girl who had been sitting in the lobby as we came in materialised in front of our table in a bellydancer's outfit, wiggling energetically. With a flourish, Oleh produced a wad of notes and stuck them in her bra. Not quite Sacher-Masoch, but getting there.

◆ CHAPTER FIVE ◆

A Meaningless Fragment: Chernivtsi

Undefined ourselves, we expected something from Time, which was unable to
provide a definition and wasted itself in a
thousand subterfuges.
– *Bruno Schulz, 1937*

OF ALL THE rag-tag foreign leavings that make up present-day Ukraine, the remotest and most obscure is the Bukovyna. Squeezed between the Carpathian alps and the river Prut, it belongs nowhere and has been ruled by everybody: first by Poles and Turks, by the Austrians through the nineteenth century, by the Romanians between the wars. 'It was cut off from every-where,' wrote the historian A. J. P. Taylor, 'a meaningless fragment of territory for which there could be no rational explanation.'[1] In 1940 it was annexed to the Ukrainian Socialist Soviet Republic by the Soviet Union, and in 1991 it duly fell to Ukraine. Its capital is Czernowitz in German, Cernauti in Romanian, Chernovtsy in Russian, Chernivtsi in Ukrainian. The Austrian novelist Gregor von Rezzori, who grew up there in

the 1920s, called it 'Tchernopol', weaving nostalgia-laden stories around its dusty streets and rainbow population for the
whole of his life. Home to 'Jews in caftans ... spur-jingling
Romanian soldiers ... colourfully dressed peasant women with
baskets of eggs on their heads' and 'solid ethnic German
burghers in ... wide knickerbockers and Tyrolean hats',[2] his
Tchernopol belongs to no one but itself; a sharp-witted, mock-
ing, slovenly place where nothing is permanent and nothing is
taken seriously. For all their imperial pomp, the Austrians never
really made the city their own; still less the parvenu Romanians.
'That Romanian interlude,' von Rezzori wrote of the interwar
years, 'was hardly more than a fresh costume-change in a setting
worthy of operetta. The uniforms of Austrian lancers were
supplanted by those of Romanian Rosiori ... and the whole
transformation was given no greater weight than the one
accorded to the changing scenery at the municipal theatre
between ... "Countess Maritza" and "The Gypsy Baron" or
"The Beggar Student".'[3] He wasn't surprised when the Romanians packed up their costumes and went home again, for 'how
can you get anything done in a town that laughs at everything?'[4]

Chernivtsi is duller now. Though its cab-drivers still juggle lei
and forints and roubles in their heads, it has lost the old,
heterogeneous population that gave it flavour. On market days,
wrote von Rezzori, the streets used to fill with a dozen different
nationalities: Jews and Armenians haggled over corn and used
clothing, Hutsul peasant-women squabbled with Swabians over
vegetables and poultry, and gypsy card-sharpers shuffled aces
under the noses of gaping mountain men with long matted hair
and faces 'tanned like old goat hams' – all to the wailing of
Caruso from the wind-up gramophones on sale beside the
Turkish Fountain, and the stench of raw sheep's hide.

Now the Jews, Armenians and Swabians have all gone,
replaced by stolid Ukrainians – less than half the Bukovyna's
population before the war – and a scattering of lonely Russians:
stranded survivors, like von Rezzori's dotty parents three-quar-
ters of a century ago, of an empire that sank beneath their feet.

The Great Synagogue ('in the Moorish style', according to Baedeker), has disappeared, as has the statue of a Bukovynan bison goring an Austrian double-headed eagle – a piece of Romanian *folie de grandeur* – that stood in the Ringplatz opposite the Rathaus and the hotels Adler and Weiss. The cafés have been given bland Soviet names, the 'Dniestr', 'Turyst' and 'Kiev' replacing Baedeker's Café de L'Europe and Café Wien. Only the 'Edelweiss' carries a reminder of an Austrian past. The old opera house – its sinuous Jugendstil façade covered in bill-posters for folksy Ukrainian operettas – has closed for lack of funds, and the Armenian church ('in a mixed Gothic and Renaissance style') has been turned into a concert hall. When von Rezzori revisited in the late 1980s, he found the city well preserved architecturally but 'devoid of soul'. Plumply uniform, its new inhabitants had nothing of the 'restlessly vivacious, cynically bold and melancholically sceptical spirit that had distinguished the children of this town and made them famous throughout the world as Czernowitzers.'[5] All the time I lived in Kiev, the sole occasion on which Chernivtsi limped into the national news was when it was discovered that one of its steep, silent streets was sliding quietly downwards into the muddy Prut.

What does survive is the landscape. To the south, the Prut runs away to the broad Moldovan plain. To the west, the furry blue Carpathians march off towards Poland and Transylvania. Bright with the fluorescent green of aspens and shiny white of silver birch, loud with the percussion of axes and woodpeckers, the mountains cannot have changed much since von Rezzori went shooting with his father as a boy, each with shirt buttoned up tight to the chin in accordance with the sacred laws of Austrian hunting etiquette. The Hutsuls – a picturesque tribe of mountain shepherds, famous for their craftsmanship – believed the forests hid *rusalkas*, green-eyed nymphs who asked riddles and tickled men to death, and witches whose long pendulous breasts, flung backward over their shoulders, gave them the ability to change shape and to fly. To keep the witches at bay they built themselves fantastical wooden churches – some tiny, dwarfed by shingled pagoda-like spires; others tall and four-square and roofed in grey tin, riding between the pines like battleships among square-riggers.

It is hard to believe now, but before the war the Bukovyna was a fashionable holiday resort, an alternative to the Alps for middle-class families from Warsaw and Vienna. Their villas – two-storey, with glassed-in verandahs and mansard roofs – are still there, scattered about the hillsides above hamlets of two-room cottages, each with fruit-trees, dungheap and barking dog. Over in the Polish Carpathians the tourists are back, together with such novelties as cars, metalled roads and refrigerated Coca-Cola. Strings of polite blond schoolchildren hike up and down signposted trails, and young couples delve about in the blueberry bushes with purple-stained carrier bags.

But on the Ukrainian side of the border, the mountains are more cut off from the world than ever. The communists' concrete sanatoria stand empty, since the Ukainian new rich, who are the only people who can afford to go on holiday at all nowadays, head straight for Ibiza or Marbella. After a disastrous attempt at a skiing holiday with my boyfriend, I could hardly blame them. An Englishman of traditional tastes, he was so traumatised by a weekend at the Yuzhtechenergo – property of the local branch of the energy ministry – that he refused ever, *ever* to come to Ukraine again. It was not so much the families cooking *shashlyki* over little bonfires in the corridors that he minded, he said, or the bits of reinforcing rod sticking out of the walls, or the strips of newspaper stuck over the cracks in the window-frames, or the cabbage-filled ravioli for breakfast, lunch and dinner, or even the ice-sculpture of an erect penis at the top of the resort's single chair-lift. It was the fact that when he got back to his room, he found a happy troop of skiers having a picnic on his bed. That they had offered him a piece of sausage on the end of a penknife was no consolation, and as soon as we got back to civilisation he was going to handcuff himself to the nearest heated towel-rail and never let go. Our ski-guide Anton, part-time drummer in a band devoted to something called 'prison rock', was unsympathetic. 'Be glad,' he told us, 'you're not at the Dynamo. That's a *real* horse-house.'

Chernivtsi's 'Romanian interlude' was a result of the First World War. When war was declared in July 1914, Ukrainians found themselves conscripted into two opposing armies – 3.5 million into the Russian, a quarter of a million into the Austrian. As ever, Ukraine turned into a battlefield, and Ukrainians often ended up fighting each other. In September 1914, after the Russians' defeat at Tannenberg in East Prussia, the Austrian army advanced north-east into Russian-ruled Poland. The Russians immediately counter-attacked, capturing Lviv and Chernivtsi. Through the following spring and summer, the Austrians and Germans fought eastwards again, occupying the whole of western Ukraine and Belarus. Another Russian offensive under General Brusilov in June 1916 resulted in the capture of 400,000 prisoners, but failed to retake its principal objective of Lviv. A year later Russia's final westward push collapsed in ignominy when the rank and file, thoroughly demoralised by poor leadership and Bolshevik propaganda, laid down their weapons and fled. Accused of collaboration by both sides, Ukrainian civilians suffered terribly throughout, being shot, deported or interned in thousands.

The Bolshevik coup of November 1917 and the collapse of Austro-Hungary twelve months later ushered in the 'Russian' Civil War, most of which really took place in Ukraine. The First World War had at least been fought between regular armies on recognisable fronts; the Civil War was chaos. For Isaac Babel, incongruously attached to a Red Army cavalry unit, it was a war of dusty roads and obscene songs, the 'odour of yesterday's blood and slain horses',[6] casual rapes and throat-slittings, charred towns and looted churches, all under a sun that rolled across the sky 'like a severed head'. It brutalised him – an intellectual with 'spectacles on his nose and autumn in his heart' – as it did everyone else: he ends one of his *Red Cavalry* stories 'begging fate for the simplest of abilities – the ability to kill a man'.[7]

For three years five different armies – Red, White, Polish, Ukrainian and Allied – rampaged through the countryside, as did dozens of anarchic 'Cossack' bands. Hiding their weapons in barns and pigsties, these peasant formations could appear and disappear at will. Machine-guns were mounted on rickety two-wheeled *tachankas*; 'haycarts,' Babel wrote, 'drawn up in battle formation, take possession of towns'.[8] The biggest, under otamans Nestor Makhno and Matviy Hryhoryev, were thousands strong and equipped with field-guns and armoured cars. On all sides, soldiers had little idea what they were fighting for, and deserted whenever they could.

For Ukraine's Jews, it was the worst period in their history since the Khmelnytsky massacres. Victimised by all sides, but by the Whites and Ukrainians in particular, they suffered looting, rape and wholesale murder. Massacres took place in Berdychiv, Zhytomyr, Odessa, Poltava, Chernihiv and Kiev, as well as dozens of smaller cities. One of the worst, the work of White troops, took place in Fastiv, a small town south-west of Kiev, in September 1919:

> The Cossacks divided into numerous separate groups, each of three or four men, no more. They acted not casually . . . but according to a common plan . . . A group of Cossacks would break into a Jewish home, and their first word would be 'Money!' If it turned out that Cossacks had been there before and taken all there was, they would immediately demand the head of the household . . . They would place a rope around his neck. One Cossack took one end, another the other, and they would begin to choke him. If there was a beam on the ceiling, they might hang him. If one of those present burst into tears or begged for mercy, then – even if he were a child – they beat him to death . . . I know of many homeowners whom the Cossacks forced to set their houses on fire, and then compelled, with sabres or bayonets,

along with those who ran out of the burning houses, to turn back into the fire, in this manner causing them to burn alive.[9]

The Fastiv massacre is said to have taken 1,500 lives; estimates of the total number of Jews killed in the Civil War pogroms range from 50,000 to 200,000.

Altogether the years 1914 to 1921 killed about 1.5 million people in Ukraine. Amid this slaughter, Ukrainians made two separate attempts at independence. One centred on Kiev, the other on Lviv. Both ended in failure.

When news of Nicholas II's abdication reached Kiev in March 1917, Ukrainian organisations in the city formed a Central Council, or Rada, in competition with the Russian-dominated Soviet of Soldiers and Workers. Over 100,000 demonstrators turned out in the Rada's support, marching under blue-and-yellow banners and pictures of Shevchenko. In April a National Congress, attended by 900 delegates from all over the country, elected as President the historian Hrushevsky, newly returned from exile in Moscow, and the following month the Rada issued its First Universal, declaring that 'without separating entirely from Russia, without severing connections with the Russian state', the Ukrainian people should 'have the right to order their own lives in their own land'.[10] In July Petrograd's Provisional Government reluctantly gave the Rada official recognition, and Britain and France sent accredited representatives.

The Rada survived less than a year. Manned by young left-wing idealists who refused to adopt the existing administrative apparatus or the army units voluntarily formed in their support, it was more a talking-shop than a government, never extending its authority much beyond the cities. From the outset, wrote a (sympathetic) observer, it was 'a real Tower of Babel ... a parliament of national elements rather than of political parties'.[11] Six weeks after Lenin's coup in Petrograd, pro-Bolshevik troops marched on Kiev, ineffectually opposed by a scratch collection of peasants, schoolboys and ex-prisoners of war under

Semyon Petlyura, a leading Ukrainian socialist and the Rada's minister for war. While the Bolsheviks bombarded the city with heavy artillery from across the Dnieper, the desperate Rada rushed through its Fourth and last Universal, declaring Ukraine unconditionally independent: 'People of Ukraine! By your efforts, by your will, by your word, a Free Ukrainian People's Republic has been created on Ukrainian soil. The ancient dream of your ancestors – fighters for the freedom and rights of workers – has been fulfilled ... From this day forth, the Ukrainian People's Republic becomes independent, subject to no one, a Free Sovereign State ...'[12] Thirteen days later the Rada fled Kiev for Volhynia, debating as it went. 'In various obscure towns along the railway line,' writes Hrushevsky's biographer, 'laws were passed about the socialisation of land, about the introduction of the New Style calendar, a new monetary system, a coat-of-arms for the Republic, Ukrainian citizenship ...'[13] After eight precarious months, the Ukrainian People's Republic was no more.

While fighting continued around Kiev, German, Russian and Ukrainian delegations were negotiating an armistice in the Belarussian town of Brest-Litovsk. Two separate agreements – one with the Bolsheviks, one with the Rada – handed Ukraine, along with the Baltics, Russian-ruled Poland and most of Belarus, to Germany. For the Bolsheviks, the Treaty of Brest-Litovsk was the only way to stop the war. For Germany, it secured a rich source of food supply and freed up troops for the Western Front. For the Rada, promised autonomy under German protection, it was a route back into government. In the event, only Bolshevik expectations were fulfilled. The Germans occupied Kiev in March 1918, bringing Hrushevsky and the Rada with them. But a few weeks of the Ukrainians' interminable bickering convinced them that the Rada was incapable of running even a puppet government. On 28 April, soldiers marched into a debate on the new Ukrainian constitution and disbanded the assembly. The next day Pavlo Skoropadsky, a Russified landowner who had earlier offered military support to the Rada and been turned down, was declared 'Hetman of All Ukraine'. Sympathetic soldiers smuggled Hrushevsky out of the city on foot, his long beard hidden inside his overcoat.

Given an illusory stability by the Germans' presence, Kiev filled with Russian refugees: 'grey-haired bankers and their wives . . . Respectable ladies from aristocratic families and their delicate daughters, pale depraved women from Petersburg with carmine-painted lips; secretaries of civil service departmental chiefs; inert young homosexuals. Princes and junk-dealers, poets and pawnbrokers, gendarmes and actresses from the Imperial theatres.'[14] Nightclubs – the 'Lilac Negro' and the 'Dust and Ashes' – opened to cater for those determined to fiddle while Rome burned. All that summer, wrote Bulgakov, 'the cab-drivers did a roaring trade and the shop windows were crammed with flowers, great slabs of rich filleted sturgeon hung like golden planks and the two-headed eagle glowed on the labels of sealed bottles of Abrau, that delicious Russian champagne'.[15]

Meanwhile, in the trenches of Flanders, the Germans were losing the war. In December they evacuated Kiev, taking Skoropadsky with them, and Petlyura's Ukrainians entered the city once again, only to flee in the face of a second Red Army advance a few weeks later. At the same time, the Allies made their sole contribution to the anti-Bolshevik cause in Ukraine, landing 60,000 French troops along the Black Sea coast in support of the Whites. They were withdrawn again four months later, after a single unsuccessful skirmish with 'otaman' Hryhoryev.

Over the next year and a half, Kiev changed hands with dizzying frequency. 'The inhabitants of Kiev reckon that there were eighteen changes of power,' wrote Bulgakov. 'Some stay-at-home memoirists counted up to twelve of them; I can tell you that there were precisely fourteen.'[16] The Ukrainians' last throw came in 1920, when Petlyura did a deal with the Polish leader Jozef Pilsudski, recognising Polish sovereignty over Eastern Galicia in exchange for a joint Polish–Ukrainian advance on Kiev. Pilsudski duly took Kiev in May, only to abandon it again just over a month later. Petlyura fought on with the typhoid-ridden remnants of his army until November, before accepting internment in Poland. In 1926 he was assassinated in Paris by a middle-aged watchmaker, Sholem Schwartzbard, in revenge for his troops' massacres of Ukrainian Jews. Despite having been arrested standing over Petlyura's body with a smoking revolver, after a sensational three-week trial Schwartzbard was acquitted. 'There are times,' he wrote in his confession, 'when private sorrows disappear in public woe, like a drop of water in the sea.'[17]

In Lviv, Ukrainian independence was even shorter-lived. In October 1918, when it became clear that Austro-Hungary was falling apart, officers from the Sich Riflemen, an all-Ukrainian unit of the Austrian army, ran up blue-and-yellow flags over the public buildings, and posted placards announcing a West Ukrainian National Republic. House-to-house fighting immediately broke out between the Riflemen and Pilsudski's Polish Military Organisation. Three weeks later the Ukrainians fled east to Stanyslaviv (now Ivano-Frankivsk), where they managed to form a rough-and-ready government and gather an army. The following summer the Poles pushed them over the river Zbruch into central Ukraine, where they joined Petlyura in defeat at the hands of the Bolsheviks.

Why did the Ukrainians fail to get independence at the end of the First World War, when the Poles, Czechs, Balts, Romanians and Albanians all succeeded? That they should fail was not a foregone conclusion. In 1918 some strands of Western opinion saw the establishment of an independent or semi-independent Ukrainian state in eastern Galicia as a real possibility, in accordance with Woodrow Wilson's principle of self-determination. Pilsudski was also initially in favour, on the grounds that an autonomous Ukrainian state, federated with Poland together with Lithuania and Belarus, would act as a buffer between Poland and Russia.

But even before the Ukrainians were beaten on the battlefield, rendering an independent Ukraine a practical impossibility, they had lost the argument at the conference table. At the Paris peace talks of 1919 the Ukrainians had to make their voice heard among a host of vociferous newly freed East European nations, all of whom based their claims more on historical precedent than Wilson's Fourteen Points. 'When Dmowski related the claims of Poland,' recalled a despairing American official, 'he began at eleven o'clock in the morning and in the fourteenth century, and could only reach 1919 and the pressing problems of the moment as late as four o'clock in the afternoon. Benes followed immediately afterward with the counter-claims of Czechoslovakia, and, if I remember correctly, he began a century earlier and finished an hour later.'[18] The Poles' argument, laid out in arch-nationalist Roman Dmowski's impressively fluent French and English, was that Poland needed sovereignty over East Galicia, the better to act as counterweight to a resurgent Germany. Ukrainian national feeling was a German invention and the Ukrainians were dangerously inclined towards Bolshevism, as witnessed by their bloody raids on Polish-owned estates. The Ukrainians could and should not, therefore, be given any sort of independence. The White representatives at the conference agreed – though of course as far as they were concerned Ukraine was part of 'one and indivisible' Russia.

Hopelessly out of their depth in the gilt and green-baize world of international diplomacy, the Ukrainians fought their corner as best they could. The head of the Ukrainian delegation, Arnold Margolin, dashed to and fro between the European capitals, vainly trying to stir up enthusiasm for the Galician cause. 'In interviews with Philip Kerr . . . chief of Lloyd George's cabinet,' he wrote in his memoirs, 'I could elicit no definite opinion in regard to events in Warsaw and the Ukraine. "*Qui vivra, verra*" was his enigmatic reply to my questions.' Herbert Asquith expressed polite interest in Ukrainian peasant customs, and asked 'which Ukrainian party corresponded to the British

Liberal Party'.[19] In Berlin, Rathenau assured him that Bolshevik Russia was bound to turn democratic; an American diplomat asked him why Ukraine and Russia didn't form 'a federation similar to our American commonwealth'. Americans in general, Margolin discovered, were 'as uninformed about Ukrainians as the average European is about the numerous African tribes'.[20]

In the end, the Allies split on the Galicia issue. Britain, with oil interests in the region, was inclined to favour the Ukrainians; France, paranoid about a resurgent Germany, strongly supported the Poles. The casting vote therefore went to the Americans. After much dithering, they too came down in favour of Poland. On 25 June the Allied Council of Ambassadors accepted Poland's right to occupy Galicia 'in order to protect the civilian population from the dangerous threat of Bolshevik bands'. In exchange Poland gave a vague promise, never fulfilled, of a plebiscite permanently to decide the region's future.

Ironically enough, one of the few Western voices raised against the decision was that of the historian Lewis Namier, a Polonised Galician Jew who had taken British nationality and spent the war working for British intelligence. Despite knowing that Ukrainian marauders had burned down the family manor-house and kidnapped his mother and sister, he wrote:

> For all my personal loss and anxieties I do insist that a grievous wrong has been done the Ukrainians. Left in peace to establish a strongly radical but decent government, they might well have organised themselves. Driven to despair, insidiously pushed daily toward bolshevism and into committing atrocious crimes, they know – and we shall see – that a Polish military occupation, as foreshadowed in the Foreign Minister's decision of 25 June, means disaster without end. And I insist that no number of atrocities, however horrible, can deprive a nation of its right to independence, nor justify it being put under the heel of its worst enemies and persecutors. If the horrifying excesses reported by the Poles are true, they only prove the intensity of the Ukrainians' detestation of them . . .'[21]

The Treaty of Versailles, signed three days after the decision on Galicia, split Ukraine in four. Galicia and western Volhynia went to Poland; the Bukovyna to Romania, and the district around Uzhorod and Mukachevo, known as Ukrainian Transcarpathia, to Czechoslovakia. Central and eastern Ukraine stayed with Russia, pending the outcome of the Polish–Soviet war. The treaty, Namier told his boss, was 'worse than incomprehensible', it was 'a scandalous letting down of the Ukrainians.'[22] Poland's border with the Soviet Union, left open at Versailles, was formalised at the Treaty of Riga in February 1921, with no Ukrainian participation whatsoever.

Namier's forebodings were all too prescient. The Treaty of Versailles created plenty of grievances among the East European nationalities. But none matched the Ukrainians', who, though numbering tens of millions, had been left with no state of their own at all. Their hostility to the Galicia settlement became one of the major factors destabilising Poland between the wars.

In 1923 the League of Nations recognised Poland's permanent sovereignty over Galicia and western Volhynia on condition that it grant the region an autonomous administration, allow the use of the Ukrainian language in government, and establish an independent Ukrainian university. But despite numerous complaints to the League, these promises were never fulfilled. Though almost a third of interwar Poland's inhabitants were non-Polish (Ukrainians made up 14 per cent of the population, Jews 9 per cent, Belarussians 3 per cent, Germans 2 per cent), Polish governments became increasingly authoritarian and nationalistic, especially after Pilsudski's coup of 1926. Ukrainian schools were closed or turned Polish-speaking, Ukrainian professorships at Lviv University abolished, Ukrainian newspapers strictly censored, Ukrainians barred from even the lowliest government jobs, and Ukrainian candidates and voters arbitrarily struck from electoral rolls. Over 300 Orthodox churches were demolished or converted to Catholicism, and up to 200,000

Polish settlers were moved into Ukrainian towns and villages. Poland's aim, according to the aptly named nationalist politician Stanislaw Grabski, should be 'the transformation . . . of the Commonwealth into Polish ethnic territory.'[23]

Predictably, far from assimilating the Ukrainians, Polonisation turned them radical. Though the largest Ukrainian parliamentary party, the Ukrainian National Democratic Union (UNDO), sought compromise and denounced the use of violence, the national movement passed increasingly into the hands of an underground terrorist group, the Organisation of Ukrainian Nationalists (OUN). Led by an ex-Sich Rifleman, OUN was neo-fascist in rhetoric and pro-German in sympathy, drawing financial support from Germany and Lithuania. In 1930, in response to hundreds of OUN-led arson attacks on Polish-owned estates, the government mounted a violent and indiscriminate 'pacification' campaign in the Galician countryside. Despite clumsy cover-up attempts (the *Chicago Daily New's* man in Lviv was trailed by 'a woman in gumboots, who spent most of her time looking bored in the vestibule of the George Hotel') the campaign provoked an outcry in the Western press:

> The 'pacificatory' system of the Polish soldiers consists of raiding a village suspected of being implicated in the destruction of the farm of a neighbouring Polish landowner. The principal men of the village – the mayor, priest, heads of co-operative societies and leaders of sports and reading clubs – are summoned before the commander of the Polish detachment. The Ukrainians are required to give information regarding acts of incendiarism and to hand over all arms. If their answers are considered unsatisfactory – and this is generally the case – they get sixty or ninety blows from the knout, which used to be employed in Poland only by emissaries of the Russian Czar. If the victims faint under the blows, they are sometimes revived by throwing cold water over them, and then flogging begins anew.
>
> The Polish soldiers have been no respecters of sex, and in many

villages women have been subjected to these merciless whippings. Sometimes in their search for arms the soldiers remove the
thatched roofs from the cottages and then depart, leaving the
hapless occupants exposed to the less brutal treatment of the
elements.

SIGNS OF NATIONALITY DESTROYED

The native Ukrainian garb and Ukrainian needlework is
destroyed wherever seen in the homes of peasants, for the object
of the Polish military commanders is ruthlessly to eradicate all
vestiges of Ukrainian nationality. For this reason the Ukrainian
co-operative stores and creameries, reading-rooms and libraries
have been destroyed. Priests are forced to cry out 'Long live
Pilsudski!' (Marshal Joseph Pilsudski, Premier and virtual dictator of Poland) or 'Hurrah for the Polish Republic' under threat of
being flogged until they are made unconscious if they refrain
from so doing. (*New York Herald Tribune*, 15, October 1930)

OUN's response was an assassination campaign. In the early
1930s OUN killed dozens of Polish policemen and officials, as
well as several prominent Ukrainian moderates. Its best-known
victim was Bronislaw Pieracki, the interior minister responsible
for the outrages in Galicia. Though OUN leaders were eventually rounded up and imprisoned, the organisation continued to
expand right up to the Second World War, when it formed the
basis of the Ukrainian partisan army.

OUN's only direct descendant in contemporary Ukrainian
politics is the Ukrainian National Assembly (UNA), a small
neo-Nazi paramilitary group which sent volunteers to fight
against the Russians in the Moldovan and Georgian civil wars.
In December 1993, just after Vladimir Zhirinovsky shocked the
world in Russia's first free parliamentary elections, my editor
told me to go and find out more about them. Was neo-fascism,
he wanted to know, about to sweep Ukraine too?

UNA's headquarters happened to be just around the corner

from my flat, in a shabby basement at the end of a boarded-up cul-de-sac. In the mornings, its khaki-clad devotees could be spotted queueing, rather self-consciously, amongst the shuffling pensioners outside the local bread shop. My interview, with the second-in-command of UNA's political wing, went like a dream. Dressed in black polo-neck, fatigues and army boots, he delivered the requisite tirade on Ukrainian cultural supremacy and Russian and American 'diabolism'. Saracens came into it, so did Nostradamus. By trying to persuade Ukraine to give up its nuclear missiles, the West was 'going in the direction of a third world war'. A Cossack mace sat in a corner, and a picture of the partisan leader Stepan Bandera hung, slightly askew, on the wall, next to a calendar from the Dniproflot riverboat company. I duly mustered my quotes and wrote my piece. That the Ukrainians should swing to the extreme right, I opined, was not only possible but 'very likely'. Prices were doubling every month, factories were closing right and left, and fuel shortages had doused the eternal flames on the war memorials. All the Weimar ingredients, in short, were there.

My Ukrainian friends read the piece and got cross. I had got things completely out of proportion, they said. UNA was a tiny group, never likely to get anywhere, and they were fed up with people like me taking down its pathetic ravings and splashing them all over the Western press. Those excitable Russians might vote for a clown like Zhirinovsky, but Ukrainians were a sensible lot who knew how to keep their feet on the ground. They were right. In the Ukrainian parliamentary elections of spring 1994, campaigning under the priceless slogan 'Vote for us and you'll never have to vote again', UNA won three out of 450 seats, and quietly dropped out of the news. I had learned my lesson in one of Ukraine's most enduring characteristics – pragmatism.

Western Ukraine produced four great writers between the wars: von Rezzori, Paul Celan, Joseph Roth and Bruno Schulz. Von Rezzori and Celan both grew up in Chernivtsi, Roth and Schulz in small towns in Polish-ruled Galicia. Von Rezzori was Austrian; Celan (born Paul Antschel), Roth and Schulz all Jews. Except for von Rezzori, who mixed with Italian literati to the age of eighty-three, they all led tragic lives. Roth died a penniless alcoholic at a café table in Paris. Celan's parents were both killed by the Nazis; haunted by survivors' guilt, he threw himself into the Seine. Schulz, having just started being published when war broke out, was shot dead by an SS officer as he walked home with a loaf of bread.

Though all save Schulz lived most of their lives abroad, none stopped writing about the strange, indefinite borderlands in which they grew up. Their work is linked by a sense of limbo and disorientation – not the disorientation of exiles, but of people whose own homeland has no fixed identity. In his wonderful novel *The Radetzky March*, Roth turns Galicia into a literal and metaphorical swamp: 'Any stranger coming into this region was doomed to gradual decay. No one was as strong as the swamp. No one could hold out against the borderland.'[24] In Schulz's surreal Drohobycz, pots and pans fly about the room, men turn into doorbells and cockroaches, and comets descend chimneys from green, millennial skies. His characters wander about in a timeless, somnambulant daze:

> Waking up, still dazed and shaky, one continues the interrupted conversation or the wearisome walk, carries on complicated discussions without end. In this way, whole chunks of time are casually lost somewhere; control over the continuity of the day is loosened until it finally ceases to matter . . . [25]

What has cut the town from its moorings is the passing of the Hapsburg empire, an empire which 'squared the world like paper . . . held it within procedural bounds, and insured it against derailment into things unforeseen, adventurous, or simply unpredictable'.[26] Even Celan, born two years after Austro-Hungary's collapse, called himself a 'posthumous Kakanier', after the Hapsburgs' omnipresent *K & K*. In von Rezzori's Tchernopol, similarly lit by the 'sunset glow of the sunken dual monarchy', Hapsburg certainties have been replaced with cynicism, with a ruthless appreciation of the grotesque. His novel *The Hussar* has an impossibly correct Austrian, a left-over from the old regime, quixotically defending his nymphomaniac sister-in-law's honour by fighting a series of duels. The incredulous city authorities duly commit him to an insane asylum:

> He couldn't help it that he was virtuous. It was the heritage of
> the world from which he came, a world that had gone under. In
> the idiom of Tchernopol, one would have said he just happened
> to be one of the slow ones who can grasp only very gradually
> that times have changed.[27]

One last magnificently Rezzori-esque figure from the pre-war borderlands deserves mention – Jan Ludvik Hoch. Hoch was born in 1923 in Slatinske Doly (now Velyky Bychkiv), a muddy little town wedged between the Carpathians and the river Tisza in what was once Czechoslovakia and is now Transcarpathian Ukraine. It had a main street, two wooden synagogues, a few shops, one bar and five cars. It didn't need a cemetery, jokers said, because everyone either emigrated or ended up on the gallows.

On birth, Jan had been called Abraham, but when the birth was registered at the town hall an official insisted that the baby take a Czech name. His father was a woodcutter and cattledealer, and probably, like the rest of the town, a part-time smuggler, ferrying shoes and clothing across the Tisza to Romania in exchange for food and alcohol. The family lived in a two-room cottage with its own wooden verandah and well but no oven; instead dough was sent to the communal bakery. The seven children shared beds and shoes, and every year gypsies cleared out the pit below the outdoor privy and spread its contents on the vegetable patch in the yard. Jan wore a skullcap and long Hasidic curls, and learned to read and write in Hebrew at the local *yeshiva*. When war broke out he reinvented himself. He cut off his hair, took the train to Budapest, and joined – it is unclear quite when or where – the Czech Legion. The

Legion took him from Palestine to Marseilles to Liverpool, and he ended the war a much-decorated captain in the British army. When he took British nationality, it was under a name chosen by his brigadier – Robert Maxwell.

One blazing Sunday afternoon forty-five years later I interviewed Maxwell on the roof of the London headquarters of his publishing empire. A helicopter gleamed on the Astroturf, and a butler in striped trousers brought up tea things on a tray. Dressed in a scarlet silk shirt that bulged like a spinnaker-sail, he was the fattest and most bombastic man I had ever seen. The lies he told about his business (the subject of the interview was the launch of a short-lived newspaper, the *European*) were transparent, superb, regal in their scope and shamelessness. Eighteen months later, as his companies crumbled around him, he vanished over the side of his motor-yacht into the Mediterranean. Enigmatic to the last, he was another true son of the somewhere in the middle of nowhere that was pre-war borderland Ukraine.

◆ CHAPTER SIX ◆

The Great Hunger: Matussiv and Lukovytsya

> The decree required that the peasants of the Ukraine, the Don and the Kuban be put to death by starvation, put to death along with their little children.
> – *Vasiliy Grossman, 1955*

MARIA PAVLIVNA KURYNO, crabbed and shrunken as a Pompeii mummy, has lived in Matussiv all her life. Her cottage has two rooms and a clay floor and smells of horse. On the wall, papered with mismatched offcuts stuck on with drawing-pins, hangs a photograph of her husband, black-bordered and framed in tin foil. He disappeared fifty years ago, somewhere on the Eastern Front. Now Maria spends her days on the warm ledge above the clay stove, dozing or watching the television that stands beneath the icons in the corner. Her daughter and granddaughter are there too – a stout middle-aged woman in a *muzhik*'s padded jacket, and a wide-eyed little girl who chews the end of her blonde pony-tail and ducks her head when we try to take a photograph. It takes a while to make ourselves understood.

'Babka, there's someone to see you, a foreigner, from *Angliya*.'

'Is she really an English girl – really, really foreign? You mustn't photograph me – look at me, I look like a monkey! I read somewhere that Ukraine borders England . . .'

'And this one's from *Kanada*.'

'From *Amerika*!'

Roma shrugs her shoulders.

'Yes, from *Amerika*!'

Maria wears a scarf over her yellow-white hair and a nylon dress held together with safety-pins. As she talks she crosses herself again and again. She was twelve years old when 'Nicholas's war' began and fifteen at the outbreak of the Russian Revolution. She can remember reaping corn with her sisters in her family's one-and-a-half-acre field, while the daughters of the local big house rode round on horseback. 'You'd cut five sheaves, keep one, and the other four would go to the Lopu-khins,' she says. 'But it wasn't so bad – at least they paid.' Neighbours worked in the local beet refinery, owned by the Brodskys, the Jewish sugar magnates who endowed, among many other good works, the Bessarabka covered market in Kiev. The village had twice as many inhabitants then, and real shops where you could actually buy things: 'Jewish *magazinchiki*. You could say – bring a bag of flour, and they would bring white or brown, right to your house, whatever you wanted.'

After the Revolution, Maria's memory gets muddled. *Bandyty* came and took people away – to the North 'where they built a canal, poor people', or to the woods, where they were shot and buried in pits. When was this? Who was doing the shooting? 'Ah, they were just bandits – such bandits.'

Matussiv's undoing, like that of thousands of other villages in central and eastern Ukraine, was not war or revolution but collectivisation, and the massive famine – the 'Great Hunger' – which followed it. Finding Ukrainians who are willing and able to talk about the famine is surprisingly hard. The younger generations have been told little about it by their parents and grandparents, for fear that such talk might compromise their careers, even their lives. 'It just wasn't something we talked about in our family' was a typical comment from Kiev friends. The old, who remember the famine at first-hand, are dying off fast, and do not like confiding in strangers.

My problem was solved by my interpreter, Sergey Maksimov. A gentle, bearded man in his early forties, he was grotesquely overqualified for his job. He had written a thesis on 'The Use of Dactyl Markers in British Legal Language' at Birmingham University, could read manuscripts in ancient Goth, and knew the whereabouts of every Scythian gravemound and ruined monastery in the country. But his teaching post at the Foreign Languages Institute only paid twenty dollars a month, so he was happy to spend hours with me in parliament translating dull debates. His lifeline – the place where he went to croon John Lennon and contemplate life – was his dacha at Lukovytsya, a village a couple of hours down the Dnieper by hydrofoil. His neighbour Hanna Hrytsay was a proper villager, not a *dachnik*, and would be happy to talk.

A spry, scrubbed old woman with pink cheeks and silver hair done up in a bun, Hanna looked as though she had stepped straight out of a fairy-tale. The whitewashed walls of her cottage were festooned with scythes, wicker baskets, enamel pots, old cartwheels and useful bits of rope and leather. Every inch of the half-acre plot behind was covered with immaculate rows of onions, sweetcorn, potato-plants and tomatoes. One small barn, walled with hurdles, stored the last of the previous year's hay; another, roofed with tarred cloth held in place by bricks hanging on wires from the roof tree, housed a brown-and-white cow with curly horns. Hanna said she would have preferred asbestos for the roof, but at a million coupons a sheet it was too expensive, and she and her husband were going to have to carry on making do with tar-paper. All Lukovytsya's running water came from a single standpipe; like Matussiv, it had dirt roads, no shops, no public transport and, in winter, no postal service.

Hanna was seven years old when collectivisation began in 1929:

People didn't want to enter these collective farms at all, but they were forced to. They took everything – land, grain, ploughs, animals. And as if that weren't enough they took the bread out of the house. My grandfather was a blacksmith; he resisted for three years. They took his horses, his smith's shop, they banged on the walls with hammers to see if he had hidden any grain. They even took the seedcorn for the next year. A barn or a stable was a symbol of wealth. If you had a metal roof on your house, you were considered a kulak, and sent away to the North. You know Tykhon's house over the road – it had an iron roof. The only reason it wasn't confiscated was because he was ill and had to have his leg amputated – the activists took pity on him.

The local church – 'it was a beautiful one, with bells' – was demolished and its icons looted. 'People protested but it didn't help. There was a man called Myron who lived right here – people used to go to his place to read the Bible and sing hymns. Then he disappeared too.'

Hanna's family sold 'everything – icons, clothes, pillows' to buy rye. But by the winter of 1932 they were living off anything they could find. 'People were eating straw and lime-tree leaves, making *kasha* out of bark, nettles. I went to see my uncle, and they served a dinner. There was a stew – I saw something strange – tails sticking out of it! It was made from mice!' Compared to most villages, the Lukovytsyers were lucky, because they could trawl – illegally, using blankets – for fish and molluscs in the Dnieper. Even so, two families died. On the other side of the river things were much worse: 'People were killing their children and eating them.'

The famine, though, was a long time ago. What Hanna really wanted to talk about were the iniquities of the present. A few years ago she and her husband had sold five cows and put the proceeds – 2,000 roubles, 'half the price of a Volyn jeep in those days' – into the bank. Hyperinflation had since reduced their value – the savings of a lifetime's work – to absolutely nil: 'not even enough to buy a box of matches'. They had been keeping the money for their funerals. Now they wished they had bought a refrigerator instead.

Exactly how many people died in the Great Hunger of 1932–3 is unclear. As Khrushchev admitted in his memoirs, 'No one was keeping count'. Contemporaries spoke of 4 or 5 million. The historian Robert Conquest uses Soviet census data to arrive at a figure of 7 million: 5 million in Ukraine, 2 million elsewhere in the Soviet Union. Another 6.5 million, he reckons, died in 'dekulakisation' immediately beforehand. If Conquest is right, the whole operation killed over twice as many people as the Holocaust – thirty-four lives not for every word, but for every *letter* in this book. These may well be underestimates, since Soviet census data are unreliable. When the post-purge census of 1937 turned up an embarrassing population deficit, Stalin promptly had the officials in charge arrested and shot. Subsequent counts, one can assume, erred on the side of optimism.

The term 'famine', with its implication of natural disaster, is the wrong word for what happened. Unlike the Irish potato famine of the 1840s, the deaths of 1932–3 were a deliberate, man-made event. Crop failure was not to blame, since the harvest of 1932 was only slightly smaller than average, and actually better than that of the previous year. Nor can it, by any stretch of the imagination, be put down to bureaucratic oversight. By the early autumn of 1932 Stalin and his ministers undoubtedly knew, because local communists repeatedly told them so, that the countryside was starving, but ordered that food requisitions continue none the less. Right through the famine, storehouses full of 'emergency supplies' were kept locked and guarded, while people died in thousands in the villages round about. During the less serious famine of 1921–2 (also the result of grain requisitions), the Soviet government had allowed Western relief agencies to provide food aid; in the far worse conditions of 1932–3, it denied that famine existed at all.

The official explanation – seconded, until quite recently, by standard Western textbooks – was that collectivisation was a painful but necessary step towards modernising the rural economy, and the famine something obdurate peasants brought upon themselves. 'You can't make an omelette,' Stalin is said to have declared, 'without breaking eggs.' But even from this point of view, collectivisation was counter-productive: deporting all the country's most successful farmers and starving the rest to death was hardly the way to go about boosting agricultural output, and Soviet farming has not really recovered from the blow even now. Like Stalin's purges, which killed hundreds of thousands of stalwart Party supporters and most of the Red Army officer corps, the collectivisation famine of 1932–3 is so incredible, so seemingly self-defeating, that it is unsurprising that many historians have interpreted it as some sort of self-perpetuating blunder, a freak act of God.

The most convincing explanation for the famine is that it was a deliberate, genocidal attack on rural Ukraine. The groups the Bolsheviks most hated and feared, and had had most difficulty subduing during the Civil War, were the peasants and the non- Russian nationalities. The Ukrainian countryside – home to the Soviet Union's largest and most turbulent ethnic minority and to its richest and most self-reliant peasantry – embodied these twin demons in one. For centuries visitors had contrasted Ukraine's 'smiling' farmhouses, so clean that 'a traveller might fancy himself transported to Holland',[1] with Russia's rural hovels. Their prosperity was not only the result of a richer soil and milder climate, but of the fact that most Ukrainian farmland was individually owned by independent smallholders, whereas Russian land was held communally, and periodically redistributed by councils of village elders. Communism – which to the peasant meant collectivisation – was thus even less popular in Ukrainian villages than in Russian ones. By 1928 there was one Party member per hundred and twenty-five peasant households in the Soviet Union as a whole, compared to only one per thousand in Ukraine.[2] When Stalin ordered collectivisation, Ukraine was where it encountered most resistance and where it was enforced most harshly. Though there was also widespread famine in the Russian Kuban (where many Ukrainians also lived), and among the Kazakhs, Don Cossacks and Volga Germans, proportionately higher grain quotas in Ukraine ensured that it bore the bulk of deaths. 'Truly, truly,' wrote Vasiliy Grossman in his autobiographical novel *Forever Flowing*, 'the whole business was much worse in the Ukraine than it was with us.'[3]

The attack on Ukraine was a reversal of policy for the regime. In the mid-1920s the official line towards ethnic minorities was *korenizatsiya* or 'taking root'. *Korenizatsiya* meant encouraging non-Russian languages and cultures (though not political organisations), with the aim of broadening communism's appeal. Ukrainian-language books and newspapers were printed in large numbers, and hundreds of new Ukrainian-language schools opened, under the aegis of Mykola Skrypnyk, a close friend of Lenin's and one of the few Ukrainians with a senior post in the Ukrainian Communist Party at the time. It was at one of these that Petro Hryhorenko, a Soviet army general who turned dissident in the 1960s, 'first saw and heard played the Ukrainian national musical instrument, the *bandore*. From them I learned of *Kobzar*, written by the great Ukrainian poet Taras Grigoryevich Shevchenko. And from them I learned that I belonged to the same nationality as the great Shevchenko, that I was Ukrainian.'[4] Even Party officials were made to take courses in the language and use it in government business. Viktor Kravchenko, an aeronautics student at the Kharkiv Technological Institute, described how *korenizatsiya* shook up the education system:

Another dimension of confusion was added to our life in the Institute soon after I entered by an order that all instruction and examinations be conducted in the Ukrainian language, not in Russian. The order applied to all schools and institutions. It was Moscow's supreme concession to the nationalist yearnings of the largest non-Russian Soviet Republic.

In theory we Ukrainians in the student body should have been pleased. In practice we were as distressed by the innovation as the non-Ukrainian minority. Even those who, like myself, had spoken Ukrainian from childhood, were not accustomed to its use as a medium of study. Several of our best professors were utterly demoralised by the linguistic switch-over. Worst of all, our local tongue simply had not caught up with modern knowledge; its vocabulary was unsuited to the purposes of electrotechnics, chemistry, aerodynamics, physics and most other sciences.[5]

Notwithstanding Kravchenko's misgivings, *korenizatsiya* was a success. It taught thousands of peasants to read and write – in Ukrainian – for the first time, and produced a brief literary renaissance. Ukrainian had its Symbolists, its Modernists, its Neoclassicists and its satirists, many of whom exercised their wit on the *korenizatsiya* programme itself. One of the most popular was Ostap Vyshnya, who lampooned his countrymen under the name 'Chukrainians':

There were lots of Chukrainians – more than thirty million of them, although most didn't know themselves who they were. If someone asked them 'what's your nationality?' they would scratch their heads and answer 'God knows – we live in Shengeriyivka, we're Orthodox' ... Academics say that ancient Chukrainians covered their milk pots with poetry books – proof of how highly developed their culture was even then ...

But even at its height, *korenizatsiya* never meant intellectual freedom. Kravchenko recalled a friend pointing at some public toilets, signed 'Men' and 'Women' in Ukrainian, and hissing, 'There's the whole of our national autonomy!' The former Rada president, Hrushevsky, was lured back to the Soviet Union in 1924 with the offer of a chair at the Kiev Academy of Sciences, only to find himself tailed day and night by the OGPU, the Bolshevik secret police. An American visitor who had applied for a job at the faculty was shocked to find that Hrushevsky took this for granted, and went straight back home again. He was right to be nervous: the OGPU had already drawn up lists of 'counter-revolutionaries' to be dealt 'a crushing blow when the time comes'. These ranged from all ex-members of defunct Ukrainian organisations to shopkeepers, traders, 'all foreigners' and 'all those with relatives or acquaintances abroad'.[6]

The 'crushing blow' – and the end of *korenizatsiya* – came with the first Stalin purges. What collectivisation was to the countryside, the purges were to the towns, the two running side by side through the late 1920s and early '30s. In Ukraine the purges started early, with the arrest in July 1929 of some 5,000 members of a fictitious underground organisation, the 'Union for the Liberation of Ukraine'. The following spring a series of show trials kicked off with the pillorying of forty-five Ukrainian writers, scholars, lawyers and priests in the Kharkiv opera house. (Close to the Russian border, Kharkiv was republican capital from 1922 to 1934; if it had remained so a few years longer, more of Kiev's churches might have been spared demolition.) The following year the OGPU 'uncovered' another conspiracy, putting Hrushevsky at its head. Though Hrushevsky himself was only exiled to Moscow, many of his colleagues and almost all his students were sent to the camps or shot. At the same time the Ukrainian Autocephalous Orthodox Church, which had re-formed in the early 1920s, was disbanded and its clergy deported.

With the arrival of Stalin's new viceroy, Pavel Postyshev, in January 1933, the purges intensified. Postyshev denounced *korenizatsiya* as a 'cultural counter-revolution' whose aim was to fan 'national enmity' and 'isolate Ukrainian workers from the positive influence of Russian culture'.[7] Entire commissariats, judicial boards, university faculties, editorial departments, theatre groups and film studios were duly arrested and sent to their deaths. Several hundred of Ukraine's wandering bards, the *kobzars*, were summoned to a conference and never seen again. Skrypnyk, the Old Bolshevik in charge of Ukrainian-language education, committed suicide at his desk, using a revolver he had kept hidden since Civil War days. At the same time, Postyshev set about decimating the Ukrainian Communist Party itself, on the ironic grounds that it had showed insufficient 'Bolshevik vigilance' during collectivisation. By the end of the year, it had lost 100,000 members. As Postyshev's report to Stalin of November 1933 boasted, 'almost all the people removed were arrested and put before the firing-squad or exiled'.[8]

Between 1937 and 1939 a third wave of terror swept the whole of the Soviet Union. Victims spanned all types: factory-workers and scientists, priests and atheists, shop-girls and Party wives. For every Party member arrested, six or seven non-Party members also went to the cells, where they were threatened or tortured into denouncing colleagues and neighbours. In one Kiev district sixty-nine people were denounced by one man; in Odessa, over a hundred.[9] The victims' actual identity mattered little, bald quotas for desired numbers of arrestees being imposed from above. Vera Nanivska, a Kiev friend, told me what happened to her grandparents:

> One night – it happened all over the place under Stalin – they were warned by friends in the local soviet that they were on the list of tomorrow's arrests. That night they left everything and fled, to another small town not very far away. You didn't have to really hide because Stalin didn't care about who was on the list and who was not on the list, it didn't matter. What the Stalin regime cared about was the constant threat, the constant fear . . .

Ironically, the system allowed some genuine anti-Communists, like Vera's grandparents, to fade into the background. Mykola Stasyuk, an ex-minister in the Rada government, took a job as a park attendant in Mariupol, surviving to become a partisan leader during the Second World War.[10]

Exactly how many people died in the purges is unclear. Conquest reckons that between 1937 and 1938, in the Soviet Union as a whole, 1 million people were executed, and 2 million died in labour camps, the total camp population at the end of the period being about 7 million, and the prison population another 1 million. Adam Ulam comes up with half a million people executed, and somewhere between 3 and 12 million sent to the camps. What percentage of these were Ukrainians we do not know. A mass grave of purge victims in the Bykivnya forest outside Kiev, rediscovered in the late 1980s, contains an estimated 200,000 bodies. Another at Vinnytsya, uncovered during the war underneath a Park of Culture and Recreation, holds at least 10,000, all shot in the back of the head. In Ukrainian villages, quite casually, one hears of other sites, forgotten by everyone but the locals, who themselves can't quite remember who shot who, or why, or when. Faced with old battleaxes prone to rhapsodising about the good old days of the Soviet Union, I found that a failsafe riposte was to inquire gently whether any of their relatives had been 'repressed' under Stalin. The answer was invariably a grudging Yes.

Rural terror ran in three overlapping stages: food requisitioning, dekulakisation and mass starvation. In the spring of 1928, eighteen months before the first batch of Ukrainian intelligentsia were put on trial in Kharkiv, requisitioning brigades started appearing in the villages, the first time this had happened since the end of 'War Communism' seven years earlier. A group of activists, some local, some from nearby towns, would arrive, call a meeting, and demand 'voluntary' surrender of a certain quantity of grain or meat. The villagers, naturally, usually voted against. Thereupon the activists denounced the village spokesmen as counter-revolutionary kulaks, and put them under arrest or confiscated their property. The meeting was kept in session until the remainder changed their minds. The confiscations provoked widespread resistance – riots, looting and the murder of several hundred requisitioning agents.

The next stage, announced by Stalin in December 1929, was the 'liquidation of the kulaks as a class'.[11] In practice, this meant the arrest and deportation of anybody who resisted collectivisation – that is to say, of any peasant who refused to give up his land, tools and livestock in favour of bonded labour at derisory wages on a state-owned farm run by a Party appointee. Singled out were richer peasants, priests, and those who could write or read – in other words, all the villages' natural leaders. Like the purges, dekulakisation proceeded on a quota system. Provincial OGPU offices came up with a total of 'kulaks' to be 'eliminated', and distributed it among local troikas made up of a soviet member, a Party official and an OGPU man, for fulfilment as they pleased. Denunciations were encouraged, giving ample scope for malice. 'It was so easy to do a man in,' wrote Grossman. 'You wrote a denunciation; you did not even have to sign it. All you had to say was that he had paid people to work for him as hired hands, or that he had owned three cows.'[12] In some places, dekulakisation was only applied to heads of households, in others to entire families. Protests – very common – from local officials that there were simply no kulaks in their area were ignored.

In the winter of 1930–31, in the Kharkiv Technological Institute, the up-and-coming Komsomolyets Viktor Kravchenko started hearing something of what was going on:

Rumours of incredible cruelty in the villages in connection with the liquidation of the kulaks were passed from mouth to mouth. We saw long trains of cattle cars filled with peasants passing through Kharkov, presumably on their way to the tundras of the North, as part of their 'liquidation'. Communist officials were being murdered in the villages and recalcitrant peasants were being executed en masse. Rumors also circulated about the slaughter of livestock by peasants in their 'scorched earth' resistance to forced collectivisation. A Moscow decree making the unauthorised killing of livestock a capital crime confirmed the worst of these reports.

The railroad stations of the city were jammed with ragged, hungry peasants fleeing their homes. 'Bezprizorni', homeless children, who had been so much in evidence in the civil war and famine years were again everywhere. Beggars, mostly country people but also some city people, again appeared on the streets.

The press told glorious tales of accomplishment. The Turk-estan–Siberian railway completed. New industrial combinats opened in the Urals, in Siberia, everywhere. Collectivization 100 per cent completed in one province after another. Open letters of 'thanks' to Stalin for new factories, new housing projects . . .

Which was the reality, which the illusion? The hunger and terror in the villages, the homeless children – or the statistics of achievement?[13]

Transferred to the Metallurgy Institute in Dnipropetrovsk, his doubts grew. Arriving home one evening, he was surprised to find a small girl, 'grey with exhaustion and prematurely old', squatting by the radiator pipes on the kitchen floor. She was called Katya, his mother told him, and she had come begging to the door. After supper she told her story:

We lived in Pokrovnaya. My father didn't want to join the *kolkhoz*. All kinds of people argued with him and took him away and beat him but still he wouldn't join. They shouted he was a kulak agent . . . We had a horse, a cow, a heifer, five sheep, some pigs and a barn. That was all. Every night the constable would come and take papa to the village soviet. They asked him for grain and didn't believe that he had no more . . . For a whole week they wouldn't let father sleep and they beat him with sticks and revolvers till he was black and blue and swollen all over . . .

Then one morning : . . strangers came to the house. One of them was from the GPU and the chairman of our soviet was with him too. Another man wrote in a book everything that was in the house, even the furniture and our clothes and pots and pans. Then wagons arrived and everything was taken away . . .

Mamochka, my dear little mother, she cried and prayed and fell on her knees and even father and big brother Valya cried and sister Shura. But it did no good. We were told to get dressed and take along some bread and salt pork, onions and potatoes, because we were going on a long journey . . .

They put us all in the old church. There were many other parents and children from our village, all with bundles and all weeping. There we spent the whole night, in the dark, praying and crying, praying and crying. In the morning about thirty families were marched down the road surrounded by militiamen. People on the road made the sign of the cross when they saw us and also started crying.

At the station there were many other people like us, from other villages. It seemed like thousands. We were all crushed into a brick barn but they wouldn't let my dog Volchok come in, even though he'd followed us all the way down the road. I could hear him howling while I was inside in the dark.

After a while we were let out and driven into cattle cars, long rows of them, but I didn't see Volchok anywhere and the guard kicked me when I asked. As soon as our car was filled up so that there was no room for more, even standing up, it was locked from the outside. We all shrieked and prayed to the Holy Virgin. Then the train started. No one knew where we were going. Some said Siberia, but others said no, the far North or even the hot deserts.

Near Kharkov my sister Shura and I were allowed out to get some water. Mama gave us some money and a bottle and said to try and buy some milk for our baby brother who was very sick. We begged the guard so long that he let us go out which he said was against his rules. Not far away were some peasant huts so we ran there as fast as our feet would carry us.

When we told these people who we were they began to cry. They gave us something to eat right away, then filled the bottle with milk and wouldn't take the money. Then we ran back to the station. But we were too late and the train had gone away without us.[14]

A few weeks later Kravchenko found himself collectivising in person. Eighty young activists were summoned to a pep talk by the local Party committee. Dnipropetrovsk region had fallen behind schedule, they were told. Kulaks were sabotaging livestock; the grain plan had not been fulfilled. What the local soviets needed was 'an injection of Bolshevik iron'. This was no time for 'squeamishness or rotten sentimentality'; they were to go forth and 'act like Bolsheviks worthy of Comrade Stalin'.[15]

Kravchenko was despatched to Podgorodnoye, a large village not far from Dnipropetrovsk. Collectivisation had already reduced it to a shambles. Crops stood unharvested in the fields; farm machinery lay scattered about in the open, rusting and broken. Emaciated cattle wandered the farmyards, unfed and caked in manure. Kravchenko spent the next weeks persuading the peasants to bring in what remained of the harvest while his colleagues went about the business of grain requisitioning and further dekulakisation. He claims – not wholly convincingly – to have been profoundly surprised and shocked when he saw at firsthand just what their methods were:

> Evening was falling when I drove into the village, with several companions. Immediately we realised that something was happening. Agitated groups stood around. Women were weeping. I hurried to the Soviet building.
>
> 'What's happening?' I asked the constable.
>
> 'Another round-up of kulaks,' he replied. 'Seems the dirty business will never end. The GPU and District Committee people came this morning.'
>
> A large crowd was gathered outside the building. Policemen tried to scatter them, but they came back. Some were cursing. A number of women and their children were weeping hysterically and calling the names of their husbands and fathers. It was all like a scene out of a nightmare.
>
> Inside the Soviet building, Arshinov was talking to a GPU official. Both of them were smiling, apparently exchanging pleasantries of some sort. In the back yard, guarded by GPU soldiers with drawn revolvers, stood about twenty peasants, young and old, with bundles on their backs. A few of them were weeping. The others stood there sullen, resigned, hopeless . . .
>
> For some reason, on this occasion, most of the families were being left behind. Their outcries filled the air. As I came out of

the Soviet house again, I saw two militiamen leading a middle-aged peasant. It was obvious that he had been manhandled – his face was black and blue and his gait was painful; his clothes were ripped in a way indicating a struggle.

As I stood there, distressed, ashamed, helpless, I heard a woman shouting in an unearthly voice. Everyone looked in the direction of her cry and a couple of GPU men started running towards her. The woman, her hair streaming, held a flaming sheaf of grain in her hands. Before anyone could reach her, she had tossed the burning sheaf on to the thatched roof of the house, which burst into flame instantaneously.

'Infidels! murderers!' the distraught woman was shrieking. 'We worked all our lives for our house! You won't have it. The flames will have it!' Her cries turned suddenly into crazy laughter.

Peasants rushed into the burning house and began to drag out furniture. There was something macabre, unreal, about the whole scene – the fire, the wailing, the demented woman, the peasants being dragged through the mud and herded together for deportation. The most unearthly touch, for me, was the sight of Arshinov and the GPU officer looking on calmly, as if this were all routine, as if the burning hut were a bonfire for their amusement.[16]

The fate of the dekulakised peasants was similar to that of the purge victims. Herded into cattle-cars, they were transported across Russia to labour camps in Siberia, Central Asia and the far north. Deprived of food, heat or water, up to 20 per cent of deportees, especially old people and children, died on the way. One of the main transit points was Vologda, where the corpses were unloaded and the survivors crammed into empty churches. 'In a little park by the station,' an eyewitness wrote of another transit town,' 'dekulakised peasants from the Ukraine lay down and died. You got used to seeing corpses there in the morning; a wagon would pull up and the hospital stable-hand, Abram, would pile in the bodies. Not all died; many wandered through the dusty mean little streets, dragging bloodless blue legs, swollen from dropsy, feeling each passer-by with doglike begging eyes . . .'[17]

From the railheads, the peasants marched or rode in wagons to their final destinations deep uncultivated forest, tundra, desert or bog. Husbands and wives were often split up with promises that they would be reunited later, never to see each other again. Some were put to work in mines and logging camps; others were dumped in the middle of nowhere and told to fend for themselves. A German communist described how in Kazakhstan, kulaks from Ukraine were simply abandoned in empty wilderness: 'There were just some pegs stuck in the ground with little notices on them saying: Settlement No. 5, No. 6, and so on. The peasants were brought here and told that now they had to look after themselves. So then they dug themselves holes in the ground.'[18]

Some deportees, especially young men, escaped. Others managed to establish viable settlements, only to find themselves dekulakised all over again. But for very many, deportation was equivalent to a death sentence. Conquest estimates that between 10 and 12 million peasants were dekulakised up to the spring of 1933, when mass deportation (though not that of individual families) was brought to an end, and that within two years about a third of them had died. 'In hardly four months,' wrote a survivor of a camp on the river Dvina, 'it was necessary to construct several cemeteries . . . cemeteries so large that it would have taken a big European city several years to have as many.'[19] When winter struck the arctic Magadan peninsula whole camps perished, down to the last guard and guard-dog.

Dekulakisation left the villages in ruins. For every group of deportees, at least half as many people again fled the countryside of their own accord. Though starvation had already set in by the spring of 1932, in July Stalin ordered that food requisitions continue:

> They searched in the house, in the attic, shed, pantry and the
> cellar. Then they went outside and searched in the barn, pig

pen, granary and the straw pile. They measured the oven and calculated if it was large enough to hold hidden grain behind the brickwork. They broke beams in the attic, pounded on the floor of the house, tramped the whole yard and garden. If they found a suspicious-looking spot, in went the crowbar.[20]

In 1931 there had still been some grain to hide. By 1932 there was none. Under a decree defining all standing crops as state property, watchtowers were set up around the fields, manned by armed guards. Anyone spotted picking corn was arrested and deported or summarily shot, as was anyone still hiding food. 'The alert eye of the GPU,' ran a typical press announcement, 'has uncovered and sent for trial the fascist saboteur who hid bread under a pile of clover.' One thousand five hundred death sentences are reported from the Kharkiv court for one month alone. A woman was sentenced to ten years, writes Conquest, 'for cutting a hundred ears of ripening corn, from her own plot, two weeks after her husband had died of starvation. A father of four got ten years for the same offence. Another woman was sentenced to ten years for picking ten onions from collective land.'[21]

That autumn Kravchenko was again summoned to Party headquarters, and despatched with a friend to Petrovo, a village seventy-five miles west of Dnipropetrovsk. Their instructions were to organise the harvest. On arrival, they were struck by the 'unearthly quiet'. All the village dogs, they were told, had been eaten. The next morning, they took a stroll:

> Again we were oppressed by the unnatural silence. Soon we came to an open space which, no doubt, was once the market-place. Suddenly Yuri gripped my arm until it hurt: for sprawled on the ground were dead men, women and children, thinly covered with dingy straw. I counted seventeen. As we watched, a wagon drove up and two men loaded the corpses on the wagon like cordwood.[22]

After a hearty meal with local Party officials, they did the rounds of the houses:

What I saw ... was inexpressibly horrible. On a battlefield men die quickly, they fight back, they are sustained by fellowship and a sense of duty. Here I saw people dying in solitude by slow degrees, dying hideously, without the excuse of sacrifice for a cause. They had been trapped and left to starve, each in his home, by a political decision made in a far-off capital around conference and banquet tables ...

The most terrifying sights were the little children with skeleton limbs dangling from balloon-like abdomens. Starvation had wiped every trace of youth from their faces, turning them into tortured gargoyles; only in their eyes lingered the remainder of childhood. Everywhere we found men and women lying prone, their faces and bellies bloated, their eyes utterly expressionless.

We knocked at a door and received no reply. We knocked again. Fearfully, I pushed the door open and we entered through a narrow vestibule into the one-room hut. First my eyes went to an icon light above a broad bed, then to the body of a middle-aged woman stretched on the bed, her arms crossed on her breast over a clean embroidered Ukrainian blouse. At the foot of the bed stood an old woman, and nearby were two children, a boy of about eleven and a girl of about ten. The children were weeping quietly ...

The nightmarishness of the scene was not in the corpse on the bed, but in the condition of the living witnesses. The old woman's legs were blown up to incredible size, the man and the children were clearly in the last stages of starvation.[23]

By spring, people were eating anything they could find – grass, leaves, acorns, snails, ants and earthworms. They boiled up bones and leather, stripped the bark from the trees and fought over horse dung for undigested seeds. Suicide, murder and cannibalism were all common: 'People cut up and cooked corpses,' wrote Grossman; 'they killed their own children and ate them.'[24] Many poisoned themselves by digging up and eating diseased horse carcasses: one account has the perpetrators being shot by OGPU soldiers as they lay dying in bed.[25]

Peasants tried to escape the famine by fleeing to the cities. Though checkpoints were set up at railway stations and on the main roads, thousands managed to evade them, only to die ignored on the city streets. 'People hurried about on their affairs,' wrote Grossman of Kiev, 'some going to work, some to the movies, and the streetcars were running – and there were the starving children, old men, girls, crawling among them on all fours.'[26] Early each morning, carts collected the dead:

I saw one such flat-top cart with children lying on it. They were just as I have described them, thin elongated faces, like those of dead birds, with sharp beaks ... Some of them were still muttering, their heads still turning. I asked the driver about them, and he just waved his hands and said: 'By the time they get where they are being taken they will be silent too.'[27]

Similar carts went the rounds in Kharkiv, Dnipropetrovsk, Odessa and Poltava.

Grain collections were officially halted in March 1933, by which time about a fifth of the entire rural population – 5 million people – lay dead. The size of the death-roll varied widely village by village. In some only one in ten families died; elsewhere whole communities perished. The euphemism used on death certificates – when they were issued at all – was 'exhaustion'. Where the bodies were too numerous for burial, squads of Komsomol members put up black flags and 'no entry' signs. William Chamberlin, Moscow correspondent of the *Christian Science Monitor*, was one of the first foreign journalists to be allowed into the famine areas, in September 1933:

Quite by chance the last village we visited was at once the most terrible and the most dramatic. It is called Cherkass, and it lies about seven or eight miles to the south of Byelaya Tserkov, a Ukrainian town south-west of Kiev. Here the 'normal' mortality rate of 10 per cent had been far exceeded. On the road to the village, former ikons with the face of Christ had been removed; but the crown of thorns had been allowed to remain – an appropriate symbol for what the village had experienced. Coming into the village, we found one deserted house after another, with window-panes fallen in, crops growing mixed with weeds in gardens with no one to harvest them. A boy in the dusty village street called the death-roll among families he knew ...

'There was Anton Samchenko, who died with his wife and sister; three children were left. With Nikita Samchenko's family, the father and Mikola and two other children died; five children were left. Then Grigory Samchenko died with his son Petro; a wife and daughter are left. And Gerasim Samchenko died with four of his children; only the wife is still living. And Sidor Odnorog died with his wife and two daughters; one girl is left. Gura Odnorog died with his wife and three children; one girl is still alive ...'[28]

Chamberlin was appalled, convinced both that collectivisation failed to justify 'organised famine', and that the famine was intentional, 'quite deliberately employed as an instrument of national policy'.[29] Nor did he hesitate to say so, in a book published soon after he left the Soviet Union. But Chamberlin was an exception. Killing more people than the First World War on all sides put together, the famine of 1932–3 was, and still is, one of the most under-reported atrocities of human history, a fact that contributes powerfully to Ukraine's persistent sense of victimisation.

The Soviet press, of course, denied that the famine existed at all. Arthur Koestler, living in Kharkiv in the ghastly winter of 1932–3, found not the slightest allusion to the disaster in the local papers:

Each morning when I read the Kharkov *Kommunist* I learned about plan-figures reached and over-reached, about competitions between factory shock brigades, awards of the Red Banner, new giant combines in the Urals, and so on; the photographs were either of young people, always laughing and always carrying a banner in their hands, or of some picturesque elder in Usbekistan, always smiling and always learning the alphabet. Not one word about the local famine, epidemics, dying out of whole villages . . . [30]

The Western press did little better. Despite a ban on foreigners leaving Moscow, the famine's existence – though not its extent – was well known in the capital. 'Few of us,' wrote the United Press correspondent Eugene Lyons,

> were so completely isolated that we did not meet Russians whose work took them to the devastated areas, or Muscovites with relations in those areas. Around every railroad station in the capital hundreds of bedraggled refugees were encamped, had we needed further corroboration . . .
>
> There was no more need for investigation to establish the mere existence of the Russian famine than investigation to establish the existence of the American depression . . . The famine was accepted as a matter of course in our casual conversations at the hotels and in our homes.[31]

None the less, it went almost unmentioned in despatches, treated at best as a sideshow, a temporary hitch in collectivisation. Though occasional full and honest reports did appear, they were far outnumbered by the dishonest, penned by reporters who feared losing their contacts and their visas, or who simply found it more convenient to swallow the official propaganda. 'Even conscientious newspapermen,' wrote Koestler, 'evolved a routine of compromise; they cabled no lies, but *nolens volens* confined themselves to official dope and expressed such comment or criticism as they dared "between the lines", by some subtle qualifying adjective or nuance – which naturally passed unobserved by anybody but the initiated reader.'[32] The result was a picture fatally distorted by half-truth, contradiction and doubt.

Lyons gives a graphic example of the reigning atmosphere of pusillanimity. The British journalist Gareth Jones, 'an earnest and meticulous little man', of the sort 'who carries a note-book and unashamedly records your words as you talk', had succeeded in making a secret tour of the Kharkiv area. On his return to London, he sent a detailed account of the horrors he encountered to the *Manchester Guardian*. The rest of the Moscow press corps duly received urgent requests from their editors for follow-ups. These coincided, however, with the opening of a sensational show trial of a group of British engineers, on charges of sabotage. 'The need to remain on friendly terms with the censors,' wrote Lyons, 'was for all of us a compelling professional necessity. Throwing down Jones was as unpleasant a chore as fell to any of us in years of juggling facts to please dictatorial regimes – but throw him down we did, unanimously and in almost identical formulas of equivocation.' At a meeting with the chief censor, Konstantin Umansky, the journalists jointly worked out a 'formula of denial'. 'We admitted enough to soothe our consciences, but in roundabout phrases that damned Jones as a liar. That filthy business having been disposed of, someone ordered vodka and "zakuski", Umansky joined the celebration, and the party did not break up until the early morning hours.'[33]

The evasions and omissions of the professional journalists were backed up by the naive fellow-travellers who came to the Soviet Union to admire the results of the first Five-Year Plan. For the marvellously acerbic Malcolm Muggeridge (another journalist who managed to travel through Ukraine during the famine, and reported what he saw), they were 'one of the wonders of our age':

There were earnest advocates of the humane killing of cattle who looked up at the massive headquarters of OGPU with tears of gratitude in their eyes, earnest advocates of proportional representation who eagerly assented when the necessity for a Dictatorship of the Proletariat was explained to them, earnest clergymen who walked reverently through the anti-God museums and reverently turned the pages of atheistic literature, earnest pacifists who watched delightedly tanks rattle across the

Red Square . . .[34]

The government tourist agency Voks laid on full-scale Potemkin tours of factories, schools, prisons and collectives, complete with singsongs, folk-dancing, politically correct film-shows and enormous banquets. Sometimes these were permanent establishments, kept especially for propaganda purposes; sometimes ordinary villages were dressed up for the occasion. An extraordinary account of the preparations made for the visit of the French Radical leader Edouard Herriot to the 'October Revolution' collective near Kiev in September 1933 is worth quoting at length:

> It was thoroughly scrubbed and cleaned, all Communists, Komsomols and activists having been mobilized for the job. Furniture from the regional theatre in Brovary was brought, and the clubrooms beautifully appointed with it. Curtains and drapes were brought from Kiev, also tablecloths. One wing was turned into a dining-hall, the tables of which were covered with new cloths and decorated with flowers. The regional telephone exchange, and the switchboard operator, were transferred from Brovary to the farm. Some steers and hogs were slaughtered to provide plenty of meat. A supply of beer was also brought in. All the corpses and starving peasants were removed from the highways in the surrounding countryside and the peasants were forbidden to leave their houses. A mass meeting of collective farm workers was called, and they were told that a motion picture would be made of collective farm life, and for this purpose this particular farm had been chosen by a film-unit from Odessa. Only those who were chosen to play in the picture would turn out for work, the rest of the members must stay at home and not interfere. Those who were picked by a special committee were given new outfits brought from Kiev: shoes, socks, suits, hats, handkerchiefs . . . The next day, when Herriot was due to arrive, now well-dressed workers were seated in the dining-hall, and served a hearty meal. They were eating huge chunks of meat, washing it down with beer or lemonade, and were making short

work of it. The director, who was nervous, called upon the people to eat slowly, so that the honoured guest, Herriot, would see them at their tables. Just then a telephone message came from Kiev: 'Visit cancelled, wind everything up.' Now another meeting was called. Shaparov thanked the workers for a good performance, and then Denisenko asked them to take off and return all the clothes that had been issued to them, with the exception of socks and handkerchiefs. The people begged to be allowed to keep the clothes and shoes, promising to work and pay for them, but to no avail. Everything had to be given back and returned to Kiev, to the stores from which it had been borrowed.[35]

When Herriot returned home, *Pravda* was able to report that he 'categorically denied the lies of the bourgeois press about a famine in the Soviet Union'.

Speaking no Russian, closely chaperoned, and travelling on special trains, visitors came into almost no contact with ordinary homes, workplaces or people. Even those not already determined to turn a blind eye to any shortcomings they might stumble upon were easily misled. The travel-writer Robert Byron, no friend of the Soviet Union (his favourite amusement was to mutter the dread initials 'GPU' in public places, and observe the horrified reactions of passers-by), failed to notice anything amiss on a train journey through Ukraine in the horrible winter of 1932 save 'a mob of maddened peasants' at a wayside station.[36]

But for most visitors, the Potemkin tours were an unnecessary precaution. They had made up their minds before they arrived. George Bernard Shaw, capering around Moscow with Nancy Astor in the summer of 1931, told a banquet in his honour that he had thrown tins of food out of the train window on crossing the border from Poland, so sure was he that rumours of shortages were nonsense. At lunch at the Metropole next day, he was upbraided by Chamberlin's wife. Waving a hand around the restaurant, Shaw asked, 'Where do you see any food shortage?'[37] Back in London he told a press conference he had not seen 'a single undernourished person in Russia, young or old'. 'Were they padded?' he wanted to know; 'Were their hollow cheeks distended by pieces of rubber inside?'[38]

Flattery was an important part of the package. Shaw was delighted to discover that the waitresses in his restaurant-car knew his work intimately and were longing to be introduced. The German socialist Lion Feuchtwanger, visiting Moscow in 1937, met 'a young girl from the land, glowing with happiness', who told him, 'Four years ago I could neither read nor write, and today I can discuss Feuchtwanger's books with him.'[39] The tract Feuchtwanger wrote on his return exhorted his readers to 'free themselves from their own conceptions of democracy' and not to indulge in 'carping, whining, and alarming' at the Soviet Union's expense, ending on a note of religious exaltation: 'It does one good after all the compromise of the West to see an achievement such as this, to which a man can say "Yes," "Yes," "Yes," with all his heart.'[40] André Gide found the front pages plastered with his picture, and was told that sales of his latest book ran into the hundreds of thousands. He was given so much spending money that he did not know what to do with it: 'Every time I got out my wallet to settle a restaurant or hotel bill, to pay a cheque, buy some stamps or a newspaper, I was brought up short by an exquisite smile and authoritative gesture from our guide: "You are joking! You are our guest, and your five companions with you."'[41]

But the palm among apologists for the horrors of the 1930s goes to a journalist – Walter Duranty of the New York Times. Of all the correspondents who denied or played down the famine, he was by far the most cynical and influential. In November 1932, as the famine took grip, he reported that 'there is no famine or actual starvation, nor is there likely to be'.[42] By March he had subtly changed his tune: 'There is no actual starvation or deaths from starvation but there is widespread mortality from diseases due to malnutrition.'[43] In August, in reply to a Herald Tribune piece estimating deaths at no less than 1 million, he wrote that 'Any report of famine in Russia is today an exaggeration or malignant propaganda'. 'Food shortage' had, however, 'caused heavy loss of life'.[44]

In September 1933 foreign journalists were allowed into the famine areas for the first time. Duranty was given a fortnight's start over the rest of the corps. When he came back, Lyons ran into him with a group of friends in a restaurant:

> He gave us his fresh impressions in brutally frank terms and they added up to a picture of ghastly horror. His estimate of the dead from famine was the most startling I had as yet heard from anyone.
>
> 'But Walter, you don't mean that literally?' Mrs McCormick exclaimed.
>
> 'Hell I don't . . . I'm being conservative,' he replied, and as if by way of consolation he added his famous truism: 'But they're only Russians . . .'

Lyons was not surprised to find that Duranty's articles on the trip failed even to acknowledge the famine's existence. When Kravchenko defected to America and published the memoirs I have quoted here, the Western press accused him of being a CIA plant. Duranty's payback was a Pulitzer Prize, awarded for the 'scholarship, profundity, impartiality, sound judgement and exceptional clarity' of his reporting.[45]

CHAPTER SEVEN

The Vanished Nation:
Ivano-Frankivsk

You were my death:
you I could hold
when all fell away from me.
– *Paul Celan, 1968*

THREE *BABUSHKI*, STOUT and sturdy as ponies, wiggle their spades under a rectangular flagstone and heave it over. The underside is inscribed in Hebrew: 'Here lies buried a righteous woman, Sarah, daughter of Shmeor. She died on 11th October 1929.' The next stone in the search also bears traces of lettering, but is too worn to read.

I am in Ivano-Frankivsk, a nondescript town in south-western Ukraine. The tombstones have been here – in a yard round the back of the railway station – ever since the war, when German troops demolished the town's Jewish cemetery and used the remains to pave what was then an army repair-shop. Locals had always known that the stones came from Jewish graves, since some lay face-up, with the inscriptions showing. 'It wasn't normal, having people walking all over them,' says one of the women, wiping her hands on her fluorescent orange apron. 'They should have been back in the cemetery where they belong.'

'So why didn't you do anything about it earlier?'

'Because nobody told us to.'

The man who chivvied the city authorities into action is Viktor – or, in the Hebrew version he prefers, Moishe-Leib – Kolesnyk, the town rabbi. Unlike most of the rabbis in Ukraine, he is not an American, but was actually born here, to a conventional Party family – father a local soviet deputy – that much disapproved of his unexpected interest in religion. Sacked from his teaching job in a village school, he earned a living touring the mountains taking photographs of peasant weddings, before being ordained by New York Lubavitchers in Moscow and sent back to Ivano-Frankivsk to reopen the town synagogue, then used as a dance-hall by the local medical institute. The familiar bureaucratic battle ensued. 'First we were given a small house in the yard – a shed really. Then, while building works were going on next door, the shed collapsed. We took all the holy books and came in here – we just said no, we wouldn't go. A year later, we got it officially.' But despite black mackintosh and patriarchal beard, rabbinical dignity is something Moishe-Leib is happy to put on and off with his homburg. Ensconced among old calendars and piles of books in a makeshift office at the back of the synagogue, he cracks open a packet of Dollar Gold cigarettes and reverts to his other incarnation, as local fix-it man and historian.

Ivano-Frankivsk, he says, was founded in the seventeenth century as a Polish frontier town. A photocopy of an old map shows the zigzag outline of a fortress, long since disappeared. On the first partition of Poland it found itself in Austro-Hungary, between the wars it went to Poland again, and in 1945 it was handed over to the Soviet Union. Until 1962 it was called Stanyslaviv, after a Polish prince; today's name is that of the Ukrainian writer Ivan Franko. But the name changes are unimportant, for the people the town really belonged to for most of its history were the Jews.

Up to 1941, over 60 per cent of Ivano-Frankivsk's population was Jewish. It had fifty-five synagogues and produced dozens of distinguished rabbinical dynasties. Proudly, Moishe-Leib reels off the names – the one I recognise is Shneor Zalman ben Baruch, one of the founders of Hasidism. With the war, 300 years of history came to a swift and savage end. Conveniently placed on the railway-line west to Poland, the town turned into a deportation centre for Jews from all over Ukraine. 'According to my calculations,' says Moishe-Leib, lighting another Dollar Gold, '120,000 people came through Stanyslaviv. Sixty or seventy thousand were killed here, the rest were taken to the camps.' It all happened amazingly quickly: Ivano-Frankivsk's ghetto opened in September 1941, three months after the German invasion, and closed again early in 1943, when there was no one left to kill.

Donning his homburg again, Moishe-Leib takes me back out through the synagogue hall. Inky wooden school-desks do duty as pews, and the walls are stencilled with patterns touchingly designed to look like real wallpaper. We climb into a battered Zhiguli for a tour of Jewish landmarks, Moishe-Leib swivelling round to point things out as we go. There is not much left to see. The old Jewish cemetery, with graves dating back to the seventeenth century, was demolished in the 1960s, to make way for a tatty Kosmos cinema. Nearly all the synagogues have gone too – of the seven surviving buildings, one is used as a laboratory, one as a school, one as a deaf-mute centre and one as a storehouse; the last two have been divided into flats and shops. The only thing marking the site of the wartime ghetto is a small metal plaque on what used to be its boundary wall. Vandals have scraped off its six-pointed Star of David.

What also remains is a mass grave. On the edge of town the road peters out into a dirt track. We clamber out of the car, and pick our way through the ruts to a patch of open ground. Surrounded by peasant cottages, each with its hens, fruit-trees and sagging chain-link fence, the only thing that distinguishes it from any other bit of suburban wasteland is a series of oddly shaped lumps and hollows. These are the ditches where, during the war, the town's entire Jewish population were shot and buried. An old woman is sweeping round a pink granite monument with a birch-broom. 'In this place,' runs the inscription, 'German Fascist invaders shot over 100,000 Soviet citizens and prisoners of war.' The number is cheapened by exaggeration, and, as at the larger Babiy Yar memorial in Kiev, there is no mention of the fact that the victims were Jews.

'It's very peaceful,' I remark, groping for something appropriate to say about this grisly and neglected spot. 'Not really,' says Moishe-Leib cheerfully, offering a strip of chewing-gum. 'People have parties here, they get drunk and fight. You can see where they've stolen part of the fence.' A concrete shelter – he calls it a chapel – marks the spot where one of the town's famous rabbis is supposed to be buried. Somebody has scratched graffiti into the paintwork: 'Yids'; 'Ukraine hates you.' 'It's nothing,' says Moishe-Leib, 'just kids playing.' My interpreter looks appalled. Though she has lived in Ivano-Frankivsk all her life, she never even knew this place existed.

There have been Jews in Ukraine since before the word 'Ukraine' existed. The Greek colonies of the Black Sea coast had their Jewish traders, and the earth embankments of ancient Kiev were pierced by a Jewish Gate. The first record we have of the existence of the city is a letter written in Hebrew by the Jews of Khazaria, an eighth-century Turkic kingdom on the Black Sea steppe, to a synagogue near Cairo. There were Jews in Lviv in the fourteenth century, and in the Volhynian town of Lutsk in the tenth. But they did not start arriving in large numbers until 1569, when the Union of Lublin allowed Poles and Jews to migrate east into the Lithuanian Grand Duchy. Through succeeding centuries, despite waves of emigration in the face of pogroms and poverty, Ukraine's Jewish population grew steadily, totalling about 3 million people – 8 per cent of the population – by the outbreak of war. When the Nazis struck, Odessa had 180,000 Jews, Kiev 175,000 – as many each as the whole of the Netherlands. Kharkiv had 150,000, Dnipropetrovsk and Lviv 100,000 each. In the sleepy *shtetlech* of Galicia and Volhynia – places like Ivano-Frankivsk – they made up 40 per cent or more of the population.

These were pious places, poor and tradition-bound. Men wore side-curls and velvet hats with squirrel-tails; their wives kept the children quiet with tales of dybbuks and golems, and shone their hair with kerosene. It was the land of miracle-working rabbis and the mystical kabbalah, of arranged marriages and strict Sabbaths full of prayer and song and ritual. The exception was bustling, brash Odessa, synonymous, in Jewish lore, with frivolity and irreligion. Odessa produced musicians and orators (among them Trotsky and the early Zionist Leon Pinsker), and from its poor Jewish quarter, the Moldavanka, a legendary tribe of gangsters. Travellers remarked on the self-confidence and dignity with which Jews walked the city streets, and if a Jew wanted to say that a man was prosperous, he might say that he 'lived like a God in Odessa'.[1]

As old as the history of Ukrainian Jewry is the history of Ukrainian anti-Semitism. One of the first written records we have of Jewish settlement in Ukraine is also a record of anti-Jewish violence. On the death of Prince Svyatopolk in 1113, according to the Rus chronicles, the Kiev mob rioted, looting the homes of Jewish merchants who had profited from Svyatopolk's hated monopoly on salt. For the next several centuries, there were too few Jews in Ukraine to be much of an issue, but with Jewish immigration following the Union of Lublin, the potential for hatred increased.

Many Jews arrived as agents to Polish landowners, who deputised to them the collection of rents and taxes, and management of taverns and mills, at which the surrounding peasantry were often obliged by law to buy their drink and grind their corn. They lived huddled under the protection of Polish palace walls, and built their synagogues like mini-fortresses, with gun-embrasures and cannon on the roof. Hence when Khmelnytsky rebelled in 1648, his peasant army's murderous fury was directed as much at Jews as at Poles. The Polish fortified towns, to which Jews fled for protection, fell like ninepins. In some places Poles shut Jews out, in others they handed them over in exchange for their own lives. Usually both groups were massacred together. In Nemyriv, Khmelnytsky's soldiers burned the synagogue, murdered Jews with their own ritual knives, and tore up the covers of their holy books to make shoes. Similar massacres took place during the uprisings of the next century, notably at Uman, seat of the Polish Potockis. Again, Poles and Jews shared jointly in the peasants' fury: a common practice was to hang a Pole, a Jew and a dog from the same tree, with the words, 'Pole, Yid and hound – each to the same faith bound.'[2]

Through the 1800s, Orthodox attitudes towards Jews hardly improved, and at the end of the century they actually worsened. While in Western Europe Jews were beginning to integrate, with spectacular success, into middle-class gentile society, in the Russian empire they remained legal and social pariahs. Save in the big cities – from which most Jews were excluded by the Pale of Settlement – the old pattern of Polish or Russian landlord, Jewish tradesman and Ukrainian peasant hardly shifted, all three groups locked together in a frozen web of mutual dependence and resentment. To the peasant, Jewry represented the alien Polish- or Russian-speaking town, the mysterious money economy which paid little for his labour and charged much for manufactured goods. Anti-Semitism became 'the socialism of the imbecile'. When pogroms broke out in Yelizavetgrad (today's Kirovohrad) in 1881, the local paper blamed the Jews' precarious dual role as money-lenders and tavern-keepers: 'Let the Jew deny a drink to a drunken or penniless peasant, and the hatred begins.'[3] Even in rich, easygoing Odessa, as the Zionist Vladimir Zhabotinsky remembered of his schooldays in the 1890s, integration was only skin-deep:

Without any propaganda, without any ideology, we ten Jews used to sit on one row of benches in class, next to one another . . . We were quite friendly with our Christian classmates, even intimate with them, but we lived apart and considered it a natural thing that could not be otherwise . . .[4]

Odessa was the site of the first modern pogroms. In 1871, on the night before Easter, drunken sailors started throwing stones at Jewish homes and shops. Though deaths were few, the looting went on for three days before the police restored order. As the decade progressed, the tsarist government increasingly used anti-Semitism to offset the rising tide of revolutionary dissent. When Aleksandr II was assassinated by anarchists in 1881, riots swept southern Ukraine. In Kiev a barefoot mob looted the Brodsky vodka warehouse and rampaged through the poor Jewish suburbs. Though police kept the peace in the wealthier districts, and here and there university students turned out to help defend Jewish property, most townspeople looked the other way. 'It was a calm and sunny Sunday holiday,' wrote an onlooker. 'Christians were strolling about. I don't know what astonished me more, the boldness of the plunderers or the shocking indifference of the public.'[5]

The 1881 pogroms, passed over in deafening silence even by liberal luminaries such as Turgenev and Tolstoy, were followed by the infamous May Laws, toughest yet in a long litany of anti-Semitic legislation. Jews were excluded from legal practice and from the officer corps, from every sort of government job, from teaching posts, from juries, from the boards of asylums and orphanages, even from military bands. They could not vote or stand in elections for local councils, and they were forced to contribute a disproportionate number of conscripts to the army. They were barred from owning or leasing land, and from the oil and mining industries. A quota system, the 'numerus clausus', made it hard to get into secondary school or university. Worst of all was the tightening-up of the Pale of Settlement, under which Jews needed special permits to live in the cities. Foreign visitors were shocked to see lines of migrant workers being driven through the streets at dawn, victims of night-time police raids. Not surprisingly, one of the chief results of the May Laws was the wholesale corruption of the tsarist police force and bureaucracy, enabled, by this mass of lunatic legislation, to extract a fortune in bribes.

As the empire began its long slide towards revolution, right-wing monarchist groups took to blaming Jews for all Holy Russia's reverses, publishing rabidly anti-Semitic pamphlets and employing uniformed thugs, the 'Black Hundreds', to beat up Jews and students. In 1905, when naval defeat at the hands of the Japanese forced Nicholas II to grant Russia's first-ever constitution, they vented their fury in a new wave of pogroms. In Odessa 302 people are known to have been killed; more deaths went unrecorded. 'On Tuesday night October 31st,' the shocked American consul reported home, 'the Russians attacked the Jews in every part of town and a massacre ensued. From Tuesday 'til Saturday was terrible and horrible. The Russians lost heavily also, but the number of killed and wounded is not known. The police without uniforms were very prominent. Jews who bought exemption received protection. Kishinev, Kiev, Cherson, Akkerman, Rostoff and other places suffered terribly, Nicolaev also.'[6]

With tsarism's final collapse a new superstition – Jew equals Bolshevik – was born. The vast majority of revolutionaries were not Jewish, of course, and the vast majority of Jews not revolutionaries, but it is true that Jews were over-represented in revolutionary organisations in relation to their numbers. (The same, paradoxically, applied to the offspring of Orthodox priests, who were also often well educated but prospectless.) When the Bolsheviks came to power in 1917, Jews were able to take government jobs for the first time – hence the connection, in the minds of peasants whose first sight of a Jew in a position of authority was a commissar come to requisition grain or conscript men for the Red Army, between Jewishness and the nastier aspects of communism. The fact that Jews – like all non-

Russian minorities – were murdered in disproportionate numbers during Stalin's purges did little to shake this perception.

Ukrainian–Jewish relations were not all bad. In 1918 the Ukrainians' short-lived Rada government declared 'national-personal autonomy' for Jews and set up a special ministry for Jewish affairs. Its banknotes were printed in four languages – Ukrainian, Russian, Polish and Yiddish – and the head of the Ukrainian delegation at the Paris peace talks, amazingly, was a Jew, Arnold Margolin. In Galicia too, Ukrainians and Jews sometimes cooperated: in 1907 four Zionists were elected to the Vienna Reichsrat with Ukrainian support (both sides hoping to shake off the Poles), and in 1922 Jewish and Ukrainian parties fought joint campaigns in elections to the new Polish parliament. But in the 1930s, as Polish democracy crumbled, attitudes hardened. Popular support for the moderate Ukrainian party UNDO fell away in favour of the underground terrorist group OUN, which borrowed its philosophy from fascist Germany. (Members swore to a Decalogue of ten commandments, the first of which was 'You will attain a Ukrainian state or die in battle for it', the ninth, 'Treat the enemies of your nation with hatred and ruthlessness.')[7] In 1940, six months after Germany and Russia had carved up Poland between them, OUN split in two – the more moderate 'Melnykivtsi', under the Civil War veteran Andriy Melnyk, and the fanatical 'Banderivtsi', under the young head of OUN's terrorist unit, Stepan Bandera. Released from prison by the Germans in 1939, Bandera explicitly declared war on Ukrainian Jewry. 'The Jews in the USSR,' an OUN congress in Cracow resolved, 'constitute the most faithful support of the ruling Bolshevik regime, and the vanguard of Muscovite imperialism in Ukraine.'[8]

For all Ukraine, the war years were ones of unparalleled violence, destruction and horror: 5.3 million of the country's inhabitants died during the war – an astounding one in six of the entire population.[9] (The equivalents for Germany, France and Britain were one in fifteen, one in seventy-seven and one in 125.)

Of these, about 2.25 million were Jews. Most died *in situ*, rounded up, shot and buried in woods and ravines outside their own home towns. Others were sent to the gas chambers at Belzec – just over the present-day border with Poland – or to the slave-labour camp on Janowska Street in Lviv. Two hundred thousand people died in Janowska Street,[10] and of all 600,000 people deported to Belzec – greeted at the railway station by a poster, 'First a wash and breakfast, then to work!'[11] – only two are known to have survived. Altogether, the Holocaust killed 60 per cent of the Jews of Soviet Ukraine, and over 90 per cent of the Jews of Galicia.[12]

For Ukrainians, the war was fratricidal. Caught between Stalin and Hitler, they split three ways. The vast majority of direct participants – 2.5 million men[13] – were conscripted straight into the Red Army. Several tens of thousands – known as 'Hiwis' – short for *Hilfswillige* or 'willing-to-helps', joined the Nazis in various capacities. At least 12,000 worked as police auxiliaries[14] helping round up, deport and massacre Jews, and others became camp guards. Survivors reported about 400 Ukrainians at Sobibor, 300 at Treblinka, and more at Sasow, Ostrow, Poniatow, Plaszow and Janowska Street.[15] Some were volunteers; others joined to escape the German prisoner-of-war camps, where death rates ran at a frightful two in five.[16] 'Russian war prisoners,' wrote Leon Weliczker, a Janowska Street survivor, 'consisted of the most varied types of characters. There were some who were really worse than the SS, but, on the other hand, there were also many who merely filled the job in order to secure for themselves a better means of livelihood.'[17] Lastly, in 1943 Germany recruited 13,000 Ukrainians – out of many more volunteers – into a new SS division, 'SS Galicia'.[18] The division was not sent into battle until the summer of 1944, and eventually surrendered to the Allies in southern Austria. After a long internment in an Italian displaced-persons camp, most of its members were allowed to emigrate to Britain, where their descendants form quite a large proportion of the diaspora population. Yet more Ukrainians – somewhere between 40,000 and 200,000 – fought both Russians and Germans, in the Ukrayinska Povstanska Armiya (UPA), the Ukrainian Insurgent Army.

In Polish-ruled western Ukraine, the war started with the Ribbentrop–Molotov pact of 23 August 1939. Nine days after the pact was signed, the Wehrmacht marched into Poland from the west; a fortnight later, the Red Army did the same from the east. By mid-October Poland had been wiped from the map for the second time in its history, and Galicia, for the first time ever, had come under Russian rule.

Initially, the change-over went peacefully. In Avhustivka, a small village east of Lviv, Ukrainians greeted Poland's demise with delight. In memoirs written after post-war exile in Siberia, the local Uniate priest, Pavlo Oliynyk, remembered them saying 'Let the devil come, as long as he isn't Polish!'[19] In Lviv, fourteen-year-old Leon Weliczker looked on with amusement as hayseed Russian conscripts wandered wide-eyed round the city's shops:

> A soldier would come into a store to buy a bar of chocolate. When he got it, he would ask if he could buy a second bar. After he got the second bar he would look around to see if anyone from the army was around, and then, in a low voice, would ask if he could get the whole box.[20]

Even the wives of the newly arrived Soviet bureaucrats were so unused to consumer goods that they mistook nightgowns for evening dresses and wore them on the street.

But Galicians quickly discovered that Soviet rule was no joke. Lvivites learned to set their clocks two hours ahead to Moscow time, and stopped talking politics or even reading the newspapers. 'The best thing,' Weliczker remembered, was 'to be as ignorant as possible'.[21] In Avhustivka villagers were summoned to a meeting, where they were told to create a 'Committee of the Poor' – the usual prelude to collectivisation – and regaled with the charms of life under communism. 'The representative,' Oliynyk wrote, 'vividly described how well people lived in the

Soviet Union, how the disabled and elderly were provided with all necessities – housing, heating, shoes, food, clothes . . .' But having seen their stores stripped bare and the contents of their village library burned in the market-place, the villagers were not fooled, quickly declaring themselves 'fed up with having to listen to these children's fairy-tales'.[22]

In October came Soviet-style 'elections' to an assembly to 'decide western Ukraine's future' – to confirm its incorporation, in other words, into the Soviet Union. All the candidates having run on a single slate, the resulting body did its job without a hitch. Nikita Khrushchev, First Secretary of the Ukrainian Communist Party and the man in charge of Sovietising Galicia, congratulated himself on the smoothness of proceedings:

> The assembly continued for a number of days amid great jubilation and political fervour. I didn't hear a single speech expressing even the slightest doubt that Soviet Power should be established in the Western Ukraine. One by one, movingly and joyfully, the speakers all said that it was their fondest dream to be accepted into the Ukrainian Soviet Republic.[23]

'At the same time,' Khrushchev goes on without a trace of irony, 'we were still conducting arrests.' The arrestees – in a terror campaign that got fully under way in the spring of 1940 – were almost the entire Galician middle class: landowners, business-men, peasants who resisted collectivisation, Polish bureaucrats and officers, Jewish refugees, lawyers, priests and politicians of all stripes, left as well as right. In a few cases, the upper grades of entire schools disappeared. As former owners of a timber yard, the Weliczkers feared being picked up themselves:

> My father and I hid every night in our basement, for we did not know whether we belonged to the 'capitalistic' group or not. When we found that our families would be arrested too, we gave up hiding, for we did not want to be separated; and to hide our whole family, seven children and two parents, would have been impossible.[24]

Among the arrestees was a cousin of Weliczker's mother, owner of a confectionary employing seven men – his six sons and himself. The whole family, including daughter-in-law and grandchild, were sent to Siberia.[25] In little Avhustivka, the NKVD took away six young men, despite the absence of any anti-Soviet protest in the area. One died of 'suffocation' in prison, four of starvation in the Urals.

Altogether, in the two years preceding the German invasion, the Soviets deported between 800,000 and 1.6 million people – 10 to 20 per cent of western Ukraine's entire population.[26] Travelling under guard in closed cattle-trucks, they were sent to farms and labour camps in Kazakhstan and Siberia, to a life of earth-floored shacks, starvation rations and forty degrees of frost in winter. Though the deportees included Jews and several hundred thousand Ukrainians, the majority of victims were Poles – inexplicably unable to grasp, according to the disappointed Khrushchev, 'that their culture would actually be enriched by the annexation of their lands to the Soviet Union'.[27]

At three o'clock in the morning on the night of 21 June 1941 Germany attacked the Soviet Union. For the Soviet border troops, the invasion came like a bolt from the blue. 'We are being fired on,' ran the desperate signals back to headquarters, 'what shall we do?'[28] Eight days later, after three nights of air-raids, the Wehrmacht marched into Lviv. Kharkiv and Dnipropetrovsk fell in August, Kiev in mid-September. Retreating in front of the overwhelming German advance, the Soviets massacred their remaining prisoners: in Lviv corpses were found piled five deep in the cellar of the NKVD gaol. 'The Poles didn't find as many "political criminals" among us in twenty years,' the Avhustivka villagers mourned, 'as "older brother" Russia did in a year and a half.'[29] Along with millions of other Ukrainians, they believed Nazi rule could not possibly be any worse than Stalinism. Photographs (some cooked up by Soviet propagandists,) show smiling Galician peasants running out of their houses to welcome the Panzer crews with bread and salt.

In the wake of the Wehrmacht came the units devoted to

slaughtering Jews – SS brigades, the Ordnungspolizei, and the Einsatzgruppen, execution squads specially drawn up by Himmler for this task. All were encouraged to recruit Ukrainians – thus aiming to preserve, as one Einsatzgruppe member later put it, 'the psychological equilibrium of our own people'.[30] On 2 July, three days after the Germans had taken Lviv, two Ukrainian militiamen arrived at the Weliczkers' house and took Leon and his father at gunpoint to their headquarters:

> A spectacle such as we could never have dreamed of awaited us. A huge heap of men, one lying on top of another, lay helpless on the floor of the room. Militiamen with truncheons in their hands moved among them. At first I thought that the men on the floor must be corpses and that we had been fetched to carry them out . . . In this confused state I reached for the foot of one of them in order to draw him out of the heap. As I did, a savage blow on the head stunned me, and I toppled among the bodies.[31]

Later – how much later Leon couldn't tell – the survivors were ordered to get up and go outside. Having been forced to perform physical jerks for the amusement of the guards, they were lined up with their hands behind their heads and marched through the streets to the town's hockey-pitch:

> Thousands of men were lying here in rows. They lay on their bellies, their faces buried in the sand. Around the perimeter of the field searchlights had been set up. Among them I caught sight of German officers standing about. We were ordered to lie flat like the others. We were pushed and shoved brutally, this way and that. My father was separated from me, and I heard him calling out in despair: 'Let me stay with my son! I want to die with my son!' Nobody took any notice of him.
>
> Now that we were all lying still, there was a hush that lasted for a moment or two. Then the 'game' started. We could hear the sound of a man, clearly one of us, stumbling awkwardly around, chased and beaten by another as he went. At last the pursued collapsed out of sheer exhaustion. He was told to rise. Blows

were rained down upon him until he dragged himself to his feet again and tried to run forward. He fell to the ground again and hadn't the strength to get up. When the pursuers were at last satisfied that the incessant blows had rendered him unable to stir, let alone run, they called a halt and left him there. Now it was the turn of the second victim . . .[32]

Night fell, and Weliczker sank into oblivion. But

the welcome state of unconsciousness passed all too quickly. I came to, and was startled by a painful stab of dazzling light . . . We sat up, one beside the other, so close we could not stir. Directly in front of me sat two men with shattered skulls. Through the mess of bone and hair I could see their very brains. We whispered to them. We nudged them. But they did not stir. They just sat there, propped up, bulging eyes staring ahead. They were quite dead.[33]

The Lviv massacre – dubbed the 'Petlyura action' in revenge for Sholem Schwartzbard's assassination of the Ukrainian Civil War general fifteen years earlier – went on for three days, killing over 2,000 people.[34] Over the next weeks, as the Einsatzgruppen swept on east, similar atrocities took place all over the country. One of the first towns to fall was Schulz's Drohobycz, a pretty little place known for its frescoed wooden churches. On 14 July a member of the local Einsatzkommando, SS Sergeant Felix Landau, recorded the events of the day in his diary:

We drive a few kilometres along the main road 'til we reach a wood. We go into the wood and look for a spot suitable for mass executions. We order the prisoners to dig their graves. Only two of them are crying, the others show courage . . . Slowly the grave gets bigger and bigger. Two are crying without let-up. I let them dig more so they can't think. The work really calms them. Money, watches and valuables are collected. The two women go first to be shot; placed at the edge of the grave they face the soldiers. They get shot. When it's the men's turn, the soldiers aim at the shoulder. All our six men are allowed to shoot. Three prisoners have been shot in the heart.

The shooting goes on. Two heads have been shot off. Nearly all fall into the grave unconscious only to suffer a long while. Our revolvers don't help either. The last group have to throw the corpses into the grave; they have to stand ready for their own execution. They all tumble into the grave.[35]

Just over a month later the Einsatzgruppen reached Uman, where notices were posted telling Jews to report for a census. Twenty-four thousand men, women and children duly assembled, and were taken in trucks to a square in front of the city airport, where ditches had already been dug and sacks of lime laid out. 'One row of Jews,' wrote Erwin Bingel, a Wehrmacht lieutenant who witnessed the scene, 'was ordered to move forward and was then allocated to the different tables where they had to undress completely and hand over everything they wore and carried. Some still had jewellery which they had to put on the table. Then, having taken off all their clothes, they were made to stand in line in front of the ditches, irrespective of their sex.' SS soldiers and Ukrainian militiamen marched down the lines with automatic pistols. Infants, wrote Bingel, were 'gripped by their little legs and put to death with one stroke of the pistol-butt or club, thereafter to be thrown on the heap of human bodies in the ditch, some of which were not quite dead'.[36]

A week later, Bingel saw two more massacres in Vinnytsya. The first, he estimated, killed 28,000 people, the second, in the town park, another 6,000.

In Kiev, the killing began on 27 September, just eight days after the city's surrender. Ordered to report for 'resettlement', the city's Jews were taken out to the suburbs, to a steep wooded ravine known as Babiy Yar. The mouth of the ravine forms a precipice; men, women and children were driven towards it in columns, and machine-gunned by SS men and Ukrainian militia from the opposite bank. In two days, according to the records of

Einsatzkommando in charge, 33,771 Jews went to the Yar. The earth shovelled into the ravine when the operation was over did not cease moving for some time after.

Through October, the slaughter continued. Four and a half thousand Jews were killed at the port of Kerch; 14,300 at the Crimean capital of Simferopol; 17,000 at the Volhynian town of Rivno, where those who refused to undress beforehand had their eyes put out. In Ivano-Frankivsk militiamen surrounded the Jewish district and marched its occupants, beaten and bleeding, to the newer of the town's two Jewish cemeteries – the same place I stood fifty-four years later with Moishe-Leib. Here the Jews were ordered to undress, hand over their valuables, and line up beside three large ditches. 'The German stormtroops together with the Ukrainian police took up their stations beside the machine guns,' remembered a survivor. 'Fifteen of the storm-troops shot, and fifteen others loaded the guns. The Jews leapt naked into the graves. The bullets hit them while jumping . . .' By the time the shooting stopped, the ditches were overflowing. 'All around lay the dead, strangled, trodden underfoot, wounded. Those of us who remained alive felt ourselves to be infinitely unfortunate.'[37]

On 23 October came the turn of Odessa, home to one of the largest and most flourishing Jewish communities in the world. Six days after the city's capture by the German and Romanian armies, a bomb exploded in Romanian headquarters, killing several officers. The next day, Romanian soldiers herded 19,000 Jews into a fenced square near the port, where they were sprayed with gasoline and burned alive. Another 16,000 were marched to the nearby village of Dalnik, where they were tied together in groups, pushed into anti-tank ditches and shot. When this method proved inefficient the Romanians drove the remainder into four large warehouses and machine-gunned them through holes in the walls. Three of the warehouses, containing women and children, were then set on fire, and the fourth demolished with artillery fire. The rest of Odessa's Jews were sent to concentration camps – Dumanovka, Bogdanovka, Atmicetka and Vertugen – sixty miles to the north, where they died, along with tens of thousands of others from central Ukraine and Moldova, of disease, starvation, cold, and in more mass executions.

The recorded examples of Ukrainians hiding or helping Jews are inspiring, but not, relative to the size of the slaughter, very numerous. Metropolitan Andriy Sheptytsky, the aged, semi-paralysed head of the Uniate Church, sheltered fifteen Jews in his episcopal palace, arranging for another 150, mostly children, to be hidden in nunneries and monasteries. Early in 1942 he wrote to Himmler protesting that 'Ukrainian auxiliary police are being forced to shoot Jews', and in November of the same year he issued a pastoral letter under the title 'Thou shalt not kill', which was read out from pulpits all over the country. At the other end of the scale a professional burglar, Leopold Socha, hid twenty-one Jews in the Lviv sewers, which he knew well having used them to stash stolen goods. For fourteen months he brought food every day – including a bottle of vodka to celebrate Stalingrad – and arranged for the weekly laundering of their clothes. He produced a Jewish prayerbook, and provided potatoes instead of leavened bread every Sabbath. Of this group, eight left the sewers and were captured immediately, one drowned, and one fell ill and died; the remainder emerged safely above ground on liberation, to be greeted by Socha and his wife with cakes and vodka. Elsewhere woodsmen, peasants, priests and ex-servants to Jewish families hid escapees in attics, under cowsheds and in hen-coops. For the rescuers, of course, discovery meant death: German reports list around a hundred such executions in Galicia alone between October 1943 and June 1944.[38]

But on the whole, as in the rest of occupied Europe, gentiles treated the slaughter going on around them as a sideshow to their own predicament. The *Sunday Times* correspondent Alexander Werth, visiting newly liberated Uman in March 1944, remarked that 'the Ukrainians in the town did not talk much about it: they seemed to look upon it as rather a routine matter under the Germans'.[39] In Kharkiv he interviewed a 'buxom young lady barber, with rouge, lipstick, manicure and perm', who described Jews being driven wailing through the streets, pushing prams and wheelbarrows. 'I could understand their wanting to send the Jews away somewhere,' she told him, 'but to kill them all in that awful way, that was going a bit far, don't you think?'[40]

Oliynyk remembered Jews from the local ghetto being shot on market days, while peasants from the neighbouring villages looked on. 'People grew so accustomed to these atrocities,' he wrote, 'that they would go home and tell their families all about them.' The children learned to play at 'shooting Jews'. 'One group of boys', Oliynyk wrote, 'would stand at the edge of the ditch, and the others would aim at them. After the call "fire" the "Jews" would fall into the ditch . . . priests had to go to great lengths to make the children give up this horrible game.'[41] Although in general Oliynyk's parishioners condemned the Jewish massacres, they were much angrier about the massacre of Ukrainians by the NKVD: 'Germans were killing their own race enemy while the *moskali* did this to their brother Ukrainians . . .'[42]

Jewish escapees to the forests – like the 2,000 people who fought their way out of the Volhynian town of Tuczyn in September 1942 – were often betrayed by local peasants, in exchange for a little sugar or a few cigarettes. Others were killed by Ukrainian and Polish partisans, who, according to Weliczker, 'hated the Jews just as much as they hated the Germans'.[43] (Yet others, paradoxically, survived the war attached to partisan units as doctors or tailors.) Gentiles who did hide Jews were scared of reprisals from neighbours. Weliczker, who spent the last months of the war huddled with twenty-three others in a cellar under a Polish farmer's barn, remembered his rescuer begging them not to come back and thank him because 'it would go hard for him if it were known that he had hidden Jews'.[44]

'When they've finished with the Jews,' Oliynyk's parishioners wondered, 'will they I begin on us?'[45] It was no idle fear – Slavs too were Untermenschen. For Erich Koch, the knout-wielding head of Reichskomissariat Ukraine, Ukrainians were 'niggers' fit only for 'vodka and the whip'. 'If I find a Ukrainian worthy of sitting at the same table with me,' he once remarked, 'I must have him shot.'[46] Himmler wanted the Ukrainian intelligentsia to be 'decimated';[47] Göring thought the solution was to kill all Ukrainian males over the age of fifteen and 'send in the SS stallions'.[48] Hitler himself, visiting advance headquarters near Vinnytsya, instructed that Ukrainian education should be restricted to 'one single sentence: the capital of the Reich is Berlin'.[49]

Ukrainian nationalists had had high hopes of Germany, believing it might back an independent Ukrainian state. In the 1930s the Nazis had provided a haven for leaders of the underground group OUN, encouraging its terrorist campaign in Poland. And in 1939 they released Bandera, leader of OUN's radical wing, from a Polish prison, allowing him to join in the training of Ukrainian troops in readiness for the invasion of the Soviet Union. By 1941 the Ukrainians seem to have believed that a declaration of Ukrainian independence would be welcomed by Germany, or at least accepted as a fait accompli.

They were wrong. Though some senior Nazis – among them von Ribbentrop and Alfred Rosenberg, head of the Ostministerium – did indeed advocate establishing a Ukrainian puppet-state as a buffer against Russia, it was the Untermensch philosophy that won out. The first sign that the Germans regarded their Ukrainian alliance as no more than a marriage of convenience was the débâcle known as the 'Republic of Carpatho-Ukraine'. In October 1938, just after the Munich agreement, Germany encouraged OUN-led Ukrainian nationalists in Transcarpathia, a sliver of ethnically Ukrainian territory attached to eastern Czechoslovakia, to declare autonomy. This they duly did, winning reluctant recognition from the tottering Czechs. But when Germany overran Czechoslovakia the following March, it allowed Transcarpathia to be taken over by

Hungary. As the Hungarians marched in, the Ukrainians proclaimed complete independence and sent a telegram to Hitler asking for acceptance as a German protectorate. No help came: the Republic of Carpatho-Ukraine lasted exactly twenty-four hours.

Much the same thing happened when Germany invaded Ukraine itself. When the Wehrmacht attacked in June 1941, it was joined by two 600-strong OUN units, 'Nachtigall' and 'Roland', recruited and drilled under the approving eye of German military intelligence. Nachtigall, clad in the field-grey of the Wehrmacht, marched into Galicia; Roland, in the uniform of the First World War Ukrainian Sich, into the southern steppe from Moldova. OUN also organised 'march groups' of young activists, who raced forward into eastern Ukraine setting up Ukrainian city administrations (many of which joined enthusiastically in the first Jewish massacres).[50] But almost immediately, the Ukrainians ran up against the limits of German tolerance. A few days after entering Lviv, a leader of OUN's Bandera faction, Yaroslav Stetsko, called a 'national assembly' in the old Prosvita building and proclaimed a 'Sovereign All-Ukrainian State'.[51] The announcement was broadcast from the city radio station, together with a message of support from Sheptytsky. Ten days later Stetsko and Bandera were arrested and sent to Berlin. The arrest and execution of dozens more OUN activists followed, and Nachtigall and Roland were both withdrawn from the Ukrainian front and sent to fight Soviet partisans in Belarus.

The honeymoon with Germany over, the Ukrainian nationalists went underground. A variety of partisan groups sprang up, the largest being the Ukrainian Insurgent Army or UPA, controlled by the Banderivtsi. Fielding up to 200,000 men, for a few months in the autumn and winter of 1943 it controlled most of north-west Ukraine, establishing a primitive administration and its own training camps and hospitals. Even more remarkably, small UPA guerrilla units carried on an assassination and sabotage campaign against the Soviet Union for years after the end of the war. The last UPA commander, Roman Shukhevych, was killed in a shoot-out near Lviv in 1950, but small detachments continued to operate in the hills and forests, despite wholesale deportation of villages suspected of giving them shelter.

UPA's methods were every bit as ruthless as those of the SS and the NKVD. During the German retreat, it massacred tens of thousands of Polish civilians in Volhynia. 'At night, and even by day,' Oliynyk recounts,

> partisans would pounce on Polish houses and kill everyone from the youngest to the oldest . . . There was an incident in our village when one of the men, Petro Vasylchyshyn, refused to join in and went home to his parents. A week later, the USB [OUN's secret police] took him to the woods and shot him. And when the USB found out that his parents were complaining, they shot them too.[52]

Fighting continued in the Bieszczady mountains of south-eastern Poland until the spring of 1947, when UPA was rounded up by the Polish army. Over the next months Ukrainian villages in the area were systematically demolished, and their inhabitants forcibly deported to the ex-German 'recovered territories' in the north and west, or to the Soviet Union.

Retreating westward in the last months of the war, the Wehrmacht marched to a gloomy Russo-German ditty: '*Es ist alles vorüber, es ist alles vorbei/Drei Jahre in Russland, und nichts ponimai*' – 'Everything's over, everything's past/Three years in Russia, and we don't understand a thing.' It was truer than the soldiers knew: one of the Nazis' biggest mistakes of the war was their treatment of Ukraine.

Germany's suppression of the OUN-led partisans affected only a relatively small group of committed, even fanatical nationalists. What turned the population as a whole against Nazi rule, initially welcomed as a deliverance from Stalinism, were two other policies: its treatment of prisoners-of-war, and the mass deportation of civilians to Germany as slave-labourers.

During its initial advance, the Wehrmacht captured vast numbers of prisoners – over 60,000, according to German records[53] – in its pincer movement on Kiev alone. Partly because the number of surrenders was so huge, partly because Slavs were Untermenschen undeserving of even basic care, few preparations were made for their reception. Instead, the Wehrmacht herded hundreds of thousands of men into 'cages' – bare enclosures surrounded with barbed-wire. The Jews and political commissars among the prisoners were executed, and since deciding who was Jewish was left up to officers' 'intuition', so too were tens of thousands of circumcised Muslims from the Caucasus and Crimea. It sufficed, according to one observer, 'for a man to have black hair and black eyes in order to be considered a Jew and shot'.[54]

Ravaged by typhus, beaten and starved, the remaining prisoners died like flies. At no camp was the death rate less than 30 per cent, and in some it was as high as 95 per cent.[55] The bodies were left lying for weeks on end, the guards only entering the verminous compounds in order to incinerate the dead and dying with flame-throwers. Cannibalism made its appearance: 'After having eaten everything possible, including the soles of their boots,' Göring joked with the Italian foreign minister, 'they have begun to eat each other, and what is more serious, have also eaten a German sentry'.[56]

In the final months of the war, thousands of prisoners were shunted west in death marches similar to those suffered by the inmates of the concentration camps. Altogether, of the 5.2 million Soviet soldiers taken prisoner by Germany during the war, 2 million are recorded as having died in camps, and another 1.3 million fell into the catch-all category of 'escapes, exterminations, not accounted for, deaths and disappearances in transit'. Taking only the most conservative figure of 2 million deaths, the Eastern Front's prisoner-of-war camps killed over a third as many people again as the entire Holocaust.[57]

Unsurprisingly, the fate of Soviet PoWs shocked the civilian population far more than did that of Ukraine's Jews. The Avhustivka villagers threw loaves of bread over the wire to prisoners in a nearby transit camp; the Jewish massacres, in contrast, were treated by some at least as entertainment. Germany's treatment of its prisoners also gave Soviet soldiers, many of whom had little or no enthusiasm for Stalinism, the best of incentives not to change sides. After the initial German advance, numbers of deserters dropped sharply – 'because', as a Soviet officer explained, 'most of the prisoners have been disappointed . . . days without food; only cursing and beating; shootings without reason, often only because the prisoner cannot understand what the Germans want from him . . .'[58]

Worst of all, from the average civilian's point of view, was the Nazis' programme of forced labour. Between the spring of 1942 and the summer of 1944, Germany deported 2.8 million Soviet civilians – 2.1 million of them Ukrainian and just over half women[59] – to the Reich as Eastworkers or Ostarbeiter. Initially recruitment was voluntary, but as news of atrocious work conditions got back home, the Germans resorted to violence, piling people into lorries as they left churches or cinemas. Thirty-eight thousand Kievans – over 10 per cent of the city's population – were delivered to the Ostarbeiter programme in the first ten months of occupation.[60] Once in Germany, they were forced to wear badges embroidered with the letters OST, barred from fraternising with Germans and from public transport, subject to punitive whippings and paid starvation wages. 'A glass of cold water,' ran an Ostarbeiter song, 'keeps you working 'til the afternoon/The soup is good – a litre of water, one grain of kasha and one little potato . . .'[61] Escapees were executed or sent to concentration camps. As the more pragmatic of Hitler's henchmen repeatedly but vainly pointed out, one of the chief results of the Ostarbeiter scheme was that more and more Ukrainians fled to the forests to join the partisans.

In Kiev's main post office I met an ex-Ostarbeiter, an old woman with gold front teeth, a furry white beret and bright blue eyes. We started chatting in the queue for stamps – she wanted to know if I believed in God. I forget how it came up that she had been in Germany during the war, but I finally persuaded her – 'You're not a communist, are you? You're not going to print this?' – to come to my flat and talk. With feet planted wide apart, and many theatrical flourishes of a tear-stained handkerchief, she told her story – a remarkable, but not, for her generation, a particularly unusual one. Her name was Lydiya Gordeyevna, and she came from a poor Kiev family; her mother was a seamstress and her father worked in a canteen. In the spring of 1942, aged sixteen – 'Oh such a long time ago, I had beautiful hair then, down to here!' – she was sent to Germany. First she weeded beets on a farm, and when summer was over she was transferred to an armaments factory, where she worked on a lathe. The norm was 450 shells an hour, which meant lifting nine and a half tonnes of metal a day. 'The Germans fed us with cabbage full of worms. When we complained they said – this is meat for you!'

In 1943, having been discovered writing to a friend that 'the Germans would run away from Russia with their trousers down', she was sent to the women's section of Ravensbrück. Had I heard of it? Yes, I had. The guards 'were like witches. They had black uniforms and rubber sticks and they hit us on the head, everywhere – real witches. Even the SS men weren't as bad as the women.' At three o'clock each morning a siren went off and the prisoners had to stand outdoors at attention for 'two or three hours – shivering and shivering'. Girls who were too ill to work were taken away on 'transports' and never seen again. 'There were rumours that patients were burned but we didn't know exactly what happened – we only saw the chimney, with black smoke coming out. We didn't know about the gas chambers.' Crippled by rheumatism, Lydiya only just escaped the chimneys herself. 'An officer came to the hospital, and insisted I should go on the transport. But the old doctor was looking around for reasons for me not to go. He said – look at her glands, she's got diptheria, she might contaminate German air!' To thank him, she gave three days' bread ration to 'a Ukrainian woman there who was a sort of sculptor. She got a bit of cardboard from somewhere, a bit of red velvet from an old dress, and some steel turnings from the factory. She made a picture of a vine – really beautiful, with leaves and grapes and everything. I hid it under my jacket and gave it to him. He was really pleased.'

The end of the war found her in another camp near Leipzig. 'In 1945 they collected up all the women and marched us off under guard. We marched day and night and slept on the ground. We were only allowed a glass of porridge a day – not even bread. Lots of people died – young girls – on the road. Crows picked at their eyes. It was a horrible sight – even the Germans cried.' Passing through woods, some of the women ran off into the trees. 'Then we saw that the younger guards were doing the same. Only the old ones were left – they had plenty of bullets but they couldn't run.' Lydiya and a friend ran too, and hid in a hay barn. 'We sat there for three days and nights. Then suddenly we heard Russian swear words – we knew our people were coming.' Their liberators were not, however, the clean-cut heroes of Soviet legend. 'The commander arrived, he said – you, come over here! I didn't know what he wanted. I saw he had all sorts of bits of gold hidden under his jacket – perhaps they'd taken it off dead bodies. Then he pointed to a bed.' Outside, German soldiers were coming out from the farm buildings with their hands up. 'I heard – bang bang!' – the old woman pretended she was holding a machine-gun – 'and they all fell down.'

Back home in Kiev – after a train journey during which officials 'collected all photos and postcards and made us throw them away so we couldn't show anyone what life was like in the West' – things were not much better. The returning Ostarbeiter were treated like pariahs. 'I couldn't get a job. The managers kept saying – were you in Germany? Then get out! They really hated us, despised us. Even now I've got a neighbour who keeps saying I'm a fascist – why? – because I was in Germany, that's all.'

Now Lydiya lives off her pension in a one-room flat with her husband and an orphaned grandson. She has been abroad once since the war, when a German organisation arranged for a group of camp survivors to go back to Ravensbruck for the fiftieth anniversary of liberation. Producing a grubby Soviet passport from inside her dress, she turned to the page with the German visa on. It was big and shiny and multicoloured; it even involved a holograph. She stroked it as if it were a piece of silk: 'Look, isn't it beautiful?'

What the worthy organisers of Lydiya's trip presumably did not know was that Lydiya is, by Western standards, a dyed-in-the-wool anti-Semite. Talking about Ravensbrück she referred to Jews as *zhidy* – yids – or, conspiratorially, to 'members of a certain nation': 'The block where the Polish members of a certain nation were kept had a terrible smell. We used to say – it's the dirty yids.' It was not the first time I had heard this sort of thing. In Odessa, I stayed with a very sweet old lady who fed me to bursting with a lethal mixture of fried fish and stewed pears, the purchase of which must have used up nearly all the five dollars a night I was paying her. Unfortunately, her conversation was heavily larded with tales of how Jews took all the best jobs, hid gold under their beds, and so on. Even young, educated Ukrainian friends were prone to throw-away jokes about Jewish cunning and Jewish parsimony, looking genuinely baffled when I explained to them, with some heat, that in Western society this would not go down well at all.

Is Ukraine still an anti-Semitic place? At the official level, definitely not. There is no Soviet-style 'nationality' entry on the new Ukrainian passports, the informal quotas on Jews entering higher education are long gone, and there are Jews in senior positions in every branch of government. Israeli and Ukrainian foreign ministers exchange cordial visits, and Odessa has elected a Jewish mayor. Synagogues are slowly being reopened (though the one on Rustaveli Street in Kiev is still subject to a rearguard action by a children's puppet theatre), and Kiev recently got its first kosher restaurant. No Ukrainian political party save the tiny UNA uses anti-Semitic rhetoric, and the country has no political figure, to its great credit, even approaching Russia's ghastly Zhirinovsky. Though Ukraine still has anti-Semites – the graffiti and the bricks through the synagogue windows testify to that – anti-Semitism is no longer an institutionalised part of its culture.

But if Ukrainian society is coming to terms with its living Jews, the same cannot be said of its dead ones. As in Soviet days, the Holocaust is one of the great unmentionables, fitting in as badly with Ukraine's new story-book self-image of doughty Cossacks and martyred poets as it did with the Soviets' square-jawed Slav brothers standing shoulder-to-shoulder against the fascist invader. 'Ukrainians don't want to talk about it,' a Jewish friend told me. 'They prefer talking about Ukrainians fighting Germans and Russians, and Ukrainians being sent to Siberia.' When Ukraine's first post-independence president, Leonid Krav-chuk, made a speech at Babiy Yar on the fiftieth anniversary of the massacre 'it was a real shock, because before that, people didn't even pronounce the word "Jew" – they used euphemisms, they talked about "individuals of Jewish nationality".' Babiy Yar has a new menorah-shaped memorial to remind passers-by that the people killed there were not just 'Soviet citizens', but hundreds of other sites round the country remain forgotten and unmarked. The subject is not taught in schools, nor much discussed in the media. This selective amnesia applies, it should be added, not only to Jews, but to all Ukraine's vanished minorities – Poles, Germans, Greeks and Armenians. All are uncomfortable muddiers of the waters in a country that has not even begun to come to terms with a history strewn with more than its fair share of blood and paradox.

Among the Ukrainian diaspora, the Holocaust is still an acutely touchy issue, alternately the subject of flaming polemic and defensive silence. The entry for Babiy Yar in a new English-language guidebook to Ukraine, published in Baltimore and obviously aimed at a diaspora readership, consists of a single astonishing sentence: 'O. Teliha (1907–42), a poetess and a leading activist of the Melnyk faction of the Organisation of Ukrainian Nationalists, executed by the Germans, is buried here.' Nazi-hunters and Ukrainian organisations have had frequent spats, the most notorious and longest-drawn-out being the Ivan Demjanjuk affair. In 1986 a Cleveland car-worker, a post-war Ukrainian immigrant, was extradited to Israel on the charge of being 'Ivan the Terrible', one of the operators of the gas chambers at Treblinka. The case collapsed (Demjanjuk having already spent seven and a half years in prison) when it was proved that prosecution evidence provided by the Soviet government had been faked.

In reality, the question of Ukrainian anti-Semitism is an increasingly academic one. There are few anti-Semites left in Ukraine, because there are few Jews. They were less than 1 per cent of the population in 1989, and are fewer still now. Back in Ivano-Frankivsk, Moishe-Leib tells me that 150 families have emigrated in the last three years – most to Israel, some to America or Germany. 'Every month another two or three lots go, and the old people left behind are dying. The rest are assimilated – half-Ukrainian or married to Ukrainians – and they don't come to synagogue.' Even on festival days his congregation numbers only fifty or so – elderly, courteous men dressed with the painstaking respectability of the old Soviet middle class. Moishe-Leib gives Sabbath school to the children and Hebrew lessons to the adults – 'so they don't arrive in Israel like wild people' – and helps with visa applications.

Wouldn't it be better, I ask, to try to get people to stay, to rebuild something of what was lost? Impossible, he says: 'The fact is, people have lost their traditions.' Besides, most of the Jews living in Ivano-Frankivsk today are Easterners who moved in after the war. The real Galician *shtetl* communities are already long gone. When he has no congregation left, Moishe-Leib will emigrate himself: 'I'm only here because there are still people I can help. Maybe in two years, maybe in five, I will have gone too.' What will happen to the synagogue and the graves then, he doesn't know.

Driving back through town, Moishe-Leib tells one last oh-so-Ukrainian story. As we bump past a routinely hideous Intourist hotel, he points to the bit of empty pavement where Ivano-Frankivsk's Lenin statue once stood. 'I've done a deal to re-use the stone for a Holocaust memorial,' he says. 'We're paying them back in their own currency.'

◆ CHAPTER EIGHT ◆

The Wart on Russia's Nose: Crimea

> The person of Selim Giray is comparable to
> a rose garden; the son who is born to him is
> a rose. Each in his turn has many honours in
> his palace. The rose garden is ornamented
> by a new flower; its unique and fresh rose
> has become the Lion of the padishah of
> Crimea, Selamet Giray Khan.
> – *Arabic inscription above the portal of the*
> *royal mosque at Bakhchisarai*

ON THE MALAKHOV bastion at Sevastopol two rows of cast-iron cannon-balls have been laid out in the shape of a cross. They mark the place where, on 28 June 1855, Admiral Paul Nakhimov, laconic, frock-coated commander of the city's defences for the previous eight months, was shot in the head by a French sniper. He had been viewing the enemy batteries through a telescope, and his last words, before the instrument fell from his hands, were 'They're shooting better today.'

It is a quiet grey day in early March. In Kiev there is still snow on the ground; down here the streets are dry and the breeze from the sea smells of spring. Showing me round are Arkady, a journalist from Simferopol, and Nataliya, a student born and brought up in Sevastopol itself. Both are typical Crimeans: Nataliya's father is a retired naval officer, Arkady's a Russian

169

bus-driver whose Stakhanovite feats of long-distance travel earned him a nice little vine-covered house in the sunny south. Nataliya's parents are less fortunate: the tap-water in their housing block is undrinkable, so they heave buckets up five flights from a pump in the yard. Do they have hot water? 'Oh yes – but only twice a week.'

All the same, Nataliya is proud of her city. 'This,' she says, pointing across a ravine with a wrecked bus at the bottom, 'is where the enemy were camped. They fired on us for 349 days before they took the hill.' Sandbags and a row of bronze cannon mark the Russian emplacements, and the whole area is dotted with monuments and memorials. A bas relief of Tolstoy, here as a young artillery-officer, shows him beardless and in profile, glaring from between jug-ears. Across the other side of the hill stands the 'Museum of the Heroic Defence and Relief of Sevastopol', a giant stone rotunda built in 1905 to mark the siege's fiftieth anniversary. Niches round the outside wall house a series of busts: whiskered generals and admirals, the surgeon Pirogov – 'the first person to use anaesthetics on the battlefield', says Nataliya – and a nun – 'Dasha of Sevastopol, our Florence Nightingale'. Inside, a woman with a white baton is talking a group of Central Asians through a 360-degree, three-dimensional diorama, all heaped bodies, gleaming bayonets and fluttering tricolors. From her commentary one would never guess that Sevastopol actually surrendered. On the way out we pass a faded little fun-fair, still closed up for winter. 'On Young Pioneers' Day,' Nataliya says, 'all the schools used to come up here. First we'd go to the cinema – it was free just for that day – then we'd come and take rides on the carousel, all in white dresses.'

Sevastopol is a holy city twice over – sacred not only to Russian military sacrifice, but also to Russian Orthodoxy. On the edge of the town, on a windy, half-drowned peninsula lined with boarded-up summer cottages, stand the remains of Chersonesus, the Greek city where the Byzantine missionaries Cyril and Methodius first landed in Rus, bringing the Gospel and the

Cyrillic alphabet with them. In the chilly dusk, we wander among sunken streets and shattered columns, lapped by a gun-metal sea. Near the shore a giant bell hangs on a wooden frame. 'Strike it,' Arkady says; 'it's good luck.' The clapper has disappeared so I throw a stone at the bell instead, producing a long, melancholy buzz. A nineteenth-century basilica marks the spot where Prince Volodymyr, converter of Kievan Rus, was once thought to have been baptised. Later the archaeologists changed their minds, and now trees are growing through the church's roof. 'They're supposed to be repairing it,' says Arkady with a shrug, 'but they haven't got the money.'

Hypnotised by its glorious past, Sevastopol is caught in a time-warp. The city is tidy in the old, dour Soviet way. There are no billboards, no money-changers or gypsy beggars, few kiosks with their jumbled rows of Western cigarettes and psychedelic liqueurs. Every third man is in uniform – the officer's handsome black and gold, or the sailor's bell-bottoms and brimless ribboned caps. The local newspapers are called things like *Glory to Sevastopol* and *The Motherland Flag*, and the clock on top of the Sailors' Club bangs out the tune 'Legendary Sevastopol' every hour. On May Day veterans gather at the railway station to lay flowers beside an old steam train painted with the slogan 'Death to Fascists'. When the Soviet Union collapsed, nearly all the naval base's officers went over to Russia, refusing to swear new oaths of loyalty to Ukraine and running up the tsarist St Andrew's Cross over the battleships rusting in the oily harbour. They also hung on to the fleet's fine neoclassical headquarters, shoving the disgruntled Ukrainians off to dilapidated barracks in the suburbs. Ashamed to let me see his office, a Ukrainian lieutenant gave me an interview outdoors in the rain. 'It's all lies what the Russians say about us having four ships and eight admirals,' he grumbled, as a birch-tree dripped on to his collar. 'These are very old political tricks – we've got *four* ships, *four* admirals.' Back in the old headquarters overlooking South Bay, a Russian officer had told us that he still couldn't quite believe that Russia and Ukraine were separate countries: 'It will take dozens of years before we realise that we live in different states. Nobody takes all these customs controls seriously.' And the Ukrainian ships? 'We're always happy when they get back to base by themselves – they don't always manage it, they're so inexperienced.' His father was with the Black Sea Fleet before him, but he didn't know where he would end up. 'Most officers think of themselves as citizens of Crimea and of Russia. As for me, I grew up in Crimea, but Russia is my Motherland.'

Until 1996 Sevastopol was a closed city. All non-residents, Ukrainian citizens as well as foreigners, needed special permits to visit. After days of fruitless run-around for the right papers in Simferopol, I got past the check-points into town with the aid of a borrowed Ukrainian passport and a discreet twenty-dollar note. 'I brought some Germans here a while ago,' Arkady said. 'They looked really Western in their big anoraks, so I took them in through the vineyards. But you look just like one of ours, so we won't bother.' I resolved to take this as a compliment. Months later I collared Sevastopol's notoriously old-guard mayor at a London conference devoted to Ukrainian economic reform. A beetle-browed, brown-suited dead ringer for Brezhnev, he looked uncomfortable among the chattering, blazered businessmen. 'So when,' I asked, 'is Sevastopol going to stop being a closed city?'

'I can't believe, Anoushka' – eyebrows raised in bonhomous concern – 'that foreigners have any problems getting in.'

'But they do – I had to bribe the *militsiya*.'

'But you should have called me! We want tourists, but élite, controlled tourism only. We can't have lots of tourists, because we have no hotels!'

'Yes, you do – I stayed in one.'

'They have no water!'

'But if you stay closed you'll never get any investment, any new jobs. Your own businessmen say so.'

'You shouldn't have been talking to these people – they're bandits, just little bandits!' What he wanted, he said, was for

Sevastopol to become a 'free economic zone – because for every economic zone you need a fence, controls. And we have all this already!' As he manoeuvred away through the crowd, his stubby hands started to shake – whether the effect of too much vodka or suppressed fury, I couldn't tell.

With its passionate Russian-ness, its stunned refusal to acknowledge the collapse of the Soviet Union, Sevastopol is the whole of Crimea in concentrated miniature. Sixty-six per cent Russian-speaking, the peninsula has not been part of Ukraine for long. Khrushchev handed it over to the Ukrainian Socialist Soviet Republic in 1954 to celebrate the 300th anniversary of Pereyaslav; Crimeans say he must have been drunk. Staid and balmy, it was the place where every Russian dreamed of going on holiday, and where Party functionaries and military types came to retire.

When Gorbachev held his referendum on maintenance of the Union in March 1991, 88 per cent of Crimeans voted in favour, the highest percentage anywhere in Ukraine. Crimeans did in fact sign up to Ukrainian independence nine months later, but on a low turnout and by a margin of only 4 per cent. Since then, the peninsula has been a continual thorn in Kiev's side. It elected a pro-Russian regional parliament, which has twice passed 'constitutions' declaring virtual independence, and voted, in an illegal referendum of March 1994, in favour of dual Russian–Ukrainian citizenship. Though the pro-Russian dema-gogue Yuriy Meshkov was easily booted out of the Crimean presidency once he got into turf-wars with his own parliament, the peninsula remains terminally unenthusiastic about being part of independent Ukraine. Unable to reconcile themselves to the new order, but nervous of demanding outright union with Russia, Crimeans daydream of turning the clock back to a rebuilt Soviet Union, to a make-believe world where Russians and Ukrainians were much the same thing. One of Meshkov's more irritating achievements was to put the peninsula on to Moscow time.

Crimea's wistfulness about Russia is reciprocated. If Russians find accepting independent Ukraine painful, taking on board the fact that Crimea – with its cyprus trees and Massandra wines, its lapis-lazuli sea and shining cliffs – is part of it, is even worse. 'Crimea is Russian, Russian!' an otherwise impeccably democratic Moscow acquaintance told me one evening. 'It's never been anything else!' And the Donbass slag-heaps? 'Oh well, that's another question.'

Russian or not, one can see why Crimea is worth making a fuss about. In my grandmother's attic, I found travel diaries written by my great-great-great-uncle, a roving Scottish MP. 'Climbing to the top of a hill overhanging the sea,' he wrote in 1878, 'I lay down under a pine tree and felt like a lotus-eater. Blue water, green trees, wild precipices, smiling orchards and vineyards, stately villas, and rude mountain villages, all lay around me in panorama . . .' Avert your eyes from the communists' shabby sanatoria, and the view from the cliffs above Yalta is just as lovely today. Another wandering Victorian, the Reverend Thomas Milner, was patronising – Crimea was no match for the Alps, and its reputation for romantic scenery due only to the flatness of everything else. But most travellers were happy to rhapsodise. 'If there exist upon earth a spot as a terrestrial paradise,' wrote the polymath Cambridge don Edward Daniel Clarke in the early 1800s,

> it is the district intervening between Kutchuckoy and Sudak, along the south coast of the Crimea . . . The life of its inhabitants resembles that of the Golden Age. The soil, like a hot-bed, rapidly puts forth such a variety of spontaneous produce, that labour becomes merely amusing exercise. Peace and plenty crown their board; while the repose they so much admire is only interrupted by harmless thunder reverberating in rocks above them, or by murmuring waves upon the beach below.[1]

Like so many ingredients of Russia's self-image, the Crimea-as-Russian-heartland story has a hole at its centre. For the happy Golden Agers Clarke was talking about were neither Russians nor Ukrainians, but Crimean Tatars – still, when he visited, the large majority of the peninsula's population.

Muslim and Turkic-speaking, the Tatars arrived in Crimea in the thirteenth century, with Batu Khan's mighty Mongol army. Intermarrying with the tribes of the interior, they ruled the peninsula for the next 500 years, first as an offshoot of the Horde, and when the Horde crumbled, as a semi-independent khanate under Ottoman protection. 'Henceforth,' Khan Mengli Giray promised the sultan in 1478, 'we are the enemy of your enemy, the friend of your friend.'[2] Though Soviet historians tried to deny the Tatars historical legitimacy by painting them as mere Turkish vassals, in fact the arrangement was a loose one. The sultan had the final say in the choice of khan, elected from among eligible Girays by the 'kurultai', a Horde-inherited assembly of Tatar nobles. But the khanate had its own legal system, bureaucracy and coinage, and above all its own army, with which it was able to exact yearly tributes from Poland and Muscovy (the Russian payments only came to an end under Peter the Great), and launch regular slave-raids deep into Ukraine.

Baron de Tott, Louis XV's envoy to 'the Kam of the Tartars', accompanied one such expedition into the Zaporozhian lands in January 1769. Armed with bows and scimitars, the Tatar horsemen rode short-stirruped, like modern jockeys, and took two or three horses into battle each, leaping from one to another mid-gallop when under pursuit. The rich wore embroidered caftans trimmed with fox or sable, the poor sheepskin coats with the wool turned outside, so that they looked like 'white bears mounted on horses'.[3] Marching under the green banner of the Prophet, they burned every village they came to, turning the snow grey and blocking out the sun. Mid-campaign, de Tott wrote, the cloud of cinders from 150 burning Cossack settlements stretched a 'full twenty leagues into Poland'.[4] A single Tatar horseman might capture 'five or six slaves of different ages, sixty sheep and twenty oxen',[5] carrying the infants in saddlebags and herding the rest along in front of him for months at a time. In this, at least, the Tatars compared favourably with the accompanying Turkish Sipharis, who 'after dragging these wretched people about with them for some time, tired of the trouble, and cut them in pieces to get rid of them.'[6]

But Tatar life was not all slave-raids. Having dreaded his posting, de Tott found that the khan's 'pretended barbarous court' had a certain rough-hewn Oriental charm. Visitors were received at sunset, after evening prayers, and entertained with clowns and musicians until midnight – a pleasure somewhat marred by the fact that nobody was allowed to sit in the royal presence. Hawking and coursing – 500 horsemen at a time – were favourite pursuits, and de Tott scored a diplomatic triumph with a fireworks display for Khan Makfoud Giray's birthday. 'Accustomed as he had been,' the envoy wrote complacently, 'to nothing but smoaky gerbs [sic], bad crackers and small rockets, badly filled and ill directed, the success of my exhibition was complete.'[7] For his grand finale he administered Makfoud and his nobles with electric shocks; for the next few days 'Nothing was talked of but electricity, and the number of the curious continually increased'.[8]

Makfoud's successor Kirim Giray, a clever, affable man with a weakness for practical jokes involving severed heads, became a close personal friend. Under de Tott's influence he developed an enthusiasm for French cuisine (especially its wine-based sauces), and requested that *Tartuffe* be translated into Turkish for performance by the court buffoons. On campaign, the two spent long evenings talking politics inside a giant crimson-lined tent, Kirim delivering his opinions 'on the abuses and advantages of liberty, on the principles of honour, or the laws and maxims of government, in a manner which would have done honour to Montesquieu himself'.[9]

By de Tott's day, the khanate was nearing its end. The Ottoman empire was in decline, and Crimea with it. Fewer successful Turkish-backed wars meant fewer infidel prisoners, and the slave-trade withered. At the same time, Russia was starting to look Crimea's way, tempted by the Black Sea ports and by the empty 'wild field' south of the Zaporozhian Sich. The eighteenth century saw a series of military expeditions against the khanate, and in 1772 the Tatars were forced to exchange Ottoman for Russian protection. Two years later, having thrown the Turks out of Kaffa, Catherine II signed a second treaty with the Porte itself, under which Crimea was not to be interfered with by either side. 'Independence' lasted less than a decade, and in 1783 Russia annexed the peninsula outright. Catherine instructed that notices be prominently posted 'to announce to the Crimeans Our receiving them as Our subjects'.[10] The Girays decamped to Constantinople, where they became courtiers to the sultan: the Crimean khanate – 'one of the most important states in eastern Europe' according to one modern historian[11] – was no more.

In their determination to cast the Tatars as little better than nomadic tribesmen, and Crimea itself as virtually unsettled land before their own arrival, the Russians tore down almost all reminders of the Tatar past – hundreds of mosques, palaces, medressas, caravanserais and hammams. One of the few buildings to have survived more or less intact is the khans' palace at Bakhchisarai, spared only because Pushkin versified about it and because Catherine II stopped there on her way to Sevastopol. (Its star attraction used to be a specially installed royal bathtub.)

Though its contents and most of the interior decoration have long gone, Bakhchisarai still carries a whiff of sybaritic glamour, of the Krim Tartary of fairy-tales. The buildings are homely, ramshackle, with stumpy minarets, fretworked eaves and open verandahs, quite lacking the aesthetic rigour of Samarkand or the spooky claustrophobia of Topkapi. When the Rev. Milner came here in the mid nineteenth century the rooms were painted with 'flowers, fruit, birds, beasts, stars, scrolls, villages and landscapes' – all vanished now, but proof, as he pointed out, that the Girays 'were free-thinking Mohammedans; for the Koran expressly forbids the representation of living objects'.[12] The empty fountains in the overgrown garden are carved with rose-bushes, goldfish and baskets of pears; the turban-topped tombstones in the royal cemetery with Arabic verses, sun-flowers and scimitars. Nothing grows there now but dusty steppe grass, but Milner saw nut-trees and lilacs. From inside an octagonal mausoleum – it once had a gilded cupola – comes the sound of hammering. 'No we're not doing repairs,' a workman tells me when I poke my head in, 'this is a carpentry shop.' Over the whole seductive complex, at the top of a flight of granite steps, looms a large grey Russian tank. Officially it is a war memorial; unofficially, a reminder of just who is – or was until recently – in charge in Crimea.

Nineteenth-century travel-writers all waxed furious at the cultural havoc Russia wreaked on its newly conquered territories. One of the most splenetic was Cambridge's indefatigable Clarke, visiting in 1800:

> We were in a Turkish coffee-house at Caffa, when the principal minaret, one of the antient [sic] and characteristic monuments of the country, was thrown down, and fell with such violence, that its fall shook every house in the place. The Turks, seated on their divans, were smoking; and when that is the case an earthquake will scarcely rouse them; nevertheless, at this flagrant act of impiety and dishonour, they all rose, breathing out deep and bitter curses against the enemies of their Prophet. Even the Greeks, who were present, testified their anger by similar imprecations. One of them, turning to me, and shrugging his shoulders, said, with a countenance of contempt and indignation, SCYTHIANS![13]

At least a third of the buildings in Bakhchisarai, he wrote, had already been demolished. Aqueducts and fountains were being stripped of their lead, and cemeteries of their tombstones, despite the fact that the country afforded 'most excellent lime-stone, capable of being removed from the quarries with almost as little trouble as the destruction of the grave-stones occasions to the Russians'.[14] Kaffa's ancient Greek remains were being broken up to build barracks, and at Chersonesus marble was up for sale by cubic measure. Clarke wanted to buy a bas-relief – on offer, 'together with a ton weight besides of other stones, for a single rouble' – but purchase was prohibited 'because we were strangers; and, worse than all, we were Englishmen'.[15] 'If it be now asked what the Russians have done in Crimea,' he concluded furiously,

> the answer is given in few words. They have laid waste the country; cut down the trees; pulled down the houses; overthrown the sacred edifices of the natives, with all their public buildings; destroyed the public aqueducts; robbed the inhabitants; insulted the Tatars in their acts of public worship; torn up from their tombs the bodies of their ancestors, casting their reliquaries upon dunghills, and feeding swine out of their coffins.[16]

Clarke exaggerated. In reality, the Tatars were no harder hit by tsarist rule than the other newly conquered nations of the expanding empire, and in some ways, they were better off. Though Russians staffed the local bureaucracy, police force and courts, the government did not interfere in religious matters or with the clergy-run schools. The old khanate lands were distributed among royal favourites – Catherine II alone gave away a tenth of the whole peninsula – but Tatars, unlike Ukrainians, were never subjected to serfdom, paying the same taxes to their new Russian landlords as they had to the old Tatar nobility.

The Tatars' response was to vote with their feet, emigrating *en masse* to Turkey. Out of a population of half a million on annexation in 1783, over 100,000 had already left by the early years of the nineteenth century. More major exoduses followed each of the four Russo-Turkish wars, especially the Crimean War of 1854–5, during which Tatars were pushed out of their farms on the fertile southern coast into the dry steppe interior. By mid-century, the Tatars made up only just over half the population, and as Crimea filled with Slav settlers with the opening of the railways, they fell into the minority. By 1897 they were down to a third of the population, by 1921, to a quarter.[17] The few Tatar noble families who did not emigrate were coopted, like the Ukrainians before them, into the Russian nobility, becoming to all intents and purposes Russians. (One such was Rasputin's murderer Felix Yusopov.) Outside the mosques, Tatar culture atrophied and died, only reviving again at the end of the century, with the first stirrings of the modern national movement under a new middle-class intelligentsia.

Through the chaos of the Russian Revolution and Civil War, the Tatars' national aspirations ran a doomed and familiar course. On Nicholas II's abdication in March 1917 the leaders of the various Tatar parties raced home from exile in Constantinople and Switzerland and began agitating for self-rule under the slogan 'Crimea for the Crimeans'.[18] In December the radical wing of the Tatar movement, the Milli Firka or National Party, held a national assembly – dubbed a 'kurultai' after the old khanate gathering – in Bakhchisarai, electing the Young Turk-affiliated Noman Celebi Cihan as head of a new Crimean Tatar government. But while the Tatars established their headquarters in Simferopol, the Bolsheviks took control among the Russian sailors of Sevastopol. In January the Bolsheviks marched on the capital, easily defeating the Tatar cavalry they met on the way. The kurultai disbanded and its members fled to the mountains or to Turkey. Celebi Cihan, who had stayed behind hoping to come to a *modus vivendi* with the new regime, was killed and his body thrown into the sea. Wholesale slaughter of Tatar and Russian civilians followed: taking over under the Treaty of Brest-Litovsk in May 1918, the German army uncovered fresh mass graves. The Germans left again in December, and for the next year and a half the peninsula was in chaos, changing hands four times before finally falling permanently to the Bolsheviks in October 1920. A new wave of terror followed, as Lenin's Cheka set about rooting Tatar partisans out of the hills, and slaughtering the Tatar and Russian intelligentsia. Sixty thousand Crimeans were killed in less than six months,[19] and another 100,000 died of starvation. An *émigré* newspaper described conditions in Yevpatoriya:

Bands of gypsies live in the suburbs of the city, dying of hunger. Robberies are innumerable during the night. The soldiers of the Red Army, in rags and bare feet and dying of hunger, attack the inhabitants at nightfall and steal their clothing. The Communists are not exempt from these attacks. The lack of fuel requires that doors and windows are used for heating . . .[20]

The 'taking root' policy of the 1920s, aimed at reconciling non-Russians to Bolshevik rule, saw a brief cessation of hostilities. Tatar schools, libraries, museums and theatres opened; Simferopol got a new university and returned to its old name of Akmecet. Permission was given for the publication of Tatar-language books, and Tatars – including many old Milli Firka members – got senior posts in local government. But the period of grace did not last long. In 1928 the Tatar Bolshevik Veli Ibrahim, leader of *korenizatsiya* in Crimea, was executed, signalling a new round of purges. Collectivisation meant the deportation of 30–40,000 Tatar 'kulaks'[21] and thousands more deaths through starvation. The Tatar alphabet was first Latinised then Cyrillicised – not just a cosmetic change, since it cut off the younger generation from Arabic-script pre-revolutionary Tatar literature. Mosques were closed, and Muslim clerics exiled to Turkey or Central Asia.

Up to the Second World War, the Tatars' experience of communism was nothing unusual. Executions, deportations, famine – these were the common lot of all Soviet subjects, including the hapless Russians themselves. But in 1944 the Tatars became one of a select group of nationalities for whom Stalin had reserved a special fate: wholesale deportation – not just of collectivisation-resistant peasants and the urban middle classes, but of the entire population.

The deportees came from eight different nationalities – about 1.6 million people in total.[22]. They were the Crimean Tatars; the Chechens, Ingush, Meskhetians, Karachai and Balkars, all Muslim nations from the Caucasus; the Volga Germans and the

Buddhist Kalmyks, from the Caspian steppe. The Volga Germans were deported in the summer of 1941, as the Wehrmacht advanced, the rest from 1943 to '44, as it retreated again. In what was by now a familiar pattern, the victims were arrested, piled into wired-up cattle-trucks and shipped, food- and water-less, to 'special settlements' in Central Asia and Siberia. In the Tatars' case, the round-up was completed in three days. Recently released NKVD statistics say that 5 per cent of Tatars died in transit, and another 19 per cent in the first five years in the settlements.[23] According to the Tatars themselves, 46 per cent of deportees died during the journey or within a year of arrival.

Nothing was publicly announced about the deportations until June 1946, when a Supreme Soviet decree, published in *Izvestiya*, announced the abolition of the Crimean and Chechen–Ingush Autonomous Soviet Socialist Republics:

> During the Great Patriotic War, when the peoples of the USSR were heroically defending the honour and independence of the Fatherland in the struggle against the German-Fascist invaders, many Chechens and Crimean Tatars, at the instigation of German agents, joined volunteer units organised by the Germans and, together with German troops, engaged in armed struggle against units of the Red Army . . . meanwhile the main mass of the population of the Chechen–Ingush and Crimean ASSRs took no counter-action against these betrayers of the Fatherland. In connection with this, the Chechens and the Crimean Tatars were resettled in other regions of the USSR, where they were given land, together with the necessary governmental assistance for their economic establishment.

A minority of Tatars had indeed collaborated. Erich von Manstein, commander of the German Eleventh Army, headquartered in Crimea until late in 1942, was able to recruit some 20,000 Tatars into anti-partisan battalions and 'village defence units', designed to protect homes from marauding Russian and Ukrainian irregulars. But more than twice as many Tatars fought alongside the Russians in the Red Army, only to be deported on discharge along with everybody else. (These included several bemused Tatar Heroes of the Soviet Union.) As for the Chechens and Ingush, their lands had never even been occupied by the Germans, so they had had little opportunity to collaborate whether they wanted to or not. The real reason for the deportations seems to have been the NKVD's desire to justify its existence, since it had not done any front-line fighting (letters from Beria to Stalin show him vigorously supporting the scheme[24]), combined with Stalin's customary paranoia about the non-Russian nationalities. As Khrushchev observed in his earth-shattering 'Secret Speech' to the Twentieth Party Congress in 1956, 'the Ukrainians avoided meeting this fate only because there were too many of them ... Otherwise, he would have deported them also.' (A statement greeted with 'laughter and animation in the hall'.[25]) Though Khrushchev condemned the deportations as 'monstrous', officially rehabilitating five of the deportee nationalities, he made no mention at all of the Tatars, Volga Germans or Meskhetians, who had to wait for the dying days of perestroika before being allowed home to their native lands.

Saide Chubukshiyeva is one of the oldest returnees. Before the war she lived with her husband and two children at 23 Rosa Luxembourg Street in Bakhchisarai. She had a job in a printing shop, under a friendly Russian boss, and her husband worked as secretary to the city council. At five o'clock in the morning of 18 May 1944, she says, the family were woken by a knock at the door. 'Two militiamen were standing there. They shouted – you have ten minutes! The children were small then – you can imagine what one could collect in those ten minutes.' By the end of the day all the Tatars in the town had been taken to the station and loaded into railway-cars. There were 133 people in Saide's wagon, 'all women and children – I can't imagine now how they managed to squash us all in'. The next morning the train set off for the east. Though Saide was occasionally let out to get food and water, there was never enough for everybody, and the older women and the children started dying – 'we just had to throw the bodies out of the window'. At the stations, she says, 'people called us traitors, betrayers – they threw stones.' Twenty-eight days later the convoy arrived at Perm in the Urals. 'We were all ordered to the forest to work as lumberjacks. The salary was in kind – they gave us 400 grams of bread a day. My youngest sister was nineteen then. She had to load those six-metre logs into wagons – can you imagine? If you didn't complete your quota for the day you weren't allowed out of the forest. There were these slogans painted on the trees – "If you don't finish your work, don't leave the forest."'

Forty-seven years later Saide made her way back to Crimea with a daughter, son-in-law and three grandchildren. Not, of course, to the old house on Rosa Luxembourg Street, but to a one-room trailer in a new Tatar shanty-town on the windswept hills above Bakhchisarai. Though the cold bites straight through the trailer's paper-thin walls, they have done their best to make it cosy. There are rag rugs on the floor, and a picture of a cocker spaniel hangs above the wood stove in the corner. Six people live here at the moment, says Saide, but last winter there were eleven. The rest of the settlement still looks like a refugee camp. Half-built houses cobbled together out of bricks and breeze-blocks alternate with tiny shacks made of sheets of polythene tacked to wooden frames. Hens and goats scratch about in the coarse dry grass, which stretches away in treeless billows to the horizon. The returnees have rigged themselves up an electricity supply, pirated from the mains, but there are no drains or standpipes. Drinking-water comes in a lorry twice a week.

When the Tatars arrived three years ago the hillside was completely deserted. 'We waited and waited for official permission to start building,' says Saide, 'but nothing happened, so we divided it into plots ourselves. They came and told us to stop, but we weren't going to move. It's so stupid – in *Glory to Labour*

I saw an article saying "the Tatars have occupied a fertile peach-orchard". Can you see any orchard here?' Relations with local government have improved a bit since, but ordinary Russians still resent the returnees. 'Quite recently I went to get my pension. Three or four other Tatar women were there too. And the girl behind the counter said – hey, you've brought the whole tribe, and you won't go away until you've taken everything! That's mostly the Russians who've arrived recently – the ones who were here before the war know the Tatars; their reaction is completely different.'

The man responsible for holding the line between Tatars and Russians is Mustafa Cemiloglu, head of the Milla Mejlis, the organisation Crimean Tatars think of as their national parliament, and one of the grand old men of the Soviet human-rights movement. After an hour's driving about the Simferopol suburbs, we found the Mejlis's headquarters in a cottage on one of the straggling streets where town starts turning into countryside. In the courtyard a group of weatherbeaten men in felt boots and padded jackets stood round a burned-out Mercedes. They were a generation younger than Saide – born in exile in Uzbekistan, they had no memory of pre-war Crimea. One had spent his life in a silk factory in Samarkand; another had worked on a collective farm, only survivor of seven brothers and sisters. The car, they said, had burned out the previous night, when somebody threw a petrol bomb over the wall.

In a back room decorated with a star-and-crescent flag and a portrait of Celebi Cihan, head of the stillborn Tatar government of 1917, Cemiloglu gravely gave me my interview. Though only in his early fifties he looked twenty years older, with draggly silver beard and an old lag's nervous nicotine-yellow fingers. 'The first time I was arrested,' he said, 'was in 1966, when they wanted to send me to the army. I told them I couldn't serve in the Soviet army because I couldn't serve the Motherland – I had no Motherland. There was nothing for me to protect. That's how I got my first year and a half's sentence.' The brave, lonely life of the dedicated 'uncorrectable' followed – seven more arrests and a total of fifteen years in prison, two in Vladivostock, three on the arctic Magadan peninsula in a camp for violent criminals. When he was released for the last time in 1986 it was thanks to the support of better-known non-Tatar dissidents. His mentors were Andrey Sakharov, who put him on the list of political prisoners whose freedom he made a condition of his return from Gorky to Moscow, and General Petro Hryhorenko, a Ukrainian army officer who, magnificently and improbably, adopted the Tatar movement for his own in middle age, suffering five years' torture in psychiatric clinics as a result. Cemiloglu lived with him between prison sentences. 'He was,' he says, 'my second father.'

In 1989 Gorbachev finally allowed the Tatars to start returning home. Now they faced a new problem: how to make themselves felt in a Crimea where they were vastly outnumbered by defensive and disoriented Russians. Around 260,000 Tatars have returned so far, giving them just under 10 per cent of Crimea's population. It is an awkward number – large enough not to be ignored, but too small to give them much electoral clout, especially since they are thinly dispersed throughout the peninsula. For a while, it looked as though things would turn violent: in October 1992 the Crimean government bulldozed a Tatar settlement on the coast, arresting and beating up several protesters in the process. ('You might consider it a violation of human rights,' a Crimean official told me, 'but we call it making order.') The Tatars responded by storming the Simferopol parliament, breaking every window in the building. The following winter two prominent Tatar moderates, a businessman and a parliamentary deputy, were assassinated – whether for political or financial reasons is unclear, since neither man's murderer has ever been brought to trial.

Since then, although officialdom still puts bureaucratic obstacles in the way of Tatars getting land and jobs, and filches Western resettlement aid, things have quietened down. In the autumn of 1993 Cemiloglu succeeded in negotiating a quota of fourteen Tatar seats in the ninety-six-member Crimean parliament – not as many as he wanted, but generous none the less – while simultaneously reining in violence-prone factions in the Mejlis. What he fears most now is pro-Russian separatism. 'It's not that we love Ukraine any better than Russia,' he says. 'We simply realise that we need a stable situation here in Crimea. Changing boundaries means war.' He has accordingly come out strongly on Kiev's side in its periodic bust-ups with Crimea's Russian nationalists, a tactic which should have earned favours for the future.

But however cunningly Cemiloglu parlays Tatar influence, their basic grievance is not going to go away. Like stateless nations everywhere, the Tatars regard themselves as a conquered people unjustly sidelined in a country morally their own. 'But how can you have a Tatar Crimea,' I ask, 'when 70 per cent of Crimeans are Russians?' Tapping his yellow fingers on the desk with the star-and-crescent flag, Cemiloglu has heard this question all too many times before. 'Of course we don't represent a majority of the Crimean population. But it isn't our fault. The fact that we were annihilated doesn't lessen our rights to our native land.'

Potemkin called Crimea 'the wart on Russia's nose', and it still itches. Were a civil war to break out in Ukraine, it would most likely begin in Crimea. So far, things have been quieter than expected. Kiev has handled the peninsula coolly, giving it substantial autonomy and resisting pressure from Ukrainian nationalists to impose direct presidential rule. Kiev's timing has been canny too: when the pro-Russian firebrand Yuriy Meshkov was elected Crimean president in January 1994, Ukraine's President Kuchma waited until Meshkov had squandered his popularity by failing to deliver on economic promises before giving him the boot. The Crimean presidency has now been abolished, and at the time of writing Kiev and Simferopol are still half-heartedly bickering over the fine print of a new Crimean constitution.

But like so much in Ukraine, Crimea's future hangs largely on what happens in Moscow. The Yeltsin government has been restrained on the issue, repeatedly declaring Crimean kerfuffles 'Ukraine's internal affair' and agreeing, as part of the 1994 deal on Ukraine's surrender of its nuclear weapons, to mutual respect of national borders. When Meshkov visited Moscow the month after his election, Yeltsin and the Russian prime minister Viktor Chernomyrdin both refused to meet him, leaving the disconsolate Crimean president boasting unconvincingly about contacts with anonymous 'big pine-cones' in the 'capital'. And though Ukraine and Russia spent five years squabbling over the fate of the Black Sea Fleet, rotting at anchor in Sevastopol, the protraction of negotiations probably had more to do with both governments' reluctance to give ammunition to their nationalists than with the fleet's actual strategic importance, which is negligible. The Chechen war has worked in Ukraine's favour, since as well as spoiling Russia's taste for imperialist adventure, it has given Ukraine the moral high ground. Having bombed its own would-be secessionists to pieces in the Caucasus, Moscow can hardly object to Kiev using a few sharp elbows in Crimea.

There is no guarantee that Russia will be sensible for ever. Many politicians would like to take a more aggressive line on Crimea, among them two of Yeltsin's likeliest successors, Aleksandr Lebed, the gravel-voiced ex-head of the Russian army in Moldova, and Yuriy Luzhkov, the populist mayor of Moscow. Both talk about the 'historic Russian-ness' of Sevastopol; Luzhkov has declared it 'the eleventh district of Moscow'. All this is music to the ears of the Russian parliament, which has twice condemned Khrushchev's transfer of Crimea to Ukraine, and in 1993 passed a resolution declaring Sevastopol to be Russian territory. Were a President Lebed or a President Luzhkov to successfully re-ignite the secessionist movement in

Crimea, it could even spark a chain reaction in Russian-speaking eastern Ukraine.

Kiev's best pre-emptive bet is to get to work on the Crimean economy. With local government dominated by conservative ex-communists, in terms of economic reform the peninsula is one of the most backward places in Ukraine. In Simferopol milk queues outnumber pavement kiosks, and until the summer of 1996 there was a moratorium on all privatisation. Nothing will stop Crimea's Russians being Russian, but if Kiev can start creating jobs and improving living standards, the lure of nationalist demagogues will be weaker.

Back in Sevastopol, in a café down by the waterfront, I asked a group of young men lounging round a card-table if they felt like Ukrainians. They looked at me as if I were mad. 'Of course not!' exploded one. 'They put new stamps in our passports without asking us – they did it by force! I don't speak Ukrainian at all – but they didn't care if you were Russian, Jewish or whatever!' It was all Gorbachev's fault: 'That man was a real bastard. He let the country collapse. No one managed it in seventy years but he managed it in one with his perestroika!' Like his friends, he was out of work – yesterday he had been offered a job as a security guard, but with a salary of less than five dollars a month it wasn't worth taking. The girl behind the counter chipped in: 'There's no sense in any of it – we should have stayed together! Suddenly me and my sister live in different countries! You've got your hard currency, you can go anywhere in the world with it – but with our coupons we can't even go to Moscow!' Grimacing, she slapped at a wad of scuzzy notes: 'It's paper, not money – what *is* this stuff? I don't know!' Her friends, she said, were all leaving – not just for Russia, but for anywhere abroad. She hadn't voted in the elections 'on principle' – because I don't believe in these borders. It's like a play – they know in advance who'll win, who'll lose.'

As I got up to leave one of the men started to laugh. 'If I was commander of the Black Sea Fleet, you know what I'd do? I'd start a war with Turkey, then surrender, and become a Turk in a leather jacket!' Russians wanting to turn into Turks? Admiral Nakhimov would be turning in his grave.

◆ CHAPTER NINE ◆

The Empire Explodes: Chernobyl

An unbreakable Union of freeborn Republics
Great Russia has welded forever to stand;
Created in struggle by will of the peoples,
United and mighty, our Soviet Land!

Hail to the Fatherland, free from oppression,
Bulwark of peoples in brotherhood strong!
The Party of Lenin, strength of the nation,
Leads us to communism steadfastly on!
– *First verse and chorus of the Soviet
national anthem*

Chernobyl helped us understand that
we are a colony.
– *Rukh leader, April 1991*

'BIG STOMACH, LOW concentration,' chuckles Stepan Lyashenko, pressing a metal funnel to his bulging waistband. The electronic read-out on the other end of the apparatus clicks up a few notches. 'Look, I'm quite safe to eat!'

Outside the greasy windows of my hired Zhiguli, the midsummer countryside rolls bucolically by. Storks mince about between sugar-bun haystacks; a barefoot toddler splashes in a puddle; an old woman waits at a bus-stop with a goat on a bit of string. But like the establishing shots of some rustic fright-movie, behind apparent normality horror lurks: Chernobyl. What we are driving through is the so-called 'Obligatory Evacuation Zone' – the amoeba-shaped strip of countryside, roughly eighty miles long by twenty-five miles wide, most seriously contaminated by radioactive fallout during the nuclear explosion of 1986. 'Obligatory evacuation' is a euphemism: according to government promises, the whole population should have been moved out years ago, but lack of alternative housing means that over 30,000 people still live here, including several hundred in the fenced-off thirty-kilometre inner zone round Chernobyl itself.

Lyashenko is a middle-ranking *apparatchik* from the agriculture ministry. His job is to persuade the Zone's collectives to use safer farming techniques. On his lap sits a bundle of booklets wrapped in newspaper and tied with string. Smudgily printed on rough paper, they instruct farmworkers to give up planting beans and buckwheat – both have shallow root systems, and hence take up high doses of the deadly caesium and strontium particles lurking in the topsoil – in favour of deeper-rooted beets and potatoes. But on this trip at least, not many are going to get the message. 'I asked for 300 copies,' Lyashenko says, 'but there are problems with the printers, and I only got a hundred.'

Down the end of a dirt road we draw up outside a dilapidated bungalow. I try out a Geiger counter on the ground – it clicks up to forty milli-roentgens, twice as high as in Kiev. Over by a drainpipe, where rainwater off the roof collects, the readout jumps to 180. The farm's radiologist, a red-faced man with gold teeth, explains that according to regulations, livestock should only be grazed on fields spread with lime, which soaks up radioactive particles, leaving fewer to be taken up by grass, and thence via milk and meat by human beings. 'The most difficult thing,' he says, 'is stopping people grazing their cows in the woods. It's cheap for them but it's very dangerous, because that's where the "traps" are, the places that have never been tested for radiation.' What's worse, his collective is now so short of cash that it can't lime its fields anyway. 'Before, we were able to treat the pastures – you could see the radiation levels going down. Now we haven't got the money and the work has stopped.' Lyashenko looks uncomfortable – the radiologist isn't sticking to the script. 'If you tested every cow near your Sellafield,' he interrupts, 'like we do here, you would find your milk is even worse than ours.'

'But what about the cows in the woods?'

A shrug. 'What do you expect? *Babushka* controls?'

Back in the car, we pass a group of farmworkers sitting on wooden benches outside the collective's single, boarded-up shop. I ask my driver Vlad to stop. Lyashenko climbs out too, grumpy but not saying anything. Straight away the complaints start flowing. An old man in dirty brown jacket and tracksuit trousers says, 'The top officials don't care about normal people – they live in Kiev and eat clean food. Here they used to send us stuff, but not any more.' Like most of the villagers, he has his own cow, but has never had its milk tested for radioactivity. The woman sitting next to him chips in: 'It's really bad here – we get terrible headaches, leg pains. There's no medicine in the shops. We thought of moving out but there's nowhere to go. And how can you worry about the food you're eating when you haven't been paid for three months?' Another woman comes up, trailed by a flock of turkey chicks. A heart-shaped religious medallion hangs round her neck, and under her arm she carries a basket of eggs.

'Are you going to eat those?'

'Of course!' – a jerk of the head at Lyashenko – 'I don't care what they say. I'm sixty-six now, so why does it matter?'

On the way home Vlad's Zhiguli packs up for the third time that day. By suspiciously artistic coincidence, we grind to a halt directly underneath a faded billboard bearing the message 'UKRAINIANS! TAKE CARE OF YOUR ENVIRONMENT!' While Vlad pokes about under the bonnet, Lyashenko and I smoke companionable cigarettes in the low evening sun.

His father, it turns out, disappeared during the purges. Thirty years later the family found out that he had been shot by the NKVD. 'The night of Chernobyl,' he says, 'I was twenty kilometres away, travelling on business. I didn't know anything about the explosion until the second day – and then I only heard about it because some friends who live near the station rang me up and asked me to get them out.' Despite all this, he had waited until 1991 to tear up his Party card, and had voted for the Communist candidate in the presidential elections.

'The way the system treated you, why didn't you leave the Party sooner?'

'I couldn't have moved up the ladder otherwise; I would have stayed in one place. The Communist idea isn't so bad – it was just badly carried out.'

From under the bonnet, Vlad jabs an accusatory finger: 'That's why this place is so fucked up – these bureaucracy pigs just sit there and do nothing. Do you think he cares? No!'

Ask a Ukrainian when he stopped believing in communism, and the answers vary. A few quote the invasion of Czechoslovakia, some the Afghan war, others the discovery of Stalin's mass graves at Bykivnya. Many, like Lyashenko, look blank, because they have not really stopped believing in communism at all. But by far the likeliest reply is 'Chernobyl'. A saga of technical incompetence and irresponsibility, of bureaucratic sloth, mendacity and plain contempt for human life, the Chernobyl affair epitomised everything that was wrong with the Soviet Union. As Yuriy Shcherbak – a doctor turned environmental activist turned Ukraine's ambassador to Washington – declared, 'Chernobyl was not *like* the communist system. They were one and the same.'[1] Imperilling everyone impartially and in the most basic and dramatic fashion, no other single piece of communist bungling did more to turn public opinion against the regime.

Chernobyl exploded at 1.23 a.m. on the night of Friday 26 April 1986. The cause was neither equipment failure nor human error, but an experiment which went wrong. In order to test how long the reactor could operate with no external power supply, engineers deliberately lifted all but six neutron-absorbing control rods out of the reactor's core, and disabled the automatic shut-down system which would have normally come into play in case of power failure. As soon as the external electricity supply had been switched off, power levels inside the reactor core surged, resulting in steam explosions, rupture of the reactor casing, and a fire.[2]

In the months after the disaster, Shcherbak toured the hospital wards collecting interviews with engineers, doctors and firemen who had been on the scene at the time.[3] Yuriy Badayev, a 34-year-old electrical engineer, was on duty in Reactor Number Four's information processing room, following the progress of his bosses' experiment on his computer screens. Shortly after 1 a.m. he was amazed to see that the reactor had been closed down. Fifteen seconds later he felt two massive shocks, one a few moments after the other. The lights went out and water started pouring through the ceiling. Racing out into the corridor, he could hardly see anything for steam and dust; the doors of the elevator had been crushed shut, and the stairs were covered in rubble. Back in his own room the telephone from one of the control rooms on the floor above started ringing; he picked up the receiver, but nobody answered. Later, Badayev saw the colleague who had made that call being carried out on a stretcher, his spine crushed by falling masonry. Another engineer in the same control room died immediately, of burns.

Hryhoriy Khmel, a fifty-year-old engine-driver with the local fire brigade, spent the evening down at the station playing draughts. He had just unrolled a mattress when a call came through that Chernobyl was on fire. Two engines set off; he drove the second. They arrived at about fifteen minutes to two, some twenty minutes after the blast. Flames were coming out of the reactor-block roof and pieces of graphite were scattered everywhere, hot to the touch and crunchy underfoot. Having spent some time trying to locate the station's hydrants – wrongly marked on the map – the younger men scaled the building and started playing twenty-metre hoses down into the burning reactor itself. After watching proceedings from the ground for some hours, Khmel was taken to the station cafeteria, given 'powders' to eat and told to strip and wash. 'We didn't have much idea about radiation,' he told Shcherbak later. 'Whoever was working didn't have any idea.'[4]

In Prypyat, the next-door town where most of the station's workforce lived, a twenty-eight-year-old doctor, Valentyn Bilokin, was finishing his rounds. It had been a quiet shift – a few drunks, a child with an asthma attack. Driving back to the clinic, he saw two flashes in the sky – lightning, he thought, or maybe shooting stars. Told there was a fire at Chernobyl, he packed his burns equipment into a bag and set off for the station – like the firemen, without any radiation medicines or protective clothing. When he arrived, people were running around everywhere. Nobody told him what to do, there didn't seem to be any burns victims to treat, and there were no other doctors on site. When a group of firemen complained that they were feeling nauseous, he finally remembered some of his radiation training from medical school. 'It seemed that I had forgotten everything,' he told Shcherbak. 'Who needed radiation hygiene? Hiroshima, Nagasaki, all that was so remote.'[5]

Having realised what was wrong, he was powerless to do anything about it: 'We had been told there were gas masks and protective suits, but there wasn't anything of the sort, it didn't work.'[6] In desperation, he rang the clinic for gauze masks, but they hadn't got any. More firemen came up, vomiting and complaining of acute headaches, some of them too weak to stand. Bilokin gave them anti-nausea drugs to treat the symptoms, but could do nothing for the radiation itself. One eighteen-year-old, stumbling and slurring like a drunk, drifted away into a coma before his eyes. As the night wore on, Bilokin tried to persuade people to stay inside the station cafeteria: 'I chased them all back into the building, but they just came out again . . . People just didn't fully realisewhat had happened.'[7] By dawn he was feeling ill himself, and got a lift back to the Prypyat clinic, where vodka bottles were doing the rounds. 'Some were drunk,' he told Shcherbak, 'and others were running around constantly washing themselves.'[8] A few hours later, having distributed iodine pills among family and neighbours, he sank into a coma himself.

That same Saturday morning, the regional Party committee held a meeting in Prypyat. Though the whole town could see black smoke belching from the reactor, it was decided that there were to be no safety warnings, and no explanations. All that day – while local Party bosses were arranging for their own children to leave for holiday camps in Crimea – life in the town went on as normal. Families went shopping and walked their dogs; fishermen lugged their tackle off to the Prypyat river; couples sunbathed round the power station's cooling ponds. Football matches went ahead, as did sixteen outdoor weddings sponsored by the Communist Youth League. The schools debated whether or not to go ahead with a planned 'Health Run', and settled on outdoor gymnastics instead. Off-duty station-workers who rang up the town hall asking for instructions were told that the fire was none of their business, and that all decisions would be taken by Moscow. The town's schoolchildren had been put through their 'civil defence' routines, designed for nuclear attack from the West, only days before. But with a nuclear disaster on their own doorstep none of the safety procedures, not even the simplest, were carried out.

Lyubov Kovalevska, a journalist on the local paper, had sat up all night writing a poem. Setting off for her literary club on the Saturday morning, she noticed two odd things: white cleaning-fluid flooding the streets, and lots of policemen about. A few weeks previously she had written an article exposing the shoddy work going into the construction of Chernobyl's fifth reactor. She could have said much more – station-workers had told her of corruption, of faulty equipment and supply shortages – but she had been afraid of losing her job. 'At the time I just hadn't the courage to write about it,' she told Shcherbak afterwards. 'I knew it had no chance at all of being published.'[9] But even she didn't realise there had been a serious accident: 'The whole day we knew nothing, and no one said anything. Well, it was a fire. But as for the radiation, that there were radioactive emissions, nothing was said about that.'[10]

On Sunday morning, Boris Shcherbina arrived in Prypyat, head of a secret emergency commission pulled together by Moscow the day before. Taking a map and a pair of compasses, he drew an arbitrary ten-kilometre circle round the station and ordered a general evacuation. The buses – yellow Icaruses from Kiev – started leaving the town at two in the afternoon, thirty-six hours after the initial explosion. Evacuees were told they would be back soon, so took few belongings with them. Though it was obvious that wind and rainfall would spread fallout over a far wider area, evacuation was not extended elsewhere for another five days.

All Sunday, there was no official announcement of any sort about the accident. Sixty miles south in Kiev, the public was completely ignorant of what had happened, noticing only that all the city's buses had mysteriously disappeared. When an announcement was finally made, it was under pressure from abroad. At 9 a.m. on Monday morning a nuclear power station in Sweden detected abnormal radiation levels in the air: a nuclear dust cloud seemed to be drifting northwards from somewhere inside the Soviet Union. All that afternoon Swedish diplomats badgered the Russian foreign ministry for information, meeting outright denials that anything was wrong. Finally, at nine o'clock in the evening, there was a short bulletin at the end of the regular television news:

> An accident has taken place at the Chernobyl power station, and one of the reactors was damaged. Measures are being taken to eliminate the consequences of the accident. Those affected by it are being given assistance. A government commission has been set up.

The head of Moscow's state-run Novosti news agency later admitted that he had known of the accident since Sunday, but, for the same reasons as Kovalevska in Prypyat, had failed to make it public. Gorbachev himself made no public statement on Chernobyl for two weeks, and when he did go on television, it was to accuse the Western media of spreading 'malicious mountains of lies'. The day before *Pravda* had published an interview with one of the country's top nuclear scientists, in which he told a horrified world that the reactor core might burn its way down through the station's foundations, poisoning the groundwater of the entire Dnieper valley and setting off a second, even larger, steam explosion – the so-called 'China Syndrome'. It was still touch and go, he admitted, whether the reactor could be brought under control at all.

Meanwhile, six days after the explosion, Kiev's May Day celebrations went ahead as normal. Trade-union representatives marched under embroidered banners, children waved flowers, military bands tootled patriotic airs. Ukrainian First Party Secretary Volodymyr Shcherbytsky reviewed the parade from a podium on Khreshchatyk; people noticed that although it was raining, he wasn't wearing a hat. The day before, the wind had swung round to the north, and it was on May Day itself that fallout over Kiev peaked. A British student who flew home just as the heavy fallout was beginning was found to have a piece of nuclear fuel attached to his shoe; a Dutch tourist had fragments of nuclear fuel on his trousers.

On 6 May, after repeated assurances that the accident posed no danger to human health, the Ukrainian health minister suddenly went on local television with instructions that Kievans should not eat green vegetables or drink milk, should stay indoors if possible, wash thoroughly, and sweep out their flats. Better-informed Kievans had already begun leaving the city; now the exodus was general. Cars jammed the roads and frightened crowds mobbed the railway station. The big Univermag store on Khreshchatyk ran out of suitcases, and Aeroflot set up special ticket offices in the ministries and Party offices, so that the *nomenklatura* could get out first. The interior ministry posted policemen armed with automatic rifles on the main roads out of town, with orders to turn back all vehicles without official passes.

The week after May Day, tens of thousands of military reservists started arriving in the Chernobyl area, conscripts in the Soviet Union's biggest manpower round-up since the Afghan war. Mostly teenage boys, their job was to sluice down streets, houses and trees, and to shovel topsoil into lorries for burial. They lived outdoors in tents, often without showers or protective clothing. According to a report in an Estonian newspaper, some were to be found washing in contaminated streams and ponds.

The most dangerous work was at Chernobyl itself, clearing away highly radioactive rubble from inside the reactor core. Groups of conscripts were ordered to run up on to the reactor-block roof, fling one shovelful each of deadly debris back through the hole in the roof on to the exposed reactor, and run down again, the whole operation not to last more than forty seconds. The boys involved dubbed themselves 'bio-robots', perfectly summing up the Soviet regime's attitude towards its citizenry. The official upper limit radiation dose for clean-up workers was twenty-five 'body-equivalent roentgen' or 'rems' – five times the annual limit for an ordinary Soviet nuclear power worker. But in practice even this high limit was frequently exceeded. Since radiation levels near the station were one rem per hour, conscripts should not have worked on the site for more than two days. In reality many stayed for months. Better-off reservists could avoid being sent to Chernobyl altogether by paying bribes, the relevant price being 500 roubles – half that of a deferment from Afghanistan.[11]

Sluggish, chaotic, profligate with human life and bolstered by the crudest propaganda, the Soviet system's response to Chernobyl has been likened to its behaviour during the Second World War. People involved in the disaster even refer to it as 'the war'; the clean-up operations were a 'campaign' and the official result a 'victory'. The old men and women who refused to leave

Prypyat, holing up in their blacked-out flats with gas-masks and biscuits, were nicknamed 'partisans'.

A war maybe, but Chernobyl was no victory. Just how many people have been killed by Chernobyl to date nobody knows. Two people died in the explosion itself; another twenty-eight, mostly firemen and engineers, of radiation sickness soon afterward. Estimates of the total number of subsequent deaths attributable to the disaster range from around 6,000 to 8,000. This does not take into account deformed births, genetic disorders, and early deaths still to come through cancer and leukaemia. A World Health Organisation report of 1995 noted a hundred-fold increase in thyroid cancers in Ukrainian and Belarussian children, but oddly, none in leukaemia or other blood disorders. If the 120 million curies of radioactive material released in the explosion – almost a hundred times more than Hiroshima and Nagasaki combined – had not been pushed high into the atmosphere, spreading thinly over a wide area, the death toll would already be much higher.

Today's uncertainty over the health consequences of Chernobyl is largely the fault of a deliberate cover-up by the Soviet authorities. Registers of clean-up workers and evacuees were left hopelessly incomplete, making post-Chernobyl medical histories hard to track, and in 1988 Shcherbina issued a decree forbidding doctors from citing 'radiation' on death certificates. Instead, deaths were put down to 'rare toxins', 'debility' and the like. (When Shcherbina himself died in 1990, having suffered a large dose of radiation organising the evacuation of Prypyat, the cause of death was marked as 'unspecified'.)

Independent research on the effects of the accident was derided or hushed up. In 1988 a group of journalists made a short film on events at collective farms round Narodychy, a small town thirty-eight miles west of Chernobyl. A foal had been born with eight legs, piglets without eyes, calves without heads or ribs. More than half the children in the district had swollen thyroids, and cancers of the lip and mouth had doubled. The government response was an outburst of vilification and denial, choreographed via Kiev's Centre for Radiation Medicine. Scientists from the Centre lambasted the film as 'incompetent'. Deformities were due to inbreeding, they said; mouth cancers to poor dental work, thyroid problems to a shortage of iodine in the diet. Eventually, after a series of angry meetings in Narodychy, fourteen villages were evacuated – all the fault, the scientists continued to assert, of the media in stirring up irrational 'radiophobia'. Later, records turned up showing that radiation levels in the area in the months after the explosion had been three times higher than round the power station itself.

In the spring of 1995, seven months after my trip to the Zone with Lyashenko, I got permission to visit Chernobyl. At the time, two of its four nuclear reactors were still operating, in the teeth of an international campaign to close the station down. The International Atomic Energy Agency had just issued a report lambasting its dangerous design, lack of back-up systems and fire-proofing, and general 'poor safety culture'. The section of the reactor-block building nearest the wrecked Unit Four, the report said, was structurally unsound, and in 'significant' danger of collapse. Backed by the European Union and America, the IAEA wanted Chernobyl shut immediately. The Ukrainian government had agreed in principle, but argued that since it still provided 6 per cent of the country's electricity, nothing could be done until the West came up with the money to complete three half-built reactors on other sites, the bill for which it put at an eye-popping $4 billion.

Again, the countryside looked uncannily peaceful, more like a nature reserve than the scene of the world's worst nuclear disaster. Baby pines sprouted in the middle of untilled fields; brambles swamped the whitewashed cottages like the roses round Sleeping Beauty's castle. Of one village nothing was left but a faded road sign and a row of grassy barrows where its buildings had been bulldozed underground. A few more years, and this would all turn back into forest.

Apart from the concrete 'sarcophagus' enclosing the remains

of Unit Four, Chernobyl itself looked like any other run-down Soviet factory. On the pot-holed forecourt, men and women stood about in flapping blue cotton jackets, smoking and chatting, and a workman dabbed at a war memorial with a pot of yellow paint. A public relations man – an innovation this – led me upstairs, past maidenhair ferns in knobbly ceramic pots and a stained-glass window of heroic cosmonauts, to meet Vitaly Tolstonogov, the station's chief engineer. The sound of 'Radio Rocks', the latest pop station from Moscow, drifted out from behind chipped plywood doors, and girls with frizzy perms and pantomime make-up stood about in the corridors staring at their nails. As we came in, Tolstonogov switched off his television.

'So what do you think about the closure rumours?'

He drew himself up, stuck out his chin. 'I don't think anything about them. The decision will be taken by the state. As a private soldier, I will implement its decisions.'

'And the IAEA report?'

'Incomplete, let us say one-sided.'

'But what about the reactor block being close to collapse?'

'The building is perfectly safe, it has been tested by the explosion already. Nothing about it has changed. It's all just a pretext for another scandal.'

'And your staffing problems; the engineers quitting for better pay in Russia?'

With the mention of cash, Tolstonogov's military pose took a dent: 'Once we knew that everyone throughout the Soviet Union got the same! But now, everyone gets different salaries even though they're in the same job! It's monkey business, monkey business!'

After lunch in a dingy cafeteria, we changed into lab coats and went to see one of the control rooms. Lined with scratched metal panels and hundreds of paint-splodged buttons and old-fashioned circular dials, it looked more like the bridge of a decommissioned battleship than the nerve centre of a modern nuclear power station. The floor was covered in wrinkled lino, and the plastic upholstery on the controllers' stools was slightly frayed. You didn't have to be the IAEA to find it a less than confidence-inspiring place.

Elbowing aside a stub-filled ashtray, the shift controller told me that he had come out of retirement to work back at Chernobyl. During the 'war' he had been in this very room, helping shut down the three surviving reactors. So far he hadn't fallen ill himself, but his daughter had problems with her bones and stomach: 'She has to go and rest before and after classes – when she was a schoolgirl she didn't need this.' The weekend of the explosion, the family had been evacuated from Prypyat to a nearby village, only to find that it was contaminated too.

'Why don't you work somewhere else?'

One of the younger men, his cotton coat undone, interrupted angrily: 'If you were Ukrainian, you'd be begging for a job here, because otherwise you wouldn't survive! The bazaars are full of teachers, doctors – educated people, all out of work.'

'Aren't you afraid of getting cancer?'

'And if I was a taxi-driver or a kiosk owner? I'd only get killed in a car crash, or by the mafia. We're safer here.' Like the rest, he wanted the station to stay open. 'If the West wants to close the old Soviet reactors it's because Western companies will get the orders for the new ones!' As we turned to go he lifted his cotton hat derisively: 'Success to you! Come back! And bring your children!'

On the way out, the PR man took me to look at an architect's model of the plant. This was how Chernobyl was supposed to be – neat and tidy, with two modern air-cooled reactors and no scorched buildings or crumbling sarcophagus. Turning to go, he knocked over a miniature chimney. 'Where did this go? Oh well, who cares.'

Chernobyl's corrosive effect on public opinion took some time to make itself felt. Kiev saw no big anti-nuclear demonstrations until the autumn of 1988, more than two years after the disaster. The popular independence movement got under way a year after that, well behind its counterparts in the Baltics and the Caucasus. Why was the opposition so slow to get off the ground?

Through the long Cold War years, Ukrainians had been in an anomalous position, simultaneously extra-privileged and extra-repressed. Like the Scots of the British empire, they acted as trusted junior partners in the Union, subordinate to Russia of course, but senior to Armenians, Uzbeks and the rest. All the post-Stalin leaders save Gorbachev had close personal ties to the republic: Khrushchev and Brezhnev were both Russians from eastern Ukraine, Andropov built his career as head of the Ukrainian KGB, and Chernenko was born of Ukrainian kulak parents in Siberia. Politburos were packed with Russians and Ukrainians, and the usual practice in the republics was to appoint a native as first Party secretary, while a Russian or Ukrainian wielded real power as number two. Ukraine, like Belarus, even had its own seat at the United Nations – though it always voted with Russia.

But Ukraine's 'younger brother' status exacted costs as well as privileges. If rewards for loyalty were higher for Ukrainians than for other non-Russians, penalties for dissent were harsher too. After the war, the hundreds of thousands of Ukrainians sent to the camps during the Soviet occupation of Galicia were joined by another half-million partisan supporters, collectivisation-resistant peasants and *religiozni*, making Ukrainians the most prominent nationality in the 1950s Gulag.[12]. Later, they made up the largest single group of political prisoners in what remained of the camps after Khrushchev's amnesty. Under pressure from renewed Russification – publication of Ukrainian-language books and journals plummeted in the 1970s, and Russian immigration increased – most Ukrainians found it easiest to conform. 'You could teach a Jew to speak Ukrainian in no time, a Russian in two or three years,' ran an old Soviet joke. 'An ambitious Ukrainian – it would take for ever.' The Ukrainian Communist Party grew from 165,000 members in 1945 to a high of 3.3 million in 1989,[13] earning itself a model reputation under arch-conservative Volodymyr Shcherbytsky, an old Dnipropetrovsk crony of Brezhnev's.

But despite all the incentives to go along with the Soviet system, Ukrainian nationalism never quite died. The first post-war generation of activists were the 'sixtiers', a group of young writers who, like the nineteenth-century 'awakeners' before them, used the language issue as a cloak for wider discontents. Under the slogans 'Speak Ukrainian' and 'Defend the Ukrainian Language', they petitioned for an end to Party meddling in literature, and for freedom to debate and experiment. Russified Ukrainians were scolded, Shevchenko-style, for cowardice and opportunism.

The summer after Khrushchev's fall in 1964, a hundred or so of the most vocal 'sixtiers' were arrested and put on trial on charges of 'anti-Soviet agitation and propaganda'. The verdicts were foregone conclusions, but to the regime's amazement, the public refused to let the writers go quietly. In Kiev the literary critic Ivan Dzyuba stood up in the middle of the Ukraina cinema and appealed to the audience to protest. In Lviv, supporters and relatives demanded to be let into the courthouse, and defied fire-hoses to shout 'Glory' and throw bouquets as the prisoners were escorted into police vans. Petitions for information and explanations included the signatures of Supreme Soviet deputies, Writers' and Composers' Union members and the famous aircraft designer Oleg Antonov. The young Komsomol journalist Vyacheslav Chornovil was so outraged by the trial's blatant bias that he sent a 200-page document to the public prosecutor and the heads of the Supreme Court and KGB, listing all their own infringements of the constitution and criminal code. Interrogation techniques, he pointed out, had not changed since Stalin's time:

> It is not obligatory to slam doors on fingers, to stick needles under fingernails, or to strike someone's face in order to force him to denounce his deeds as terrible crimes, or to confess everything that the investigator needs to complete the evidence

he has contrived beforehand. All that is needed is to lock the man inside a stone sack with bars, a privy, to forbid him any contact with close relatives for half a year, to hammer into his head, day after day, for several hours at a time, the feeling of great guilt and, finally, to drive that man to such a state of mind that he would not at first recognise his wife if she came to visit him . . .[14]

In due course Chornovil was sentenced to three years of hard labour in a closed trial of his own, but not before his *Petition* had been smuggled out of the country for publication in the West.

With Shcherbytsky's appointment in 1972 came a second, more successful crackdown. Hundreds more writers, teachers, artists and scientists were arrested, and dealt far harsher sentences than the 'sixtiers'. At the same time Shcherbytsky purged the Ukrainian Communist Party, expelling 37,000 Party members, and sacking half the Ukrainian Politburo. In 1977 he rounded up almost the entire membership of the Ukrainian Helsinki human-rights group, founded with help from Russian dissidents the previous year. 'I was certain,' the Tatar-rights campaigner General Hryhorenko recalled in his memoirs, 'that the authorities would react with particular sensitivity to the creation of a Ukrainian group, since such a group could not avoid touching on the question of nationality, the most sensitive of all issues for the Soviet Union.'[15] He was right. Twenty-two Ukrainian Helsinki Group members were despatched to the Gulag, to serve terms of between three and fifteen years. Two were sent into internal exile, and five, including Hryhorenko himself, were forced to emigrate. Put to work as slave labourers in camp factories and farms, deprived of proper clothing, washing facilities or medical care, and kept in a continuous state of semi-starvation, the prisoners' lives narrowed to bare survival. 'The con's diary in prison is simple,' wrote one inmate. 'Bread–breakfast–dinner–supper, day after day, month after month, year after year.'[16] Suicide, self-mutilation, random beatings and long spells in freezing punishment cells were all common. The Soviet Union did not release its political prisoners until 1987. For many, like the poet Vasyl Stus, who died with three other Ukrainian Helsinki Group members in a Mordovan camp in 1985, amnesty came too late.

By the time Gorbachev launched perestroika, Ukrainian nationalism looked like a thing of the past. The movement's best-known leaders were exiled, in prison, or dead. Save for the hard-core North American diaspora, protest at home and abroad had fizzled out. 'By and large,' the historian Orest Subtelny wrote wistfully in 1988, 'it seems that most Soviet Ukrainians accept the Soviet regime as their legitimate government and identify with it. Because of the government's monopoly on information and intensive propaganda, they are, at best, only vaguely aware of the hardships that Ukrainians have suffered at Soviet hands in the "ancient" past . . . Many Soviet Ukrainians take pride in the power and prestige of the USSR of which they are an important part.'[17]

Subtelny's analysis was perfectly correct. The number of active Ukrainophiles was negligible, and had been so for the last thirty years – a few thousand out of a population of 52 million. Advocates of outright independence could be counted on the fingers of one hand. Open national feeling was restricted to a small intelligentsia clique; ordinary Ukrainians remained stolidly uninvolved. 'The simple citizen,' one activist complained, 'resembles a hypnotised rabbit.'[18] To any reasonable observer, independence looked like a Quixotic dream. Yet within three years of Subtelny's putting pen to paper Ukraine had, to universal amazement, become a fully independent, democratic state.

Did the Soviet Union collapse under pressure from national independence movements, or did the independence movements fill a vacuum left by Soviet collapse? It is a chicken-and-egg question: the phenomena fed off one another. But the two factors – popular opposition at the periphery, political weakness at the centre – had different relative weights in different republics. The Baltics, Georgia, Armenia and Azerbaijan all possessed Popular Fronts so strong that it was obvious they could not be kept in the Union without use of force. But in the case of Ukraine, where the independence movement was real and persistent, but only ever involved a minority of the population, it was never clear that this was so. For separatism to succeed, the centre had to fail. This it did in August 1991, when an attempted coup in Moscow left the Ukrainian Communist Party's conservative bosses with the choice between the Soviet Union and military dictatorship, or democracy and the Ukrainian nationalists. When it became clear that the coup had misfired, they accepted the inevitable, and went with the nationalists. Until that moment, there was no point at which one could confidently declare 'From now on, Ukrainian independence is inevitable'.

None of it would have happened without Galicia. For a hundred years Galicia had been the heartland of Ukrainian nationalism. It was where the remnants of the partisan army had fought on after the war, where Uniate priests still held secret masses in woods and barns, and where Ukrainian was most widely spoken. It had no Russian population to speak of, and since the war, no Poles either. It produced many of Ukraine's Cold War dissidents, and later, most of the leaders of Rukh, the opposition coalition that led the popular independence movement. Galicia was never strong enough to take Ukraine to independence on its own: the region was too small and sparsely populated for that. But without it – if, say, it had stayed under Polish rule after the war – Ukraine might never have become independent at all.

Ukraine's first big anti-communist demonstrations took place in Lviv. In June and July 1988 a characteristic medley of independent organisations – the Ukrainian Helsinki Union, the Committee in Defence of the Uniate Church, the Ukrainian Language Society and a student group – organised a series of illegal mass meetings, attended by between 20,000 and 50,000 people, underneath the Ivan Franko statue in front of the university. Newly-released dissidents made speeches calling for an end to Party privileges, closure of the KGB and release of remaining political prisoners. Though there were demands for more republican autonomy, there was no talk as yet of independence: some demonstrators even waved Gorbachev banners in the belief that perestroika was being obstructed by local communists. The meetings were broken up by interior ministry troops, and several of the organisers arrested. Kiev followed Lviv's lead in November, when 10,000 marchers stood in the rain listening to speeches mixing protests against nuclear power with appeals for a Popular Front. When plainclothes KGB men switched off the sound system the crowd refused to budge, chanting '*Mikrofon, mikrofon.*'

With Shcherbytsky's forced retirement in September 1989, the demonstrations turned into a political movement. The same month, a range of nonconformist organisations – the Ukrainian Writers' Union, the Ukrainian Language Society, the Helsinki Union, Green World and the historical campaign group Memorial – formed a loose coalition titled the 'Ukrainian Popular Movement in Support of Perestroika' or 'Movement' – Rukh in Ukrainian – for short. Predictably, most of the delegates at Rukh's inaugural congress came from the intelligentsia and from central and western Ukraine: there were few representatives from the farms, the factories, or the Russian-speaking east and south. Though the camp veteran Levko Lukyanenko told the hall to 'abolish this empire as the greatest evil of present-day life'[19] (the only speech not reported by *Literaturna Ukraina*, the country's most outspoken paper), the bulk of delegates were far more cautious, voting a programme that called for 'a sovereign Ukrainian state' within a 'new Union treaty'.[20]

While Rukh met in Kiev and students scuffled with riot police in Lviv, the Orthodox Church, hitherto the moribund province of KGB stooges and pious grannies, burst into uproar. Led by the SS Peter and Paul Church in Lviv, parishes all over the country started declaring themselves members of the Ukrainian Autocephalous Orthodox Church, last heard of in 1930. At the same time, a campaign got under way for legalisation of the Uniates, liquidated after the war. Refused a meeting with Supreme Soviet officials in Moscow, six priests went on hunger strike, and on 17 September, the fiftieth anniversary of the Ribbentrop–Molotov pact, 150,000 Uniates held candlelight vigils in memory of the victims of the Soviet annexation of western Ukraine. By December around 600 parishes and 200 priests had applied for registration as Uniates, finally winning official recognition following Gorbachev's meeting with Pope John Paul II. The following summer, the reborn Autocephalous Orthodox Church held its first Council for sixty years, with a service in Santa Sofia. Metropolitan Mstyslav, head of the diaspora church in America, had been refused a visa to attend, but was elected Patriarch *in absentia*. In October Gorbachev capitulated and the Autocephalous Orthodox were legalised too. In just over a year, Ukraine had progressed from one official church to three. Unchristian battles promptly broke out over ecclesiastical property. Rival congregations marched on the churchyards, and it was quite common for priests to be stoned.

Meanwhile, in March 1990, Gorbachev initiated the final, fatal phase of perestroika, allowing semi-democratic elections to the republican Supreme Soviets, among them Kiev's Verhovna Rada. Fighting on a platform of 'real political and economic sovereignty' – though not outright independence – Rukh and its allies won 108 out of 450 seats. Predictably, they did much better in Galicia and central Ukraine than in the Donbass and the south: a human chain, high point of the campaign, had stretched from Lviv to Kiev, but no further east. Despite being in a minority, Rukh's presence revolutionised Rada proceedings, hitherto a rubber-stamp for Party orders. 'The democrats represent only a third,' wrote an observer, 'but they are always at the microphones and dominate the hall as if they constituted a majority.'[21]

The literary scholar Solomea Pavlychko recorded the events of 1990 in a series of letters to a friend in Canada. Over and over, she contrasted Kiev's defeatism with the reigning sense of optimism and excitement in western Ukraine. In Kiev, she wrote in May, 'morale is low. Everyone criticises everything, yet at the same time people are apathetic . . . Some people are in despair, others are demoralised . . . Servility is alive and well.'[22] But on holiday in Galicia, she was amazed to find villagers avidly following Rada debates on television, and blue-and-yellow banners flying in the local town. The gossip was all of independence and even the local drunks sank their vodka with the toast 'Glory to Ukraine!' 'They believe in aid from the West,' she wrote. 'How naive!'[23]

By autumn, Kiev was catching up. On 30 September, opening day of the Rada's second session, the city was brought to a halt by its biggest anti-government demonstration yet:

> The meeting opened at three o'clock near the Central Stadium. It began despite the fact that all the roads into Kiev had been closed, with armoured cars at the approaches to the city on the pretext that the soldiers in these military vehicles had come to collect the harvest. Ten huge army trucks were positioned on Repin, my street, alone . . .
>
> At 5.00 p.m. a protest march departed from the stadium along Red Army and Khreshchatyk streets. At least 200,000 (and perhaps 500,000) people in enormously wide, tightly packed columns, singing and yelling slogans – 'Freedom for Ukraine! Down with the CPU!' – moved out on to Lenin Komsomol Square. The column came to a halt near the two monuments of Lenin and people began chanting 'Down with the idol!' Near one of the monuments a ring of defenders took up their positions, among them decorated veterans and, probably, KGB men in disguise. Foreign television correspondents paced about. Police stood in ranks around the second Lenin statue which, in April, had been decorated with a wreath of barbed wire . . .
>
> My feet felt battered and burned from the long hours of standing and walking; my head was buzzing from all the shouting and slogans. Yet we could barely drag ourselves away . . .[24]

Two days later students from Kiev and Lviv universities went on hunger strike, camping out under tents on what had been October Revolution and was now renamed Independence Square. They demanded new parliamentary elections, no military service outside Ukraine, nationalisation of all Party property and the removal of Vitaly Masol, the republic's prime minister. Passers-by, not all of them enthusiastic, watched proceedings from behind rope barriers. 'Some scolded the layabouts,' wrote Pavlychko, 'others passed flowers across the rope, still others said that it wouldn't make any difference, and why were they wrecking their health?'[25] On 10 October the students were joined by eight opposition deputies, and on the 17th, after a protest march by workers from the Arsenal weapons factory, scene of a pro-Bolshevik uprising in 1918, the government caved in. There would be no more military service outside Ukraine, a commission would be created on the nationalisation of Party property, and Masol would go. When the terms were read out in the Rada, deputies applauded.

With the marches and the hunger strikes, Kiev's popular independence movement peaked. 'Remember,' a friend told me, 'that a lot of these demonstrators came in buses from Lviv. We were proud of them, we would support them, definitely. But when they left, that was it.' Rukh was splintering, leaving behind a slew of quarrelsome, disorganised factions. 'The public,' Pavlychko wrote despairingly in December, 'doesn't give a damn ... it demands something to eat, but nothing very special, anything will do.'[26] With her parents on New Year's Eve, she decided that independence was still ten, twenty or even thirty years off. Her four-year-old daughter Bohdana might be the only one to live to see it.

What the Pavlychkos did not realise was that while the opposition lost momentum, the communists themselves were edging towards a change of heart. The shooting of unarmed demonstrators in Vilnius and Riga in January revealed a split between pro-Moscow hardliners, led by First Party Secretary

Stanyslav Hurenko, and an emerging bloc of 'national communists' under Leonid Kravchuk, a former Party ideology chief and
chairman of the Rada. While the Rada condemned Moscow for
its 'inadmissible . . . use of military force', the Party's Central
Committee accused the Lithuanians of extremism and provocation.[27] In March Kravchuk joined forces with the opposition to
vote in an ambiguously worded supplementary question to
Gorbachev's referendum on a new Union Treaty. Gorbachev
asked voters whether they wanted to 'preserve the USSR as a
renewed federation of equal sovereign republics'; Kravchuk
asked if they wanted to be 'part of a Union of Soviet Sovereign
States'. In Galicia, Rukh-run local soviets added a third question
of their own: 'Do you want Ukraine to become an independent
state which independently decides its domestic and foreign
policies?' True to their mixed feelings towards the Soviet Union,
Ukrainians gave all three questions large Yes votes: 71 per cent
for Gorbachev's USSR; 80 per cent for Kravchuk's 'Union of
Sovereign States', and 88 per cent in Galicia for outright
independence. As usual there was a clear split between east and
west, with 85 per cent support for Gorbachev in Donetsk,
compared to 16 per cent in Lviv.[28]

To come to any sort of decision on independence, it was clear,
Ukraine needed a mind-concentrating jolt from outside. On the
6 a.m. television news on Monday 19 August, Moscow delivered
the goods: President Gorbachev had been taken ill, the
announcer said, and a 'State Committee for the State of
Emergency', headed by the defence and interior ministers and
the chief of the KGB, had taken power. At 9 a.m. Kravchuk and
Hurenko were visited by General Varrenikov, head of the Soviet
Union's ground forces and one of the five men who had taken
Gorbachev prisoner in his Crimean dacha the evening before. If
they failed to cooperate, Varrenikov told them, the state of
emergency would be extended to Ukraine – the Ukrainian
government, in other words, would be overthrown.

The choice now facing the Ukrainian communists was as

follows: to throw in their lot with the junta, risking resubordination to Moscow if the coup succeeded and complete loss of credibility if it failed; or to come out for Yeltsin and democracy, leading in all probability to the total collapse of the Soviet Union. Scared of both options, their response was prevarication. At 11 a.m. a delegation of opposition deputies asked Kravchuk to condemn the coup; Kravchuk refused. On Ukrainian television at 4 p.m. he stressed that the state of emergency did not extend to Ukraine, but avoided either condemning or condoning the coup, and asked the public to be 'calm and patient'. On Russian television that evening he was even more equivocal, saying 'what was bound to happen was bound to happen'. He also refused repeated opposition requests for an emergency meeting of the Rada.

All next day, as crowds faced down the tanks round Moscow's White House, the Ukrainians continued to stall. The Rada's twenty-five-member Praesidium voted a panicky resolution defending Ukraine's 'sovereignty', but again failed explicitly to condemn the coup. Despite Rukh calls for a general strike – not carried in the official press – the streets stayed quiet. While Muscovites rushed to the barricades, Kievans sat tight at home, their radios clamped to their ears. 'We were scared,' a friend told me, 'but we were fatalist. We thought – if dictatorship's going to come, it's going to come, and it's no use protesting.'

But the worst was not to happen. Drunk and disorganised, the coup leaders had lost their nerve. On Wednesday, when it was clear the coup was failing, Kravchuk finally climbed off the fence, going on television to demand Gorbachev's release. 'The so-called Emergency Committee,' he intoned, 'no longer exists . . . and actually never existed. This was a deviation from the democratic process, from the constitution and the legal process.' That evening Gorbachev flew back to a revolutionised Moscow, and the coup leaders were put under arrest.

With Soviet power in tatters about their feet, Ukraine's communists now either had to take Ukraine to independence themselves, or wait for the opposition to do it for them. On

Saturday 24 August Kravchuk resigned all his Party posts, and the Rada met in emergency session. At midday the speaker read out the next item of business: Ukrainian independence. Pandemonium broke out, and the speaker announced a twentyminute break. Nationalists raced up to the third floor, communists down to a cinema in the basement. Upstairs the atmosphere was ecstatic; downstairs, deputies were stunned and afraid. 'I don't see why we should be independent,' one communist said, 'we've done nothing wrong!' As the hubbub died First Party Secretary Hurenko stood up and said slowly, in Russian: 'Today we will vote for Ukrainian independence, because if we don't we're in the shit.'[29] When the deputies reassembled, all save one – from Donetsk – obeyed. 'In view of the deadly threat posed to our country on the night of 18th–19th August,' read the final declaration, 'and continuing the thousand-year-old tradition of state-building in Ukraine . . . The Verhovna Rada solemnly proclaims the Independence of Ukraine . . . From now on only the Constitution and laws of Ukraine will be in force on its territory.' A lifeboat for the Communists, a Mayflower to a new world for the nationalists, Ukraine thus floated to freedom.

◆ CHAPTER TEN ◆

Europe or Little Russia?
Ukraina

'What's the meaning of all this silence,
lads?' said Bulba, finally, awaking from his
reverie. 'Just like a couple of monks! Come
along, pull yourselves together! To the devil
with thinking! Put your pipes in your
mouths and light them up, then spur on
your horses and let us fly forward so that no
bird can catch us!'
– *Gogol, 1835*

IN A CONSTRUCTION shed in an industrial suburb of Kiev stands the skeleton of the world's biggest aeroplane. Spanning 260 feet wing-tip to wing-tip, 250 nose to tail, it covers more ground than a football pitch. Its sister-plane was the star of the 1989 Paris Air Show, but funds for this second model ran out long ago, and it will almost certainly never leave the ground. Inside the cockpit, engineers have mocked up control panels in wood, and pasted up posters of birch-forests in place of a windscreen. The plane's name is the Antonov AN-225 *Mriya* – in Ukrainian, the 'Dream'.

The *Mriya* may never fly. But what about that even bigger dream, Ukraine herself? Ukrainians won independence on 24 August 1991 by default. Many had dreamed of independence, but none had expected it; none had prepared for it. Like the *Mriya*, the country was a drawing-board dream sprung to life. Suddenly, Ukrainians had a state, but they had no idea if it could keep to the air, and if it did, where they wanted to fly it.

Ukraine's situation was not unique. The collapse of the Union came as a shock to all the Soviet nationalities, including the Russians themselves. Each newly independent republic had to reshape itself top to bottom. Where Ukraine was worse off than others was in the vague but vital matter of national identity. Elsewhere, the past provided inspiration. The Balts had the interwar years to look back on; the Central Asians had Islam and the nineteenth-century khanates; the Russians, more problematically, a mighty 400 hundred-year-old empire. All Ukrainians could come up with was the Rada débâcle of 1918, the violent, failed heritage of the Cossacks, and even further back, the misty, disputed splendours of Kievan Rus. Split between rival powers for centuries, talking about history at all only emphasised disunity. Poles, Hungarians, Czechs and Balts all knew they were rejoining Europe; Ukrainians were not sure where they belonged or even where they wanted to belong. In academic jargon, they were faced with two tasks – 'state-building' and 'nation-building' – at the same time. The first – the creation of the institutional paraphernalia of statehood – they shared with all the other ex-Soviet nationalities. The second – the creation of a workable idea of what it meant to be a 'Ukrainian' – was theirs alone.

Independence was the result of an unspoken deal between Ukrainian nationalists and the republican Communist Party. In exchange for support for independence, which they lacked the strength to achieve on their own, the nationalists gave the communists control over the new government. In effect, there was no real change of power. In elections held on 1 December 1991 Leonid Kravchuk, former communist number two, became Ukrainian president, setting up his administration in red-carpeted Party headquarters. Vyacheslav Chornovil, the fiery ex-dissident who led the rump of Rukh, won only 23 per cent of the vote, mostly from Galicia. Communist-appointed ministers carried on in the same old posts behind the same old desks, and the Rada turned, without fresh elections, into the new national parliament.

Having spent their lives taking orders from Moscow, few of these people had a clue how to run an independent state. Speaking of his colleagues in the foreign ministry, the first British ambassador to Kiev, Simon Hemans, told me, 'When I arrived in Ukraine it was a brand-new country and didn't know quite how to be one. I was a brand-new ambassador and didn't know quite how to be one either. We learned together.' For many, it was far too late to learn new tricks: despairing Western agency officials dubbed Ukraine's first post-independence finance minister 'cement-head'. Though Ukraine had its liberals and reformers, they were – and still are – few and far between, the result of decades of brain-drain to Moscow. None has ever had the influence of a Balcerowicz in Poland or a Gaidar or Chubais in Russia.

The result was three years of stasis. Caught between Russian-speaking east and nationalist west, whatever direction Kravchuk took Ukraine in he was sure to antagonise one side or the other. 'We thought – we'll go independent and everything will change,' a Rukh deputy told me. 'The communists thought – we'll go independent and everything will stay the same.' A grey-faced bureaucrat who delivered platitudinous speeches in a robotic monotone, Kravchuk's instinctive response was to do nothing at all. Ukraine acquired a new flag and a new national anthem, but no new policies. Initially, Ukrainians interpreted their president's immobility as shrewd caution. Kravchuk's nickname was 'the sly fox'; he didn't need to carry an umbrella, wags said, because he could dodge between the raindrops. Nationalists, keen to idolise the man they credited with leading Ukraine to freedom, excused him on the grounds that 'nation-building' had to come before 'state-building'. It was expecting too much, they argued, for Ukraine to launch reforms before it had even digested independence.

But Kravchuk's mystique soon wore thin. By the end of 1993 Ukraine was reeling under higher inflation than any country anywhere not actually at war. Shops were empty, wages had gone unpaid for months, public services and most factories had collapsed. In new presidential elections in the summer of 1994, brought forward in the face of miners' strikes, Kravchuk was duly booted out in favour of Leonid Kuchma, an ex-missile factory director with a shaky grasp of Ukrainian but a snazzy line in green checked suits, a brisk platform manner – 'I only take questions from real men, and you're not one, so I'm not answering!' he told one (male) reporter – and a reputation for getting things done. As usual, voting patterns split dramatically between west and east. Kuchma won less than 4 per cent of the vote in Galicia, over 80 per cent in Donetsk and Luhansk.

Since Kuchma's election, domestic politics have increasingly become, as in Russia, a matter of behind-the-scenes manoeuvring between shady regional-industrial clans. In the summer of 1996 a bomb exploded under prime minister Pavlo Lazarenko's car. Lazarenko (since sacked) blamed the assassination attempt on 'criminals' angry at his closure of loss-making coal-mines; more likely it was the work of groups disgruntled by the handout of a multi-billion-dollar gas distribution duopoly to allies from his own and the president's home-town of Dnipropetrovsk. A few months later Yevhen Shcherban, parliamentary deputy for Donetsk and another of Ukraine's richest men, was shot dead in Donetsk airport. Nobody has yet been charged with either crime.

Corruption in high places is taken for granted. Eyebrows were scarcely raised when an ex-prime minister, Yuhym Zvyahilsky, fled abroad in November 1994, accused of having pocketed tens of millions of dollars of public money via illegal oil exports. Three years later he reappeared as a Rada deputy, safe from prosecution thanks to a vote for parliamentary immunity. The foreign trade minister shows off snaps of skiing holidays that he could not possibly afford on his salary to fellow-passengers on transatlantic flights; Kravchuk is rumoured to own property in

Switzerland. 'We used to look at Kravchuk's Mercedes,' a friend who had been at university with the president's son told me, 'and we worked out that he would have had to work non-stop for 136 years to pay for it.' Investigative journalism on such issues is scarce, since most national media are controlled by the government. The two nationwide television channels are state-owned and overseen by a presidential appointee; critical news programmes are short-lived. What pluralism there is in the media reflects rivalry between government factions. Scandal only comes to light when they fall out. Other authoritarian hangovers include the bizarre *propiska* system, whereby Ukrainians need official permission to move house, and a gruesome enthusiasm for capital punishment: in 1996 no fewer than 167 criminals were executed, by firing squad, in Ukrainian gaols.

Ukraine's democracy is not perfect; perhaps it is naive to think it could be. But violence and corruption – both worse than in most of Central Europe, but less widespread than in Russia – are only half the story. On the plus side, democracy looks secure. The presidential and parliamentary elections held so far have all been free and – bar some ineffectual manipulation of state-owned television – fair. Parliament is due for re-election in 1998, Kuchma in 1999. A new constitution strikes a sensible balance of power between the two, and will make cancellation of either election hard. Best of all, political infighting has never turned into tanks on the streets – a great point of pride for Ukrainians, who like to contrast their opaque but clubby way of getting things settled with dramatic convulsions in Moscow. 'It's all very Slav – just like getting past some concierge,' says Hemans. 'First you have a shouting match, then you give her five dollars, then you come to an agreement and tell her what a help she's been.' And of course – though Ukrainians will never admit it – it is all far, far better than anything they have had before.

Independent Ukraine's big success story is the ethnic issue. In the winter of 1993, when hyperinflation was at its worst, a leaked CIA report predicted growing ethnic tension between nationalists in the west and Russians in the Donbass and Crimea. Ukraine, the spooks said, might turn into another Yugoslavia. They were wrong. Automatically given full citizenship on independence, Russian-speakers always felt more at home in Ukraine than their cousins elsewhere in the 'near-abroad'. They were never forced to take language tests to get the vote, and Ukrainianisation of the education system has been piecemeal and largely voluntary. The new constitution of 1996 confirmed Ukrainian as the sole 'state language', but also guaranteed continued funding for Russian-language schools. Ethnic Russians have their fair say and more in national politics. A Donbass miners' strike brought forward the elections that threw out Kravchuk, and it was the weight of eastern votes that replaced him with Kuchma. The current presidential administration is packed with men from Russian-speaking Dnipropetrovsk. Roman Waschuk, a Ukrainian-Canadian diplomat, actually fears backlash more from the Ukrainian than the Russian side. The emerging market economy, he thinks, is concentrating wealth in Kiev and the eastern industrial cities, leaving the old west-Ukrainian intelligentsia out in the cold: 'There is an increasing crankiness in the Ukrainian cultural milieu. They think – why doesn't the state help us? Well – the government isn't able to help them. And the guys in the Jeep Cherokees aren't really that interested in nineteenth-century Ukrainian poetry . . .'

Disillusioned Shevchenko-lovers apart, Ukraine's fuzzy sense of national identity has paradoxically turned into something of an advantage. Lviv may be unmistakably Ukrainian and Donetsk unmistakably Russian, but the vast swathe of country in between is neither quite one nor the other. The population is thoroughly mixed – not only in the Bosnian sense that two different peoples have lived there side by side for a long time, but also in the sense that there is no longer any sharp cultural dividing line between them. The typical twenty-something Kievan speaks a mixture of Russian and Ukrainian at work and to his children, Russian to his parents, and Ukrainian to his grandmother down at the dacha at weekends. All share Orthodoxy, a potent force in pulling Russians and Ukrainians together ever since Khmelnytsky signed up to Russian protection at Pereyaslav.

Another potential liability with an unexpected upside is the sheer bloodiness of Ukraine's recent history. Wracked by a century of suffering and upheaval, Ukrainians long for peace and stability. Lvivites may cultivate angry Russophobia, but the man on the Khreshchatyk omnibus's instinct is to stay out of politics at all costs. After all, for several generations any Ukrainian who made himself conspicuous had a good chance of being shot. 'My house is outside the village,' runs a proverb; 'I don't know anything.' If one word sums up the national character, it is 'stolid'. Get into a lift with a Russian, and you will be deep into debate on the theory of capitalism or the existence of God before you reach the top floor. Chat up a Ukrainian, and he will tell you about his mother-in-law's stomach problems and the prospects for next year's tomato crop. All through the hyperinflationary winters of 1993–5, when lights went out and flats froze, Kiev remained eerily quiet. There were grumbles but no big demonstrations, still less riots. '*Eto sytuatsiya*,' people said with a shrug – 'It's the way things are.' Visiting journalists, ghoulishly anticipating Weimar-style disintegration, went home disappointed.

If Ukraine's success story is the ethnic issue, its disaster story is the economy. When the Soviet Union broke up, Ukraine was supposed to be the republic with the best chance of doing well economically. It produced a third of the Union's steel, nearly half its iron ore, over half its sugar. It lacked Russia's oil wells and gold mines, but its workers were well educated and its 'black earth' fabled for fertility. A World Bank report said it had the potential to become one of 'the richest countries in the world'.

By the time I arrived in Ukraine in the winter of 1993,

whoever wrote those words must have been wishing them unsaid. The 'bread-basket of Europe' had turned into an economic basket-case. Financed by the printing presses, the budget deficit stood at 40 per cent of gross domestic product. Prices were doubling every month, and one enterprising factory was using the national currency, the aptly named coupon, for the manufacture of lavatory paper. Save for the lucky few with dollars, the country's savings had been wiped out. Living in Kiev was like watching a textbook lesson on the evils of inflation come to life. All day long, as I sat with my feet propped inside the oven for warmth, old men in once-respectable overcoats dug through the rubbish-bins outside my kitchen window. Sometimes I ran down and shamefacedly persuaded one of them to take some grubby notes: a handful was worth less than a dollar, the lower denominations fractions of a cent. In the outdoor markets, women stood in the snow for hours, holding out a glassful of sunflower seeds, a single garlic bulb or a pathetic handful of plastic bags – all they had to sell. Even with money enough, supplying oneself with basic necessities required wartime determination and ingenuity. Each week, wild rumours swept the city: matches were about to go into shortage – sugar, flour, postage stamps – and everyone raced to stock up. Step on to a trolley-bus with a loaf of bread under your arm, and people crowded round to ask where you had bought it, then leapt out and dashed for the bakery themselves. Flash a dollar note in public and everyone stiffened, as if you had produced a suitcase full of gold or a loaded gun.

That winter and next, the only thing that saved Kiev from starving was its remarkable ability to grow its own food. Most urban Ukrainians are only a generation or two away from the farm, and still have access to their own or relatives' plots of land somewhere in the countryside. Come each spring, seed packets ousted Snickers bars from the oddments stalls in the metro ticket-halls, as Kievans trekked off to dig over their potato-beds and plant out tomatoes. Even people like my scholarly, relatively well-off interpreter Sergey spent their summers growing and bottling industrial quantities of fruit and vegetables, to tide them over the long winters when the shops emptied and prices in the private bazaars shot sky-high. The last time Kiev had emptied in this way was during the war, when 60 per cent of the population fled to the villages to escape Nazi food confiscations.

By the time Kuchma took office in the summer of 1994, it was obvious to the most bone-headed central planner that without drastic changes, Ukraine would turn back into a nation of peasant farmers. With Russia knocking at the door for unpaid oil and gas bills, it might even lose independence. In October the new president accordingly announced a comprehensive economic reform programme. He would liberalise prices and exchange rates, lift restrictions on trade, privatise state-owned firms and cut subsidies to loss-making farms and factories. In return, the International Monetary Fund promised a $1.5 billion loan, most of which was to go on paying Ukraine's fuel debts to Russia.

Kuchma has done much of what he promised, but not all. His great achievement has been to end hyperinflation. In September 1996 the government was able to ditch the loathsome coupon in favour of the 'hryvnya', named after the currency issued by the Rada government of 1918, and by early 1997 price rises were down to around 2 per cent a month. Were it not for the subsidy-guzzling industrial and farming lobbies in parliament, the economy would be turning around faster. As it is, deficit targets have repeatedly been missed, forcing the IMF to hand out aid in grudging monthly dollops. Average wages have doubled to around fifty dollars a month, but overall production – black economy included – is still shrinking.

Privatisation is progressing in fits and starts. Though small businesses – shops, cafés, hairdressers and the like – are out of the government's hands, most were handed over to existing cooperatives, who carry on running them as badly as before. Central Kiev has lots of shiny new supermarkets full of overpriced Twinings tea and Bahlsen biscuits, but in the suburbs and the provinces shops are as drab as ever, brusquely promising

'Milk' or 'Fruit and Vegetables' on the outside, and offering nothing but giant jars of murky brown pickles within. Few big firms have been privatised at all. Every six months or so, the government announces an impressive target of so many thousand companies to be publicly auctioned, in exchange for free privatisation vouchers, by the end of the year. Amid much fanfare, a few semi-bankrupt factories are indeed sold off. Parliament then votes to take 'strategic' firms – meaning anything from steel-mills to bakeries – off the list. The industrial ministries put absurdly high reserve prices on the remainder, and the government's target is quietly shelved. Ukrainians are convinced that the whole process is nothing more than a public relations exercise: one in three have not bothered to pick up their privatisation vouchers.

Farming, potentially Ukraine's economic mainstay, is as backward as ever. Over 80 per cent of agricultural land is state-owned, and so inefficiently farmed that it only produces half the country's total agricultural output. The rest comes from small private plots, planted, hoed and harvested by hand. Go-ahead collective bosses – they do exist – find their efforts to develop new markets stymied by state-owned monopolies over storage, processing and distribution. 'The worst,' a depressed EU consultant told me, 'are the local ministry people. They just want their cut, and give absolutely nothing in return.' Like everywhere else in the ex-Soviet Union, land privatisation is political anathema. Aleksandr Moroz, the powerful speaker of parliament, calls it 'an evil idea'. Collective workers themselves fear – with good reason – that it would simply mean their bosses scooping the farm.

Stagnation in the state sector would matter less if a new private sector were growing to replace it. In Poland, where privatisation is still not complete, small start-up firms got the economy growing soon after inflation had been brought to heel. In Ukraine, it is not happening. To blame is the sheer red tape involved in running a legal private business. A survey by the World Bank's Kiev office lists the problems: Byzantine licensing requirements, a constantly changing tax code, complicated restrictions on exports and foreign exchange. One small knitwear manufacturer found it had to get fourteen different permits to legally export a sock.[1]

The regulations stay because they allow the extraction of bribes. In March 1996, according to another World Bank survey, registering a business cost $175, a fire certificate $40, an export licence $125, a phone line $900 in a smart district of Kiev, $200 or $300 in a suburb.[2] A Spaniard's account of the shenanigans involved in exporting a shipload of sunflower seed, delivered over a seven-dollar beer at one of Kiev's fast-multiplying ex-pat bars, is typical:

> I got my first licence back in November, and lost it when the law changed. I got a second licence – and lost it; a third – and lost it again. Now I'm on my fourth. For all this I've had to get signatures from twenty-five different people. I'm paying one high-up guy's son a salary, and next week somebody else's kids are going on holiday to Spain, out of my pocket.

On top of officials, there is the mafia to be paid off. A basic requirement for anyone going into business in Ukraine is an 'umbrella' – an agreement with one or other local gang whereby they take a percentage of profits in exchange for 'protection'. Even big Western firms are not immune. Coca-Cola posted men in fatigues in its reception area after armed men walked in demanding a 'partnership agreement'; the American lawyers Baker & McKenzie had to pay $2,500 a month to a 'security firm'.

The result, not surprisingly, is that Ukraine has attracted little foreign investment – far less than the Czech Republic or Hungary, both a fifth of its size. The only Western firms with the stomach for doing business in the country tend either to be big multinationals prepared for years of losses, or plucky little one-man bands. Both regularly get ripped off by their Ukrainian partners. The head of the first venture-capital fund into Ukraine says that 'Companies keep three sets of books – one for the taxman, one for the Western investor and one for themselves'. Going to the court is futile: 'You choose your lawyer not for his legal skills, but because he knows the judge.'

For all this, Ukraine really is potentially a rich country. Politicians may burble about the necessity for 'gradualism' or a mythical 'Ukrainian way', but there is no technical reason why it should not have gone about reform as swiftly as Poland or the Baltics. With the arguments on how to make the transition to a market economy long over, Ukraine should in theory be benefiting from others' experience. 'Whatever they need to learn from Europe,' says Roman Szporluk, head of Ukrainian studies at Harvard, 'they can learn from Warsaw and Cracow. But they have a kind of amnesia, a blank spot.' If and when Ukraine does see the light, its economy could pick up fast. Western developing-markets funds would be only too happy to pump money into Ukrainian stocks if a proper stockmarket existed (the Kiev bourse only trades a handful of shares), and black-marketeers tell pollsters they would turn legal if the tax and licensing systems allowed them to do so without going bust.

Politically, none of it will be easy. Kuchma still has central-planning fundamentalists to face down in parliament, and ending subsidies to loss-making factories means throwing people out of work. Re-igniting public enthusiasm for reform will be well-nigh impossible: after years of broken promises, Ukrainians are sick of the word. On the other hand, they have already proved their stoicism in the face of hardship, and an end to subsidies would mean that the government could afford to pay for things such as pensions, heating and hospitals again. Kuchma faces re-election in 1999. If he gets his reform programme moving again quickly, he has a reasonable hope of seeing an improvement in living standards before then.

Sorting out its economy is something Ukraine can do for itself. What it cannot alter is its geography. With a bearish Russia to its east, and an expanding NATO and European Union to its west, Ukraine remains, as ever, a disputed borderland between rival powers. Ukrainians try to view their position as a blessing. They talk about being a 'crossroads', a 'doorway', a 'lever', a 'bridge'. But bridges, in this part of the world, tend to get marched over or blown up. As long as Russia and the West simmer with mutual distrust, to maintain its independence Ukraine has to pull off a fine diplomatic balancing act between the two.

For two years after independence, Ukraine's relations with the West were mired in mutual misunderstanding. Ukrainians resented the blandishments poured on Yeltsin's new democratic Russia, and had not forgotten Bush's insulting 'Chicken Kiev' speech of August 1991, when he warned against 'suicidal nationalism based on ethnic hatred'. The West, for its part, had difficulty taking Ukraine seriously at all. Russophile Sovietologists widely predicted, to Ukrainians' fury, that the country was bound to rejoin Russia before long. It was a tradition – chippiness on the Ukrainian side, ignorant dismissiveness on the West's – that dated back to the Paris peace talks of 1919, when Margolin deplored the crowds of 'urbane and polished' Russian and Polish exiles who undermined Allied support for the Ukrainian government in Galicia.

Relations worsened when the nuclear powers demanded that Ukraine sign up to the START-1 arms reduction treaty, committing it to surrendering the Soviet-inherited nuclear missiles stationed on its soil. Nationalists smelt a plot to neuter their fragile new state: 'If nuclear weapons are such a bad thing,' a Rukh activist asked me, 'why don't you give up yours too?' Utterly failing to appreciate the strength of Western feeling on the issue, Kravchuk allowed his country to turn into a virtual pariah-state before capitulating, in a 'Tripartite Agreement' with Russia and America, in January 1994. Under the agreement, Ukraine promised to ship its warheads to Russia for dismantlement, in exchange for nuclear fuel for its power stations and a Russian commitment to respect 'existing borders'.

With the Tripartite Agreement, Ukraine's diplomatic standing improved dramatically. Seeing Moscow's White House wrecked by shell-fire, Zhirinovsky triumphant in Russian parliamentary elections, and civil war raging in Yugoslavia, America belatedly realised that Ukraine was too important to be left out in the cold. Keeping Russia democratic meant keeping Ukraine independent, and keeping Ukraine independent meant doing something about its economy. In 1994 Ukraine became the fourth-biggest recipient of American aid after Israel, Egypt and Russia itself. The following spring the IMF backed Kuchma's reform programme, and twisted Russia's arm into rescheduling Ukraine's fuel debts, by making a deal an unspoken condition of Russia receiving its own IMF loan. In October 1994 Kuchma was given the full-scale red-carpet treatment on a trip to Washington, and returned the compliment five months later when Clinton made a flattering three-day state visit to Kiev.

Despite campaign promises of closer relations with Russia, Kuchma met the West's overtures with enthusiasm. In his first two and a half years in office he visited Brussels, Bonn, Paris, London, Tokyo, Ottawa, Warsaw and Budapest, many of them several times. He has asked for associate status in the Western European Union, the EU's embryonic defence arm, and is even talking about one day applying for membership of the EU itself. Ukraine is still capable of dreadful diplomatic gaucheries: European relations remain soured by its perverse refusal to close down Chernobyl, and in July 1996 the government chose the day before a meeting on a new multimillion-dollar aid package to send police to occupy the World Bank's Kiev offices. But, for the time being, Ukraine's age-old tightrope-walk has acquired a definite westward tilt.

But much as Kuchma cosies up to Clinton and Kohl, Ukraine's future chiefly hangs, as always, on what happens in Moscow. If the West has had a hard time coming to terms with Ukrainian independence, Russia has hardly begun. 'Russians have still not accepted, deep in their hearts, that Ukraine is a legitimate phenomenon,' says Szporluk. 'Whether your name is Zhirinovsky, Yavlinsky or Gaidar, somewhere in your mind you think that Ukraine is a fake, a phoney.' So far, Russian grouchiness at Ukrainian independence has not translated into action. The Yeltsin government has agreed to respect Ukraine's borders, rescheduled – albeit under pressure from America – Ukraine's fuel debts, and refrained from stirring up trouble in Crimea. Ordinary Russians put all foreign-policy issues at the bottom of their list of concerns in polls, well after crime and jobs.

Poor and demoralised, Russia currently lacks the will or resources for adventures abroad. Even re-integration of Belarus, which would be popular with the majority of Belarussians, but cost Russia billions of dollars at the exchange rate Belarus is demanding, has been put on hold in favour of Russia's own reform programme. The big, unanswerable question is whether, as Russia regains wealth and self-confidence, it will try to rebuild its empire, or come to terms with its loss as Britain and France did fifty years ago. Most doyens of Western opinion are optimistic. Richard Pipes, the hawkish Harvard history professor who served on Reagan's National Security Council and has spent a lifetime denouncing Russian polity through the ages, thinks the national psyche profoundly changed by the loss of the Cold War. 'There's a Turgenev story,' he says. 'A man is lying on the grass in the sun. A milkmaid comes along and gives him bread, milk. He thinks to himself – "Why do we need Constantinople?" Russia is the same about places like Crimea now.'[3] Tim Colton, another Harvard academic and an expert on the Russian army, thinks progress will be bumpy, but broadly in the right direction: 'Ukraine is a pretty secondary issue in Russia now. Governments will alternate between the common-sense approach and taking swipes just for the fun of it.'[4]

If the optimists are wrong, there are plenty of ways Russia could try to force Ukraine back into the fold. Nobody expects tanks to roll into Kiev as they did into Grozny, but Russia could stir up secessionism among ethnic Russians in Crimea and the Donbass, as it did in Moldova, Georgia and Tadzhikistan. Once an alternative westward pipeline through Belarus is completed, it could also cut off Ukraine's oil and gas supplies – both moves to which Ukraine remains very vulnerable until it has sorted out its economy. Russia is already pressurising Ukraine to join more closely in CIS institutions, and squabbles over Sevastopol meant repeated postponement of a Friendship Treaty reconfirming mutual borders, finally signed in May 1997.

Ukrainians fear that the catalyst for renewed Russian aggression will be the eastward expansion of NATO. 'They see themselves as non-aligned,' says Hemans, 'but worry that it'll be hard to stay that way if the West is playing the expand-the-alignment game. They're scared that when the Central Europeans are taken into NATO Russia will – not lash out, but loom all over them. And the West will allow it, because it doesn't really care if Ukraine stays in the Russian half of Europe.' Though Ukraine participates in joint exercises with NATO troops under America's Partnership for Peace programme, and won consultation rights, similar to Russia's, at the Madrid summit of July 1997, there is no serious talk as yet of Ukraine applying to join NATO itself. Any such move would be guaranteed to lash Russia into a bearish fury, and American public opinion is quite unprepared to extend security guarantees to the Ukrainian–Russian border. Even if Kuchma were to ask for inclusion, it is far from certain that he could take his country with him. Poised precariously between Russian-ness and European-ness, Ukrainians simply do not see themselves as part of the West in the same way that Poles, Czechs, Balts and Hungarians do. Senior politicians do talk in private about applying for NATO membership one day, but not until Russia's own relations with the West are far friendlier.

What kind of place will Ukraine be in ten years' time? At worst, it will be a fragile, poverty-stricken buffer-state in a new divide between an introverted West and an aggressive, unstable Russia. At best, it will be a rich, heavyweight democracy in a continent-wide partnership of friendly like-minded states. Given Russia's positive progress so far, and Ukraine's remarkable political and ethnic stability, the latter looks – cross fingers – rather likelier than the former. The West's role should be to slap down any renewed Russian pretensions to empire, and keep on prodding Ukraine, with a mixture of sticks and carrots, towards economic reform.

Forecasting is a mug's game. But without a doubt, Ukrainians now have their best chance ever of building a free and prosperous state of their own. If they succeed *Ukraina* will be a misnomer, for they will have ceased to inhabit a country 'on the edge', a borderland to other nations. In his novella *Taras Bulba*, Gogol has his Cossack hero ride off into the steppe with his two sons to fight the Poles:

> The day was grey and overcast; against this grey the grass stood out a vivid green; the singing and chirping of the birds sounded somehow discordant. After riding some distance they looked behind them: the village appeared to have been swallowed up by the ground until all that could be seen were the two chimneys of their modest cottage and the tops of the trees . . . At last all that remained, sticking up against the sky, was the tall, solitary pole over the well, with a wagon-wheel fastened to the top; and then the flat plain across which they rode rose up like a hill to obscure all else from view.[5]

The steppe has long been put to the plough, and Bulba never existed. But Bulba's dream of an independent Ukraine was real, and has come true. Gogol's story ends in tragedy. One son is captured and broken on the wheel in Warsaw; the other turns traitor, and is killed by his own father. Bulba himself is burned at the stake. This time, the Ukrainians' journey looks like having a happier ending. After a thousand years of one of the bloodiest histories in the world, they surely deserve it.

◆ PART TWO ◆

CHAPTER ELEVEN

The Rise and Fall of the Orange Revolution

ON 24 FEBRUARY 2022, a quarter-century after I wished Ukrainians a happy ending, the worst happened: Russia launched a full-scale invasion. Six weeks in, in mid-April, Russian forces have just retreated from Kyiv's outskirts. Residents who fled have not yet returned, so the streets are eerily empty. At junctions, concrete blocks and 'hedgehogs' made from lengths of steel girder force the few cars into chicanes, and windows are crisscrossed with white tape, like in photos from the Second World War. Here and there a café or small shop has re-opened, but mostly, their owners say, for the sake of having something to do. There are no children anywhere.

Today, I am attending a funeral. The deceased, Sasha, was a 46-year-old gardener employed by the parks department of Bucha, a leafy new commuter town fifteen miles to the capital's north-west. Like hundreds of other civilians in the area, he was not killed in the fighting but murdered. The perpetrators in Sasha's case were a Russian tank crew, who on encountering his silver hatchback fired at it without warning, then drove over it with him inside. He had been on his way home after taking a neighbour to hospital. My new friend Dmytro – in normal life the co-owner with his wife of a language school, now a fixer for foreign journalists – had heard of the case on Facebook, contacted Sasha's widowed mother, and made it his job to give him a decent burial.

It takes all day. First we pick up Sasha's sister, Valentina, from peeling Khrushchev-era housing on one of the main roads out of Kyiv. Like her brother, she used to live in Bucha, where she worked as a nurse in a rehabilitation centre for wounded soldiers. On the first night of the war Russian planes dropped two bombs on the centre. One landed relatively harmlessly in the car park, but the other knocked out its central heating. In their own and volunteers' cars, staff started moving patients to Kyiv, completing the evacuation over a terrifying fortnight. When I ask if the health ministry helped, Valentina smiles properly for the first time: 'The *ministry*? Pah!' The centre is now operating again in temporary premises.

Leaving town, the first checkpoints have an oddly festive air, the podgy sandbags, seaweed-like camo netting and fluttering Ukrainian flags reminiscent of days on the beach. The volunteers manning them – older men, unmistakeably civilian – wave us through with smiles. Further on, the *blokposty* get bigger and more purposeful, with thick walls and pine-log roofs. New-dug ditches to the side of the road, I realise, are not roadworks but trenches. Abruptly, we come to the first of the war damage: a burned-out car, an electronic billboard broken and askew, a petrol station with sun-blinds flapping and fascias hanging loose. A long windowless building – a warehouse maybe – sags in the middle, a tangle of heating ducts exposed. A roller-coaster dip and rise over a half-collapsed concrete bridge, and here the devastation is near-total. One in two buildings are burned out, and nearly all have suffered shell damage – some missing corners, others surreally punctured by large round holes. Rubble and twisted sheets of metal cover the ground. Telephone wires hang in tangles. Hardly an intact window is to be seen, the blank openings toothed with broken glass. As we pass Valentina's rehab centre she puts her hand to her mouth. The complex is hidden by trees, but the entrance lodge – a pretty little nineteenth-century building – is wrecked. She points to a once-smart new housing block opposite, now burned out top to bottom: 'Over there, that's my flat. It was so nice and quiet here, so green. And I could walk to work.' A friend has been into the block and sent her pictures. In the black hole that was once Valentina's living room, I can make out the remains of a chair; in the bathroom, of a washing machine. Sasha, she says, did the bathroom tiling. Abruptly she swipes to another photo, of a small boy proudly holding up two giant mushrooms. 'That's my grandson. He's abroad now. Who knows when I'll see him again.'

Sasha's widowed mother, Ustina, lives in a semi-rural district next to Hostomel military airport, the object of fierce fighting on the first day of the new war. The lanes around its perimeter are lined with ramshackle one-storey cottages, with well-loved gardens and brightly painted metal fences, now lacy with shrapnel holes. Ustina's house, when we reach it, has got off more lightly than most, with only a gatepost down and the front door half off its hinges. We wait in silence – a dog barks, a cock crows – and she comes out carrying a shopping bag containing Sasha's best clothes: grey trousers, a grey acrylic jersey and trainers. We drive to the undertakers, and I wait outside among shiny gravestones (hearts, roses, gold paint) while she chooses a coffin. A woodpecker is drumming somewhere, and the new house opposite has lost its roof, the faux-tile sheeting half torn away like the top of a clumsily opened cardboard box. Valentina joins me and lights a cigarette. After the first few days of bombing, she says, she stopped being scared. 'We got used to it. We're in the hands of God. Who, what, where – it's written.' And in a different tone, doing a bicep curl, 'We're strong! We're Ukraine!'

Our next stop is the morgue, an hour's drive away because all in the region are overflowing. When we arrive three mourning parties are already gathered in the car park, around open coffins sitting on wrought-iron trestles. When the coffins disappear into buses – yellow, with 'Ritual Services' signs taped to the windscreens – four more appear. While Dmytro and Valentina tackle the bureaucracy, I sit with Ustina in the waiting room. Her cottage, it turns out, was earned with a lifetime of manual labour. For twenty years she worked on a collective farm, first milking cows, later with a 'brigade' out in the fields. Then she got a job in a cigarette factory, a lucky move since when a German firm bought it from the state she netted $12,000, with which she was able buy a plot of land and build her *domchik*. Her final job was in a truck repair shop, checking vehicles in and out. She used to have three sons, but two died of cancer, aged thirty-nine and forty-one, probably because they had worked on the Chernobyl clean-up. Sasha was the middle one. 'He always helped. You rang, and he came. He could fix anything – the hot water, the lights.' Valentina was good too; she did her best, 'But that's man's work.' After a two-hour wait Sasha's remains are finally released, from an unrefrigerated long-distance lorry container parked round the back. Unzipping the body bag, it is obvious that there is no hope of re-dressing him. Ustina just slips in the clothes she has brought, laying them on his chest.

The funeral itself is as good as it can be. It is a still, golden evening, and the cemetery is a nice one, with a view of fields and woods. Since Ustina's three daughters-in-law and nine grandchildren and great-grandchildren have all fled to Poland or further, the only other attendees are Sasha's colleagues from the parks department, in their logoed workman's jackets. Amazingly, Dmytro has managed to find a priest – they are working round the clock – who hangs his bag over a railing, quick-changes into a gold cape and sings the liturgy, the words rising and falling to the swing and rattle of an incense burner. Next to Sasha's grave are his brothers' – the cheaper sort, welded metal crosses instead of engraved granite. Ustina walks back and forth between them, fussing with candles or laying her head on the coffin to weep. Further down the path is a shell crater, a reminder that we must all be home before curfew. The gardeners get out their spades, and Dmytro and Valentina coax Ustina back into the car. 'He was so good,' she keeps saying on the way back; 'So good.' This is one bereavement among thousands.

The invasion of 2022 is the latest and by far the most aggressive of three successive attempts by Russian president Vladimir Putin to bring Ukraine to heel. 'The big unanswerable question,' I wrote back in the mid-1990s, 'is whether, as Russia regains wealth and self-confidence, it will try to rebuild its empire or come to terms with its loss.' At the time the signs were rather positive. Yeltsin was friendly, and Russians in general seemed to have other things on their minds. That all changed in 2000, with the coming to power of a short, whey-faced ex-KGB man from St Petersburg. Through the 1990s the presidency had been weak, dependent on oligarchs for campaign funding and on the IMF to keep the lights on and public-sector salaries paid. But the following decade, rising oil prices fuelled an economic boom, freeing Putin to turn on international lenders and tap into what turned out to be a deep well of Russian nationalism.

The West initially gave Putin a cautious welcome, his controlled style a welcome change from Yeltsin's booziness. But relations worsened sharply from 2003 to 2005, during which time popular revolutions brought pro-Western governments to power in Georgia and Kyrgyzstan as well as in Ukraine. They cooled further in April 2008, when a NATO summit in Bucharest held out the promise of future membership to Georgia and Ukraine, though without activating a Membership Action Plan. ('Don't you understand, George?' Putin reportedly raged at Bush, 'Ukraine isn't a real state!') Four months later Russia invaded Georgia, on the pretext of protecting its Ossetian minority. With brilliant timing, the hawkish British Russia-watcher Edward Lucas brought out a book titled *The New Cold War*, detailing Putin's dirty tricks abroad and strangulation of democracy at home. Previously, the title would have seemed overdramatic; now it began to open eyes.

For the Ukrainian side of the story, we need to return to Leonid Kuchma, the missile factory director elected president in 1994. For though Ukraine's Russia problem is of course overwhelmingly due to Russia – plus Western greed and naivety – also to blame is the ghastliness of Ukraine's own post-Soviet ruling class.

It was hoped that given his managerial background, Kuchma would usher in a new era of modernisation and reform. Instead, he brought in Russian-style oligarchy, handing out contracts, subsidies, cheap loans and cut-price privatisation deals to political allies and cronies. The most lucrative of these arrangements was the gas scam, whereby profits from Russian and Turkmen gas sales to Ukraine were diverted, via otherwise wholly unnecessary intermediary companies, into the pockets of Russian, Ukrainian and Turkmen politicians.[1] What emerged from the grab-fest were depleted budgets and a hollowed-out political system, with political parties acting as fronts for semi-criminal businessmen. The best-investigated case from the period is that of ex-prime minister Pavlo Lazarenko, who having milked the gas scam, fell out with Kuchma and fled to California (where he bought a mansion that had once belonged to Eddie Murphy). Prosecuted for money-laundering by the US government, he was sentenced to eight years in gaol, the court hearings turning up $250m hidden in a spider's web of codenamed accounts in Switzerland, Guernsey, Antigua and the Bahamas.

In the bits of the country with most to fight over – the industrial east and the tourism honeypot of Crimea – the scramble for assets descended into outright gangsterism, featuring protection rackets, assassinations, and armed raids on rivals' factories and offices. Most notorious for criminality was Donetsk. Its reigning oligarch, Rinat Akhmetov, rose to vast wealth after senior mobster and fellow-Volga Tatar Akhat Bragin, otherwise known as 'Alik the Greek', was killed, together with five bodyguards, by a large bomb in the city's Shakhtyor football stadium. (His remains, according to legend, identifiable only by his Rolex.)[2] Even among Ukraine's nothing-if-not-tolerant business elite, this raised eyebrows. In his high-rise office in Dnipro (then still Dnipropetrovsk), a property-developer carefully explained to me how post-Soviet wealth creation was a natural process akin to erosion: 'It warms, it cools – then what happens? A rockfall, an avalanche. And of course, the rocks land in some laps, but not in others.' Ordinary Ukrainians, I countered, didn't quite see it that way. He went slightly pink: 'Poor people lack knowledge, they think primitively! They only see the surface, they don't analyse!' When it came to Akhmetov, though, even he thought they might have a point: 'He didn't create, privatise, consolidate – not anything! He just took! Alik the Greek founded a criminal empire. Then the day after he's killed in the stadium' – arms spread, a footballer's strut – 'Akhmetov – the great capitalist!' (Today, Akhmetov is Ukraine's richest man, worth around $6.5 billion, even taking into account the new war's destruction of his steel mills.)[3]

During his second term, won with the help of flagrant media manipulation and the suspiciously convenient death of Rukh leader Vyacheslav Chornovil in a car crash, Kuchma was hamstrung by a spectacular series of scandals. On 2 November 2000 a decapitated body was discovered in woods fifty miles south of Kyiv. It proved to be that of Georgiy Gongadze, young editor of the investigative online paper *Ukrainska Pravda*, who had not been seen since leaving his girlfriend's flat six weeks previously. Next the leader of the Socialist Party, Oleksandr Moroz, announced to parliament that a member of Kuchma's security detail, ex-KGB man Major Mykola Melnychenko, had secretly recorded the president's private conversations, using a digital recorder hidden inside an office sofa. Melnychenko having fled to a secret location in Europe, Moroz went on, it was now his patriotic duty to play an excerpt – whereupon voices similar to those of Kuchma and his interior minister, Yury Kravchenko, were heard discussing Gongadze's disposal. 'The Chechens,' growled Kuchma, 'should kidnap him, drag him off to Chechnya by his dick, demand a ransom! Take him there; strip him, the fucker; leave him without his trousers on!' In reply, Kravchenko assured the president that he was working on the problem and had just the men for the job, who would 'do whatever you want'.

Over the next two years, Melnychenko released the Kuchmagate tapes bit by tantalising bit. In one, Kuchma was heard ordering the head of the tax inspectorate to help him rig the 1999 presidential vote:

> You should get together all your fucking tax inspectors ... and warn them: those who lose the elections in their districts will not work after the elections ... You should sit down with every [collective-farm] head and fucking tell them – either you sit in fucking jail – because I've got more compromising material on you than anyone else – or you produce some votes.[4]

In others, he demanded $45m in campaign funding from the boss of a state-owned gas intermediary, and agreed with the head of the state arms export agency secretly to sell advanced anti-aircraft systems to Saddam Hussein's Iraq. Though Kuchma conceded that the voice on the recordings was his, he claimed that the conversations themselves were cut-and-paste fakes. Western experts declared them genuine, but were hampered by Melnychenko's refusal to release the recordings in their entirety.[5] Either way, by 2002 Kuchma's international reputation had become so toxic that NATO's Secretary General specifically asked him not to attend a summit celebrating the admittance of seven new Baltic and Central European members. Kuchma turned up anyway, telling an interviewer that otherwise, 'people would have said "Kuchma didn't come because he's guilty. He's afraid to come and look his partners in the eye."'[6] At NATO summits, representatives are seated according to their countries' alphabetical order, putting Ukraine, in the normal course of things, next to the United Kingdom and the United States. This time, the organisers switched the country names into French, banishing Kuchma to the lower end of the table.

The scandals didn't topple him, but they weakened him sufficiently so that in 2004, instead of trying to change the constitution so as to run for a third term, he picked a loyal successor. The man he chose, Viktor Yanukovich, had risen from a dirt-poor background in a miserable Donbass steel town to become governor of Donetsk, on the way serving two prison terms, one for assault, the other allegedly for rape (the court records have disappeared). He was probably also linked to the KGB, there being no other way an ex-convict could have got Communist Party membership. Going to meet him, in the words of former British ambassador Roland Smith, was 'a bit like going to meet Al Capone. There was a roomful of burly men in dark glasses and him. He knew enough to be reasonably polite, but his story was "We know how to run this part of Ukraine. We don't need any advice from you. Hope you enjoy your visit."'

Yanukovich's main rival, and the great hope of Ukraine's liberals and the West, was a much more presentable figure, Viktor Yushchenko. The clever, good-looking son of provincial teachers, he had built a steady career in Soviet-era banking before being made chairman of the central bank by President Kravchuk, in which role he married a Ukrainian-American former State Department official and brought an end to hyper-inflation. Kuchma briefly made him prime minister, so as to woo the IMF. Friendly and famously disorganised, he was loved by journalists for letting interviews spill way over their allotted time, and chided by his staff for always running late.

The campaign was vicious. Touring the regions, Yushchenko would arrive in a town to find his speaking venue closed on the grounds of fire hazard, or subject to mysterious power outage. At one point a travelling circus preceded him from place to place, occupying the squares where his supporters had planned rallies.[7] State-controlled television either ignored him, or derided him as 'Bushchenko', lackey of the US. Claiming to have found explosives in a raid on the headquarters of student pro-democracy group Pora! ('It's time!'), the police arrested dozens of Pora! members, releasing them again without charge or explanation after a few days in custody. In the pretty cathedral city of Chernihiv, a fake bomb was planted in an activist's flat, justifying more raids, and in Lviv, the offices of the pro-Yushchenko newspaper *Postup* burned down in an arson attack. Putin, by then four years in power, was closely involved on the Kuchma/Yanukovich side from the beginning, sending in a team of experienced Kremlin 'political technologists', and making seven trips to Ukraine himself. The point man for the operation was Dmitri Medvedev, then head of the presidential administration, later prime minister and place-holder president. (And when the 2022 war began, head of Russia's Security Council.)

In the early hours of 6 September 2004, seven weeks before the first round of the elections, the dirty tricks hit a whole new level when Yushchenko was taken violently ill on his way home from supper with the head and deputy-head of the Ukrainian security service. The next day, the then British ambassador Robert Brinkley remembers, Yushchenko's staff

> called an urgent meeting with all the Western ambassadors, and said 'Yushchenko's been poisoned'. I thought – No, it's just another gimmick. There had been quite a lot of this, trying to get the international community on side. But I couldn't have been more wrong. He nearly died. He was flown to a clinic in Vienna, where they discovered that it was pure dioxin – not an industrial by-product: something made in a lab, deliberately. We still don't know whether it was Ukrainians or Russians who did it.[8]

A fortnight later, Yushchenko discharged himself from hospital and went back on the stump, caked in make-up to disguise hideous skin damage, and kept upright by painkillers fed intravenously via a portable drip. Before speaking, he explained later, 'I disconnected it, so the public wouldn't see me with it. I had about twenty minutes, no more. I knew that after twenty-two, twenty-three minutes I would pass out.'[9]

The first round of the elections went ahead as scheduled on 31 October. The official results, announced a whole ten days later, put Yushchenko very narrowly ahead. On the eve of the second round, what appeared to be another assassination attempt was foiled when police found a car full of plastic explosives parked outside Yushchenko's Kyiv campaign headquarters. Undeterred by Yushchenko's by now immense popularity, or by platoons of indignant international election observers, Kuchma and Yanukovich rigged the second round too, arranging crude ballot-stuffing and multiple absentee voting in the pliant east and south. At dozens of polling stations, opposition observers were attacked when they made complaints, either by groups of thugs as the police stood by, or by the police themselves. In Donetsk, turnout was declared to have skyrocketed to 96 per cent; in Luhansk, to 90 per cent. Independent exit polls had given Yushchenko an eleven-point lead; the official result put Yanukovich three points ahead. Putin sent his congratulations on the Monday morning, before it had even been announced.

This blatant electoral robbery sparked the mass protests that became known as the Orange Revolution, after Yushchenko's campaign colour. On the Monday morning after the second-round poll, the opposition called a rally in Kyiv's Independence Square – known simply as 'the Square' or Maidan. That day, numbers were estimated at 200,000–300,000, and within twenty-four hours the protest had turned into a well-organised camp, occupying the whole of the Maidan and spilling over into surrounding streets. Numbers swelled as more supporters arrived from the west of the country, and by the Saturday reached over half a million. Three large public buildings – the Trades Union Building on the Maidan itself,

Ukraine House (once a Lenin museum) on next-door European Square, and city hall on Khreshchatyk – were peacefully
taken over and used as collecting points for donated mat-
tresses, food and clothing.

Like the even bigger Maidan protests nine years later, the
Orange Revolution was an expression not just of party political allegiance, but of frustration with dreadful government
and insult at being taken for fools. Though the government
dominated mainstream media (hence the Orange slogan 'Kill
the TV within yourself'), the protestors were far nimbler
and funnier on the internet and social networks, circulating
Yanukovich jokes – 'Yanekdoty' – prank videos, satirical ani-
mations and video games. Times and locations of rallies were
communicated by text, as were reminders that no drinking
was tolerated on the Maidan, and that demonstrators should
not react to provocations. A sound stage hosted the country's
best-known pop and rock groups, and the revolution's slogan
Razom nas bahoto – 'Together we are many!' – was turned
into a rap and released on MP3. Jackets embroidered with the
words 'Made in the USA' mocked Yanukovich's claim that
the protests were paid for and organised by the West. Laughs
were had by all when Yanukovich's wife, beret askew, made
an almost pathetically illiterate speech to a rally in Donetsk,
in which she claimed that in Kyiv she'd seen protestors eating
their way through 'nightmare mountains' of drug-injected
'orange oranges', leading to a mass outbreak of meningitis.
Perhaps the best moment in what Ukrainians now look back
on as a gentle and innocent revolution was when the sign-
language interpreter on state television's evening news told
her deaf audience not to believe a word that the Electoral
Committee said, that Yushchenko was their rightful president, and that she was ashamed of having told them lies
before and wouldn't do so any more.

Despite all the fun, the Orange Revolution almost ended
in violence. 'From day to day,' remembers Brinkley, 'one
didn't know how things were going to work out. There

were coachloads of thuggish-looking men parked up by the Caves Monastery, near my house. It was obvious that they were awaiting orders to go and beat people up.' Interior ministry troops mustered in the suburbs, as did forty thousand Donetsk miners outside the main railway station. Though Kuchma later claimed the credit for turning them back, another version of events has it that he ordered the head of the security service, Ihor Smeshko, to attack, and that Smeshko disobeyed.

What is certainly true is that at 2 a.m. on Wednesday 24 November Kuchma made an agitated call to Polish president Alexander Kwasniewski, who immediately flew to Kyiv to broker talks. On the Friday, under intense diplomatic pressure from the West, Kuchma and Yanukovich finally climbed down, agreeing that the legality of the elections be referred to Ukraine's Supreme Court. On 26 December the second round of the elections was run again, Yushchenko winning by a comfortable 8 per cent margin. Checking out of his hotel, one of Putin's 'technologists' wrapped an orange scarf around his neck for camouflage before making his way through wildly celebrating crowds to the airport.[10]

The Orange Revolution raised enormous hopes. 'Yushchenko was treated like a Messiah,' remembers Brinkley. 'People were euphoric; their feet really left the ground.' For a few months things seemed to go well. His martyrdom for democracy etched on his very features, Yushchenko did a victory lap of Western capitals. In Washington, Congressmen cheered him with the same three-beat 'Yush-chenk-KO!' his supporters had chanted on the Maidan. One of Kuchma's most notorious insider privatisations – of Kryvorizhstal, a Zaporozhiye steelmaker – was reversed. Earlier sold to Kuchma's son-in-law, Viktor Pinchuk, for a fraction of its market price, the company was renationalised and resold to India's Mittal Steel for six times more. The proceeds, for once, actually went into the state budget.

But soon, things started to fall apart – in particular, Yushchenko's relationship with his prime minister, Yuliya Tymoshenko. Nicknamed the 'Gas Princess', Tymoshenko was as striking a figure as the president – beautiful and immaculately dressed, with ash-blonde hair coiled round her head in a trademark plait. She and her husband made their first money in Dnipro, selling bootlegged video cassettes (pornographic, said the unkind), and went on to head the first of the gas-importing intermediaries, under the patronage of Lazarenko. After Lazarenko fled abroad with his millions, Tymoshenko reinvented herself as a pro-democracy opposition leader, her credibility greatly boosted by forty-two days spent in custody on tax-fraud charges after she too fell out with Kuchma. In her new guise, she charmed her way into the hearts of the Western foreign policy establishment. Invited to meet her for dinner, British ambassador Roland Smith was surprised to find that she had booked the whole restaurant:

> The only people there were a dozen waiters, an orchestra, and us. I should have asked, 'If you're so anti-corruption, how come you've got the money to hire this whole restaurant, and have all those cars with smoked-glass windows outside?' But she isn't, or isn't only, an oligarch in a skirt. I was gobsmacked by how critical she was of Kuchma – this was when Kuchma was president, and she was a deputy prime minister in Yushchenko's government. And she talked about corruption in exactly the same way I would have done. Basically, I wanted to believe her – she was the best hope I could see. Maybe she just knew how to talk to Westerners, but at least that was something. Not everybody did.[11]

Within months, she and Yushchenko fell out, and in September 2005 Yushchenko dismissed the entire government. The split was partly over policy – Tymoshenko a free-spending populist, Yushchenko an economic conservative. But mostly it was simply a personality clash. The rudderless Rada made a spectacle of itself, with punch-ups in the chamber, and parliamentary elections the following year produced the usual mish-mash of small personality-based parties, independents available for hire, and out-and-out criminals for whom the chief attraction of a political career was immunity from prosecution. All through that spring and summer, Ukraine had no government at all.

Yanukovich, meanwhile, tried to clean up the image of his Party of the Regions. His chief backer, Akhmetov, recommended the Washington lobbyist Paul Manafort (whose client list already featured Ferdinand Marcos and Jonas Savimbi), for what a leaked US diplomatic cable called 'an extreme makeover effort'. Yanukovich also started bribing Rada members onside – offering, according to Tymoshenko, $1m–$1.5m per switch.[12] In July 2006, while Yushchenko was away on one of his regular trips to Switzerland for medical treatment, Yanukovich scored a coup by persuading Socialist Party leader Moroz to come over to him in exchange for speakership of the Rada. On his return, Yushchenko finally did the unthinkable and endorsed Yanukovich as prime minister. Predictably, they immediately fell out. A snap parliamentary election was called and Tymoshenko came in again, whereupon she and Yushchenko resumed feuding where they had left off.

Amid the mess, almost nothing got done. Still ill and chronically disorganised, Yushchenko let reforms founder, wasting energy on second-order issues such as memorialisation of the Great Famine, now termed the 'terror-hunger' or Holodomor.[13] After Kryvorizhstal, no more insider privatisations of the Kuchma years were reversed. Pinchuk was able to hang onto Nikopol Ferroalloy, another steelmaker dubiously acquired during his father-in-law's presidency.[14] Dmitri Firtash, Putin-connected owner of the latest of the gas-scam intermediaries, continued operating as normal – aided, it was rumoured, by Yushchenko's brother.[15] The president's teenage son partied his way into the tabloids, double-parking his

BMW outside Kyiv nightclubs, flashing a platinum iPhone and claiming trademark ownership over Orange Revolution logos. (Less predictably, Tymoshenko's daughter married a middle-aged Yorkshire biker, frontman of a band called the Death Valley Screamers.) None of the high-profile crimes of the Kuchma years was properly investigated, not least Yushchenko's own poisoning.

The final nail in the coffin of the Orange Revolution was the 2010 presidential election, which Yanukovich won, reasonably fairly, in a narrow run-off against Tymoshenko, who was disadvantaged by having been head of government during the 2008–9 recession. As usual the country split, with Kyiv and the west going to Tymoshenko, and the east to Yanukovich. So thoroughly did Yushchenko loathe Tymoshenko by this stage that he tacitly connived in her defeat. Kicked out himself in the first round with only 5 per cent of the vote, he promptly approved an alteration to the Electoral Law that made ballot-rigging easier, and made the Nazi-sponsored OUN leader Stepan Bandera a posthumous Hero of Ukraine – a move that outraged and galvanised Yanukovich's ethnic-Russian base in the east. In return Yushchenko was granted continued use of an official residence, which he only quit four years later.[16]

President at last, Yanukovich grabbed at power and money with the avidity of a mobster who knows that he too may be bumped off at any minute. His first move, in what amounted to a constitutional coup, was to give himself greatly increased control of the judiciary, completely subordinating it to the executive. His second was to begin criminal proceedings against Tymoshenko. Charged with 'abuse of office' over a gas deal with Russia, in October 2011 she was fined $188m and sentenced to seven years in prison, where she was joined by thirteen of her former officials. For the West she was a political prisoner; many Ukrainians quietly muttered that she was in the right place for the wrong reasons. Police, army and the security services were all brought firmly under the president's hand, several Russian appointees being issued with Ukrainian passports for the purpose.[17]

Yanukovich also started making himself seriously wealthy. The basic mechanisms – the gas scam, insider privatisations, overvalued government procurement contracts, cheap loans from state-owned banks – remained the same as under Kuchma. But he took a bigger slice and ran the scams directly, instead of balancing competing clans. The proceeds went to a tight group of associates known as 'the Family'. Yanukovich's dentist son Oleksandr became an overnight multi-millionaire, valued by *Forbes*, prior to his father's fall, at $510m. It has been calculated that just taking into account tax and excise fraud, overpriced infrastructure projects and the gas scam, the Family sucked $8 billion–$10 billion out of the state budget annually. Altogether, during the four years of Yanukovich's presidency, as much as $100 billion may have been stolen, most of which went abroad.[18]

Best symbol of Yanukovich's reign is Mezhihoriya, the private home he built himself just outside Kyiv. When I visit, in April 2014, he has just fled the country and it has been thrown open to the public. Walking through the gates is like stepping inside a crazed lottery-winner's head. The grounds – once those of a monastery – are enormous, spread over a hillside overlooking the Dnipro River. Amid flowerbeds and ornamental lakes, a variety of buildings are dotted about, connected by winding pink paths. Wandering round, it takes a bit of time to work out what's what. This one – ropework railings, Art Nouveau windows, an umbrella-stand made out of crossed oars – seems to be a barbecue lodge. That one – boulders, a glass dome, a mosaic-lined plunge pool – is a spa. There are rockeries, rotundas, wrought-iron bridges picked out in gold, a giant hexagonal cage – for pet squirrels, a fellow-visitor tells me – and a full-sized mock-up of a classical ruin. In one direction the gardens morph into a golf course; in the other, into an orchard, high-tech glasshouses and a private zoo. Next to one enclosure, children are feeding grass to an antelope; by another, a woman crouches to admire a pair of Japanese cranes.

The tour of the vaguely chalet-style main house lasts two and a half hours. We take in a cocktail bar; a three-lane bowling alley; a gym and boxing ring; indoor tennis courts; a swimming pool with an artificial waterfall; a basement rifle range; a conservatory containing palms and a stuffed lion; a relaxation room lined with stalactites made of salt crystal; a neo-Gothic cinema featuring reproduction suits of armour; two dining rooms – one Tudor, the other Rococo; two billiard rooms and an Orthodox chapel. I tick off five white pianos before losing count. Everything that can be is tasselled, gilded, engraved, inlaid or otherwise embellished. The grand finale is Yanukovich's bedroom suite, one of a matching pair he shared with his girlfriend, reportedly the sister of his cook. In his bathroom, we all take photographs of each other sitting on the presidential toilet – not, contrary to legend, actually gold-plated.

Back in Kyiv, the National Gallery is displaying some of Mezhihoriya's contents. Bemused Ukrainians wander from room to room in silence, taking photos on their mobile phones: of inlaid cabinets, candelabra, gold-plated caviar sets, a dried crocodile skin, a carved mammoth tusk and a complete Hermes dinner service, still in its orange boxes. Showroom stickers identify some of the furniture as from Baldi – a Florentine firm which boasts, I discover from its website, of being able to veneer a Bechstein grand with malachite, or carve a bathtub out of rock crystal. There is a whole roomful of Yanukovich portraits – in beaten metal, dried beans, tapestry, porcelain and amber. An oil painting shows his prosecutor-general, Viktor Pshonka, as Napoleon on the field of Borodino, in tight white breeches and thigh-length boots. There's another of Pshonka's wife as Empress Elizabeth, bottle blonde and showing lots of bust. When photos of it all appear on the internet, Ukrainians coin a new word for the mixture of hilarity and dismay they produce – it's called 'being Pshonked'.

Less entertaining is how much it cost. Two of Yanukovich's Baldi tables (one sporting winged lions, the other pointy-breasted goddesses) retail, the firm says, for £75,895 and £36,200. For two of several giant cut-glass urns on display it quotes £28,315 and £17,490. A large reproduction ormolu clock sports a cream auction tag, identifying it as Lot 177 in Christie's 'Opulent Eye' sale, held at the firm's South Kensington showrooms in September 2013. It sold, according to Christie's website, for £20,000. Further on, another Christie's tag hangs from the ankle of one of a set of four fake-bronze neo-classical statues – £265,875. From earlier sales came an Aivazovsky seascape (June 2008; £301,250), and a radically out of place Picasso vase (*Les Danseurs*, June 2012; £265,250). The other London auction houses have not neglected the Ukrainian kleptocrat market either. *Maples at Abramtsevo*, by Cézanne imitator Pyotr Konchalovsky, fetched £240,000 at Sotheby's in May 2005. A large turn-of-the-century history painting, *Jesus and the Woman Taken in Adultery*, by Vasiliy Polyenov, went for £4.07m at Bonhams in November 2011. Aptly, the English version of its title is 'Let he who is without sin, cast the first stone'.

Not everything, the exhibition's curator explains, was bought by Yanukovich himself. Many of the items were bribes from fellow politicians or businessmen: 'I give you a million-dollar picture today, you give me a good contract tomorrow.' She and her colleagues know who gave what, having found the details among the president's abandoned paperwork. But they don't want to name names, for fear of 'problems for our museum'. What about Firtash and Pinchuk? 'I don't remember.' A rare sixteenth-century book was a present from the head of the tax office, and 'a lot', she lets slip, came from Akhmetov. One of the few covetable objects on view, a large Bronze Age terracotta jar painted with a bold design of interlocking spirals, was given by Yushchenko. The curator smiles at my surprise: 'Of course. They all did it. And Yushchenko loves archaeology – he's got a whole museum at home.' What's the most valuable object here? She leads me back to the room full of presidential portraits. Among them, slouched on a velvet draped chair, sits a life-size dummy of the president, dressed in a Formula One driver's suit. 'Him. But not the most valuable. The most *expensive*.'

◆ CHAPTER TWELVE ◆

The Maidan

In the autumn of 2013, Mezhihoriya was still hidden behind its security fence. Though known to all as grotesquely corrupt, Yanukovich seemed firmly in charge. The economy had recovered slightly from the 2008–9 crash, the media were cowed (though less so than in Russia), and the opposition still dispirited by the failure of the Orange Revolution. The next potential flashpoint was assumed to be the presidential election due in 2015.

What changed all that, to near-universal astonishment, was a trade agreement. Ever since independence, Ukraine's relations with Russia had been scratchy, soured by endless squabbles over gas payments and the Black Sea Fleet. They worsened dramatically after the Orange Revolution, as Yushchenko tried to tip Ukraine westwards, pleading with NATO for a Membership Action Plan, and opening negotiations on a wide-ranging trade deal, known as an Association Agreement, with the EU. Campaigning for the presidency in 2010, Yanukovich promised to 'rebalance' Ukraine's foreign relations: Ukraine was to be a 'non-bloc state', neither in one camp nor the other. This chimed with public opinion, which was in favour of EU membership but split on NATO.

As president, he let negotiations over the Association Agreement – seen as a prelude to full EU membership – continue. It was popular with the public – the prospect of visa-free travel

257

a major draw – and it gave him leverage over the Kremlin, which was trying to put together its own free-trade area, the 'Eurasian Economic Union'. A sticking point was the EU's insistence that Tymoshenko be let out of gaol. By October 2013 the two sides were close to a compromise – Tymoshenko would be released, but despatched for medical treatment to Germany – and the Agreement seemed set to go ahead. Putin, however, was having none of it. Threatening a wider trade war, he slapped restrictions on Ukrainian food exports, holding up hundreds of Ukrainian trucks and goods wagons at the Russian border. On 21 November, a week before a scheduled signing ceremony at an EU summit in Vilnius, Yanukovich caved in, announcing that the Agreement would not go ahead for 'national security reasons', and that Ukraine was resuming talks with Russia.

Kyivans were unsurprised by the U-turn, but bitterly disappointed. What mattered was not so much the Association Agreement itself – the content of which was deadly dull and nobody understood – as the sense of doors closing, and hope for change receding. Typically fatalistic was the novelist Andrei Kurkov. 'Closer ties with Europe,' he wrote in his diary on hearing the news, 'have been abandoned. Now, we are going to love Russia again.' Unable to concentrate on work, he headed to his local café and ordered a restorative cognac: 'It didn't make me feel any better.' Trawling for distraction on the internet, he noted that a Swiss traveller had just ridden into Tbilisi on a camel, 'an animal from which he has not been separated for more than thirty years . . . Here, everything is simpler and sadder. Once again, we have had our future taken away from us.'[1]

Others were more proactive. The first to post a Facebook appeal for demonstrators to gather at the Maidan was Mustafa Nayem, a 32-year-old, Kabul-born journalist on the same online paper, *Ukrainska Pravda*, which Georgiy Gongadze had founded, and co-leader of the youth group Pora! That first evening, only a few dozen students assembled, sheltering from the rain under a tarpaulin. As one remembers,

> We all knew about Nayem's post, and were waiting to see what would happen. Then on Twitter I saw a photo of three guys standing under the statues. One was a friend. So I went along, and there were five of us, and we stood discussing what we wanted for our city. We sent out more invitations on Facebook, and the next day there were two hundred people. Why did they come? It was like a wave. First you felt angry, then sad. Then you understood that you had to take steps, do something. That's how I was motivated.[2]

Though the protests grew substantially over the next few days (to around 100,000 on the first Sunday, 24 November), what turned them into a mass movement was the government's clumsy use of violence. At 4 a.m. on Saturday the 30th, the police moved in with riot sticks, diving into tents full of dozing young people and indiscriminately beating them up. One group of students was cornered in a dead-end street, where they sang the national anthem as police dragged them into vans. Another ran uphill to St Michael's of the Golden Domes, whose monks let them into the courtyard and helped them barricade the gates. (Demolished by Stalin, the monastery was rebuilt in exact replica in the late 1990s. Part, vitally, of the Kyiv rather than the pro-Putin Moscow Patriarchate of the Orthodox Church, it subsequently served as a protestors' first-aid centre and hostel.)

The brutality of the attack mobilised people who had previously only grumbled from the sidelines. In the words of a forty-something ex-banker friend, 'It was the police beating up the students that got me involved initially. I was really enraged – first of all because it was so stupid. It was a cold night, and there were only a few dozen of them. If the police had left them alone they would probably have dispersed, as had happened before. Basically, Yanukovich decided to spit in the face of the nation. It was so idiotic, and so unprovoked.'

The following morning, Sunday 1 December, he decided to

join the protestors – the first time he had done so since the Orange Revolution. Borrowing an EU flag, he walked down to the Bessarabsky covered market:

> I looked up Shevchenko Boulevard – it was full of people, as far as the eye could see. And along Khreshchatyk – full of people. There must have been a million at least. I was thrilled. When you are part of a demo like that you feel you can do anything. The atmosphere was very peaceful. People were extra polite towards each other, careful not to step on each other's feet . . . It was a wonderful feeling – almost like going to church, though I'm not a believer. You went to feel better, to make yourself better. It didn't matter who you were, or what language you spoke; you knew that everyone there was a good person. Whatever bad things they had done in life, being on the Maidan redeemed them.[3]

From then on, the Maidan convulsed the nation. Initiated by students and young professionals, it grew to encompass young and old, rich and poor, and every region of the country. Even Donetsk had its own mini-Maidan, a few hundred demonstrators braving harassment from police and pro-Russian thugs. For the hundreds of thousands who participated, it was a life-changing experience. As a young volunteer at one of the starburst of new charities the movement spawned told me, 'Before the Maidan, I was totally different. You make new friends, and other people stop being friends. You learn new values. You start talking to people who you'd never have had anything to do with before, because they support you, even if perhaps your own family doesn't.' A year on, she still felt a rush of emotion every time she got out at the Khreshchatyk metro stop: 'It has a particular smell; I don't know what of. But it all comes back, and my heart starts racing.' A colleague chipped in; for her the trigger was woodsmoke: 'When you got home after a night on the Maidan your clothes would be full of it, from the cooking fires.' Like almost everyone I interviewed on the subject, they wiped away tears as they spoke.

*

Bounded by barricades, the protests initially had a music festival air. On the Maidan itself, canvas tents filled the area
round the fountains where in normal times old men gather
to play chess. Facing the Stalinist Ukraina Hotel, a covered
sound stage hosted a round-the-clock stream of speakers and
performers. Ruslana, winner of the 2004 Eurovision Song
Contest, appeared night after night, leading the crowds in the
national anthem. So did rock bands, folk singers, children's
choirs, Cossack drummers and a seemingly endless procession of poets. Priests – Orthodox and Uniate together – told
Yanukovich to repent of his crimes, and Ukrainians in general to repent of paying and taking bribes. Performances were
punctuated with shouts of 'It's time!', 'Down with the criminal gang!' and 'Glory to Ukraine!'; the roared reply: 'Glory to
the heroes!' In the Trades Union Building, an 'Open University' popped up, at which lecturers from the most progressive
of Kyiv's universities, the Mohyla Academy, gave media
training and held seminars on economic and constitutional
reform. Outside city hall, students from the Convervatoire
took turns on a blue-and-yellow-painted upright piano,
while inside, a mass of volunteers prepared and distributed
hot drinks and sandwiches, or handed out sleeping bags and
winter clothing.

In contrast with the Orange Revolution, politicians made
little of the running. Ukrainian flags, rather than party leaders' faces, waved above the crowd, and though opposition
MPs spoke regularly from the stage, they got a lukewarm
reception: 'They aren't with us in the tents,' a 'Cossack' protestor told an interviewer. 'Look at them all shouting today
– "We're one, we're one!" But once they've got their noses in
the trough, they've forgotten all about it.'[4] Only 8 per cent of
participants, according to pollsters, attended as part of an organised group, or in response to an appeal by a political party.

With the approach of New Year, the atmosphere began to
harden. On 8 December protestors threw a lasso around the

neck of the Lenin statue at the end of Khreshchatyk, pulling it to the ground and smashing it to pieces with sledgehammers. Long gone in the west of the country, Lenins now started tumbling in the central provinces, scandalising the east. ('It was horrid,' a Donetsk teacher told me later, 'seeing part of Lenin's head, or a finger, for sale on the internet. Uncultured.') In the small hours of 11 December, when freezing temperatures had thinned protestor numbers, the security services mustered for a second attempt to clear the area. News of impending attack spread via Facebook and the bells of St Michael's, which rang the alarm from 4 a.m. until dawn. Alerted by the world's oldest and newest communications technologies, tens of thousands of Kyivans immediately headed for the Maidan, separating and immobilising the police squads, which eventually retreated.

As well as raiding activist and opposition-party offices and making hundreds of arrests, the authorities increasingly resorted to extra-judicial violence. They seemed especially riled by the 'Avtomaidan', a network of car-owners who used their vehicles to picket government buildings. After a thousand-strong motorcade descended on Yanukovich's Mezhihoriya on 29 December, hundreds of drivers were stripped of their licences, or woke to find their cars vandalised. Later the Avtomaidan's chief spokesman was kidnapped and held for a week, during which time he was beaten into 'confessing' that he was a CIA spy, before being dumped in woods minus part of an ear. Similarly targeted was the radical activist Tetyana Chornovol, famous for climbing into the Mezhihoriya grounds and posting photographs of them on the internet. On 25 December she was driving into the city when a Porsche SUV forced her off the road. Several men jumped out, dragged her out of her car, and beat her savagely about the head before leaving her for dead in a ditch. Photographs of her pulped face shocked the nation.

Encouraged by Putin, on 16 January Yanukovich rammed a 'dictatorship law' through parliament, passed on a chaotic show of hands. Modelled on repressive measures Putin had taken against his own pro-democracy demonstrators two years earlier, it made illegal, among many other things, convoys of more than five cars, the erection of tents without police permission, and the wearing of hard hats during public demonstrations. The protestors responded by donning kitchen colanders. Nor did they take any notice when the prime minister resigned and the dictatorship laws were toned down: it was not enough, and politicians did not speak for the people.

On the 19th police used water cannon. It was Epiphany, traditionally celebrated with an icy dip in the Dnipro, and the soaked protestors jeered 'Baptism!' in reply. From now on, the protests turned into near-nightly riots: police firing rubber bullets, stun grenades and tear gas; protestors replying with cobbles, fireworks and petrol bombs. Instead of sweets and tea, volunteers were asked to bring pieces of forked wood and leather for catapults, and condoms and ammonia for tear-gas pellets. The barricades surrounding the Maidan's tented city were built up into massive, twelve-foot-high bulwarks, and supplemented with burning tyres. As the missiles flew and black smoke billowed, shouts and explosions combined with the sound of sticks beating empty oil drums, the long-long-short-short-short rhythm standing for RE-VO-lut-si-ya.

Organised into 'hundreds' (an old Cossack term), the hard core of fighters was increasingly made up of working-class men from western Ukraine, an over-publicised minority of them members of the nationalist far right. The riot police or 'Berkut', conversely, came increasingly from the east, as the authorities brought in extra forces from the Donbass. They were supplemented by titushki – tracksuited thugs, a mixture of football hooligans, fight-club members and petty criminals, given small cash handouts to rough up and intimidate.

The original middle-class protestors split. Disliking the violence, some peeled away. But others stayed put, fighting, giving first aid, helping reinforce the barricades or ferrying supplies. If one defining image of the Maidan is a teenager in a crash helmet lobbing a stone, another is a respectably dressed middle-aged woman passing bricks along a human chain, or filling sacks with rubble. As a twenty-something Odessan who had spent the winter on the Maidan told me proudly: 'In Ukraine now, every little girl knows how to make a Molotov cocktail.' Her own apartment was a mix of girly clutter and street-fighting gear: corn dollies and china frogs next to shin guards and a flak jacket; bandage rolls and a loudhailer alongside a box set of *Friends*. It wasn't just a pose – she really had been in the thick of the fighting, and had seen friends seriously hurt. Outside Kyiv's old Dynamo football stadium, a home-made siege engine, built of rope and metal girders, looked as though it had come off the set of *Game of Thrones*. But it actually worked, flinging rocks hundreds of feet over the police lines.

On 22 January the Maidan's first killings took place, when police beat to death two protestors on Hrushevsky Street, just down from the National Gallery. The same day the bound and beaten body of an activist from Lviv – in ordinary life a seismologist at its Geological Institute – was found in woods near Boryspil airport. The previous evening he had been in hospital, waiting for treatment for an eye injury, when a group of men burst in and frogmarched him into a van, together with a journalist from *Ukrainska Pravda*. The two were driven to a garage hidden in woodland and violently interrogated, the questions variations on 'Who's organising the Maidan?' and 'Are you getting money from America?' The journalist was driven to another part of the woods and released; the geologist was left to die of his injuries and hypothermia.[5]

The last act played out in the third week of February, sharing the world's TV screens with Russia's Sochi Winter Olympics. On Tuesday 18 February an initially peaceful rally outside the Rada, led by opposition MPs and demanding a more democratic constitution, ended in running battles as police pushed protestors downhill towards European Square.

Far-right fighters (or, as many claim, provocateurs) invaded and set fire to the Party of Regions' offices near the Rada, reportedly killing two people.[6] Around eight o'clock in the evening, the anti-terrorism unit known as the 'Alfa Group' did the same to the Trades Union Building, then serving as a protestors' field hospital and hostel. Most people escaped safely with the help of the fire services, but unknown numbers did not: one eyewitness reported seeing medics remove four charred bodies.[7] *Titushki* killed six protestors outside St Michael's monastery, and later that night plain-clothes police took a journalist from a taxi outside Saint Sofia Cathedral, beat him up and shot him dead. The (probably undercounted) official death toll for the day was twenty-six – sixteen demonstrators and ten police.

The next day the two sides regrouped. The government announced a nationwide 'anti-terrorist operation' – in effect a state of emergency – but also reopened talks with the parliamentary opposition. The protestors reinforced their barricades. (Supporters delivered so much food, remembers one, that most of it went uneaten.) In six western and central provinces, meanwhile, pro-Maidan mobs stormed police stations, security service headquarters and city halls. In Lviv, cars and several buildings were set on fire.

The climax came on Thursday the 20th. Early in the morning, protestors attacked the police lines on Hrushevsky and Institutska Streets, trying to take back ground lost two days before. This time, the response was rifle fire, from uniformed snipers – a mixture of Berkut, Alfa and Interior Ministry forces – stationed uphill from the Maidan on the roofs of the Central Bank, the Ukraina Hotel and the Cabinet of Ministers. (The snipers are also credibly rumoured to have included men from Russia's Federal Security Service, though this has not been proved.)[8] Amazingly, the protestors continued to press forwards, relying on sheer force of numbers to overwhelm the better-armed opposition. Whether or not they also fired back is unclear. One rooftop Berkut was filmed being hit by a round[9] and guns taken from Lviv police barracks over the previous two days were certainly making their way to Kyiv.[10] But the overwhelming impression given by video footage and witnesses is of an *intifada*-style battle between trained and well-armed professionals and determined but disorganised and ill-equipped amateurs. British academic Andrew Wilson was on the ground:

> This was not an armed revolution: the Maidan 'hundreds' were barely armed, or even protected. I saw an advertising hoarding being ripped down for use as a shield. Protestors hid behind trees. This time, for obvious reasons, I stayed further away; but I was still close enough to the edge of the Maidan to have to stumble aside at the regular shouts of *korridor!* – 'make way' – for the wounded or already-dead to get through . . . The protestors won with rocks and Molotov cocktails against snipers . . . When one of their number was shot, they were prepared to keep going.[11]

My ex-banker friend also saw the fighting at first hand: 'The attack on Institutska was suicidal, completely suicidal,' he told me. 'Armed with sticks and stones, they were advancing up a hill defended by professional snipers. I watched them do it – just collecting up the dead, and carrying on. I was awestruck – they were ordinary people, people just like me. Some were [the far-right party] Svoboda, but only a minority.'

Initial estimates for the day's dead were 70 killed and 166 missing. Over the next weeks the death toll rose, as information came in about the missing and the most seriously injured died. A martyred 'Heavenly Hundred' became 107. Altogether, it is now reckoned, 111 people – 94 civilians and 17 police – were killed just in the Maidan's final four days.

The slaughter – or rather its ineffectiveness – destroyed Yanukovich. That same Thursday evening, his Party of the Regions finally deserted him. Twenty-two MPs formally left the party. The rest, as Wilson puts it, 'had other things to do, with documents to destroy and businesses to protect'. A half-empty Rada voted overwhelmingly to sack the interior minister and send the security forces back to barracks.

At the same time the Polish, French and German foreign ministers, plus a Putin representative, flew in to broker emergency talks between Yanukovich and the parliamentary opposition. Negotiations continued all night, and a deal was finally reached at seven on Friday morning. There would be a new 'national unity' government, a new constitution, and presidential elections would be brought forward from March 2015 to December. The agreement nearly fell apart again when the opposition leaders, realising that the Maidan would view it as a sell-out, failed to turn up to a signing ceremony scheduled for 11 a.m. 'It wasn't an easy deal for them to accept,' Polish foreign minister Radek Sikorski later admitted. 'Basically what we were proposing was that the person who had just killed a hundred people would stay on as their president for almost a year.'[12] But without it, he argued, Yanukovich would order an even bloodier crackdown. At 3 p.m. the opposition leaders finally shook hands with Yanukovich for the cameras, and were duly booed when they appeared on the Maidan later in the day.

Whether the deal would have held is hypothetical, because in the small hours of the following morning, Yanukovich boarded a helicopter and skedaddled. Why he did so is unclear. One possible explanation is that Putin ordered him to leave, so as to escalate the crisis and create a pretext for the invasion of Crimea, which began less than a week later. Another is that Yanukovich feared mutiny, having sacked the head of the armed forces three days earlier. His chief financial backer, Akhmetov, claims to have withdrawn support as soon as the police started shooting, but we have only his word for it, which should be taken with a bucketful of salt. The then US ambassador to Moscow, Michael McFaul, recalls astonishment:

We were like: Where did he go? We don't know! He's in Crimea? Why's he there? Get the vice-president on the 'phone to tell him to go back ... That's not Putin's view. Putin thinks we chased him out. But that's not our view. He left.[13]

Flying first to Kharkiv, where he discovered that the mayor had already high-tailed it to Russia, then to Donetsk, where airport officials refused to let him board his private jet, on 28 February Yanukovich re-emerged just over the border in Russia's Rostov-on-Don, where he told assembled journalists that he was still the rightful president of Ukraine, and the victim of a US-sponsored far-right coup.

◆ CHAPTER THIRTEEN ◆

Putin Strikes Back

APRIL 2014, and the Maidan has turned into a shrine cum tourist attraction. Hrushevsky is lined with bright masses of colour: cellophane-wrapped flowers, flickering icon lamps, cross-stitched scarves. Tree trunks flutter with handwritten prayers and poems; rosaries loop from railings and branches. Framed photographs take up a section of pavement, each encircled with a twiggy wreath: it is the 'Heavenly Hundred', with their crowns of thorns. People wander quietly from one to another, pausing to read the names and lay flowers.

Halfway down the hill come the first of the barricades, their height and variety of ingredients – sandbags, tyres, bricks, metal gates, a bicycle wheel – giving them the air of manically outsize pieces of installation art. Outside a canvas tent stands an elderly man, blearily rubbing his stubble. Would I like to share a beer? A bit early? In that case, how about a couple of cigarettes in exchange for a lesson on throwing a Molotov cocktail? Picking up a bottle with a loop of wire for a handle, he takes me to a nearby public lavatory – used, he explains, for training during the fighting. A match to a rag, an overarm swing, and it flies the length of the stalls and smashes against the far wall, flames licking against sooty tiles.

Down on the Maidan itself, underneath the burned-out Trades Union Building, stalls have set up selling patriotic souvenirs: blue-and-yellow scarves, hairbands decorated with plastic sunflowers, *salo* key-rings. There are fridge magnets in the shape of Yanukovich's golden toilet, and doormats stencilled with his face. A couple of months later, the stalls are touting a new line: rolls of toilet paper printed not with the ex-president's face, but with Vladimir Putin's.

Putin hated the Maidan. He had not thought much of Yanukovich, publicly snubbing him on various occasions and apparently getting on much better with flirtatious Tymoshenko during her days as prime minister. But he disliked triumphant people power a great deal more. The protests, the Russian foreign ministry and state-controlled television repeated again and again, were the work of European intelligence agencies and the CIA, all part of a grand plan to trap and declaw the peaceable Russian bear. The Russian public, according to polls, lapped it up.

With Yanukovich gone, there were to be no more negotiations. Instead, Putin invaded Crimea. The opening move was the arrival in Sevastopol of Berkut men on the run from Kyiv, who in a public meeting on Sunday 23 February announced a 'people's mayor'. On the 26th, scuffles between pro- and anti-Kyiv demonstrators outside the Simferopol parliament building ended in two deaths, and the following day it was taken over by gunmen in unmarked uniforms – probably also Berkut. MPs – the large majority of whom belonged to Yanukovich's Party of Regions – obediently voted in a local gangster turned Russian-nationalist politician, locally nicknamed 'the Goblin', as Crimea's prime minister.

The same evening a full-scale invasion began, with up to 35,000 unbadged Russian troops – some already stationed at the Sevastopol naval base, others shipped in – taking over police stations, airports, and the road linking Crimea to the Ukrainian mainland. Outnumbered and given no orders, the 20,000 or so Ukrainian troops stationed on the peninsula swapped sides, or surrendered without a fight. (An air force colonel became a national hero when instead of giving up his

airbase, he marched his men, unarmed, out to meet the be-
siegers. The Russians let him stay for three weeks.)[1] The few
ships of the Ukrainian navy simply ran down their Ukrainian
flags and ran up Russian ones – one captain explaining as he
did so that he and his crew all had at least half-Russian an-
cestry. Extra-judicial violence squashed civilian protest. On
3 March a 39-year-old Tatar activist, Reshat Ametov, was
holding a peaceful one-man protest outside a government
building in Simferopol when paramilitaries bundled him into
a van. A fortnight later his body was found, showing signs of
torture. Six days later a further seven pro-Maidan activists
and journalists were arrested by militiamen, two at Simferopol railway station, five at a checkpoint as they tried to
enter Crimea by car. They were roughed up but later released.
In May four more activists, including the filmmaker Oleh
Sentsov, were arrested on terrorism charges, transferred for
trial to Moscow, and sentenced to between seven and twenty
years.[2]

The takeover may have been improvised, but more likely
it was the opportunistic putting into action of a long-planned
operation, perhaps originally meant for Ukraine's 2015
presidential elections. Either way it succeeded brilliantly,
achieving full control of Crimea, almost bloodlessly, in less
than a month. The West's initial response to this stunning
fait accompli was stern words, but no action. (A cartoon in
the *Financial Times* showed one NATO general saying to
another, 'We're not just talking tough on Russia, we're threatening to act tough too.') On the one hand, this was a clear
breach of international law, and of the 1994 'Tripartite Agreement' under which Russia promised to respect Ukraine's
borders in exchange for its Soviet-inherited nuclear warheads.
On the other, wasn't Crimea sort of Russian anyway? Even
more confusingly, the Kremlin flatly denied that the silent,
anonymous soldiers patrolling Crimea's towns had anything
to do with it. They were local 'self-defence forces', protecting
the peninsula from anarchy in Kyiv. Western media parroted

the line for far too long, the BBC continuing to refer to 'un-identified armed men' well after sources on the ground had established exactly which Russian units they were from. Derisively, the Ukrainians nicknamed the occupiers 'little green men': did we think they had arrived from Mars?

On 16 March the Kremlin consolidated its hold by staging a pseudo-referendum on the reunion of Crimea with the Russian Federation (the organisers some of the same Kremlin 'political technologists' who helped rig Ukraine's 2004 presidential vote). Given Crimea's sizeable pro-Kyiv Ukrainian and Tatar minorities, the result – a 97 per cent vote in favour on a turnout of 83 per cent – was obviously bogus. But even a fair count, without intimidation, might have produced the same verdict. Sevastopol erupted in celebration, and even in less militaristic and more ethnically mixed Simferopol, footage of cheering crowds – endlessly replayed by Russian television – did not have to be faked.

Two days later, in Moscow's Grand Kremlin Palace, an 'Accession Treaty' was signed in front of the joint houses of the Russian parliament. Preceded by trumpet fanfares, Putin spoke of Volodymyr's baptism at Khersonesus and of 'legendary Sevastopol'; of Khrushchev having handed Crimea to Ukraine 'like a sack of potatoes'; of the Maidan 'coup', using 'terror, violence, murders and pogroms', carried out by 'neo-Nazis, nationalists and anti-Semites'. The West seemed to believe that it was 'entrusted by God to decide the fates of other peoples', but Russia had 'her national interests . . . and if you press the spring too hard, it will recoil'. The audience broke into frequent bursts of what in Stalin's day would have been called 'stormy applause'. The Goblin, stubble neater than usual, looked as if he were pricing up the hall's giant chandeliers. On 20 March every Russian MP but one voted to ratify the treaty, and soon after, without explanation or apology, Putin blithely admitted that he had sent troops to Crimea after all.

*

In Kyiv, meanwhile, the three largest opposition parties formed a new interim government, approved by the Rada on 27 February. Far from being the neo-Nazi junta of Kremlin demonology, the coalition was led by Tymoshenko's liberal, pro-European 'Fatherland' party, and represented Ukraine's ethnic diversity well. The prime minister came from famously mongrel Chernivtsi; the interior minister was by background Armenian and had built his career in Russian-speaking Kharkiv; a deputy prime ministership went to the young Jewish mayor of Vinnytsya. The interim president, appointed until new elections could be held in May, was a Baptist from Russian-speaking Dnipro.

Less happily, three ministries went to the far-right Svoboda party, rewarding its part in February's street-fighting but far more than it deserved given its minimal public support. Another blunder was a parliamentary vote, the day after Yanukovich's flight, to downgrade the official status of the Russian language. It was recognised as a misstep straight away: the interim president suspended the measure four days later, and Lviv city council declared a solidarity-boosting 'Speak Russian Day'. Russian propagandists nonetheless made hay, claiming that Russian-speakers were to be stripped of citizenship and Russian-language schools closed, and that even doctor's prescriptions would have to be written in Ukrainian.

The second half of Putin's double-punch was an insurrection in the Russian-speaking industrial east. Acknowledging the region's more balanced ethnic mix and local, rather than Moscow-centric, patriotism, the tactics chosen were different from those used in Crimea. Instead of sending in troops, Moscow would let the Party of Regions stage a mirror-image simulacrum of the Maidan. And instead of the protestors asking for reunion with Russia, they would call, initially at least, for autonomy within Ukraine.

It half succeeded. In a string of Russian-speaking eastern cities, demonstrators – some bussed-in and paid, others local and sincere – held anti-Maidan rallies and tried to take over government buildings. In Kharkiv and Dnipropetrovsk the protests were quickly snuffed out by the local authorities, who had decided to throw in their lot with the new government. Kyiv also cannily sent in loyal oligarchs as regional governors: Igor Kolomoisky, a notoriously unscrupulous corporate raider from Dnipro, raced home from Switzerland to secure the city, forming his own militia, the Dnipro-1 Battalion, and posting billboards promising '$10,000 for a *moskal'* (Ukrainian slang for a Russian). Where the tactics did work was in Yanukovich's long-time political heartland, the Donbass. In Donetsk, Luhansk and the rust-belt towns in between, police and local authorities cooperated or stood aside as gunmen in unmarked uniforms, backed up by locals armed with chains and baseball bats, took over government buildings and declared 'People's Republics'.

On 1 May, I watched the 'seizure' of the Donetsk regional prosecutor's office. By the time I got there its ground floor windows had been smashed in, and a group of men carrying police-issue riot shields stickered with Russia's double-headed eagle stood guard on the steps leading up to the front door. A ring of journalists lay on their stomachs photographing the burning remains of a *tryzub*, Ukraine's trident-shaped national emblem. 'Prettier like this!' a man joked, poking it with a stick to give them a better shot. The journalists giggled. A small crowd, no more than a couple of hundred strong, milled around a flag showing a bare-chested Stalin cradling a giant assault rifle. Car-top speakers thumped out a marching song – '*Marsh, marsh, marsh, Russkiy marsh*' – and a woman danced along, trying to get everyone to join in. Nobody did. Thirty yards away, waiters tacked between tables on the terrace of the 'New York' pizzeria. When nothing seemed to be happening I went and got myself a cup of tea. Finally a line of uniformed policemen emerged from the building, looking unruffled and a little bored. Later more police went in, then came out again, then hung about on the corner of the street. Asked what was going on, one said he didn't know himself.

Another muttered a misappropriated slogan from the Maidan: 'The police are with the people.' The crowd, and the car with banner and speakers, I began to understand, were for show. If there hadn't been any journalists there, probably nobody would have bothered with burning the *tryzub* or breaking the windows.

But even with the Donbass local authorities onside, Yanukovich could not engineer a genuine popular revolution. Rallies were small – only a few thousand on Donetsk's Lenin Square on May Day, for example. An opinion poll taken in mid-April showed the majority of Donbassers disapproving of the armed seizure of public buildings (72 per cent in Donetsk province, 58 per cent in Luhansk province), not wanting to join Russia (52 per cent in both provinces), and in case of armed incursion by Russia, intending to 'stay at home and not interfere' (55 per cent in Donetsk, 43 per cent in Luhansk[3]). The results chimed with my bus-stop vox-pop interviews: what most people said they wanted was not independence or reunion with Russia but *federalisatsiya* or *avtonomiya*, the clunky words taken vaguely to mean any sort of arrangement involving paying less tax to Kyiv. Several assured me that they were not *separatisti*, the word still carrying Soviet overtones of treachery and extremism. Least likely to support the People's Republics were the educated middle classes, who were furious with Kyiv for failing to nip the insurrection in the bud ('Three *babushki* with fly-swats could have done it!'), and whose whispered nickname for the thugs taking over their streets was 'orcs'.

I met Donetsk's new rulers in the regional administration building. Fronting a park, it was surrounded by barricades and covered in handwritten posters and white-blue-red Russian flags. The dozen or so men hanging about the entrance had taken their look – bandanas, death-metal T-shirts, camo accents – from *Call of Duty*. Some wore balaclavas and nearly all carried baseball bats. The rest of the city seemed to be doing its best to pretend they were not there. Among neat municipal flowerbeds – tulips going over, roses coming into leaf – headscarved gardeners were planting out marigolds, and passers-by – sixth-formers carrying sketchpads, a woman in peep-toe gladiator boots pushing a stroller – walked past without giving them a second glance.

Negotiating entry took a while. While I waited I read the posters. Several were in English: 'America, Hands off Eastern Ukraine!', 'No to Fascism!' and 'Yankee Go Home!' Another contrasted a couple kissing on a Gay Pride float with goose-stepping military cadets, above the question 'Which parade will your son be in?' Inside, the lobby stank of dirty lavatories. In one corner, blankets and sleeping bags lay in a heap, underneath framed photographs of old regional First Party Secretaries. In another, beer bottles stuffed with rags clustered round a startled-looking cheese plant, together with a canvas gas-mask and a plank spiked with nails. The lifts were broken, which meant climbing eleven flights of stairs. My escort, all eyes and teeth beneath his balaclava, paused to clasp fists with everyone we passed on the way, giving me time to catch my breath. We stood aside for a posse coming down, at its centre a man in a suit. Who is he? A shrug: 'A *pomochnik*' – a political assistant. A crowded meeting room and a show of niceties. Would I like tea or coffee? How many sugars? The tea arrived in a china cup and saucer, accompanied by cellophane-wrapped ginger biscuits.

My interviewee, who would not give his name or role, was in his mid-thirties, with a shaven head, gaunt stubbly cheeks, and red eyes. In normal life, he said, he was a lorry driver, and spent eight months of the year in Magadan, the Far Eastern town that was once a hub of Stalin's Gulag. Pay was better there and petrol cheaper, leaving him with enough money to send home to his family. Others gathered round and slightly reluctantly admitted to being a builder, a warehouseman, a 'sportsman' and a miner. The miner, more wired up than the rest, took out pen and paper and scribbled an outline of 'our' – heavily ironic – Ukraine, bisected by the Dnipro. 'Here'

– jabbing at the eastern half of the country – 'we make coal,
steel, chemicals, rockets, tanks! There' – jabbing at the west
– 'all they have is agriculture and tourism. We send all our
money to Kiev, and only get half of it back! What do they
do? They work abroad, pay no taxes, then come home and
build themselves two-storey houses. Me, I haven't even got
one storey!' More scribbles, of NATO countries encircling
the old Soviet Union. The break-ups of Czechoslovakia and
Yugoslavia were part of an American grand plan, and so was
Greece's debt crisis. Even the Great Famine was the West's
fault: 'Stalin had to buy arms from you, and you demanded
grain and potatoes in return. Children were dying! What did
England do? Nothing!' What does he think of the new pro-
European government in Kyiv? He scribbles down the names
of various MPs, stabbing at them with the point of his biro.
'Him' – stab – 'gay. And him – gay. Him – gay AND a Jew.'
'And a paedophile,' one of the others chips in; 'it's on the
internet.' 'That's right. Gay' – stab, stab – 'AND a Jew, AND
a paedo.'

The only Russian-speaking city where large-scale violence
broke out was Odesa. In a gift to Putin's propaganda machine,
on May 2 street fighting between pro-Kyiv and pro-Russian
demonstrators ended with forty-three pro-Russians dying in
a fire. I got to the site – a pillared Trades Union Building in
a park next to the railway station – two days later. On the
entrance steps flowers were piled high, and rain-smudged notices read 'Glory to the saintly heroes of Odessa!' and 'Russia,
save us! Odessans are not kebabs!' Inside, mourners and the
curious crunched their way through the wrecked, soot-black
lobby and up the main staircase. The smells were of wet lilac
– laid on a windowsill next to crossed baseball bats – charcoal
and melted plastic. There were no police anywhere, nor even
any police tape.

Earlier in the day, a local activist had walked me along
the route of the fighting. It started, she said, when pro-Kyiv

marchers – a mixture of locals and out-of-town football supporters in the city for a match – were attacked on Greek Street
by pro-Russians armed with pistols and baseball bats. The
pro-Kyiv group fought back, throwing broken paving stones.
Here, in front of the Great Moscow Hotel, they set light to a
fire engine. Over there, by the Perle Belle restaurant, the one
with the petunias, they set up a barricade using café tables
and wheelie bins. The bins, she said, were 'wonderful. You
wheel them into place, then fill them with stones to make
them heavier. They were the real heroes of the day.' And it
was out of that broken window there, above the wig shop,
that the pro-Russians started shooting, killing two, maybe
three. In revenge, some of the pro-Kyivans decided to destroy
the pro-Russians' protest camp, which had been set up in
the park a few weeks earlier. They set light to the tents and
chased whoever they found into the Trades Union Building.
But they weren't responsible for the building itself catching
fire: the pro-Russians had clumsily started the blaze themselves, while mixing Molotov cocktails on the second floor.

But looking at the building, the last part of her story didn't
make sense. The fire had obviously begun not on the second
floor, but in the ground floor lobby, suggesting that it was
caused by incoming petrol bombs rather than outgoing ones.
Upstairs, the central corridors were black with smoke, but
those in the wings untouched. Why hadn't the pro-Russians
taken shelter there? And who broke down the doors into
otherwise undamaged offices? Looters, or did fighting also
take place inside the building, as some survivors claimed?
What about the Ukrainian Security Service's seemingly crazy
claim that the whole thing was a provocation, and that the
deaths were caused by a poisonous gas? Why did the police
and fire service not turn up until 8 p.m., well after the fire
started?

By leaving the building completely unsecured, the city authorities seemed to be doing their best to make sure none
of these questions was answered. As I picked my way back

down the staircase, a man came up to talk. I hesitated: earlier, stones had been thrown at a British journalist here. But there was no need. 'Stupidity,' he said, shaking his head, 'just stupidity. Odessans are clever – this isn't Odesa.'

On 25 May, buttressed by thousands of international observers, Ukraine held new presidential elections. The landslide winner was Petro Poroshenko, an oligarch best known for his ownership of a large confectionery company. A supporter of the Orange Revolution via his television channel, he had taken ministerial positions under both Yushchenko and Yanukovich before coming out strongly for the Maidan. Relieved that the vote had passed off peacefully, Ukrainians tried to look on the bright side. On the one hand, Poroshenko was Ukraine's sixth-richest man and indisputably part of the old system. On the other, he had made his fortune in consumer goods rather than monopolistic, subsidy-guzzling commodities, and had a reputation as a capable manager and team-builder. Though his share of the vote was markedly lower in the east than in the west, it was hoped that being genuinely bilingual and hailing from central Vinnytsya province, he might also be in a good position to unify the country. To everyone's relief, the two far-right candidates did hopelessly, with less than 2 per cent of the vote between them. So did newly released Tymoshenko, her combination of martyr's halo and Louboutin heels ultimately unconvincing.

Excluded from the elections were the voters of the Donbass, where the People's Republics intimidated district election committees into closing down. Instead, on 11 May, they held a Crimea-style 'referendum', asking voters to approve a *samostoyatelniy* republic. Literally translated as 'self-supporting', this could be taken to mean either 'independent' or 'autonomous'. The result, to nobody's surprise, was announced to be an overwhelming Yes.

I interviewed the organiser, a young 'political technologist' called Roman Lyagin, shortly afterwards. Dressed in jeans and loafers and toting a man-bag, he looked uncomfortable in the still-chaotic Donetsk administration building, where an obscene rhyme had been scribbled on his office wall and the door kept swinging open because someone had shot through the lock. A graduate of Donetsk State University, he had worked as a campaign manager for Yanukovich during 2004's rigged presidential elections. Now, he said, he was an unpaid volunteer

> for the structure that is the core of the Donetsk People's Republic, but I won't tell you its name . . . Our task is to destabilise Ukraine. It's like a virus we want to spread there. People in Kiev are fools. We're waiting for the third revolution. It will happen soon. Why? They've got an oligarch in power, and his cronies. And in Kiev we try to raise the mood against oligarchy. We've been planning this since 2006.

Far-right Svoboda, he said, had at one stage been 'bought by the Party of Regions. Why? Because when they make Russophobe comments it just fuels pro-Russian feeling here. We share an aim – destabilising Ukraine.' He segued on to the importance of creating 'leaders of public opinion' and making 'simple people' feel involved: 'We deliberately didn't provide pens to the polling stations, so as to give them a chance to contribute something themselves.' Later, I asked my local fixer how much of what Lyagin said about Svoboda and the Party of Regions I should believe. She snorted. Lyagin's ex-wife and son lived comfortably in Düsseldorf, and one thing she knew for sure – he wasn't working for nothing.

Over the same month the insurrection turned into a war, as the People's Republics acquired guns and artillery, and Kyiv belatedly sent in the Ukrainian army. Bolstered by volunteer battalions drawn from the hard core of the Maidan, the army cleared the separatists from the Donbass's mainly rural west and north, and fought a successful battle for Donetsk's new-built airport. It also retook the Azov Sea port of Mariupol, the region's third-largest city and an important staging post between the Donbass and Crimea.

By mid-June the Donbass had a frontline atmosphere. In Donetsk, many shops and nearly all cashpoint machines had closed, and a curfew emptied the streets in the evenings. In the bar of the Park Inn, where World Cup games played on a big screen to empty tables, a Reuters team pored over maps, working out the safest way round hotspots to the latest news story. OSCE officials held *sotto voce* meetings in an annexe, discussing the freeing of colleagues kidnapped by one of the ever-multiplying People's Republic militias.

Fancifully named – the Ghost Brigade, the Don Cossacks, the People's Levy – these now numbered around thirty. A group calling itself the Russian Orthodox Army had commandeered the Security Service headquarters, plus a looted cash-and-carry on the road to the airport. Vostok ('East'), rumoured to be funded by Akhmetov, had just left town to take control of the railway line to his steel works at Mariupol. (Asked whether Akhmetov was behind Vostok, his corporate PR man, a genial Scot, denied it. But would he know? A pause: 'Maybe not.') Oplot – 'Stronghold' – guarded the mayor's office and the television tower, now broadcasting only Russian channels.

Outside the tower's sandbagged gates half a dozen young men hung about in the sunshine, wearing black T-shirts emblazoned with a Halloween bat and the English words 'Live Strong'. One, in beard and flip flops, was varnishing the stock of his rifle, which was decorated with a roundel of a rhinoceros – 'The strongest animal,' he explained, 'and peaceful unless you annoy it.' When I asked why Ukrainian channels were being blocked, a slightly unhinged-looking older man butted in, sour-breathed and beginning to shout. 'You should watch Russia 24! You know what the Kiev junta's doing? It's building concentration camps. There'll be *filtratsiya* – women and children in one camp, men in the other. Then they'll give our flats to *Banderivtsi* from the west! When they captured Shchastye they used gas, they killed two hundred people! They're killing children! Little girls, twelve years old, thirteen years old!'

Not wanting to join the OSCE people in a basement somewhere, I didn't mention Stopfake, a Kyiv-based student initiative dedicated to exposing misinformation in Russian media. Typical of its recent scalps was a photo of a man, billed as a Ukrainian militia member, diving into an ice-hole cut in the shape of swastika. Stopfake had shown that the photo had actually been taken in Russia, and that the hole had been in the shape of a cross. Routinely, footage of supposed victims of Ukrainian shelling turned out to have come from Iraq or Syria. The wildest stories – such as an interview, on Russia's main state-run channel, with a woman claiming to have watched a pro-Kyiv mob crucify a toddler in the middle of the Donbass town of Slovyansk – were immediately proved untrue not only by the Ukrainians but by independent Russian media. (The 'crucifixion witness' even got the name of Slovyansk's central square wrong.) But still the stories kept coming, their purpose less to convince than to inflame and confuse.

In Luhansk – still reachable by ordinary passenger train – the Ukrainian army had pushed so close that one could hear the artillery fire: giant, stomach-shaking rumbles like the sound of an approaching thunderstorm. In the leafy square outside the city administration building, a series of small craters marked where a Ukrainian fighter jet had botched a rocket attack, killing eight passers-by. (Taking a leaf from the Kremlin's playbook, the ministry of defence was blaming the separatists, claiming that they had misfired an anti-aircraft gun.[4]) Inside a glass-fronted civic bulletin board, fresh notices read 'The Ukrainian army kills peaceful people!', 'Don't fire on children, fascists!', and 'Mothers of Ukrainian soldiers, spare your children! They are cannon fodder!' At the university an archaeologist – a boyish man, happier talking about Neolithic midden heaps than war – was making up his mind to become a refugee. Tipping a handful of delicate flint blades from an envelope, he explained that most of his colleagues had left already. So had his students, their accommodation block given over to 'Chechens' – catch-all slang for professional gunmen from the Caucasus. There would be no field trips for him this summer: one of his digs was in Crimea, the other in the midst of fighting to the north. But if he left, where would he go, and what was to prevent his flat from being looted? His wife didn't want to leave either. She worked at the Luhansk museum; already the militias had been in to confiscate an old Second World War gun, and she was worried that they would cotton on to its collection of ancient gold and silver coins.

The only local journalist still in town explained that he didn't dare speak Ukrainian in public, and asked me to tear out his name and number from my notebook. He was brave to meet me at all: between mid-April and July 2014, according to the UNHCR, 222 civilians were abducted by separatist paramilitaries in the Donbass, and four killed. The real total was certainly higher, since victims' families often kept quiet so as to facilitate ransom payments. After release, they variously reported being beaten, electrocuted, cut with knives, burned with cigarettes, made to clean out blood-stained vehicles, or threatened with rape or execution. In a preview of worse horrors to come, when the Ukrainian army recaptured Slovyansk from separatists in July, fifty hostages were found in police and security services headquarters, and twenty bodies in a mass grave in the old Jewish cemetery.

There, as in other liberated towns, the Ukrainian authorities faced a daunting reconstruction task. In the main square, Lenin was still standing, though he wore a yellow and blue necktie. The newly installed pro-Kyiv mayor told me that despite the killings, about half the population would be pleased to see the Donetsk People's Republic back again. Even the anti-separatists, he said, hadn't much love for the Ukrainian government: 'Their attitude is – First they failed to defend us, then they shelled us, and now they're doing nothing to help.'

One such was the owner of a small ceramics factory, home-built in a corner of a derelict chemical works. He was managing to keep production going – his best line now a vodka bottle in the shape of a Kalashnikov – but took me to see what had happened to his other business, an out-of-town restaurant run by his wife. Hit by a Ukrainian shell the previous month, nothing was left of it but ragged walls and the remains of an outdoor pizza oven. Neighbouring businesses – a petrol station and a garden centre – had been utterly destroyed too. So had a large psychiatric hospital up on the hill. Most expressive of the force of the blasts were the roadside trees: fully grown poplars, smashed like thistles swiped with a walking stick. He laughed when I asked about compensation. For a flat, you might be lucky, but not for a restaurant; he wasn't even bothering to apply.

Even harder to repair would be Slovyansk's social fabric, split between those who had fled separatist rule and returned, and stay-behind collaborators and supporters. An administrator at a building firm explained to me how in the early days of the insurrection, she used to speak freely with other mothers when dropping off her daughter at school. 'I said what I thought – that what was happening was completely illegal. There were different reactions. Some agreed with me. Others said I didn't understand, that the DPR would be better. But a third lot said – If you carry on talking like this, we'll report you to the Security Council.' She never was arrested, but still had to meet those same women at the school gate every morning. At work, where most of her colleagues were anti-Kyiv, there was an unspoken agreement not to mention the war. 'Because otherwise, there's an explosion' – throwing her hands wide – 'Bfffff!'

On 17 July, the fact that this was now a proper war involving proper weaponry came horribly to the world's attention when a Malaysia Airlines passenger jet, on its way from Amsterdam to Kuala Lumpur, was shot down over separatist-held territory, killing all 298 on board. Two-thirds of the dead were Dutch, and eighty children. The Kremlin immediately whipped up its usual dust cloud of conspiracy theories: the Ukrainians shot the airliner down deliberately, so as to blame Moscow; or they mistook it for Putin's private jet; or it was the same Malaysia Airlines plane that had disappeared four months earlier over the Pacific; or it was all a CIA hoax, the passengers dead before they even boarded. Subsequent international investigations established that it was hit by a Russian mobile anti-aircraft battery that had crossed the border earlier that morning, and the Dutch prosecution service has charged four people with the murders, including the Donetsk People's Republic then 'defence minister', a Russian militia leader called Igor Girkin. The atrocity prompted European governments belatedly to match new US sanctions on Russia, the most important being the exclusion of Kremlin-connected banks and companies from Western bond and stock markets.

At the end of August, when it looked as if the People's Republics might be crumbling, Putin tipped back the scales by sending in tanks and large convoys of military equipment – spotted by spy satellites, war reporters and locals with smartphones but all, according to the Kremlin, either non-existent or containing humanitarian aid. Any Russian military in the Donbass, the Kremlin insisted, were volunteers, fighting while on leave. Ten Russian paratroopers captured by the Ukrainians in August had got lost on exercises. One of several Russian human rights groups to set about proving this nonsense was the Committee of Soldiers' Mothers, a thorn in the Kremlin's side ever since the Afghan war. The authorities were having none of it. The 73-year-old head of the Committee's southern branch, having started making inquiries about men gone missing from nearby bases, was arrested for fraud and held for three days while prosecutors searched her office. In north-western Pskov – home of Russia's elite 76th Airborne Division – a local opposition politician who started looking into a rash of military funerals was beaten unconscious on the street, and threatened with charges of financial misconduct.[5]

By September, after a bloody defeat at the town of Ilovaisk, on the railway line between Donetsk and the Russian border, Kyiv was worried enough to consent to peace talks. At a meeting in Minsk on the 5th, representatives from the two sides agreed a protocol: they would stop shooting, pull back their heavy weaponry from the front line, and release all captured fighters and hostages. Control of the border would be handed back to Ukraine, the whole to be monitored by the OSCE. The agreement dampened the fighting for a few months, but no more than that. No heavy weapons were pulled back, nor border crossings handed over, and both sides continued to exchange fire around Mariupol and Donetsk. A second Minsk agreement, reached on 11 February 2015 after frantic summitry between Putin, Germany's Angela Merkel and France's François Hollande, was immediately followed by the fall of Debaltseve, a town straddling road and rail links between Donetsk and Luhansk.

Thereafter the two sides dug in, turning the front line into a static 'line of contact'. Around one and a half million residents fled the war zone, about a third to Russia and two-thirds to Ukraine. The occupied territories turned into legal and economic limbo-lands, dependent on Russian handouts and unrecognised by the rest of the world. In Donetsk and Luhansk, Moscow continued to rule via the People's Republics, the original militiamen put into suits or replaced with more presentable figures. In Crimea, the bureaucracy of full integration went ahead. Businesses were required to re-register – those belonging to pro-Kyiv oligarchs confiscated in the process – and residents given a month to opt out of automatic Russian citizenship, losing their right to residency, or to work in any sort of government job, if they chose to do so. Remaining opposition figures were chased out with the usual detentions, disappearances and police raids.[6] Worst hit were the Crimean Tatars, their representative body, the Mejlis, closed down and their political leaders arrested on various spurious charges. The veteran dissident Mustafa Cemiloglu, whom I had last interviewed in Simferopol back in the 1990s, I met again in Kyiv, in exile once more seventy years after being deported from Crimea as a baby. It was easier, he remembered, being in opposition in Soviet times: 'Then there was a procedure at least – arrest, trial, off to the camps. Now, people disappear and reappear as corpses.'[7] By the end of 2014 about 20,000 Crimeans had already left for the Ukrainian mainland, about half of them Tatars.

Putin, it was assumed, had now got what he wanted: a hike in his domestic ratings (the seizure of Crimea was extremely popular with the Russian public, that of the rust-belt Donbass less so), and a hold over Ukraine that he could tighten or loosen at will. Though Crimea was shackled directly to Moscow – most visibly by the construction of a bridge over the Kerch Strait – his retention of proxies in the Donbass kept open the option of withdrawal if convenient. Instead of openly taking control of the region, Putin seemed to have adopted the subtler strategy of keeping it violent and unstable, so as to have leverage over Kyiv and prevent Ukraine from turning into the kind of Poland-style success story that would show up his regime. As Andrew Wilson put it, he had created a 'variable temperature conflict, to control whoever is in power in Kyiv: sometimes with a little bit more war, sometimes with a little bit more negotiation, but fundamentally on and on indefinitely.'[8] Just how high and how crudely Putin would turn up the temperature seven years later nobody guessed.

◆ CHAPTER FOURTEEN ◆

Between Battles

IN THE MEANTIME, Ukraine did rather well. Helped by fresh IMF loans and its Association Agreement with the EU (finally signed in June 2014), the economy picked up, growing steadily until 2020's Covid pandemic. In Kyiv, club and food scenes took off, and for the first time Western tourists started coming, not least for frisson-inducing outings to Chernobyl. Though in the east a few soldiers were still being killed every week, the war felt far away.

Progress was most dramatic in Lviv, its post-Soviet melancholy swept aside by booms in clothing manufacturing (Spain's Zara opened a factory), food processing, tourism and IT, all boosted by a modernising mayor. In 2015, the marketing director of one of over 130 software firms in the city showed me round its offices, an open-plan mini-Googleplex – bean bags, ping-pong tables – converted from an old television factory. She reeled off the names of her clients – Canadian, Swedish and British. The fighting in the Donbass, she admitted, put off some: 'We explain to them that it's 800km away, but they're still nervous.' But she was hoping for a sanctions windfall, as US firms directed business away from Russia. A bigger problem was the still-opaque tax system: 'Fix that, and we'll cope with everything else. We can wait a couple of years for new roads.' Why did Western firms outsource to Lviv rather than to cheaper India? 'It's called near-shoring. The time difference is small, and people like coming and spending time in our coffee shops.'

Strolling round cobbled Market Square, this was easy to believe. There were tandems and Segways for hire, a chocolatier and an art glass studio, posters for a klezmer concert and an Italian film festival. At Veronika's, a wood-panelled delight overlooking pollarded plane-trees and swoony Secessionist facades, a French visitor's letter of appreciation hung framed on the wall: 'Your décor is in very good taste, and your patisseries *exquise*. Even in Paris, few patisseries are as good as this.' The past was having a revival too. Sacher-Masoch had got his statue. The Armenian cathedral, once a warehouse for confiscated icons, was a working church again. A Uniate theological college had returned from exile in Rome, and was using diaspora money to build a sleek new campus. A German conservation charity was rescuing historic buildings, researching earlier inhabitants as it did so. 'Five years ago,' said an organiser, 'you'd tell someone that a Jewish family used to live in their house, and they'd say "Jews here – ridiculous!" Now it's no longer taboo.' The site of the medieval Golden Rose synagogue, demolished by the Nazis and used as a car park by the Soviets, had been turned into a memorial garden.

Less happily, the city also now had a statue of Stepan Bandera, leader of the Nazi-sponsored terrorist group OUN. Tourist shops sold Bandera mugs and T-shirts. Even the most pro-European Lvivers, I discovered, didn't necessarily disapprove. What about his anti-Semitism? His followers' massacre of Polish villagers? I was taking him out of context, I was told. It was the 1940s; it was wartime; the Poles massacred Ukrainians too. Of course Bandera's ideology is completely unacceptable today, but all the same, he fought for Ukraine. A local historian sighed when I brought up the subject. It was still impossible, he said, to debate Bandera objectively. He was just relieved that the statue had gone up in an out-of-the-way park, and not in the centre of town.

The biggest change was that Ukraine now felt indisputably like a real country. Though plenty of people would have got cross if you had said so, back in the 1990s it had had something of a make-believe, provisional air. With a quarter-century of independence and two patriotic revolutions under its belt, that was all gone. The change was most obvious among the under-thirties, who could not even remember the Soviet Union. In Yanukovich's hideous Mezhihorya a teenage fellow-visitor had looked startled when I asked if he really thought Ukraine could make it: 'Of course I do! I'm Ukrainian! I was born here, I've always lived here, and I'm not planning on moving anywhere else!' Outside Slovyansk, a young soldier standing guard at a pontoon bridge in a freezing wind could not have been more straightforwardly patriotic if the state whose passport he held had existed for centuries. Was he nervous about a possible new offensive? 'Nervous? No!' Would he resist? 'Of course! That's what we're here for!' He wore a blue and yellow ribbon on his coat, and turned out to be from Russian-speaking Dnipro.

The spirit of the Maidan – now christened the 'Revolution of Dignity' – very much lived on. Everywhere, groups of mostly young people carried on campaigning, organising, fund-raising – keeping an eye on the new government, helping refugees from the Donbass, gathering supplies for the front – all seemingly without a care as to how they would pay the rent. As a middle-aged Lviv environmentalist put it to me, it felt as if the country was starting over: 'Ukraine only became truly independent when the Maidan began. That was when social consciousness changed, when the Soviet Union inside us died.' He was proud that his 21-year-old daughter had camped out with the protestors. He had been afraid for her safety, naturally, but 'understood her need for change. She was born after independence. She has nothing Soviet inside her at all.'

The biggest disappointment of the post-Maidan period was the persistence of corruption. Early signs were hopeful.

Parliamentary elections in October 2014 got rid of some of the worst of the old Party of Regions hacks, and let in a group of bright young reformists. The resulting coalition took months to form, but came up with a bold programme, and made some imaginative technocratic appointments from abroad. In 2015 a new National Anti-Corruption Bureau (NABU) was launched, together with a transparent online tendering system for government contracts. A computerised asset declaration system, covering more than a million public servants, went live the following year. President Poroshenko, however, turned out to be only partially on board. He closed but did not sell, as promised, his Russian factories, and in 2016 the Panama Papers leak revealed that while his soldiers had been dying at Ilovaisk, he had been busy setting up a holding company in the British Virgin Islands. NABU found itself blocked by the courts and the prosecution service, and the foreign technocrats one by one resigned.

Instead, Poroshenko played the Ukrainisation card. His first move was a package of 'de-Communisation laws'. Passed by parliament in April 2015, they banned Soviet (and Nazi) symbols and propaganda, and gave local authorities six months to remove Communist monuments and change remaining Communist place-names. Criticised abroad were a ban on the Ukrainian Communist Party or its offshoots standing in elections, and a law 'Honouring the Memory of Fighters for Ukraine's Independence in the Twentieth Century'. Listing dozens of organisations – from the 1917–18 Rada government, to Bandera's OUN and the wartime Ukrainian Insurgent Army, to Rukh in 1989–91 – it made anyone 'publicly showing contempt' for them 'responsible under law', though without specifying penalties. 'Public denial of the legitimacy of the struggle for independence of Ukraine in the twentieth century' was also declared to be 'unlawful', but again without specifying penalties. (To date, the law has thankfully not led to legal actions. Of more practical import was a clause throwing open Ukraine's KGB archives. Russia's having closed again, they became a prime resource for historians of the Soviet period generally.)

In 2017 came a new education law, which gave Russian-language schools three years to introduce Ukrainian-language teaching for all children in Year 5 and above (Russian language and literature lessons excepted). Poroshenko's last piece of legislation – signed when he had already lost the 2019 presidential election – was a sweeping State Language Law. Though it guaranteed the 'free development and use' of Russian, it decreed that Ukrainian should become the language of all local as well as national government. Russian-language newspapers and books were to be published in parallel Ukrainian-language versions; in cinemas, 90 per cent of showings were to be dubbed into Ukrainian; Russian was not to be used in theatres except in cases of 'artistic necessity'. Websites were to pop up in Ukrainian first, and in shops, staff were to address customers in Ukrainian unless requested otherwise. The changes were to be phased in over five years.

Similarly of great long-term but less immediate significance was a split between the Ukrainian and Russian Orthodox churches. Since the seventeenth century, the Kyiv Patriarchate had come under the Moscow one, an arrangement now made untenable by Moscow Patriarch Kirill's lickspittle Putin-boosting. (And hypocrisy: in one notorious photograph, the luxury watch on his wrist is Photoshopped out, but not its reflection in a shiny table.) Encouraged by Poroshenko, in 2016 the Kyiv Patriarchate applied to Orthodoxy's leader, the magnificently titled Bartholomew I, Ecumenical Patriarch of Constantinople, for autocephaly or self-government. In October 2018 Bartholomew granted the request, prompting furious Kirill immediately to break with him. Ukrainian parishes were able to choose whether to join the new Orthodox Church of Ukraine or stay with the (much better funded) old Moscow one. They split, Moscow scoring the majority of parishes, but Kyiv most churchgoers. Perhaps the most important and certainly the most popular of Poroshenko's Westernising moves was his negotiation of *bezviz*, or visa-free travel to the European Union. Previously subjected to expensive and insulting visa application processes, from June 2017 Ukrainians could spend ninety days travelling freely throughout the Schengen Area on just their passports. They jumped at the opportunity, applying in millions for new biometric ones.

Though many were disappointed in Poroshenko, when the next presidential election approached at the end of 2018 he seemed on track to win. That was until the surprise late entry of a stocky, mobile-faced everyman called Volodymyr Zelensky. Forty-one years old, Jewish and a native Russian-speaker from the central industrial city of Kryvyi Rih, Zelensky was not a politician but a television entertainer, well known in Russia as well as Ukraine for his comedy team Kvartal 95. In the 2000s he had won the local version of *Strictly Come Dancing* – toreador suit for Ravel's *Boléro*; fuchsia Elvis costume for 'Blue Suede Shoes' – and after the Maidan turned political with *Servant of the People*, a long-running satire in which he played an idealistic schoolteacher catapulted by chance to the presidency.

Announcing that he wanted to be president for real, live on screen at five minutes to midnight on New Year's Eve, he upstaged Poroshenko from the start, eschewing stump speeches in favour of tweets and short person-to-person chats on YouTube and Instagram (where he already had over a million followers). The pro-European intelligentsia were mostly unconvinced. Zelensky was totally inexperienced, and what better gift to Putin, who thought Ukraine a joke, than electing a clown? Another worry was his relationship with the oligarch Kolomoisky, whose television channel hosted *Servant of the People* and whose personal lawyer had become one of the candidate's chief advisors. The hero of the hour back in 2014, when his heavies saved Dnipro from going the same way as Donetsk, Kolomoisky had fallen from grace when his bank, one of the country's largest, turned out to be a giant Ponzi scheme. Poroshenko had nationalised it, and Kolomoisky was now using Zelensky, it was assumed, to get revenge. None of this, however, much bothered the wider public, and in April 2019 Zelensky won by a landslide. Parliamentary elections in July consolidated the victory, when his party – also called Servant of the People – won a clear majority of seats, the first time any had done so since independence.

Immediately, fate threw a brickbat, in the shape of a phone call from American president Donald Trump. Ostensibly he was ringing to congratulate Zelensky on winning the parliamentary elections, but really to pressure him to dig dirt on his Democrat rival Joe Biden's son Hunter, who had been given a lucrative seat on a Ukrainian gas company's board while Joe was vice-president. The two opened with mutual compliments, Zelensky telling Trump that he was 'a great teacher' and that he too wanted to 'drain the swamp'. Trump replied with the observation that unlike Europe, America had 'been very, very good to Ukraine . . . very, very good.' Zelensky agreed that Trump was right, 'not just 100 per cent but 1000 per cent', and asked for more Javelins, a type of shoulder-held anti-tank missile. Then Trump moved on to his real business: 'I would like you to do us a favour.' In fact it was two. First, Zelensky was to take a call from Trump's attorney general, who was looking into the theory (being pushed by Manafort, by now in gaol for tax fraud) that it was Ukraine rather than Russia that had hacked into Democratic Party servers during the 2016 US presidential election. Zelensky assured Trump that investigations would be 'open and candid', that he was ready for 'any future cooperation', and that in Kyiv the President had 'nobody but friends'. Trump's second request was that Ukraine's chief prosecutor follow up a 'lot of talk' about 'Biden's son . . . a lot of people want to find out about that, so whatever you can do with the Attorney General would be great.' In response Zelensky said that he was appointing a new prosecutor, who would be '100 per cent my person, my candidate', and joined Trump in criticising Obama's ambassador to Kyiv. He wrapped up with more flattery: last time he had been in New York he had enjoyed staying at Trump Tower, and it would be wonderful if the President were able to tack a visit to Kyiv onto an upcoming summit in Warsaw: 'We can either take my plane or your plane, which is probably much better than mine.' Leaked by a White House staffer, the call prompted the Democrats to start impeachment proceedings against Trump in Congress, for soliciting foreign interference in the upcoming US elections. In Ukraine there was less of a storm. People winced at Zelensky's obsequiousness but on the whole let him off, judging that he had been in a tough spot, and had avoided committing himself while keeping Trump onside.

The big disappointment of the new presidency, as ever, was its failure to tackle corruption. Like his schoolteacher alter ego, Zelensky had promised not just legislation but a whole new start, a complete change of culture. In his inauguration speech he had summoned the nation to the fight: 'Europe starts with us, [not] somewhere over there, but' – tapping his head – 'right here . . . Each one of us is responsible.' To government officials: 'No portraits of me, please, in your offices . . . Hang photos of your kids instead, and look at them each time you make a decision.' Even cynics were rather moved.

Some progress was made. A bill lifting MPs' immunity from prosecution sailed through the Rada, and Zelensky broke with Kolomoisky, who soon found himself being investigated by the FBI for money-laundering. (The billions stolen from his depositors allegedly went into Midwestern real estate.) Many of Zelensky's appointments, though, felt dubious – too many old regime figures; too many cronies from Kvartal – and worst of all he let the new anti-corruption agencies introduced by Poroshenko run into the ground. The Kyiv District Administrative Court, notorious for biased rulings, continued to operate; the directorship of the Specialist Anti-Corruption Prosecutor's Office was left empty; and an Ethics Council of international experts, supposed to vet the membership of a new body to hire and fire judges, failed to convene. The West's darling, NABU, was attacked by the Constitutional Court, which in August 2020 sparked a crisis by ruling that NABU's director should stand down, and that the new electronic asset declaration system should be closed. The IMF threatened to withdraw and the EU to cancel *bezviz* if the decision was not reversed, and the Ukrainian foreign minister got a forthright phone call from US Secretary of State Antony Blinken. Things were patched up, but in October of the following year the mass-leaked Pandora Papers revealed that Zelensky, though nowhere near as rich as Yanukovich or Poroshenko, co-owned his TV production company via a network of shells registered in the British Virgin Islands, Cyprus and Belize. To add to the sense of *déjà vu*, gunmen had just tried to assassinate one of his co-owners, an old comedy buddy turned presidential aide. (The case is still unsolved.) Their on-screen wish-fulfilment president, Ukrainians decided, had not translated into real life, and Zelensky's approval ratings dropped to a disenchanted 25–30 per cent.[1]

◆ CHAPTER FIFTEEN ◆

The New War

THAT WAS THEN. On 24 February 2022, foreseeably yet astonishingly, Putin launched a full-scale war on Ukraine. Four months later it has transformed the post-Soviet world order and is still bloodily ongoing. Russia holds about a fifth of Ukraine's total territory, up from a twentieth (including Crimea) before the new invasion. Ukraine does not publish numbers for its military losses, and civilian ones in places taken by the enemy can only be guessed at. But military deaths to date number at least 10,000, and confirmed civilian ones nearly 5,000, with the UN warning that the real total is many thousands higher. Dozens more are being killed every day.

Unlike in 2014, when Russia's 'little green men' seemed to spring from nowhere, this time the build-up was gradual and in plain sight. The first smoke signal rose above the Kremlin battlements in July 2021, in the unlikely form of a long quasi-historical essay. Published under Putin's name, it set out its stall in its opening sentence: Russians and Ukrainians were 'one people, a single whole', and periodic estrangements the work of foreigners, seeking to divide and rule. Its first sections, covering the tenth century to the nineteenth, were calm in tone and faithful, albeit selectively, to the facts. But from the Russian Revolution onwards it descended into post-truth absurdity. The Great Famine was referred to, once and in passing, as a 'common tragedy'; Stalin and Hitler's 1939 joint invasion of Poland became the 're-gaining of lands earlier seized by Poland'; Stalin's name was not mentioned at all. Into the present, and no reference to the 2014 seizures, or to the ongoing war in the Donbass. Instead Ukraine's desire to join Europe was down to the West's 'anti-Russian project', which had 'set up the Ukrainian political system in such a way, so that although presidents and members of parliament change, the separatist, anti-Russian attitude stays the same.' Pro-Russians were being 'intimidated, driven underground . . . also killed', a 'forced change of identity . . . comparable in its consequences to the use of weapons of mass destruction against us'. Ukraine could only have 'true sovereignty' it wound up, 'in partnership with Russia . . . For we are one people.' In other words, Ukrainians weren't just part of Russia's patrimony – they didn't even really exist.

Little noticed on publication, the essay took on sinister significance from October, when Russian troops, armour and heavy weaponry started moving west towards the Ukrainian border – according to the Kremlin, on training exercises. As autumn turned to winter troop numbers grew, from 90,000 at the start of November to 100,000 in December, some coming all the way from the Russian Far East. American intelligence agencies started publicly to warn that invasion was possible, and to publish satellite images of ranked trucks, tanks and tents. The British foreign policy establishment was doubtful. No, Putin hadn't gone mad in lockdown. Why would he take such a risk, and throw away thirty years of economic integration? He was the same cautious old fox as always, and open warfare wasn't his style; he preferred proxies and deniability. What about his bombing of Aleppo? That was Arabs; he wouldn't bomb fellow Slavs. The maximalist prediction was that Putin might make a push in the south-east, to create a land link between the Donbass and Crimea. Absolutely nobody suggested that he might march on Kyiv.

By the end of January, however, it was clear that if this was a bluff, it was an extraordinarily thorough one. Troop numbers had risen to 130,000 – 30,000 of whom were moving into Belarus and massing at the point on its border nearest to Kyiv. Six amphibious assault ships arrived in the Black Sea from the Baltic and the Arctic, and satellites spotted pontoon bridges and radio masts going up. US warnings became more urgent – invasion was now not only possible but imminent. The Kremlin responded with sneers about 'hysteria' and 'alarmism', and accused Washington of 'provocations' designed to distract from its own planned attack.

On 4 February the war drums paused for the Beijing Winter Olympics. On the day of the opening ceremony, Putin and China's Xi Jinping met and made a joint statement deploring NATO expansionism and Taiwanese separatism. Though Ukraine was not mentioned, the message was clear: if Russia invaded, China would not interfere. Lasting just over a fortnight – during which time, it was assumed, Putin would not steal Xi's thunder by attacking – the Games created a diplomatic breathing-space. French president Emmanuel Macron and German chancellor Olaf Scholz both took the opportunity to fly to Moscow, only to find themselves seated twenty feet away from Putin at the other end of a freakishly long conference table. In Kyiv, meanwhile, remaining staff at the Western embassies packed up and left.

Having not been there since Covid, I took advantage of the hiatus. The flight was perfectly normal, and so was the city, looking its best under a blue sky and fresh snow. All the restaurants were open, and all the shops. Nobody was panic-buying; there were no crowds outside the banks, and no demonstrations. The only queue was outside the Pinchuk Art Centre, for the opening of an exhibition showcasing young artists from around the world. My favourite was a video piece by an Afghan. The film was of five small boys in a desert in a howling gale, blowing toy trumpets while trying to balance on a rock. They kept being blown off it and gamely climbing back on again. A metaphor for Afghanistan, and for Ukraine too.[1]

At breakfast the next morning – in a hipster haven of houseplants and fresh-ground coffee – I got chatting to an IT guy over French toast spritzed with peppermint and scattered with geranium petals. How worried was he about an invasion? Had he laid in supplies? He looked slightly sheepish. 'Maybe I should. But I don't want to believe that anything's going to happen. And if I have a pile of stuff sitting in the corner of my flat, I'll have to.' A real-estate lawyer told me that last time around, in 2014, she had panic-bought rice and pasta. But now people had lived with the Russian threat for eight years already, and they were carrying on as normal. Only one friend – the same ex-banker who joined the Maidan protests – had made preparations, laying in not only food and water but bulletproof vests. Yet even with him, discussing invasion scenarios felt completely unreal, as though we were scriptwriters brainstorming a war movie.

It was the same in Chernihiv, two hours' drive to the north and only forty miles from the Belarussian border. In one of its lovely churches, a priest looked offended when I asked if his parishioners were anxious. No, he wasn't organising special services, and he prayed for peace every Sunday anyway. When I asked a taxi driver if he expected invasion he shook his head and rubbed together forefinger and thumb – it was all a game, about money. The regional governor wasn't mentioning the war either. 'Of course we must control the borders, but the most important thing is that nobody panics, that we keep cool heads.' His office had done an 'audit' of potential air-raid shelters but not equipped or stocked them, and he pooh-poohed when I asked about military volunteers: 'What would we do with them?'[2]

On 20 February the Winter Olympics closed, and the following day Putin made an hour-long broadcast that amounted to a declaration of war. Looking stressed – taking deep breaths, gripping a table edge with both hands – he told viewers that Ukraine was under 'foreign external management' and 'just like a colony'. With Western help it was developing nuclear weapons, and its armed forces reported straight to NATO headquarters. NATO 'lied and swindled' when it took in new members after the Cold War, and rebuffed Russia's own friendly offer to join. Now Ukrainian entry was 'almost a done deal', and would allow the alliance to strike Samara or Volgograd. Russia was being 'blackmailed . . . for a single purpose: to put Russian back, to stop it developing. Just because we exist.'

At five o' clock in the morning of Thursday, 24 February, it finally happened. In Kyiv, Kharkiv and Mariupol, people were woken by the sound of explosions. Just outside the capital, Russian paratroopers landed at the Hostomel military airport, briefly capturing it before being driven off by Ukrainian units. (The giant cargo plane *Mriya* or 'Dream', restored and proudly back in service, was destroyed in the fighting.) At 2 p.m. Russian troops arrived outside Chernobyl's administrative headquarters, twelve miles inside the border, and started digging trenches in its highly contaminated Red Zone. In the south, units rolled out of Crimea and into the Dnipro estuary port of Kherson. One of the first civilians to be injured was a middle-aged nursery-school teacher, when a shell hit her building in a Kharkiv suburb. Except of course for Russian state media, which said she was an actress, a photograph of her bloodied face marked the war's awful transition to reality. All over the country, people pushed their way into trains or joined westward-pointing traffic jams, in Europe's biggest refugee flight since the end of the Second World War.

As the rockets began to fall, the leaders traded broadcasts. Zelensky got in first, on the eve of the attack. Speaking in Russian, he appealed directly to the Russian public, asking them to use their common sense – 'How could I be a Nazi?' – and to pressure their leadership not to go to war. War was 'pain, dirt, blood, death, thousands of deaths . . . Who will suffer most? The people. Who wants it least? The people? Who can stop it? The people.' Putin responded with a barely veiled nuclear threat: 'Whoever tries to hinder us . . . should know that Russia's response will be immediate. And it will lead you to such consequences you have never encountered in your history.'

If Putin hoped to frighten the West into sitting on its hands, it didn't work. The reaction was immediate, and nothing like the feeble protests of 2014. The US and EU announced their first sanctions packages on 28 February, and ramped them up over the following weeks, the most significant early moves being the ejection of Russian banks from the international payments system, SWIFT, and the freezing of Russian central bank reserves held abroad. At an emergency session of the General Assembly of the United Nations, 141 countries backed a motion condemning the invasion, and Russia managed to rally only four – Belarus, Syria, North Korea and Eritrea – against. (China and more disappointingly India both abstained.) Most to the point, the West finally began sending arms in quantity, starting with seventeen thousand anti-tank missiles in the invasion's first week. The most striking turn-around was Germany's. In the run-up to the invasion, Scholz had been derided for answering Zelensky's pleas for weapons with a batch of helmets. Now he announced that the world had come to a *Zeitenwende* or turning-point, and that it was time for Germany to abandon seven decades of pacifism. No more would German-made weapons not be sent to war zones, and an €100 billion new defence fund would be created, making her the third-biggest military spender in the world.

The public response, too, was remarkable. London's first rally – in Whitehall, on a wet afternoon on the invasion's second day – was small and sad. Everyone looked shocked and sick; many were in tears. A friend had stayed up all night making flags on her sewing machine. She lent me one, and I draped it over my shoulders against the drizzle. I bumped into a professor from my old university, fresh from protesting outside the Russian embassy. The last time he had done this, he said, was in 1968, during the crushing of the Prague Spring. One of his graduate students came up – a bracing person, bright and gutsy. She was supposed to be going to Arkhangelsk, to research the Russian poet Josef Brodsky's exile up there. Now she wasn't sure if she would get her grant. Go, I said; flex your credit card. Silly words, I realised almost as they left my mouth. What if she's arrested? Or what if meeting her gets my Arkhangelsk contacts into trouble? It felt absurd – a return to the 1930s. But it wasn't.

The next day there was a much bigger rally, in Trafalgar Square. Weaving through tourists on the way from the Tube, I resented their obliviousness. Why weren't they wearing yellow and blue? How could they think about anything else? But the whole of the square – lions, fountains, steps, balustrade – was packed tight, and the whole of the plaza in front of the National Gallery. A thick belt of onlookers, not quite joining in but interested, ringed the main crowd. This time it was a sunny day, and the mood was strong and almost jubilant. Up front, people bounced in unison, laughing and shouting 'Jump or you're a *moskal*!' – a chant from the Maidan. A long banner read 'When the last Ukrainian soldier falls, Putin will come for YOU', and placards 'Close our Sky' (a plea for a no-fly zone), 'Hongkongers Stand with Ukraine' and 'Putin Go Home'. The occasional – very occasional – cardboard sign read 'I'm Russian; I'm sorry', or 'I'm Russian; I'm ashamed'. A man was handing out daffodils. Did he have any connection to Ukraine? No, he just felt he had to. The Canadian Embassy looked on kindly; even more than usual, it was nice having it there.

For all the flag-waving, for the first three weeks the Russian advance looked unstoppable. In the south, troops fanned out from Crimea, pushing east towards Mariupol and west towards Odesa. On 4 March a long-range shell set fire to the nuclear power plant at Enerhordar, on the lower Dnipro bend – luckily, only to an administrative building. In the east Kharkiv was pummelled – a university library burned, all the windows of the city art gallery broken – and in the north the Russians surrounded dozy Chernihiv and pushed on towards the capital. The commuter town of Bucha was occupied on 27 February, and next-door Irpin, after fierce fighting, on March 6th. Shells started hitting Kyiv's high-rise Left Bank, smoke rising in the distance as war reporters made their broadcasts from the roof-terrace of the Intercontinental. Over their shoulders peeped the bell-tower of Saint Sofia's. For how much longer would the cathedral's Madonna stand 'from morning to morning'? After a thousand years, was she about to be pulverised into harebell-blue dust?

Soon, all my Kyiv friends had left except for Sasha, the music impresario with whom I had recorded a New Year's Eve song thirty years earlier. Astonishingly, I was able to keep WhatsApping him, even as the Russian army cut all but the southern roads out of the city. Disdaining to sleep in the metro – 'AN-na! Come ON!' – he and his partner Sveta camped in their hall corridor, away from the kitchen and living-room windows. At night they tried their best to sleep through the rumbles and shudders, and by day, Sasha walked with a backpack in search of open shops – edgy volunteer patrols a danger – wrote an online diary and composed. His new songs were quite unlike his usual output; some very sad, others very angry. On the phone, he would break off so that I could hear the mooing air-raid sirens. Sitting in workaday London, it was like telephoning back in time to the Blitz.

That morale didn't collapse in the first shocking days was due largely to Zelensky. His decision to stay in the capital, in the words of MP Alyona Shkrum, was 'a game changer. He took the lead, and the rest followed. The war began at 5 a.m., and that morning we held a session in our usual chamber – super-fast, just for half an hour, because the aircraft guns were going. But it was super-important to do it, to show that there was no power vacuum.'[3] To communicate with the public, Zelensky returned to his old campaign format of short to-camera talks, broadcast on YouTube. In the first, released on the third day of the war, he walked about in front of Chimera House, with its frogs and rhinos. No question, everyone could see, that he was anywhere but Kyiv. A leak from the US military did the rounds: they had offered to help Zelensky get safely out, but he had told them that he wanted 'ammo, not a ride'.

Zelensky's style and bravery also galvanised the West. His first big speech was to the annual Munich Security Conference, six days before the war began. Going straight to the point, he told delegates that 'in the twenty-first century, there are no more foreign wars'. Indifference made them accomplices, and appeasement did not work: 'The question "Why die for Danzig?" turns into "Now I have to die for Dunkirk."' They squirmed, and gave him a standing ovation. As Russian troops poured over the border he continued to press obvious but effective buttons. Speaking by video-link from a bunker and wearing what became a trademark khaki T-shirt, he gave the House of Commons a snippet from Churchill's 'We will fight them on the beaches'. Congress got 'I have a dream' – of weapons systems – and the Bundestag the Berlin Wall. Russia was trying to build a new one between freedom and slavery, and until Germany called off the Nord Stream 2 gas pipeline, she was reinforcing the barrier with barbed wire.

Together with the awful pictures coming out of Ukraine – of heavily pregnant women, stomachs bloody, being stretchered out of Mariupol's maternity hospital; of a mother and teenage children, neat with their day-packs and wheelie-cases, lying dead on a pavement next to Irpin's half-wrecked bridge – the speeches also galvanised the general public. Every day, friends called with offers of spare rooms (and followed up). Along the street, crayoned Ukrainian flags appeared in front windows, and children set up stalls selling outgrown toys and homemade lemonade. Though Britain was stingy with visas (put to shame by Ireland, which lifted all requirements immediately), so many people started driving vans filled with donations to the Polish border that the Ukrainian ambassador put out a tactful plea that they raise money instead. News desks and the think-tank world came good too. For years, it had been Brits wearing Russian goggles – ex-ambassadors to Moscow, ex-Moscow bureau chiefs – who opined on the various 'Ukraine crises' in the media. Now at last Ukrainians themselves filled the airwaves. The 2014 'annexations' became seizures or invasions, the 'referenda' became faux referenda, and antiquated 'the Ukraine' finally died a death. Especially heartening, somehow, was the sight of packs of Chicken Kyiv rather than Kiev in the chilled foods aisle at Sainsbury's. If that mighty supermarket had got it, Middle England had too.

About three weeks into the war, towards the middle of March, it became possible to hope that Ukraine would not be overrun after all. Unlike the Afghans the previous summer, the Ukrainians were not deserting or surrendering. On the contrary, they were fighting hard and nimbly. On a road north of Kyiv, a forty-mile-long Russian mechanised column initially seemed to spell the city's doom. But as small Ukrainian units mounted on quad bikes knocked out vehicles at its front and rear, it began to look more like a giant traffic jam. Russian lorries turned out to have cheap, quick-to-burst tyres. Abandoned tanks, stuck in the spring mud, were towed away in triumph by local farmers, using their tractors. Also, the army was making good use of the weapons beginning to arrive from the West. America's Javelin proved so popular that a Saint Javelin – haloed and cradling a bazooka – made her debut, and at least one baby girl was christened Javelina. Russian morale, judging by radio intercepts, began to droop. Soldiers complained that they hadn't got enough food or fuel, and that at night they couldn't turn on their engines for warmth for fear of heat-seeking drones. Their casual early tactics – 'bimbling in', as a British general put it, 'and seeing what would happen' – suggested that they really had expected to be welcomed as liberators.

On 29 March, that things weren't going to plan for the Kremlin was confirmed by the announcement that as a 'good-will gesture' Russian troops were 'repositioning' from the north to the Donbass. Their hurried pullback – from around Kyiv, Chernihiv, Kharkiv and Sumy – revealed horrors. In the Kyiv commuter town of Bucha, dozens of civilians were found lying dead, shot as they walked or bicycled along the streets, or as they came out of their houses into their front yards. Some had their hands tied behind their backs, and many showed signs of torture. In Motyzhyn, a village off the main road west of Kyiv, the village council leader and her husband and son, all abducted by Russian troops ten days earlier, were found bound and half-buried in woods. In the small farming village of Yahidne, near Chernihiv, 360 residents had been imprisoned in a school basement for twenty-five days, in the course of which seven were shot dead and ten, mostly elderly, died of cold and exhaustion. Rape reports started coming in, the first in the Western press an interview with a 33-year-old from a village near Kyiv. A pair of drunken soldiers had shot dead her husband and the family dog, then repeatedly raped her while her four-year-old son cried in the next-door room.[4] In the first two weeks after the withdrawal, the Ukrainian authorities recovered 765 civilian corpses in the Kyiv region alone, thirty of them children.[5] Everywhere, Russian troops had robbed and vandalised, stealing televisions, microwaves, clothes and children's toys – sometimes, as radio intercepts revealed, fulfilling the wish-lists of wives back home. Doors were sprayed with Russia's new 'Z' symbol, or booby-trapped with grenades so as to kill or cripple if homeowners returned.

When I visited Bucha and Irpin a fortnight after liberation, it felt as if they could never be happy again. In Irpin, every building was torn, charred, skeletal; the ground around heaped with shattered brick and concrete, and glittery with broken glass. In front of a wrecked block of flats, flowerbeds were strewn with the contents of peoples' kitchens – a bar of soap, tins of peas and of tuna, a big jar of home-pickled tomatoes, walnuts spilling from a bag, Christmas decorations, a wall clock. Amid the detritus, spring bulbs were coming up – daffodils already in flower, hyacinths in bud. The symbolism was illusory. One family had come back, but only to board up windows and retrieve any salvageable belongings. A reason they could not stay, as they showed me, was that a small rocket had crashed through their living-room wall and was sitting, unexploded, next to their rubble-covered sofa. They were the lucky ones. Elsewhere, a young man took us to where his 48-year-old mother and two neighbours had been killed by a shell as they went to fetch water. The crater was surprisingly small, in the middle of a parking space. His father had buried his mother nearby – the wooden cross over there, under the tree. Best not to try to interview him: 'He sits on that bench all day. He's not speaking, even to me. And when evening comes he starts to drink.' His parents used to run a market stall selling cleaning products. A birthday photograph showed them together, smiling; her in a smart coat, him carrying a bouquet. The son's own small business, a car parts shop, had been robbed and trashed. 'What they could take they took, and what they couldn't they broke.' Because the family flat was gone – a wave at a blackened block – he was sleeping in his Audi, his only remaining possession. Twenty-six years old and still blank-faced with shock, he had no idea what the future held, and in the meantime was using his car to give people lifts. He wouldn't take money, but reluctantly allowed us to buy him petrol – which didn't work, because the petrol station's emergency generator had broken down. Other dead had been taken to a mass grave in the grounds of Bucha's new church, organised by the local hospital while fighting was still ongoing. A broad trench perhaps forty yards long, it contained two or three layers of corpses, most in body bags, a few not. An exhumation team were working their way along it with shovels, and had so far unearthed ninety-five.

Perhaps the hardest of Bucha's sights to process were the shot-up cars in which families had tried to flee. Shiny new

people-carriers and shabby old Ladas, they had white cloths
tied to their radio aerials and hand-written 'Children' signs
taped to windscreens or painted on bonnets. They also still
contained their owners' possessions: a luminous green child's
scooter, a hairdryer, a litter tray and scoop, a ring binder with
a woman's medical records, a bottle of Head and Shoulders
shampoo, a remote control, a packet of fish food, a child-
sized yellow T-shirt, laundered and folded flannels in a neatly
knotted bag. Firing directly at passenger windows and windscreens, the killers must have been able to see their victims'
faces. Unlike their predecessors in 1944–5 they had not been
brutalised by years of war. Nor were they getting revenge for
atrocities committed against their own country. The people
they were killing spoke their own language. How, how could
they do this? What was going through their heads? Ukraine's
first war crime trial, of a captured 21-year-old tank driver,
took place in May. The accused said he had shot dead an unarmed elderly man on a bicycle because the man had been
on the phone, and because the other soldiers he was with
were shouting at him to do so. He was sorry. In the photos he
looked runtish, dim and pathetically young. But what else did
he do, and how sorry would he be were he safely back home
in Russia? He was sentenced to life imprisonment.

Shortly followed by the killing, by missile strike, of fifty-
nine people in a refugee-packed railway station, the Bucha
revelations provoked a wave of revulsion worldwide. The
Kremlin's response was to accuse Ukraine of fakery, and to
ramp up its rhetoric. On 3 April, the day after the first photographs from Bucha hit the internet, the state-owned news
agency RIA Novosti published an editorial that would have
done Goebbels proud. The whole population of Ukraine, it
said, needed re-education, which would take at least a generation. The country would have to be directly ruled by Russia,
with no pretence at autonomy, and the very word Ukraine
could not be retained. The 'Banderite' leadership would be
'liquidated', and its accomplices executed, imprisoned, or

sentenced to forced labour. Only thus could Ukraine – 'an artificial anti-Russian construct', with 'no civilizational content of its own' – be freed 'from the intoxication [and] temptation . . . of its so-called European choice'. On the 20th the Kremlin underlined its nuclear threats by testing a new intercontinental ballistic missile.

A resumption of talks, clearly, was not on the cards. As British prime minster Boris Johnson told journalists on the day that Putin showed off his new rocket, 'How can you negotiate with a crocodile when it's got your leg in its jaws?' Instead, a procession of Western leaders took the train from Poland to Kyiv to show support. The Polish, Czech and Slovenian prime ministers had made the trip already – bravely, while the city was still encircled. Now they were followed by the European Commission's Ursula von der Leyen, who wore a flak jacket to look at Bucha's mass graves. The next day it was Johnson, who Zelensky took for a walkabout on Khreshchatyk, and assured that Ukrainian soldiers shouted 'God Save the Queen!' as they fired their NLAWs, the British version of the Javelin. A few days later Justin Trudeau reopened the Canadian embassy and got to pat Patron, a bomb-detecting Jack Russell terrier. On 24 April it was the turn of the men who really mattered – US Secretary of State Antony Blinken and Defense Secretary Lloyd Austin. No walkabouts for them, but three hours in a windowless conference room. Back in Poland, they spoke to the press in a warehouse stacked with aid. There would be 'massive support for Ukraine, massive pressure on Russia', the aim being to 'weaken [Russia] to the degree that it can't do the kinds of things that it has done'. The following day Austin hosted a meeting of defence ministers from forty donor countries at a US airbase in Germany, telling them that they needed to send arms 'at the speed of war'.

Through April into May, the hardest fighting was for Mariupol, in the south. Pulverised by heavy artillery, large parts of the city were flattened, drone footage showing nothing left but the outlines of buildings and roads. Its last defender was

the Azov Regiment, the regularised descendant of a far-right
volunteer brigade that helped keep the city out of Russian
hands in 2014–15. Holed up in Akhmetov's steelworks, it
held out for eighty-two excruciating days, its increasingly
gaunt commander uploading videos on how his wounded men
were dying of thirst and blood poisoning. They finally surrendered on 17 May. How many civilians perished in the siege
of Mariupol is unknown. Russian forces did not allow 'green
corridors' for evacuation except towards the end, and then
only into Russia itself. (Ukrainians are furious that the Red
Cross cooperated in what amounted to deportations.) Car-
owners could try to drive out but often died in the attempt,
either caught in shelling or deliberately killed, as in Bucha, by
Russian troops. The majority of residents were trapped under
bombardment. The 'cause of death' column in a database
compiled by a relatives' group gives a pale idea of what they
underwent. Entries include 'died when apartment bombed',
'bombed while trying to get water', 'died while putting out
a fire', 'froze to death', 'shot dead' and 'died from shrapnel
wounds', alongside deaths from starvation, lack of medical
treatment, heart attack, Covid and stroke.[6] The Ukrainian
government's estimate of 22,000 civilians dead (5 per cent of
Mariupol's pre-war population) may be an undercount, and
the latest fear is a cholera outbreak, if unburied and haphaz-
ardly buried bodies contaminate the water supply.

Currently the world's attention is on the Donbass, where
at the end of June Russia took the town of Severodonetsk and
now threatens Slovyansk. Slow and grinding, the fighting
mostly consists of old-fashioned unguided artillery barrages,
in which Russia has a clear advantage, firing about 20,000
shells a day compared to Ukraine's 6,000. Both sides have
good air defences, so that neither can safely fly over the other's territory. And both knock out the other's reconnaissance
drones, the Ukrainians using Western-supplied surface-to-
air missiles, the Russians electronic jamming to make the
drones crash. (The average lifespan of a Ukrainian drone is

only about seven days.) The balance will change as more Ukrainians are trained on American GPS-guided mobile rocket launchers, which are just arriving on the battlefield. As of 12 July, they have scored twenty hits on Russian ammunition dumps, as well as on command posts and barracks.[7] Russia also continues to terrorise areas outside the immediate war zone, landing cruise missiles on the Kyiv, Kharkiv, Sumy, Dnipro and Odesa regions. Some are aimed at military targets but many not, one of the latest atrocities being the killing of twenty people in a mid-afternoon hit on a shopping centre.

To be able to take the offensive, a new study by the Royal United Services Institute[8] explains, the Ukrainian army needs more howitzers and ammunition, more secure radios, more armoured cars, drones that can seek out and destroy jamming equipment, and better air defences against cruise missiles. It also needs more infantry and staff training, so that units can coordinate at scale. ('Orders groups', the authors tut, 'are more akin to debates, in which the commander's statement of the mission objective results in a chaotic discussion enabling all participants to raise questions, concerns and ideas.' At platoon and company level this produces innovation, but 'battalion and brigade-sized actions [need] unity of command [and] a clear orders process'.) The West needs to coordinate too, so that Ukraine is not landed, as is currently happening, with many slightly different sorts of gun, which even if they take the same size shell need different fuses, charges, spare parts and maintenance regimes. Without all this, Ukraine risks getting stuck in an attritional, 'last army standing' conflict, which given Russia's vast military stockpiles it cannot win.

The next development may be a behind-the-lines partisan war. Though the fronts are still moving, Russia is already trying to establish permanent rule in the parts of the south it holds, using techniques honed in Crimea. In Kherson – the only regional centre to have been captured apart from devastated

Mariupol – 'Kherson is Ukraine' protests were tolerated for a few weeks, then broken up with tear gas. The uncooperative mayor was replaced with a stooge and has recently been detained. Hundreds have been arrested, in particular army and volunteer battalion veterans, local government officials, police officers, priests, journalists and activists. At checkpoints people's phones are examined, and they are made to undress so as to reveal patriotic tattoos. Schools are being ordered to swop to the Russian curriculum, and Ukrainian radio and television stations have been blocked and replaced with Russian ones. Internet and mobile phone services are assumed to be tapped. ('The way you tell people you are OK,' says a friend, 'is by posting pictures of your cat.') In prospect is a fake referendum and a declaration that the region is a People's Republic or a Russian province.

Holding the south down, though, may not be easy. There have been at least three political assassinations in Kherson. Two pro-Russian activists were shot dead in March, when unknown assailants fired at their car, and on 24 June an official in the regional administration was killed by a car bomb. An earlier bombing seriously injured the newly installed 'people's mayor' of Enerhodar.[9] The centre of behind-the-lines resistance is Melitopol (halfway between Kherson and Mariupol), which has seen several more guerrilla attacks on collaborators and on Russian soldiers, and sabotage of railway tracks and a radar station. Ukraine aims to retake Kherson, and has pushed close to the city outskirts. But in areas of the south that Russia continues to hold, attacks like these may ramp up – and with them, reprisals.

◆ CHAPTER SIXTEEN ◆

What Next?

IN MAY A Ukrainian rap-cum-folk band won the Eurovision song contest. Everybody – except banned Russia – was delighted, and the runner-up – a Brit for once – wore a pink bucket hat for his homecoming press conference, in homage to the group's lead singer. Zelensky said next year's contest would be in liberated Mariupol.

Ukraine will need a lot more, though, than the supportive wearing of pink hats. The new war has already destroyed over $200 billion worth of infrastructure, plus who knows how many billions worth of private property. The economy is about half the size it was pre-invasion. A new IMF package, capital controls and limits on cash withdrawals have prevented a currency crash and kept the banking system afloat, but more financing will be needed. The government's budget deficit is running at $5 billion per month, currently being plugged by the sale of war bonds and by direct grants, mostly from America. A problem for the whole world is Russia's blockade of Odesa, for now Ukraine's only large Black Sea port. Grain that should be being shipped to overseas buyers is still sitting in silos, leaving no storage space for this year's harvest. The blockade is pushing up food prices everywhere, but the countries that will be hardest hit are Egypt, Ethiopia, Lebanon and Yemen, all unstable or war-torn already. The Kremlin may even calculate that a new migrant crisis will help turn the West in favour of pressing Ukraine to submit.

Another expensive problem is unexploded ordnance. Before the new war, the British de-mining charity the Halo Trust reckoned it had twenty years' work ahead of it clearing nasties left over from 2014–15. Now the task is many times bigger, and more complicated because so much of the fighting has been in urban areas, leaving behind ruins seeded among other things with small but lethal cluster bombs. 'I've seen it in Syria,' says the head of Halo's Ukraine operation, Mairi Cunningham: 'They have a high failure rate and curious kids pick them up. They're only about the size of tennis balls, but they cause multiple casualties.' One of her priorities is a public information campaign, so that returning internal refugees ('internally displaced people' or IDPs) know what to look out for: 'Accident risks are highest when people come back. They haven't witnessed the fighting, so they're not aware of the threats. That's when we expect a spike.' Another is training up more de-miners – not a problem since there is no shortage of good applicants. At the beginning of the invasion, when most of the clearance programme had to be halted, her local staff of their own accord swopped over to setting up field hospitals and driving in aid. 'We just came in to formalise and amplify . . . It's quite humbling what they're doing. And humour amidst it all. Dignity in the middle of all these horrendous things. It's been an honour working with them.'[1]

Will the West keep coming up with the cash as well as the arms to help Ukraine? There are plenty of reasons to worry that it might not. As the conflict drags on and higher food and fuel prices bite, sympathy may falter. The bellwether will be Poland, which identifies passionately with the Ukrainian cause, but is also having to cope with 1.2m Ukrainian refugees. (The next most popular host countries are Germany, with 867,000, and the Czech Republic, with 388,000. France has 92,000, Britain 91,000.)[2] Marine Le Pen's runner-up place in the French presidential elections in April was a reminder of how fickle the public can be. Despite having been a long-time

Putin supporter, and taken loans from a Russian bank, she won 42 per cent of the vote. China and India are sitting on the fence, buying Russian oil and gas but not (as yet) selling arms to Putin. By far the most important player in Ukraine's camp is America – currently providing the vast majority of financing as well as of weapons. Broad bipartisan support in Congress will see the effort through the next two years, but Trump – a professed Putin admirer, and menacer of Zelensky in the notorious 2019 phone call – could be back in the White House in 2024.

As of July 2022, however, the Western alliance is strong. In May, Biden signed a 'Lend-Lease Act' removing restrictions on military aid, $6.8 billion worth of which has been sent or committed since the war began. Europe's most important and hardest task is to switch away from Russian energy, and on 31 May the European Union announced that it would cease all sea-borne import of Russian oil (two-thirds of the total) by the end of the year. Though Hungary's Putin-emulating Viktor Orban blocked an EU-wide agreement on piped oil, Germany and Poland have said that they will stop buying it. The promises are vaguer on gas. Imports would be reduced by two-thirds in twelve months, the EU said in March, but there has been no detail on how this will happen. Instead the pressure is going the other way, as Russia threatens Europe with a cold winter by reducing flows itself.

While still not as tough as they could be, sanctions are having an effect. Russian GDP is forecast to fall by 10 per cent in 2022, and another 4 per cent the year after. Inflation is running at 17 per cent. And though the war is no longer on the front pages every day, the Western public are still squarely in Ukraine's corner. (Even my 77-year-old mother, resident in rural Dorset and long puzzled by my persistent interest in an odd part of the world, has learned the national anthem, in Ukrainian, with her local choir. A refugee mother and daughters taught them the words, and burst into tears during the final rehearsal.) Zelensky helps keep the essentials in view with his video-link speeches – for the Grammys, 'What's most opposite to music? The silence of ruined cities'; for Cannes, a line from Charlie Chaplin's satire *The Great Dictator*. At an international tech conference he appeared in hologram and quoted *Star Wars*: 'We will defeat the Empire too.' Not least, he hosts visiting celebrities. Bono started the trend by busking in the Kyiv metro, and has been followed by Angelina Jolie, Ben Stiller, Sean Penn and Richard Branson.

In the chandeliered ticket hall of Kyiv's central railway station, posters have been stuck up showing favourite memes. One is a map of Europe with Russia missing, in its place an 'Ocean of Dreams'. But much as Ukrainians might wish it, the country is not magically going to disappear.

Hopes, at the start of the war, that Russians might protest against it in overwhelming numbers quickly died. For a few weeks there were indeed demonstrations in dozens of cities. But they were small – never more than a few thousand strong – and shrivelled in the face of mass detentions. (Given legal cover by a new law criminalising criticism of the army, these became progressively more absurd. People were manhandled into police vans for holding up blank pieces of paper, or for standing and reading a book.) A prima ballerina quit the Bolshoi, but only one, and when a TV newscaster leapt onto camera with a placard reading 'They are lying to you', the rest of the studio crew carried on with their jobs. The reaction of tens of thousands was not to try to change Russia but to leave it, and join new diasporas in Tblisi and Istanbul. Unfairly but understandably, Ukrainians are cynical about Russian liberals – they would put the word in inverted commas. Many cheered, they correctly point out, when Russia seized Crimea in 2014 and are only unhappy now, they think, because their access to Nike trainers and holidays abroad is threatened. Nothing makes Ukrainians madder than liberal Russian victimhood – 'We know we're not being bombed of course, but . . .' – and the vague 'No to war' slogan, implying as it does that the two sides are equally responsible for the conflict.

It is not Russia's few and persecuted liberals, though, that Ukraine has to worry about. It is the Russian public in general, who seem so far to be mainlining Putin's Make Russia Great Again story. The last reliable polling organisation in the country, the Levada Centre, showed Putin's approval rating jumping twelve points (from 71 per cent to 83 per cent) after the invasion, and it has stayed up since. (Against received wisdom, the war is least popular among the poorest, probably because they suffer most from recessions and are least able to bribe their way out of conscription.) Focus group-style studies show ordinary people repeating formulae from state television, or locked in denial: '"We don't know anything" was a thesis put forward by many. Women would say that they were praying for someone in particular, but trying not to have an opinion about the situation overall. It felt like the whole population had chosen to be like children who didn't understand anything.'[3] This chimes with the experience of Ukrainians with Russian relatives. Aunts, cousins, even siblings and parents often flatly refuse to believe it when told on the phone that that their army is murdering civilians and bombing peaceful cities. Cross-border family contacts had shrivelled already – to awkward New Year's chats about the kids and the weather. They have now usually been dropped altogether.

While the Russian public are behind Putin, there seems to be little chance either of a palace coup. In the first weeks of the war a general was dismissed and an intelligence chief put under house arrest, but because they had misread Ukraine's military readiness, not because they were suspected of disloyalty. There has been only one high-profile government defection – by Anatoly Chubais, Putin's climate envoy and in a past life Yeltsin's economics guru. Only one oligarch has spoken out, and was immediately forced to sell his bank to a Putin loyalist at a knockdown price.[4] Notwithstanding seizures of super-yachts and Mediterranean villas, the vast

majority of the elite seem to either support the war or be resigned to it. It may not matter much what they think anyway.
As an unhappy politics professor puts it: 'We have only two
levels now: the tsar and subjects of the tsar.'[5]

There is a theological but mind-focusing debate about
whether Russia now qualifies as a fascist state. Ukrainians
– who arguably know best – certainly think so. They have
been calling Putin 'Putler' for years, and a new nickname for
Russian soldiers – alongside the old 'orcs' and 'pigdogs' – is
rashisti, from 'Russian' plus fashist. It depends on how you
define fascism, but the regime certainly ticks much of the
checklist. As the historian Timothy Snyder puts it, 'It has
a cult around a single leader, Vladimir Putin. It has a cult of
the dead, organised around World War II. It has a myth of a
past golden age of imperial greatness, to be restored by a war
of healing violence.'[6] The language and rituals are there too:
the warnings about traitors and fifth columnists, the likening
of critics to insects or parasitic worms, the schoolchildren
denouncing their teachers, the choreographed mass rallies,
the chants: 'For the army! For Putin! For Russia!' In a popular
video, children dressed in police uniforms sing about getting
Alaska back for the Motherland, the chorus 'We prefer peace/
But if our commander in chief calls us to the final battle/
Uncle Vova, we are with you!' – with a fist-pump on the
final line. The song is being taught in kindergartens country-
wide. The new 'Z' symbol looks like half a swastika, or an SS
lightning-bolt. Thugs paint it on dissidents' doors.

Overlooked abroad is the hate-filled lunacy of Russian
state television. Already virulently anti-Western, its news
programmes now merge fact with the fantasies of far-right
pulp fiction and computer games. On the country's ostensibly serious flagship current affairs show, two hours long and
broadcast six evenings a week, academics and members of
parliament talk about how the spetzoperatsiya in Ukraine is
a warm-up for the 'demilitarisation' of NATO. The 'ephem-
eral' Baltics should have been 'choked' or 'run over' back in

1991. Russia should 'tame' the Lithuanians by seizing a land corridor to Kaliningrad. Berlin is within reach of Russian bombers and needs to 'learn the lessons of history'. Dutch oil ports would be 'hard to miss . . . we don't even need a Kalibr, a torpedo would do it'. A nuclear strike off the UK's coast would sweep the country with a 'radioactive tsunami'. People who 'wave [NATO's] Article 5 in the air can roll it up and shove it you know where'; we are already entering World War Three. With bar-room expansiveness, the show's host, a veteran propagandist called Vladimir Solovyov, eggs them on. No guest demurs, or even raises an eyebrow.[7]

How long will Ukraine keep fighting? Behind the mantra that it is up to Ukraine to decide, the brute reality is that the West will dictate, since it is supplying the weapons. In public, Zelensky's position is that all Ukrainian territory must be recovered, including Donetsk, Luhansk and Crimea. Sixty-one per cent of Ukrainians, according to a late-May poll, agree with him (though that drops to 45 per cent in the east of the country).[8] Barring dramatic regime change in Russia, however, it will not happen. And since active pro-Ukrainians and much of the educated middle class left those territories after 2014, it is not clear that the majority of their present-day populations would even want it to.

On the West's side, the debate can be framed as between the 'peace' and 'justice' parties, the former believing that the Ukrainian government should be urged to start talks as soon as possible, the latter that if Putin is allowed a victory he will grab more of Ukraine, and probably other countries too. Ukrainians find the 'peace' argument, as a gay-rights activist puts it, 'very painful to read. It's like – you're being beaten by your partner, and the neighbours come and say "You should accept it, because we don't like violence."'[9] It also revives bitter memories of 1994's Tripartite Agreement, when the West strong-armed Ukraine into giving up its Soviet-inherited nuclear warheads, in exchange for what turned out to be worthless security guarantees. Most of all, unfortunately, the 'peace' argument underestimates the scale of Russian revanchism, recent Kremlin rhetoric being of 'recovering' not only Ukraine, but the whole old Soviet bloc. That is wildly overblown – Russia has not the means – but Putin could very well attack Georgia or Moldova, or even, if he thinks the West will blink, the NATO-member northern Baltics. The most cogent 'peace' argument is that if battlefield humiliation threatens, Putin might actually use a nuclear weapon. It sounds fantastical – but six months ago, so did where we are now.

And what for Ukraine when the war is over – or as Ukrainians say, when victory is won? If the rebuilding effort is anything like the war effort, the bulk of the country could spring back surprisingly quickly. Self-organised via social media, Ukraine's home front is as impressive as its military one, and as inspiring as places like Bucha are horrific. Everywhere, volunteers are doing what has to be done: driving in aid from Poland, manning information points at railway stations, packing up museum collections and storing them in basements, converting disused buildings into housing for IDPs. When I returned to my favourite Kyiv breakfast spot, I found the staff busy clingfilming cheese rolls and styrofoam tubs of grated cabbage salad, ready for distribution to hospitals and the army. The manager, in his thirties and wearing a bush-ranger's hat, said that he had joined a network of twenty-three restaurants in the city which between them were preparing thirteen thousand meals daily. His customers had become his volunteers and funders. Mostly in IT, they were able to keep doing their normal jobs online at night and help out here in the day.

Similarly typical of the times is Kateryna Mikhalitskyna, a translator and writer whom I last interviewed ten years ago, when the Lviv-based publishing house for which she works, Old Lion, was just starting up. Since then it has flourished, and before the new war published 130 titles annually – all Ukrainian-language – and employed over a hundred full-time staff. We meet in in one of its bookshop-cafés, one of eight country-wide. When Russia invaded, Kateryna says, she and her husband held a family council. They decided that instead of leaving, they would stay and do what they could. Now her days are spent sorting medical supplies in a warehouse, or helping random people in need:

> My phone just rings – a man's voice: "My name's Andriy, you helped my friends last week. My family is at the train station; can you meet them?" So I go and find them and help them to get on the bus to Poland or wherever . . . All you are doing a lot of the time is talking and connecting people, but by the evening you can't even remember your own name.

Her sixteen-year-old son, who sublimates general anxiety into worrying whether summer exams will happen, likes to join the camo-net knotting circle in the public library: 'It's meditative in a way. You can share experiences, and not sit alone.' Her own best therapy is a craft club that she runs for IDP children: 'We had a session last Sunday, just after the Bucha photographs came out. I pulled myself together and went, and together we made good monsters, not bad ones. I don't know if I helped the children, but they certainly helped me.' She goes to a shelf and takes down one of her own recent translations – Hemingway's *The Snows of Kiliman-jaro*. It's a gorgeous edition, with original illustrations and luxurious endpapers. When next season's list will come out, heaven knows. Their usual printers have stopped working, and Polish ones are too expensive. But in the meantime Old Lion has formatted thirty titles as downloadable files, free for anyone who wants them. Maybe electronic is the way to go with everything, I suggest. She looks a little sad – 'But people love these books' – before pinning her smile back on with one of the war's catchphrases – *Vsye budye dobrye* – 'Everything will be fine.'

Ukrainians are also beginning to think ahead to how they will rebuild their country. In Kyiv, husband-and-wife MPs

Dmytro Natalukha and Alyona Shkrum are infectiously positive. Where do they think Ukraine will be in a year's time? 'We're not allowing ourselves to think of frozen conflict,' says Shkrum immediately. 'We want to come out stronger.' Natalukha quotes Zelensky's 'big Israel' idea, of a Ukraine well armed, closely allied with America, and with an economy centred on IT. Worries the pair spin as positives. Will the five million Ukrainians now abroad come home? It will depend on whether there are jobs for them, of course, but those that don't can be granted dual passports, so that they keep their links and keep paying Ukrainian taxes. And those that do will have learned new languages, made new contacts and generally broadened their horizons, all good for them and for the country. They are also completely confident that despite the suspension for now of party politics, Ukraine will remain robustly democratic. Shkrum even predicts that Zelensky will lose the 2024 presidential election: 'It'll be like Churchill after the Second World War – "Thank you and goodbye."' Natalukha cites a big poster that used to hang over the Maidan. 'It said "Freedom is our Religion", with a picture of a broken chain. I used to think it was so cheesy and banal. But it turns out that for Ukrainians freedom actually *is* their religion. Especially, the freedom to say what you want, to anyone. That's why the "Russian warship, go fuck yourself" slogan is so popular.' (This dates to the first day of the war, when a Russian cruiser radioed to the thirteen defenders of Snake Island, a speck of rock off the Danube estuary, to surrender or be fired upon. In the recording of the exchange, one Ukrainian soldier whispers to another, 'This is it then. Shall I tell them to go fuck themselves?' The other replies, 'Might as well.' Their answer to the ship – fabulously rude in Ukrainian – was celebrated by the issue of a commemorative postage stamp.)

It is easy to dismiss talk about love of freedom as morale-boosterism. But one thing the war has definitely done is forge new solidarity between Ukraine's east and west. It is the gritty, Russian-speaking eastern cities – battered Kharkiv, martyred Mariupol – that are the country's frontline heroes. No longer can Lviv look down its pretty little nose at them for not being Ukrainian enough. Innumerable personal ties are being created too. At Lviv's main aid distribution centre, in the grounds of an aristocratic Polish mansion, two IDP families, unmistakeably eastern and urban, were swopping grumbles about the city's ballooning rents. But there were instant grins and thumbs-up signs when I asked about the village where the authorities had found them a cottage. 'People are so kind! They bring us cabbages! And look!' – phone held out – 'Storks! On their nest!'

The idea of a moral sea-change, of a Maidan-like passion for the better, comes up in many conversations too. 'We feel big anger and big hate,' says the Old Lion's founder, Mariana Savka,

> but big love too. We should do what we can do, each of us. It depends on each of us. I am very, very happy that all my friends are good people. It's very important for me. I know that with these people I can rebuild my company, my society, our future, everything. The war is killing people. But it's also making people. It's really true.[10]

In a pale, London-sized way, I knew what she meant about friends. For me, one of the most upsetting events of the first weeks of the war, ridiculously, was an encounter with an old and pleasant acquaintance, a successful barrister, who turned out to be helping a Russian oligarch try to get off the UK sanctions list. He saw nothing wrong with this, even found it amusing. Friends hosting refugees, conversely, made me tear up.

It doesn't do to get sentimental. For Ukraine to build back better, one big thing above all needs fixing – corruption. Things have improved a lot since the Maidan. Watchdogs and campaign groups have multiplied, and a generational culture change is underway. (As a twenty-something programmer puts it, 'A woman who works in the tax office has a new Ford.

My father says, "She works in the tax office. Why shouldn't she?" But I say, "Why *should* she?"') But still it was no great surprise, early in the war, when an ex-MP's departing wife was discovered to be carrying $28m in cash in her luggage. Transparency International's 2021 Corruption Perceptions Index ranked Ukraine one down from Zambia, and one up from Gabon. If the billions now being poured into the country are not to go into private pockets, an extremely close eye will need to be kept on how they are spent, even if that means offending Ukrainian *amour-propre*.

Whereas corruption needs a zero-tolerance regime, what needs careful handling is the 'de-Russification' movement. Not surprisingly, the 1990s' easy-going attitude to identity is a thing of the past. Since the new war began, more statues have been tumbling, and not only Lenins. Kyiv's crass but photogenic *Brotherhood* – a pair of muscled workers, jointly holding aloft a hammer and sickle emblem under a giant arch – has been pulled from its plinth. So has Kharkiv's General Zhukov, victor of the Great Patriotic War. Three Pushkins have been removed, by town councils in the west. It is the Pushkins that are most controversial, one side pointing out that it's not the poet bombing Ukraine, the other that Moscow used his cult as a territory-marker, and that he was an imperialist, romanticising the conquest of the Caucasus and writing virulently against the 1831–2 Polish rising.

Hardest to get right will be the language politics. Some are still sore at Poroshenko's education and language laws. 'We Russian-speakers', complains a Kharkiv historian and writer, 'are being turned into third-class citizens. The goal is to exclude Russian from the public sphere, to turn it into a street language.' Like Bulgakov in *The White Guard*, he sneers at the Ukrainian-language intelligentsia. They are 'very emotional, chauvinistic. Tolstoy, Dostoyevsky – they hate the fact that Ukraine hasn't got anyone comparable.' (Though one of Dostoyevsky's grandfathers, he points out, was a Uniate priest from near Vynnytsa.) He's unreasonable. Bilinguality is still the norm, and Zelensky himself is a native Russian-speaker. He's also talking about tensions within a small sliver of society, the literary intelligentsia. But there is no denying his feelings: 'I'm under attack on two sides. Russia is bombing my city, and my fellow citizens are attacking me for my culture and language. I've lost the ground from under my feet.' A new catchphrase – 'There are no good Russians' – alarms him. 'Of course they mean people who support Putin, but it could easily be extended to people like me.' He is *Ukrainian*, he repeats, 'a borderlands person'. Though in his forties, in his whole life he has only been to Moscow three times.

Governments need to acknowledge and assuage those feelings. But often, even Ukrainians whose first language is Russian don't want to speak it anymore. In Kyiv, I meet my musician friend Sasha and his partner Sveta at a Tatar restaurant, the first in the city to reopen. Having just emerged from six weeks hiding from bombing in their hallway they are a little disoriented, blinking at the packed tables – half the world's press is here – and hurrying waitresses. Sveta has lived in Kyiv most of her adult life, but was born in Russia's Rostov, just over the border. Rostov, Donetsk and Mariupol were a trio then, she says wistfully; people hopped back and forth between them without thinking twice. But when I ask, jokingly, how her Ukrainian is getting on, she grimaces and circles her throat with her hands: 'Russian. Ugh. I never want to hear it again.' She is trying to get Sasha to speak Ukrainian at home, so that hers improves. Another friend reminds me of Lviv's 2014 'Speak Russian Day': 'It would never happen now. Before, we cared how we looked on Russian TV. Now people have chosen their side. Anyone who disagrees you can't persuade.'

Four months in, the war is sculpting a new world order. Finland and Sweden – the latter neutral since the Napoleonic Wars – have applied to join NATO. And on 23 June, stunningly, Ukraine was granted candidate status by the European

Union. Whether or not the EU actually steps up in the end – Ukraine's poverty and potential voting weight may prompt second thoughts – it is a powerful gesture, and will help nudge the country into reforms it needs anyway.

We don't know for how long we will have to cope with Putin. Maybe he has cancer. Maybe he will be shuffled aside by a cabal. Or maybe he will stay in power for years. Whatever happens, some basic facts need to be kept in mind. One is that Russia is not nearly as powerful as it pretends. Its economy is only the size of Spain's. Half of its export income comes from oil and gas, since thirty years after the end of Communism it still does not make much that the rest of the world wants to buy. Its population is large, but less than half the size of America's, and a quarter the size of the rest of Europe's. Most of its imposing landmass is barely inhabited forest and bog. Another fact is that the perhaps always naïve hope of the 1990s – that Russia would turn into a normal European country – is comprehensively dead. Instead it has become a revanchist autocracy, vicious at home and abroad. Blind eye-turning has only eased it down this path. Without sea-changes in the regime and in Russian society, new attempts at 'reset' will be futile. As the anti-aircraft rockets now pointing up at the sky round Polish airports attest, we are back to containment, whether we like it or not.

A third, more cheering fact is that Ukraine really does deserve the West's help. For all its faults it is a free country, fighting for values we all share, for the kind of lives we all want live. The opening line of the national anthem – 'Ukraine is not dead yet' – no longer prompts a snigger. Sung, as it was on the Maidan, by hundreds of thousands of people – Ukrainian and Russian-speaking, Uniate and Orthodox, Jewish and Muslim, of every age and class, bareheaded in the snow – it brings tears to the eyes. Betraying the country would be moral and strategic failure on a par with the crushed Hungarian Rising or Prague Spring – and with much less excuse. And even if we care only for ourselves, letting Putin come away victorious would make the whole world a more dangerous place. How long, if he is allowed to smash Ukraine, before China attacks Taiwan, or Serbia Kosovo? And how long before we have a clutch of new nuclear powers, who have taken the lesson that only warheads guarantee security? Victory for Ukraine, conversely, might even – one can only hope – usher in a new, better regime in Russia itself. The old Polish slogan – 'For Our Freedom and Yours' – still applies.

At the end of April 2022, I take the train back from Kyiv to Poland. It is a smart modern one – South Korean, the man sitting next to me explains. Though the refugee flows are nothing like they were, the open-plan carriage is packed with families, children and cats in sleepy heaps. On overhead screens, cartoon Cossacks alternate with warnings not to touch unexploded ordnance: Don't pick up the shiny rocket, or the teddy under the tree; they might go bang. Instead tell your mummy to call this number. Outside the window, the countryside is much as it was thirty years ago. Churches have been restored, their walls white and domes shiny. Here and there, a house has a new spray-painted metal roof – a crisp rectangle of orange or purple dropped into the landscape's smudgy greens and browns. But the small roads are still gravel, and the villages still have their sentry-box privies and wandering geese and wells with hoists like upraised arms. Bicycles are as common as cars, and I even spot a V-bottomed cart, the horse grazing while the driver cuts brushwood. During the fortnight I've been in Ukraine, spring has arrived. Trees are coming into leaf and the ground has dried. A wood is scattered with anemones, thick as confetti. In new-turned vegetable plots people straighten up to watch the train go by. As we draw into Lviv station I look for damage from rockets that landed nearby early in the morning, killing seven. There is none to be seen, though when the doors open there is a slight smell of smoke. People get off and people get on, quietly so as not to disturb the sleeping children. The doors hiss shut again, and we move on west.

◆ ACKNOWLEDGEMENTS ◆

Many people contributed to the various editions of this book. On the first, written in the mid-1990s, especial thanks to the sadly now late Sergey Maksimov, and to Tanya Lipnitska, Svetlana Rusnak and Sasha Sparinsky for their help and warm friendship in Kyiv. Yulya Khoroshilova, Roma Ihnatowycz, Vlada Tkach and Roman Waschuk were generous with encouragement and ideas. Professor Timothy Colton, Dr Peter Duncan, Prince Jezzar Giray, Dr Lubomyr Hajda, Simon Hemans, Professor Geoffrey Hosking, Dr Daniel Kaufmann, Professor John LeDonne, Professor Richard Pipes, Professor Roman Szporluk, Professor Adam Ulam and Professor Andrew Wilson gave illuminating interviews, and Jonathan Ford a ruthless and invaluable critique of the manuscript. Dr Chiara Mayer-Rieckh, Julian Ellison, Jean de Sola Pool and Chris and Annabel Wrenn all hospitably put me up, and the staffs of the School of Slavonic and East European Studies Library, the London Library and the British Library were patient and helpful. Heartfelt thanks in particular to my then agent Peter Robinson, without whose support this book and my subsequent writing career would never have happened. And the same to Rebecca Wilson, then of Weidenfeld & Nicolson, who put a bet on a no-name young journalist.

For the 2015, post-Maidan edition, I was fortunate to be able to pick the wise and well-stocked brains of Duncan Allen, Robert Brinkley, Laurence Broyd, Robert and Larissa Homans, Andriy Kyrchiv, Yuri Lukanov, Ihor Olekhov, Nick Piazza, Roland Smith and Andrei Terekhov. My grateful thanks to all of them, and to the late Marta Kolomayets. In the Donbass, Lyudmila Bortok of Donbass TV, Sergei Garmash of the online paper ostrov.org, Professors Vladimir Kirpen and Ihor Todorov of Donetsk University, Dr Serhiy Telizhenko of Luhansk University, and Katerina Zhemchuzhnykova of ngo.donetsk.ua were kind enough to give me interviews at an extremely difficult time. Since then, they have all become refugees. So has the Crimean Tatar leader Mustafa Dzhemilev, whom it was an honour to meet again. For organisational help in the east, my grateful thanks to Katerina Malofeyeva, Viktoria Moroz and Oksana Parafeniuk, and especially to Vladimir Podmogilny.

In Lviv, Ben Kern and Mariana Kuchlevska of the Gesellschaft für Internationale Zusammenarbeit, Andriy Kyrchiv, Mariana Savka and Kateryna Mikhalitsyna of the Old Lion Publishing House, Bohdan Shumylovych of the Center for Urban History, Olga Sivak of Citadel Capital and Olha Zarichynska of the Ukrainian Catholic University all helped me reacquaint myself with their beautiful city. Vika Sibir looked after me in her equally lovely Odesa. Elsewhere Yuliya Andrusiv, Sir Antony Beevor, Peter Bejger, Marina Denysenko, Jim Donnet, Andrew Hunder, John Peet, Kate Smith and Noah Sneider were generous with contacts and advice. The Eurasia Circle, founded by Edward Salazar and now chaired by Ian Bond, continues to be a rich source of debate and information, as do Chatham House's Ukraine and Russia programmes, my fellow trustees at the Ukrainian Institute London, and the Institute's director Olesya Khromeychuk and deputy director Maria Montague.

For the 2022 edition, written as Ukraine defends itself against a full-scale Russian invasion, thanks again to many of the above, and to the following, for interviews, updates, thoughts and contacts at an extraordinarily distressing and frantic time: Konstantin Akinsha, James and Natasha Butterwick, Vyacheslav Chaus, General James Cowan, Mairi Cunningham, Claire Denholm, Richard Ensor, Natalya Fylevich, Ihor Garmash, Yevgeniya Gubkina, Owen Hatherley, Yuliya Hetman, Pavlo Huk, Artyom Hurzhii, Yuliya Kabanets, Sveta Komisarova, Igor Kozhan, Chris Lockwood, Sergei Lunin, Artem Lyashenko, Olena Lysenko, Dr Daria Mattingly, Roman Metelsky, Anna Morgan, Olha Mukha, Dmytro Natalukha, Oleksandr Shevchenko, Zhenya Shidlovska, Alyona Shkrum, Jacek Stawiski, Constance Uzwyshyn, Lyuba Vinogradova and Dr Tatiana Voronina.

In Lviv, Andriy Avramenko organised brilliantly. Jeff Wills kindly showed me round the ever-expanding Ukrainian Catholic University, and introduced me to the inspiring social enterprise group Ukrainian Education Platform. In Kyiv, Dmytro Prytulenko took me to his ruined hometown of Irpin, and to Hostomel and Bucha.

Natasha Fairweather and Matthew Marland of Rogers, Coleridge & White have been wonderful as ever, as has Ed Lake at Weidenfeld. Last of all, thank you as ever to my dear husband, Charles, to whom this book is dedicated.

◆ NOTES ◆

CHAPTER ONE ◆ *The New Jerusalem: Kiev*

1   *The Russian Primary Chronicle Laurentian Text*, trans. and ed. Samuel Cross and Olgerd Sherbowitz-Wetzor, Cambridge, Mass., 1953, p. 59.
2   Robert Byron, *First Russia, then Tibet*, London, 1985, p. 121.
3   Michael Hamm, *Kiev: A Portrait 1800–1917*, Princeton, 1993, p. 15.
4   *Primary Chronicle*, p. 93.
5   Ibid., p. 94.
6   Ibid., p. 97.
7   Ibid., p. 111.
8   Ibid., p. 111.
9   Ibid., p. 116.
10 Volodymyr Sichynskyi, *Ukraine in Foreign Comments and Descriptions from the VIth to the XXth Century*, New York, 1953, p. 37.
11 George Vernadsky and Michael Karpovich, *A History of Russia: Vol. 2 Kievan Russia*, Newhaven, 1948, p. 83.
12 *The Song of Igor's Campaign: an epic of the twelfth century*, trans. Vladimir Nabokov, London, 1961, p. 45.
13 Hamm, *Kiev*, p. 5.
14 Ibid., p. 18.
15 Michael Hrushevsky, 'The Traditional Scheme of "Russian" History and the Problem of the Rational Organization of the History of the East Slavs', pub. 1903 and reprinted in English in *Slavistica: Proceedings of the Institute of Slavistics of the Ukrainian Free Academy of Sciences* No. 55, Winnipeg, 1966, pp. 8–9.
16 Vernadsky, *History of Russia*, p. 309.
17 Richard Pipes, *Russia Under the Old Regime*, London, 1974, p. 75.
18 *The Travels of Macarius: Extracts from the Diary of the Travels*

*of Macarius, Patriarch of Antioch, written in Arabic by his son
Paul, Archdeacon of Aleppo; in the years of their journeying
1652–1660,* London, 1936, p. 20.

19 Ibid., pp. 20–21.

20 Ibid., p. 91.

21 Ibid., p. 94.

22 Byron, *Russia, then Tibet,* p. 40.

23 Ibid., p. 123.

24 John Steinbeck, *A Russian Journal,* London, 1994, pp. 53–4.

25 Mikhail Bulgakov, *The White Guard,* trans. Michael Glenny,
London, 1971, p. 55.

26 Ibid., p. 62.

27 Ibid., p. 302.

CHAPTER TWO ◆ *Poles and Cossacks: Kamyanets Podilsky*

1 Adam Czartoryski, *Memoirs of Prince Adam Cartoryski,* London,
1888, vol. I, p. 38.

2 Sophia Kossak, *The Blaze: Reminiscences of Volhynia 1917–1919,*
London, 1927, p. 13.

3 Norman Davies, *Gods' Playground: A History of Poland, Vol. I:
The Origins to 1795,* Oxford, 1981, p. 145.

4 Gillaume Le Vasseur, Sieur de Beauplan, *A Description of Ukraine,*
Cambridge, Mass., 1993, p. 106.

5 Adam Zamoyski, *The Polish Way,* London, 1987, p. 164.

6 De Beauplan, *Ukraine,* p. 14.

7 Zamoyski, *Polish Way,* p. 161.

8 H. Luzhnytsky, *Ukrainska tserkva mizh skhodom i zakhodom,*
Philadelphia, 1954, p. 307.

9 De Beauplan, *Ukraine,* p. 14.

10 Ibid., pp. 12–13.

11 Volodymyr Sichynskyi, *Ukraine in Foreign Comments and
Descriptions from the VIth to the XXth Century,* New York,
1953, p. 90.

12 De Beauplan, *Ukraine,* p. 11.

13 *The Travels of Macarius: Extracts from the Diary of the Travels*

of Macarius, Patriarch of Antioch, written in Arabic by his son Paul, Archdeacon of Aleppo; in the years of their journeying 1652–1660, London, 1936, p. 21.

14   Sichynskyi, *Ukraine in Foreign Comments*, p. 57.

15   Ibid., p. 90.

16   *Travels of Macarius*, p. 16.

17   Subtelny, *Ukraine: A History*, Toronto, 1988, p. 127.

18   Davies, *God's Playground, Vol. I*, p. 532.

19   Zbigniew Brzezinski, 'The Premature Partnership', *Foreign Affairs, Vol. 73*, No. 2, pp. 72, 80.

20   Interview with the author, November 1996.

CHAPTER THREE ◆ *The Russian Sea: Donetsk and Odessa*

1   Orest Subtelny, *The Mazepists: Ukrainian Separatism in the Eighteenth Century*, Boulder, 1981, p. 20.

2   Volodymyr Sichynskyi, *Ukraine in Foreign Comments and Descriptions from the VIth to the XXth Century*, New York, 1953, p. 113.

3   Subtelny, *The Mazeppists*, p. 37.

4   Orest Subtelny, *Ukraine: A History*, Toronto, 1988, p. 164.

5   Ibid., p. 172.

6   *Poems by Adam Mickiewicz*, ed. George Noyes, New York, 1944.

7   Nikolai Gogol, *Village Evenings near Dikanka and Mirgorod*, trans. Christopher English, Oxford, 1994, p. 257.

8   Anton Chekhov, *The Chekhov Omnibus: Selected Stories*, trans. Constance Garnett and Donald Rayfield, London, 1994, p. 32.

9   Vincent Cronin, *Catherine, Empress of All the Russias*, London, 1978, p. 249.

10   Kyrylo Rozumovsky, quoted in Cronin, *Catherine*, p. 247.

11   Patricia Herlihy, *Odessa: A History 1794–1914*, Cambridge, Mass., p. 34.

12   Ibid., p. 115.

13   Mark Twain, *The Innocents Abroad or the New Pilgrim's Progress*, London, 1897, p. 355.

14   Herlihy, *Odessa*, p. 123.

15 Alexander Pushkin, *Eugene Onegin*, trans. James Falen, Oxford, 1995, p. 223.

16 Isaac Babel, *Collected Stories*, trans. David McDuff, London, 1994, p. 59.

17 Zenon Kohut, *Russian Centralism and Ukrainian Autonomy: Imperial Absorption of the Hetmanate*, Cambridge, Mass., 1988, p. 263.

18 Nikolai Gogol, *Village Evenings*, p. 221.

19 Subtelny, *Ukraine*, p. 210.

20 Stefan Zweig, *Balzac*, London, 1947, p. 360.

21 Kohut, *Absorption of the Hetmanate*, p. 291.

22 Sichynskyi, *Ukraine in Foreign Comments*, p. 197.

23 Kohut, *Absorption of the Hetmanate*, p. 274.

CHAPTER FOUR ◆ *The Books of Genesis: Lviv*

1 Joseph Roth, *The Radetzky March*, trans. Joachim Neugroschel, London, 1995, pp. 131, 152.

2 Norman Davies, *God's Playground: A History of Poland, Vol. II: 1795 to the Present*, Oxford, 1981, p. 155.

3 Clifford Sifton, quoted in Orest Subtelny, *Ukraine: A History*, Toronto, 1988, p. 546.

4 Michael Hrushevsky, *A History of Ukraine*, ed. O. J. Frederiksen, New Haven, 1941, p. 480.

5 Alexander Pushkin, *Eugene Onegin*, trans. James Falen, Oxford, 1995, p. 70.

6 Pavlo Zaitsev, *Taras Shevchenko: A Life*, trans. George Luckyj, Toronto, 1988, p. 43.

7 Ibid., p. 55.

8 Ibid., p. 47.

9 Taras Shevchenko, *Song Out of Darkness: Selected Poems*, trans. Vera Rich, London, 1961, p. 38.

10 Zaitsev, *Shevchenko*, p. 59.

11 Ibid., p. 68.

12 Ibid., p. 63.

13 Ibid., p. 89.

14 Ibid., p. 144.

15 Shevchenko, *Song Out of Darkness*, p. 113.

16 Ibid., p. vii.

17 Paul Robert Magocsi, *A History of Ukraine*, Toronto, 1996, p. 369.

18 Subtelny, *Ukraine*, p. 315.

19 Ivan Franko, *Poems and Stories*, trans. John Weir, Toronto, 1956, p. 151.

20 Thomas Prymak, *Mykhailo Hrushevsky: The Politics of National Culture*, Toronto, 1987, p. 29.

21 Ibid., p. 31.

CHAPTER FIVE ◆ *A Meaningless Fragment: Chernivtski*

1   A. J. P. Taylor, *The Habsburg Monarchy: 1809–1918*, London, 1964, p. 284.

2   Gregor von Rezzori, *The Snows of Yesteryear*, trans. H. F. Broch de Rotherman, London, 1990, p. 98.

3   Ibid., p. 276.

4   Gregor von Rezzori, *The Hussar*, trans. Catherine Hutter, London, 1960, p. 8.

5   Von Rezzori, *Snows of Yesteryear*, p. 281.

6   Isaac Babel, *Collected Stories*, trans. David McDuff, London, 1994, p. 91.

7   Ibid., p. 222.

8   Ibid., p. 129.

9   Richard Pipes, *Russia under the Bolshevik Regime 1919–1924*, London, 1994, p. 109.

10 Orest Subtelny, *Ukraine: A History*, Toronto, 1988, p. 346.

11 Arnold Margolin, *From a Political Diary: Russia, the Ukraine and America 1905–1945*, New York, 1946, p. 30.

12 Thomas Prymak, *Mykhailo Hrushevsky: The Politics of National Culture*, Toronto, 1987, p. 158.

13 Ibid., p. 172.

14 Mikhail Bulgakov, *The White Guard*, trans. Michael Glenny, London, 1971, p. 57.

15 Ibid., p. 58.

16 Mikhail Bulgakov, *Manuscripts Don't Burn*, ed. J. A. E. Curtis, London, 1991, p. 1.

17 Sholem Schwartzbard, 'Memoirs of an Assassin', in Lucy Dawidowicz's *The Golden Tradition: Jewish Life and Thought in Eastern Europe*, London, 1967, p. 455.

18 Alan Sharp, *The Versailles Settlement: Peacemaking in Paris, 1919*, London, 1991, pp. 26–7.

19 Margolin, *Political Diary*, p. 59.

20 Ibid., pp. 39–41.

21 Julia Namier, *Lewis Namier, a Biography*, Oxford, 1971, p. 144.

22 Ibid., pp. 144–5.

23 Mykola Neskuk, Volodymyr Repryntsev and Yevhen Kaminsky, 'Ukraine in Foreign Documents and Strategies in the Twentieth Century', *Politichna Dumka* 2–3. 95, p. 176.

24 Joseph Roth, *The Radetzky March*, trans. Joachim Neugroschel, London, 1995, p. 129.

25 Bruno Schulz, *The Street of Crocodiles & Sanatorium Under the Sign of the Hourglass*, trans. Celina Wieniewska, London, 1988, p. 249.

26 Ibid., p. 180.

27 Von Rezzori, *Hussar*, p. 326.

CHAPTER SIX ◆ *The Great Hunger: Matussiv and Lukovytsya*

1 Edward Daniel Clarke, quoted in Volodymyr Sichynskyi, *Ukraine in Foreign Comments from the VIth to the XXth Century*, New York, 1953, p. 187.

2 Robert Conquest, *The Harvest of Sorrow*, London, 1986, p. 104.

3 Vasiliy Grossman, *Forever Flowing*, trans. Thomas P. Whitney, London, 1973, pp. 148–9.

4 Petro Grigorenko, *Memoirs*, trans. Thomas Whitney, London, 1983, p. 14.

5 Viktor Kravchenko, *I Chose Freedom*, New York, 1946, p. 63.

6 OGPU memoranda, quoted in Conquest, *Harvest of Sorrow*, p. 72.

7   Orest Subtelny, *Ukraine: A History*, Toronto, 1988, p. 419.

8   Ibid., p. 419.

9   Robert Conquest, *The Great Terror*, London, 1990, p. 253.

10 Ibid., p. 259.

11 Conquest, *Harvest of Sorrow*, p. 117.

12 Grossman, *Forever Flowing*, p. 143.

13 Kravchenko, *I Chose Freedom*, p. 63.

14 Ibid., pp. 88–90.

15 Ibid., pp. 91–2.

16 Ibid., pp. 104–5.

17 Conquest, *Harvest of Sorrow*, p. 138.

18 Ibid., p. 139.

19 Kravchenko, *I Chose Justice*, London, 1951, p. 80.

20 Conquest, *Harvest of Sorrow*, p. 229.

21 Ibid., p. 226.

22 Kravchenko, *I Chose Freedom*, p. 113.

23 Ibid., p. 118.

24 Grossman, *Forever Flowing*, p. 164.

25 Kravchenko, *I Chose Justice*, p. 75.

26 Grossman, *Forever Flowing*, p. 162.

27 Ibid., pp. 162–3.

28 William Henry Chamberlin, *Russia's Iron Age*, London, 1935, p. 368.

29 Ibid., pp. 369, 88.

30 Arthur Koestler, *The Yogi and the Commissar and other essays*, London, 1965, p. 128.

31 Eugene Lyons, *Assignment in Utopia*, London, 1937, p. 574.

32 Koestler, *Yogi and Commissar*, p. 129.

33 Eugene Lyons, *Assignment in Utopia*, pp. 575–6.

34 Paul Hollander, *Political Pilgrims: travels of Western intellectuals to the Soviet Union, China, and Cuba*, Lanham, New York, London, 1990, p. 102.

35 Conquest, *Harvest of Sorrow*, pp. 314–5.

36 Robert Byron, *First Russia, then Tibet*, London, 1985, p. 116.

37 Lyons, *Assignment in Utopia*, pp. 428–30.

38 Conquest, *Harvest of Sorrow*, p. 316.

39 Lion Feuchtwanger, *Moscow 1937*, trans. Irene Josephy, pp. 28–9.

40 Ibid., pp. 83, 164, 174.

41 André Gide, *Retouches à Mon Retour de l'URSS*, Paris, 1937, p. 57.

42 Conquest, *Harvest of Sorrow*, p. 319.

43 Lyons, *Assignment in Utopia*, p. 572.

44 Ibid., p. 573.

45 Conquest, *Harvest of Sorrow*, p. 320.

CHAPTER SEVEN ◆ *The Vanished Nation: Ivano-Frankivsk*

1 Patricia Herlihy, *Odessa: A History 1794–1914*, Cambridge, Mass., 1986, p. 300.

2 Michael Hamm, *Kiev: A Portrait 1800–1917*, Princeton, 1993, p. 118.

3 Ibid., p. 124.

4 Herlihy, *Odessa*, p. 255.

5 Hamm, *Kiev*, p. 126.

6 Herlihy, *Odessa*, p. 306.

7 David Marples, *Stalinism in Ukraine in the 1940 s*, New York, 1992, p. 74.

8 Philip Friedman, *Roads to Extinction: Essays on the Holocaust*, New York and Philadelphia, 1980, p. 179.

9 Orest Subtelny, *Ukraine: A History*, Toronto, 1988, p. 479.

10 Samuel Drix, *Witness: A Holocaust Memoir*, London, 1995, p. xii.

11 Martin Gilbert, *The Holocaust*, London, 1986, p. 476.

12 Lucy Dawidowicz, *The War against the Jews 1933–45*, London, 1975, Appendix B, p. 479.

13 Marples, *Stalinism in Ukraine*, p. 58.

14 Friedman, *Roads to Extinction*, p. 201.

15 Ibid., pp. 186, 202.

16 Alexander Dallin, *German Rule in Russia 1941–1945: A Study of Occupation Policies*, London and Basingstoke, 1981, p. 427.

17 Leon Weliczker Wells, *The Janowska Road*, London, 1966, p. 92.

18 Subtelny, *Ukraine*, p. 472.

19 Pavlo Oliynyk, *Zashiti*, Kiev, 1995, p. 63.

20 Weliczker Wells, *Janowska Road*, p. 26.

21 Ibid., p. 28.

22 Oliynyk, *Zashiti*, p. 67.

23 Nikita Khrushchev, *Khrushchev Remembers*, trans. Strobe Talbot, ed. Edward Crankshaw, London, 1971, p. 129.

24 Weliczker Wells, *Janowska Road*, p. 29.

25 Ibid., p. 279.

26 Marples, *Stalinism in Ukraine*, pp. 39–40; and Subtelny, *Ukraine*, p. 454.

27 Khrushchev, *Khrushchev Remembers*, p. 125.

28 Alan Clark, *Barbarossa: the Russian-German Conflict 1941–45*, London, 1995, p. 44.

29 Oliynyk, *Zashiti*, p. 76.

30 Daniel Goldhagen, *Hitler's Willing Executioners*, London, 1996, p. 149.

31 Weliczker Wells, *Janowska Road*, pp. 37–8.

32 Ibid., pp. 40–41.

33 Ibid., p. 41.

34 Gilbert, *Holocaust*, p. 173.

35 Ibid., p. 171.

36 Ibid., pp. 197–8.

37 Ibid., p. 212.

38 Friedman, *Roads to Extinction*, p. 190.

39 Alexander Werth, *Russia at War*, London, 1964, p. 787.

40 Ibid., p. 613.

41 Oliynyk, *Zashiti*, p. 75.

42 Ibid., p. 76.

43 Weliczker Wells, *Janowska Road*, p. 117.

44 Ibid., p. 239.

45 Oliynyk, *Zashiti*, p. 75.

46 Subtelny, *Ukraine*, p. 467.

47 Dallin, *German Rule*, p. 127.

48 Ibid., p. 123.

49 Ibid., p. 459.

50 Friedman, *Roads to Extinction*, pp. 199–200.

51 John Armstrong, *Ukrainian Nationalism*, Colorado, 1990, pp. 56–7.

52 Oliynyk, *Zashiti*, p. 87.

53 Clark, *Barbarossa*, p. 143.

54 Dallin, *German Rule*, p. 418.

55 Ibid., p. 415.

56 Ibid., p. 415.

57 Ibid., p. 427.

58 Ibid., p. 422.

59 Ibid., pp. 452, 453.

60 Armstrong, *Ukrainian Nationalism*, p. 89.

61 Oliynyk, *Zashiti*, p. 86.

CHAPTER EIGHT ◆ *The Wart on Russia's Nose: Crimea*

1 Edward Daniel Clarke, *Travels in Various Countries of Europe, Asia and Africa: Part the First – Russia, Tatary and Turkey*, London, 1811, pp. 537–8.

2 Alan Fisher, *The Crimean Tatars*, Stanford, 1978, pp. 10–11.

3 Gillaume Le Vasseur, Sieur de Beauplan, *A Description of Ukraine*, Cambridge, Mass., 1993, p. 44.

4 Baron de Tott, *Memoirs of the Baron de Tott on the Turks and the Tatars, vol. I*, London, 1785, p. 478.

5 Ibid., p. 475.

6 Ibid., p. 482.

7 Ibid., p. 371.

8 Ibid., p. 372.

9 Ibid., pp. 449–50.

10 Fisher, *Crimean Tatars*, p. 69.

11 Ibid., p. 17.

12 Thomas Milner, *The Crimea, its Ancient and Modern History: The Khans, the Sultans, and the Tsars, with notices of its scenery and population*, London, 1855, p. 182.

13 Clarke, *Russia, Tatary and Turkey*, pp. 454–5.

14 Ibid., p. 465.

15 Ibid., pp. 502–3.

16 Ibid., p. 480.

17 Figures from Andrew Wilson, *The Crimean Tatars: A Situation Report on the Crimean Tatars for International Alert*, pp. 6, 36.

18 Fisher, *Crimean Tatars*, p. 114.

19 Ibid., p. 132.

20 Ibid., p. 137.

21 Robert Conquest, *The Nation Killers*, London, 1970, p. 99.

22 Ibid., pp. 64–5.

23 Vera Tolz, 'New Information About the Deportation of Ethnic Groups in the USSR during World War II', in *World War 2 and the Soviet People*, ed. John and Carol Garrard, London, 1993, pp. 167–8.

24 Ibid., pp. 165–6.

25 Khrushchev, *Khrushchev Remembers*, trans. Strobe Talbot, ed. Edward Crankshaw, London, 1971, p. 540.

CHAPTER NINE ◆ *The Empire Explodes: Chernobyl*

1 David Remnick, *Lenin's Tomb*, New York, Toronto and London, 1993, p. 245.

2 See David Marples, *The Social Impact of the Chernobyl Disaster*, London, 1988, pp. 12–19, for an excellent account of the technicalities.

3 Yuri Shcherbak, *Chernobyl: A Documentary Story*, trans. Ian Press, London, 1989.

4 Ibid., p. 33.

5 Ibid., p. 42.

6 Ibid., pp. 41–2.

7 Ibid., p. 44.

8 Ibid., p. 46.

9 Ibid., p. 21.

10 Ibid., p. 56.

11 Marples, *Impact of the Chernobyl Disaster*, p. 191.

12 Orest Subtelny, *Ukraine: a History*, Toronto, 1988, p. 489.

13 Taras Kuzio and Andrew Wilson, *Ukraine: Perestroika to Independence*, London, 1994, p. 43.

14 Vyacheslav Chornovil, *The Chornovil Papers*, New York, 1968, p. 21.

15 Petro Grigorenko, *Memoirs*, trans. Thomas Whitney, London, 1983, p. 437.

16 Anatoly Marchenko, *My Testimony*, trans. Michael Scammell, London, 1969, p. 120.

17 Subtelny, *Ukraine*, p. 53.

18 Kuzio and Wilson, *Ukraine*, p. 105.

19 Ibid., p. 111.

20 Ibid., p. 112.

21 Solomea Pavlychko, *Letters from Kiev*, trans. Myrna Kostash, New York, 1992, p. 14.

22 Ibid., pp. 6–7.

23 Ibid., p. 40.

24 Ibid., pp. 77–9.

25 Ibid., p. 84.

26 Ibid., p. 138.

27 Kuzio and Wilson, *Ukraine*, p. 158.

28 Ibid., p. 161.

29 *Economist*, 7 May 1994.

CHAPTER TEN ◆ *Europe or Little Russia? Ukraina*

1 Daniel Kaufmann, 'Diminishing Returns to Administrative Controls and the Emergence of the Unofficial Economy: a Framework of Analysis and Application to Ukraine', World Bank, Kiev, 1994.

2 Daniel Kaufmann, 'The Missing Pillar of a Growth Strategy for Ukraine: Institutional and Policy Reforms for Private Sector Development', Harvard Institute of International Development and the World Bank, October 1996, p. 6.

3 Interview with the author, November 1996.

4 Interview with the author, November 1996.

5 Nikolai Gogol, *Taras Bulba*, in *Village Evenings near Dikanka* and *Mirgorod*, trans. Christopher English, Oxford, 1994, pp. 251–2.

CHAPTER ELEVEN ◆ *The Rise and Fall of the Orange Revolution*

1 Oliver Bullough, 'Looting Ukraine: how East and West teamed up to steal a country', Legatum Institute, July 2014. Global Witness, *It's a Gas: Funny Business in the Turkmen-Ukraine Gas Trade*, Washington DC, April 2006.

2 Taras Kuzio, 'Crime, politics and business in 1990s Ukraine', Communist and Post-Communist Studies 47 (2014), pp.196–210. Andrew Wilson, *Ukraine's Orange Revolution*, London, 2005, pp.9–12.

3 Bloomberg Billionaires Index, July 2022.

4 Andrew Wilson, *Ukraine's Orange Revolution*, p.44.

5 For detailed accounts of the still-murky Gongadze affair, see Wilson, *Ukraine's Orange Revolution*, pp. 51–6, and Askold Krushelnycky, *An Orange Revolution: a Personal Journey through Ukrainian History*, London 2006, pp.129–67.

6 Kuchma, interviewed in the BBC's *Putin, Russia and the West: Democracy Threatens*, first broadcast January 2012.

7 Yushchenko's campaign manager Oleh Rybachuk, interviewed in the BBC's *Putin, Russia and the West*.

8 Interview with the author, September 2014.

9 Yushchenko, interviewed in the BBC's *Putin, Russia and the West*.

10 Gleb Pavlovsky, ibid.

11 Interview with the author, September 2014.

12 Wikileaks, 06KIEV1992, 25 May 2005, 'Ukraine: Farewell call on PM – Hopeful Tymoshenko on Eve of Rada Opening'.

13 For an excellent essay on the use of the famine as a political football in the period, see Wikileaks, 06KYIV4414, 30 November 2006, 'Ukraine: the Holodomor and the Politics of Remembrance: the Legacy of Stalin's 1932–33 Famine'.

14 Wikileaks, 06KIEV456, 2 February 2006, 'Ukraine: Oligarch Pinchuk on Nikopol Ferroalloy and Post-Election Politics'.

15 For detail on Firtash's business background, see Reuters, 'Special Report: Putin's allies channelled billions to Ukraine oligarch', 26 November 2014. Also Wikileaks, 08KYIV2294, 21 November 2008, 'Ukraine: Firtash uses crisis to expand into banking'.

16 Andrey Kurkov, *Ukraine Diaries*, trans. Sam Taylor, London, 2014, p.249.

17 Andrew Wilson, *Ukraine Crisis: What it Means for the West*, London 2014, pp.112–13.

18 Anders Aslund, 'Payback time for the "Yanukovych Family"', Peterson Institute for International Economics, RealTime Economic Issues Watch, 11 December 2013. Wilson, *Ukraine Crisis*, pp.52–7.

CHAPTER TWELVE ◆ *The Maidan*

1 Andrey Kurkov *Ukraine Diaries*, trans. Sam Taylor, London 2014, p.5.

2 Katerina Zhemchuznykova, interview with the author, Donetsk, April 2014.

3 Andrei Terekhov, interview with the author, November 2014.

4 *Maidan: Voices from the Uprising*, eds. Natalya Vorozhbit and Andrei Mai, trans. Sasha Dugdale, Royal Court Theatre, 2014.

5 Human Rights Watch, 'Ukraine: police beatings, kidnappings in Kiev', 24 January 2014.

6 Wilson, *Ukraine Crisis*, p.87; Kurkov *Ukraine Diaries*, p.119. 19 February.

7 *Voices of Ukraine*, 27 February 2014, www.maidantranslations. com

8 *Kyiv Post*, '6 years on, Euromaidan investigations are unlikely to bring justice', 6 February 2020.

9 See Serhiy Loznitsa's documentary *Maidan*, 2014.

10 Lviv activist Andriy Porodko, interviewed in Reuters, 'Special Report: Why Ukraine's revolution remains unfinished', 23 October 2014.

11 Wilson, *Ukraine Crisis*, p.91.

12 Reuters, 'Special Report: Why Ukraine's revolution remains unfinished', 23 October 2014.

13 Michael McFaul, 'Russia, Ukraine and the West: is confrontation inevitable?', seminar at the Royal Institute of International Affairs, 25 June 2014.

CHAPTER THIRTEEN ◆ *Putin Strikes Back*

1 *Time*, 'The Standoff at Belbek: inside the first clash of the second Crimean War', 4 March 2014.

2 Amnesty International, *Abductions and Torture in Eastern Ukraine*, London, July 2014, pp.8-9. *Kyiv Post*, 'Putin's drive to destroy Ukraine: Crimean crimes', 3 April 2014. Office of the United Nations High Commissioner for Human Rights *Report on the human rights situation in Ukraine: 1 December 2014 to 15 February 2015*, p.24.

3 Kiev International Institute of Sociology, 'The Views and Opinions of South-Eastern Regions [sic] Residents of Ukraine: April 2014'. Available on www.kiis.com.ua

4 Radio Free Europe/Radio Liberty, 'Despite denials, all evidence for deadly explosion points to Kiev', 4 June 2014.

5 *Guardian*, 'The soldiers who were never there: families of troops killed in Ukraine face official silence', 20 January 2015. *Moscow Times*, 'Silent Deaths: the price of a Russian soldier's life', 27 October 2014. Rights in Russia, 'Harrassment of Lev Shlosberg continues in Pskov', 8 October 2014, www.rightsinrussia.org. BBC, 'Ukraine conflict: Russian families look for soldier sons', 28 August 2014.

6 Human Rights Watch, *Rights in Retreat: Abuses in Crimea*, 17 November 2014.

7 Interview with the author, November 2014.

8 Andrew Wilson, *Ukraine Crisis: what it means for the West*, London 2014, p.143.

CHAPTER FOURTEEN ◆ *Between Battles*

1 See for example Olga Rudenko, 'The Comedian-Turned-President is seriously in over his head', *New York Times*, 21 February 2022.

CHAPTER FIFTEEN ◆ *The New War*

1 Aziz Hazara's *Bow Echo*, 2019.

2 Vyacheslav Chaus, interview with the author, 4 February 2022.

3 Alyona Shkrum, interview with the author, 17 April 2022.

4 *The Times*, 'Russian soldiers raped me', 28 March 2022.

5 *Guardian*, 'Bodies of 765 civilians recovered so far in Kyiv region', 13 April 2022.

6 *Guardian*, 'Makeshift graves and notes on doors', 1 June 2022.

7 *The Economist*, 'Deep battle', 16 July 2022.

8 Jack Watling and Nick Reynolds, *Ukraine at War: Paving the War from Survival to Victory*, RUSI July 4 2022.

9 *Meduza*, 'Two months of terrorism: a despatch from Kherson', 27 April 2022. *Meduza*, 'Meet the collaborators', 16 May 2022. *The Economist*, 'Hide and Seek', 11 June 2022.

CHAPTER SIXTEEN ◆ *What Next?*

1 Mairi Cunningham, interview with the author, 10 April 2022.

2 The UNHCR's 'operational data portal: Ukraine refugee situation'. Figures as of 21 June-5 July 2022.

3 *Meduza* 'Feeling around for something human: Why do Russians support the war against Ukraine?' by Shura Burtin. May 3 2022.

4 *The Times*, 'Russian billionaire Tinkov denounces "crazy war"', 19 April 2022.

5 Professor Nikolai Petrov, Chatham House seminar, 3 May 2022.

6 Timothy Synder, 'We Should Say It. Russia is Fascist', *New York Times* May 19 2022.

7 For subtitled daily highlights, see @JuliaDavisNews. For an overview, see Masha Gessen's 'Inside Putin's Propaganda Machine', *The New Yorker*, 18 May 2022.

8 Kiev International Institute for Sociology, 'Most people refuse to compromise on territory', 17 June 2022. Available on www.kiis.com.ua

9 Anna Dovgopol, interview with the author, April 2022.

10 Interview with the author, April 2022.

◆ SELECTED BIBLIOGRAPHY ◆

The standard surveys, covering Ukraine from prehistoric times to independence, are Orest Subtelny's *Ukraine: A History* (Toronto 1988), Paul Magocsi's equally magisterial *A History of Ukraine* (Toronto, 1996), and most recently, Serhii Plokhy's *The Gates of Europe: A History of Ukraine* (London, 2015).

George Vernadsky's *Kievan Russia*, volume two of his multi-volume *A History of Russia* (New Haven 1948), is a thorough, though now rather dated, account of medieval Rus. James Billington's *The Icon and the Axe* (London 1966) gives an original overview of Rus art and culture; Richard Pipes's *Russia under the Old Regime* (London 1974) traces the effects of Mongol suzerainty.

For the history of Polish rule in Ukraine, I relied on Norman Davies's two-volume *God's Playground* (Oxford 1981) and Adam Zamoyski's *The Polish Way* (London 1987). Roman Szporluk's 'After Empire: What?' in *Daedalus*, vol.123, no.3, stresses Ukraine's enduring Polish ties. Subtelny's *The Mazepists* (Boulder 1981) details the rise and fall of Mazeppa, and Robert Massie's *Peter the Great* (London 1981) includes a lively account of the events surrounding the battle of Poltava. Geoffrey Hosking's *Russia: People and Empire* (London 1997) throws light on tsarist imperialism, as does Plokhy's *Lost Kingdom: A History of Russian Nationalism from Ivan the Great to Vladimir Putin* (London 2018). On Shevchenko's career, I used Pavlo Zaitsev's *Taras Shevchenko: A Life*, written in the 1930s and reprinted by the University of Toronto Press in 1988. Translations of Shevchenko's poetry are taken from Vera Rich's *Song Out of Darkness* (London 1961). Hugh Seton-Watson's *Nations and States* (London 1977) and John Armstrong's *Ukrainian Nationalism* (Colorado 1990) thoughtfully analyse late Soviet-era Ukrainian nationalism.

Pipes's *Russia under the Bolshevik Regime: 1919–1924* (London 1994) covers the Civil War in Ukraine, as, marvellously, do Isaac

Babel's short stories and wartime diary, and Mikhail Bulgakov's *The White Guard*. *Memories: From Moscow to the Black Sea* (New York 2016, trans. Robert and Elizabeth Chandler et al.) is the satirist Teffi's account of refugee life in Kyiv and Odesa at the time. Jeffrey Veidlinger's *In the Midst of Civilised Europe: The Pogroms of 1918–1921 and the Onset of the Holocaust* (London 2021) is a much-needed new study of an overlooked subject.

On Stalin's famine and purges, Robert Conquest's *The Harvest of Sorrow* (London 1986) and *The Great Terror* (London 1990) are the classic ground-breaking works. Anne Applebaum's *Red Famine: Stalin's War on Ukraine* (London 2017) updates the former, using data from Ukrainian archives to make the argument that the famine was aimed at Ukrainian nationhood rather than at the peasantry as such. Daria Mattingly's thesis, *'Idle, Drunk and Good-for-Nothing': The Rank-and-File Perpetrators of the 1932–33 Famine* (Cambridge 2019) uses the archives to analyse perpetrators' origins and motivations. Victor Kravchenko's *I Chose Freedom* (New York 1946) and Lev Kopelev's *The Education of a True Believer* (New York 1980) are outstanding first-hand accounts of the period. Paul Hollander's *Political Pilgrims* (New York 1981) is a blackly comic round-up of Western apologists for communism, and Eugene Lyon's *Assignment in Utopia* (London 1937) a fascinating memoir of life as a journalist in 1930s Moscow.

Timothy Snyder's *Bloodlands: Europe between Hitler and Stalin* (New York 2012) ties the dictators' atrocities together, seeing them as a continuum of terror. Balanced accounts of the Ukrainian war record include David Marples's *Stalinism in Ukraine in the 1940s* (New York 1992) and Philip Friedman's *Roads to Extinction: Essays on the Holocaust* (New York 1980). Martin Gilbert's *The Holocaust* (London 1986) details Jewish massacres month by month and town by town. Among survivors' memoirs, Leon Weliczker Well's *The Janowska Road* (London 1966) and Anatoly Kuznetsov's *Babi Yar* (London 1970) stand out.

Conquest's *The Nation Killers* (London 1970) covers the deportation of the Crimean Tatars; Vera Tolz's article in *World War 2 and the Soviet People* (London 1993) incorporates glasnost-era research on the subject. Alan Fisher's *The Crimean Tatars* (Stanford 1978) is a general history of khanate. The Transcarpathian débâcle of 1939 is hilariously described by Michael Winch in his *Republic for a Day: an Eye-Witness Account of the Carpatho-Ukraine Incident* (London 1939). Petro Grigorenko's *Memoirs* (London 1983) cover, among much else, the Tatar liberation movement and the beginnings of Ukrainian dissidence.

Eyewitness accounts of the Chernobyl disaster are taken from Yuri Shcherbak's *Chernobyl: A Documentary Story* (London 1989). There are more in Nobel Prize-winning Svetlana Alexievich's *Voices from Chernobyl* (Illinois 2005). The best general analyses of the accident are *The Chernobyl Disaster* by Viktor Haynes and Marko Bojcun (London 1988), Marples's *The Social Impact of the Chernobyl Disaster* (London 1988), and Plokhii's *Chernobyl: History of a Tragedy* (London 2018). Kate Brown's *Manual for Survival: A Chernobyl Guide to the Future* (London 2019) is a consensus-busting study of the accident's long-term health effects.

Ukraine: Perestroika to Independence by Taras Kuzio and Andrew Wilson (London 1994) details the tumultuous years 1987–1991; Solomea Pavlychko's *Letters from Kiev* (New York 1992) capture the atmosphere of the time. Zbigniew Brzezinski's 'The Premature Partnership', in vol.73, no.2 of *Foreign Affairs*, and Szporluk's 'Belarus, Ukraine and the Russian Question: a Comment' in vol.9, no.4 of *Post-Soviet Affairs* presciently stress Russia's non-acceptance of loss of empire, and urge continued Western support for Ukrainian independence.

Ukraine's post-independence history is authoritatively and comprehensively covered in Andrew Wilson's *Ukraine's Orange Revolution* (London 2005) and his *Ukraine Crisis: What It Means for the West* (London 2014), which takes events up to the autumn of that year. On the Maidan and its aftermath, Tim Judah's *In Wartime: Stories from Ukraine* (London 2015) paints a broad and vivid picture. Owen Matthews's *Thinking with the Blood: Scenes from Ukraine's Revolution* (Newsweek Insights, 2014) concentrates on the extremists on both sides and on the Donbass, but is good on how the Maidan prompted a sharp new turn towards nationalism and repression in Russia. Andrey Kurkov's mordant *Ukraine Diaries* (London 2014) give the novelist's view.

For an understanding of the social and political dysfunction that laid the groundwork for the 2014–2015 Donbass war, watch Jakob Preuss's superb, light-touch documentary *The Other Chelsea* (2010). Sergei Loznitsa's *Maidan* (2014) lacks commentary but provides a sumptuous visual record of the 2013–14 protests. The BBC's *Putin, Russia and the West: Democracy Threatens* (2012) covers the international ramifications of the Orange Revolution, and includes interviews with many senior players.

Among travel books, Anne Applebaum's *Between East and West* (London 1995) and Neal Ascherson's *Black Sea* (London 1995) both movingly cover parts of Ukraine. Patricia Herlihy's *Odessa: A History 1794–1914* (Cambridge, Mass. 1986) and Michael Hamm's *Kiev: A Portrait, 1800–1917* (Princeton 1993) are excellent city histories. Lviv stars in Philippe Sands's *East West Street: on the Origins of Genocide and Crimes Against Humanity*, and in Józef Wittlin's nostalgic post-war memoir, *City of Lions* (both London 2016).

◆ INDEX ◆

Anna Reid was Kiev correspondent for the *Economist* and the *Daily Telegraph* from 1993 to 1995 and has since covered Ukraine for *Newsweek* and the *Spectator*. She is the author of *The Shaman's Coat: A Native History of Siberia* and *Leningrad: Tragedy of a City Under Siege, 1941–44*, which has been translated into eighteen languages and shortlisted for the Duff Cooper Prize. From 1992 to 1996 she ran the foreign affairs program at the London-based think tank Policy Exchange. She is a trustee of the Ukrainian Institute London.